CLOUD COMPUTING

Shailendra Singh
Professor
Department of Computer Science and Engineering
National Institute of Technical Teachers' Training & Research, Bhopal

OXFORD
UNIVERSITY PRESS

Oxford University Press is a department of the University of Oxford.
It furthers the University's objective of excellence in research, scholarship,
and education by publishing worldwide. Oxford is a registered trade mark of
Oxford University Press in the UK and in certain other countries.

Published in India by
Oxford University Press
22 Workspace, 2nd Floor, 1/22 Asaf Ali Road, New Delhi 110 002

© Oxford University Press 2018

The moral rights of the author/s have been asserted.

First published in 2018
Fifth impression 2023

All rights reserved. No part of this publication may be reproduced, stored in
a retrieval system, or transmitted, in any form or by any means, without the
prior permission in writing of Oxford University Press, or as expressly permitted
by law, by licence, or under terms agreed with the appropriate reprographics
rights organization. Enquiries concerning reproduction outside the scope of the
above should be sent to the Rights Department, Oxford University Press, at the
address above.

You must not circulate this work in any other form
and you must impose this same condition on any acquirer.

ISBN-13: 978-0-19-947738-8
ISBN-10: 0-19-947738-8

Typeset in Times LT Std
by Cameo Corporate Services Limited, Chennai
Printed in India by Rakmo Press, New Delhi 110 020

For product information and current price, please visit www.india.oup.com

Third-party website addresses mentioned in this book are provided
by Oxford University Press in good faith and for information only.
Oxford University Press disclaims any responsibility for the material contained therein.

This book is dedicated to my wife, Dr Neelu Singh, my daughter, Ms Navodita Singh, and my son, Mr Aryan Pratap Singh.

Shailendra Singh

Features of

Learning Outcomes

Learning Outcomes

After completing this chapter, students will be able to:

- comprehend online analytical processing (OLAP)
- explain performance monitoring tools
- list quality of service (QoS) issues in cloud computing
- describe sky computing
- understand various cloud computing platforms like Xen cloud platform
- discuss service-level agreement
- describe various computing platforms
- describe third-party technology
- explain MapReduce in cloud computing
- comprehend Hadoop

Each chapter starts with 'Learning Outcomes' that describe the knowledge readers would acquire after going through that chapter's content.

Figures

All the chapters in the book include enough 'Illustrations' that support the text.

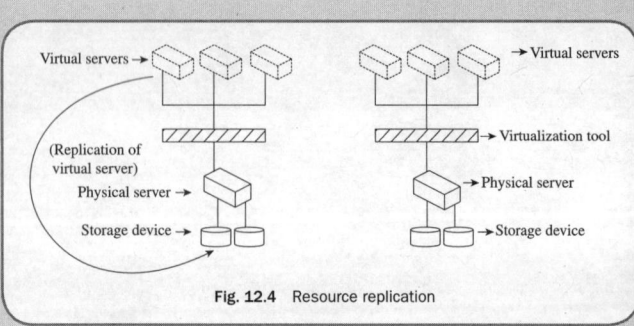

Fig. 12.4 Resource replication

Exercises

Multiple-choice Questions

1. A file that keeps a log of virtual machine activities is/are called:
   (a) BIOS file
   (b) Log file
   (c) Virtual disk file
   (d) None of these
   (c) Hardware portability
   (d) All the above
7. The advantage of physical to virtual convertor is:
   (a) Reduction in set-up time
   (b) Enabling of migration (operating system)
   (c) Enabling migration (hardware)

Review Questions

1. What do you understand by compute virtualization?
2. What is a virtual machine?
3. What are the advantages of compute virtualization?
4. What are the various components of a hypervisor?
5. What do you understand by resource management? Explain the different tools available for it.
6. How is a physical machine converted into a virtual machine using hot and cold process?
7. What are the various steps to convert a traditional data center to a virtualized data center?
8. What is a hypervisor? Explain the various categories of hypervisors in detail.

The 'Exercises' section in the book comprises Multiple-choice Questions and Review Questions for enhancing learning and for testing the knowledge of readers.

the Book

Appendices

The book comes with 'Appendices A-H' covering important topics such as study on Aneka, Amazon Network, Microsoft, etc.

- Appendix A: Abbreviations
- Appendix B: Study on Amazon Network
- Appendix C: Microsoft's Cloud
- Appendix D: Study on Salesforce.com
- Appendix E: Study of Hypervisors
- Appendix F: Study on Eucalyptus
- Appendix G: Study on Cloud Simulators
- Appendix H: Study of Aneka

Model Question Papers

'Model Question Papers' are added at the end of this book for students to test their skills.

MODEL QUESTION PAPERS
SET A
UNIT – I

Q.1 (a) What do you know about Computing Cluster? [3]
(b) Distinguish between traditional Computer and Virtual Machine. [4]
(c) Explain the architecture of Cloud Computing. [4]
(d) Define MapReduce in detail. [4]

Points to Remember

Quick recapitulation of the topics discussed is provided as 'Points to Remember' at the end of each chapter.

Points to Remember

1. Six elements of the cloud environment are physical machine, network, hypervisor, image storage, and cloud management software.
2. Service oriented architecture (SOA) manages software systems and consists of various interacting services.
3. Online analytical processing (OLAP) is a method that is used for answering multi-dimensional queries in a computing environment.
4. The financial and functioning features supported by cloud business intelligence (BI) comprise execution and installment speed, elasticity, concentration on core power, lower overall charge of possession, and on-demand accessibility.

Key Terms

Important 'Terms' used in each chapter are defined at the end of the chapter.

Key Terms

CaaS Communications as a Service delivers a Session Initiated Protocol (SIP)-based audio collaboration and on-net web conferencing over a virtual private network (VPN) using a hosted model.

CcaaS Compute Capacity as a Service means that the resource runs applications with the assistance of basic computing components. Compute basically consists of physical and logical components. By physical components, we mean hardware devices, whereas logical refers to software and protocols used.

Cloud Compliance as a Service This offers compliance collection and facilitates your cloud applications as per corporate policies or organization requirements.

Preface

Cloud Computing is an emerging technology in today's world. It provides access to inexpensive software, infrastructure, and platform through very simple APIs that are based on a pay-per-use model, so that renting these resources is much cheaper then acquiring dedicated new ones. It is a practice that allows use of shared resources through a network of remote servers, which store and manage the data on the Internet. Of late, it has become very important for businesses as it provides services such as data security, scalability, easy accessibility and sharing of data, zero maintenance, and easy data recovery. Since the focus has shifted from PCs to data centers, and with growing competition, there are many cloud computing platforms and technologies available in the market.

ABOUT THE BOOK

This book on 'Cloud Computing' explains the fundamentals of cloud computing, migration services, virtualization as also the various cloud security issues faced. It discusses the principles followed by cloud service companies and platforms available in the market. Apart from the basics, various advanced technologies such as Big Table and IoT are also covered in this book.

The book follows a bottom-up approach with systematic flow of concepts covered in 12 chapters and 8 appendices. It is meant for the undergraduate computer science and information technology students of all Indian universities for an introductory course on the subject.

KEY FEATURES

- Student friendly and easy to understand
- Lucid, simple, and conversational language
- Focuses on the latest developments in cloud computing
- Discusses cloud computing models, cloud data center, virtualization technology both at the system and network level, and the architecture in detail
- Covers topics such as Cloud Platforms and Security, that are central to the subject, in separate chapters
- Provides a well-written points-to-remember section, review questions, key terms with explanation, and multiple-choice questions at the end of every chapter.
- Includes appendices with study of Amazon network, Microsoft, Salesforce.com, Eucalyptus, Aneka, and Hypervisors
- Comes with Model Question Papers from different universities

CONTENT AND COVERAGE

An attempt has been made to write this book in simple and lucid language with self-explanatory illustrations. The brief content of the book is as follows:

Chapter 1 provides an *Overview of Cloud Computing*. It starts with the history, need, and evolution of cloud computing, and then explains the benefits of this practice. It also discusses the limitations of cloud computing and throws some light on the vendors available in the market, elastic computing, enterprise cloud computing, etc.

Chapter 2 explains the *Factors Affecting Cloud Computing*. It highlights various cloud data center requirements and introduces architectural, technological, and operational influences on cloud computing. Topics such as issues in scalability of cloud architecture and applications, and influence of cloud computing on business companies are also discussed.

Chapter 3 on *Cloud Computing Architecture* discusses cloud computing architecture on the basis of load balancing, disk provisioning, storage management, hypervisor installed, migration, service relocation, cloud balancing, virtual switches of load balancing, and failure detection and recovery. Key design aspects of cloud architecture, similarities and differences between grid and cloud computing, and characteristics of cloud computing are also explained in this chapter.

Chapter 4 introduces the various *Models of Cloud Computing*. Software as a Service (SaaS), Platform as a Service (PaaS), and Infrastructure as a Service (IaaS) are discussed in detail. This chapter also covers four cloud deployment models—public clouds, private clouds, community clouds, and hybrid clouds. Topics such as alternative deployment models, CloudStack, and cloud storage are also touched upon in this chapter.

Chapter 5 presents to its readers the *Traditional Data Center and Cloud Data Center*. It begins with the core elements of traditional data center and then discusses storage network technologies used. Important topics such as cloud backup, cloud and disaster recovery, replication technologies, and cloud analytics are also dealt with in this chapter. In the later part, traditional data center management is also discussed.

Chapter 6 on *Virtualization Technology (At Server)* covers virtualization reference model, types of virtualization, server/compute virtualization components, need of server/compute virtualization and its advantages, and techniques used. Hypervisor taxonomy, resource management tools, and conversion from physical machine to virtual machine (P2V) are also explained in this chapter.

Chapter 7 deals with *Virtualization Technology (At Network)*. It highlights tools used in network virtualization, its benefits, and components such as virtual switches and virtual LAN. Traffic management and its techniques, and virtual machine migration services are also covered.

Chapter 8 describes *Virtualization Technology (At Desktop and Application)*. It emphasizes on the drivers used in virtualization, the techniques used such as remote desktop services and virtual desktop infrastructure, and the components of desktop virtualization. Application virtualization, hardware virtual machine, and virtual machine provisioning are also discussed.

Chapter 9 explains *Cloud Infrastructure Management and Migration*. Cloud suppliers including RightScale, Kaavo, Zeus, Scalr, and Morph are discussed in this chapter along with the components that constitute the framework of cloud infrastructure. It also discusses unified management software, processes involved in cloud service management, technique used to access cloud, and challenges in migration to and from the cloud.

Chapter 10 makes readers understand the various *Security Issues of Cloud Computing*. Security threats and vulnerabilities in cloud computing, cloud security design principles and objectives, and cloud security services are explained in detail. Cloud testing and its requirements, secure development practices, virtual machine security techniques, challenges faced, and legal issues involved in cloud computing are also dealt with.

Chapter 11 *Computing Platforms* such as XCP, T-Platform, Force.com and Salesforce.com, Apache VCL, Enomaly Elastic Computing Platform, MapReduce, Hadoop, OpenNebula, Nimbus, Google App Engine, Microsoft Hyper-V, Microsoft Azure, AJAX, EMC, and NETAPP, are discussed in this chapter. It also explains service level agreement, OLAP, ISVs, and Sky Computing.

Chapter 12 is devoted to *Advanced Technologies in Cloud Computing*. It covers cloud deployment tools, groupware clouds, mobile cloud computing, cloud descriptor language, green computing, third-party technology, Intercloud, Azure cloud services, BigTable, IoT, CometCloud, and T-Systems.

Appendix A lists the various acronyms and abbreviations used in the book.

Appendices B-H cover study on Amazon Network, Microsoft, Salesforce.com, Hypervisor Network, Eucalyptus, Cloud Simulators, and Aneka.

ONLINE RESOURCES

To aid teachers and students, the book is accompanied with online resources that are available at https://india.oup.com/orcs/9780199477388. The content for the online resources is as follows:

For Faculty
Chapter-wise PPTs

For Students
Additional MCQs with answers
Two Model Questions Papers

ACKNOWLEDGEMENT

I wish to express my deepest gratitude to Dr C. Thangaraj, Director, National Institute of Technical Teachers' Training and Research, Bhopal for his valuable guidance and support. Without his inspiration, effort, and advice, this book would not have been possible. I am very grateful to my source of inspiration, Prof. Sunil Kumar Gupta, Vice Chancellor Rajiv Gandhi Proudygiki, Vishwavidyalaya, Bhopal, India for his motivation. I am very grateful to Dr Sanjay Silakari, former I/C Director, UIT, RGPV, Dr Geetam Singh Tomar, Director, THDC-IHET Tehri, Uttarakhand, Dr Sanjiv Sharma, Head School of IT, RGPV, Bhopal and Dr Ravindra Patel, Head, MCA, RGPV, Bhopal for motivating me to write this book.

I would like to give special thanks to my Ph.D scholar Mrs Sunita Gond who helped me in each and every chapter of this book. She has supported me in every respect.

Special gratitude is expressed for Dr K G Srinivasa, Associate Professor, Department of Information Technology, Ch Brahm Prakash Government Engineering College, Jaffarpur, New Delhi, for his contribution to chapter 12 of the book.

I would also like to thank other reviewers, Sudip Sahana, Department of CSE, Birla Institute of Technology, Mesra, Ranchi; A. Dennis Ananth, Assistant Professor, Department of Information Technology, Bannari Amman Institute of Technology, Alathukombai, Tamil Nadu; U. A. Deshpande HOD, CSE, NIT, Nagpur; Dr S. Mary Saira Bhanu, Associate Professor, Department of Computer Science & Engg., National Institute of Technology, Tiruchirappalli; and S.D. Madhu Kumar, HOD, CSE, NIT, Calicut.

I would like to express my heartiest thank to my beloved wife Dr Neelu Singh for her invaluable, endless support. I owe thanks to my loving children, Navodita and Aryan, who were a constant support.

All suggestions for the improvement of the book are welcome and can be sent to ssingh@nitttrbpl.ac.in

Shailendra Singh

Brief Contents

Features of the Book iv
Preface vii
Contents xi

1. Overview of Cloud Computing 1
2. Factors that Affect Cloud Computing 31
3. Cloud Computing Architecture 48
4. Models of Cloud Computing 72
5. Cloud Data Center 98
6. Virtualization Technology (At Server) 119
7. Virtualization Technology (At Network) 143
8. Virtualization Technology (At Desktop and Application) 160
9. Cloud Infrastructure Management and Migration 176
10. Security Issues of Cloud Computing 196
11. Computing Platforms 230
12. Advanced Technologies in Cloud Computing 254

Appendix-A 289
Appendix-B 292
Appendix-C 296
Appendix-D 299
Appendix-E 302
Appendix-F 305
Appendix-G 308
Appendix-H 310
Model Question Papers 315
Index 321
About The Author 327
Related Titles 328

Contents

Features of the Book   iv
Preface   vii

1. **Overview of Cloud Computing**   1
   1.1 Introduction   1
   1.2 Essentials of Cloud Computing   1
   1.3 Need of Cloud Computing   4
      1.3.1 Reduced Costs   5
      1.3.2 Scalability   6
      1.3.3 Remote Access   6
      1.3.4 Disaster Relief   7
      1.3.5 Ease of Implementation   7
      1.3.6 Skilled Vendors   8
      1.3.7 Response Time   8
      1.3.8 Easy to Customize   8
      1.3.9 Virtual Provisioning   8
      1.3.10 Fully Automated Storage Tiering—FAST   9
   1.4 History of Cloud Computing   9
      1.4.1 Client-Server Technology   9
      1.4.2 Peer-to-Peer Approach   10
      1.4.3 Distributed Computing   11
      1.4.4 Evolution of Cloud Computing from Grid Computing   11
      1.4.5 Autonomic Computing   14
      1.4.6 Platform Virtualization   14
      1.4.7 Service Oriented Architecture—SOA   14
      1.4.8 Utility Computing   15
      1.4.9 Web 2.0   15
      1.4.10 Parallel Computing   15
   1.5 Business and Information Technology Perspective   16
      1.5.1 Electronic Faxing   17
      1.5.2 Voice on Clouds   17
      1.5.3 Commerce on Clouds   17
      1.5.4 Distributed Hosting on Clouds   17
      1.5.5 Accounting and Online Banking   17
   1.6 News on Clouds   17
   1.7 Benefits of Cloud Computing   18
   1.8 Limitations of Cloud Computing   18
      1.8.1 Availability of Services   19
      1.8.2 Data Lock-in   19
      1.8.3 Data Segregation   19
      1.8.4 Privilege Neglect   20
      1.8.5 Scaling Resources   20
      1.8.6 Data Location   20
      1.8.7 Deletion of Data   21
      1.8.8 Recovery and Backup   21
      1.8.9 Offline Clouds   21
      1.8.10 Unpredictable Performance   21
   1.9 How to Develop Cloud Infrastructure   21
   1.10 Vendors of Cloud Computing   23
      1.10.1 Amazon Web Services—IaaS   23
      1.10.2 Google—SaaS, PaaS   23
      1.10.3 Microsoft Azure Service Platform—PaaS   23
      1.10.4 Rackspace—Cloud Hosting   24
      1.10.5 Salesforce.com—SaaS, PaaS   24
   1.11 Elastic Computing   24
   1.12 Social Networking   25
   1.13 Enterprise Cloud Computing   25

   Points to Remember   26
   Key Terms   27
   Multiple-choice Questions   28
   Review Questions   29
   References   30
   Answers to Multiple-choice Questions   30

2. **Factors that Affect Cloud Computing**   31
   2.1 Introduction   31
   2.2 Cloud Data Center Requirements   31
      2.2.1 Architectural Influences   32

2.2.2 Issues in Scalability of Cloud Architecture and Applications 35
2.2.3 Technological Influences 38
2.2.4 Operational Influences 40
2.3 Influence of Cloud Computing on Business Companies 42
2.3.1 Business Alignment 43
2.3.2 Governance 43

Points to Remember 44
Key Terms 45
Multiple-choice Questions 46
Review Questions 46
References 47
Answers to Multiple-choice Questions 47

3. Cloud Computing Architecture 48

3.1 Introduction 48
3.2 Grid Framework Overview 48
3.3 Grid Architecture 49
3.3.1 Advantages of Grid Computing 50
3.3.2 Challenges of Grid Computing 51
3.4 Cloud Computing Architecture 51
3.4.1 On the Basis of Load Balancing 53
3.4.2 On the Basis of Disk Provisioning 54
3.4.3 On the Basis of Storage Management 55
3.4.4 On the Basis of Hypervisor Installed 55
3.4.5 On the Basis of Migration 56
3.4.6 On the Basis of Service Relocation 57
3.4.7 On the Basis of Cloud Balancing 58
3.4.8 On the Basis of Virtual Switches Load Balancing 59
3.4.9 On the Basis of Failure Detection and Recovery 59
3.5 Key Design Aspects of Cloud Architecture, Cloud Services, and Cloud Applications 59
3.6 Similarities and Differences Between Grid and Cloud Computing 60
3.7 Characteristics of Cloud Computing 62
3.7.1 On Demand Self Services 63
3.7.2 Broad Network Access 63
3.7.3 Resource Pooling 64
3.7.4 Quick Elasticity 64
3.7.5 Calculated Service 64
3.7.6 Multi-persistence 64
3.7.7 Dynamic Computing Infrastructure 65
3.7.8 IT Service-centric Approach 65
3.7.9 Self-service Based Usage Model 65
3.7.10 Self-managed Platform 66
3.7.11 Elasticity and Scalability 66
3.7.12 Standardized Interfaces 66
3.8 Cloud and Dynamic Infrastructure 66
3.9 Impediments to Cloud Adoption 68

Points to Remember 68
Key Terms 69
Multiple-choice Questions 69
Review Questions 70
References 70
Answers to Multiple-choice Questions 71

4. Models of Cloud Computing 72

4.1 Introduction 72
4.2 Cloud Service Models 72
4.2.1 Software as a Service 73
4.2.2 Platform as a Service 76
4.2.3 Infrastructure as a Service 80
4.2.4 Cluster as a Service 82
4.3 Cloud Computing Sub Service Models 83
4.3.1 Everything as a Service 83
4.3.2 Compliance as a Service 83
4.3.3 Identity as a Service 84
4.3.4 IaaS: DataBase as a Service (DBaaS) 84
4.3.5 Paas: Storage as a Service (STaaS) 84
4.3.6 SaaS: Communications as a Service (CaaS) 84
4.3.7 SaaS: Security as a Service (SECaaS) 84
4.3.8 SaaS: Monitoring as a Service (MaaS) 84

  4.3.9 PaaS: Desktop as a Service (DTaaS) 84
  4.3.10 IaaS: Compute Capacity as a Service (CCaaS) 84
 4.4 Cloud Deployment Models 85
  4.4.1 Public Clouds 86
  4.4.2 Private Clouds 87
  4.4.3 Community Clouds 89
  4.4.4 Hybrid Clouds 90
 4.5 Alternative Deployment Models 92
  4.5.1 Linthicum Model 92
  4.5.2 Jericho Cloud Cube Model 92
 4.6 CloudStack 93
 4.7 Cloud Storage 93

Points to Remember 94
Key Terms 95
Multiple-choice Questions 95
Review Questions 96
References 97
Answers to Multiple-choice Questions 97

5. Cloud Data Center 98

 5.1 Introduction 98
 5.2 Cloud Data Center Core Elements 98
  5.2.1 Application 99
  5.2.2 Database Management Systems 99
  5.2.3 Compute 100
  5.2.4 Storage 100
  5.2.5 Network 103
 5.3 Storage Network Technologies and Virtualization 104
  5.3.1 Components of Fibre Channel SAN 104
 5.4 Object-based Storage Technologies 105
 5.5 Unified Storage 106
 5.6 Business Continuity 107
 5.7 Cloud Backup 107
 5.8 Cloud and Disaster Recovery 108
 5.9 Replication Technologies 109
 5.10 Traditional Data Center Management 110
 5.11 Information Life Cycle Management 112
 5.12 Cloud Analytics 114
 5.13 Computing on Demand 115

Points to Remember 115
Key Terms 116
Multiple-choice Questions 117
Review Questions 117
References 118
Answers to Multiple-choice Questions 118

6. Virtualization Technology (At Server) 119

 6.1 Introduction 119
 6.2 Virtualization Reference Model 119
 6.3 Advantages of Virtualization 120
 6.4 Server/Compute Virtualization 120
  6.4.1 Server/Compute Components 122
 6.5 Need of Server/Compute Virtualization 125
 6.6 Virtual Clusters 126
 6.7 Advantages of Server/Compute Virtualization 127
 6.8 Techniques of Server/Compute Virtualization 127
 6.9 Virtual Machine and Hardware Components 128
 6.10 Hypervisor Taxonomy 129
 6.11 Resource Management and Tools 129
 6.12 Physical Machine to Virtual Machine (P2V) Conversion 131
  6.12.1 Converter Components 132
  6.12.2 Conversion Process 132
 6.13 Logical Partitioning 134
 6.14 Types of Virtualization 134
  6.14.1 Data Center Virtualization 134
  6.14.2 Server Virtualization 135
  6.14.3 Storage Virtualization 135
  6.14.4 Sensor Virtualization 136
 6.15 Storage Area Network 136
 6.16 Network Attached Storage 138

Points to Remember 139
Key Terms 140
Multiple-choice Questions 141
Review Questions 141
References 142
Answers to Multiple-choice Questions 142

7. Virtualization Technology (At Network) 143

- 7.1 Introduction 143
- 7.2 Exploring Network Virtualization 143
- 7.3 Tools Used In Network Virtualization 145
- 7.4 Benefits Of Network Virtualization 145
- 7.5 Features of Network Components 146
  - 7.5.1 Virtual Switches 146
  - 7.5.2 Virtual LAN 148
- 7.6 Traffic Management and its Techniques 149
  - 7.6.1 Technique 1: Balancing Client Workload—Hardware 150
  - 7.6.2 Technique 2: Balancing Client Workload—Software 150
  - 7.6.3 Technique 3: Storm Control 151
  - 7.6.4 Technique 4: NIC Teaming 152
  - 7.6.5 Technique 5: Limit and Share 152
  - 7.6.6 Technique 6: Traffic Shaping 152
  - 7.6.7 Proposed Load Balancing in Cloud Computing 153
- 7.7 Virtual Machine Migration Services 155

Points to Remember 157
Key Terms 158
Multiple-choice Questions 158
Review Questions 159
References 159
Answers to Multiple-choice Questions 159

8. Virtualization Technology (At Desktop and Application) 160

- 8.1 Introduction 160
- 8.2 Understanding Desktop Virtualization 160
- 8.3 Drivers Used in Virtualization 163
  - 8.3.1 Features of Desktop Virtualization Drivers 163
- 8.4 Techniques Used for Desktop Virtualization 163
  - 8.4.1 Remote Desktop Services 164
  - 8.4.2 Infrastructure for Desktop Virtualization 165
- 8.5 Components for Desktop Virtualization 166
- 8.6 Application Virtualization 167
  - 8.6.1 Tools Used for Application Virtualization 168
- 8.7 Hardware Virtual Machine (HVM) 169
- 8.8 Understanding Machine Imaging 171
- 8.9 Porting Application 171
- 8.10 Virtual Machine Provisioning 172
- 8.11 Virtual Machine Migration Services Management 172

Points to Remember 173
Key Terms 173
Multiple-choice Questions 174
Review Questions 175
References 175
Answers to Multiple-choice Questions 175

9. Cloud Infrastructure Management and Migration 176

- 9.1 Introduction 176
- 9.2 Administrating Clouds 176
- 9.3 Cloud Management Products 179
- 9.4 Unified Management Software 180
- 9.5 Processes in Cloud Service Management 182
  - 9.5.1 Service Benefit and Configuration Administration 183
  - 9.5.2 Capacity Administration 183
  - 9.5.3 Performance Administration 183
  - 9.5.4 Incident Administration 183
  - 9.5.5 Problem Administration 184
  - 9.5.6 Availability Administration 184
  - 9.5.7 Service Catalog Administration 184
  - 9.5.8 Financial Management 185
  - 9.5.9 Compliance Administration 185
- 9.6 Cloud Providers and Traditional IT Service Providers 185
- 9.7 How to Access the Cloud 187
  - 9.7.1 Platforms 187
  - 9.7.2 Web Applications 187
  - 9.7.3 Web Application Programming Interface 188
  - 9.7.4 Web Browsers 189

9.8 Migrating to Clouds 191
  9.8.1 Challenges in Migration to and from the Cloud 192
9.9 Banking on Cloud Economics 193

Points to Remember 193
Key Terms 194
Multiple-choice Questions 194
Review Questions 195
References 195
Answers to Multiple-choice Questions 195

10. **Security Issues of Cloud Computing 196**
    10.1 Introduction 196
    10.2 Security Concerns of Cloud Computing 196
      10.2.1 Threats to Infrastructure, Data, and Access Control 198
    10.3 Cloud Information Security Objectives 199
      10.3.1 Confidentiality 200
      10.3.2 Cloud Computing Environment and Accessibility 200
      10.3.3 Organizational Security and Privacy Requirements 200
      10.3.4 Client-side Computing Environment Requirement 201
      10.3.5 Cloud Security Services 201
      10.3.6 Integrity 201
    10.4 Cloud Security Design Principles 201
    10.5 Cloud Security Services 204
    10.6 Secure Cloud Software Testing 205
      10.6.1 Need for Cloud Testing 206
      10.6.2 Types of Testing 206
      10.6.3 Importance of Cloud Testing 207
      10.6.4 Forms of Cloud-based Software Testing 207
      10.6.5 Internet-based Software Testing vs Cloud Testing 208
      10.6.6 Cloud Testing Environment 208
    10.7 Secure Cloud Software Requirements 209
    10.8 Secure Development Practices 210
    10.9 Vulnerability Assessment Tools for Clouds 213
    10.10 Cloud Architectural Consideration 213
    10.11 Secure Execution Environment and Communications 214
    10.12 Identity Management and Access Control 214
    10.13 VM Security Recommendations 214
      10.13.1 VM Security Techniques 215
    10.14 Challenges to Cloud Security 215
      10.14.1 Computer Security Incident Response Team 216
    10.15 Risk Issues 217
    10.16 Physical Security of Systems 217
    10.17 Input Validation and Content Injection 218
    10.18 Database Integrity Issues 218
    10.19 Regulatory Issues 218
    10.20 Legal Matters in Cloud Computing 219
    10.21 Information Privacy and Laws 221
    10.22 Common Threats and Vulnerabilities 221
    10.23 Logon Abuse 221
    10.24 Inappropriate System Uses 222
    10.25 Network Intrusion 222
    10.26 Session Hijacking Attacks 222
    10.27 Fragmentation Attacks 223
    10.28 Cloud Access Control Issues 223

Points to Remember 225
Key Terms 225
Multiple-choice Questions 227
Review Questions 228
References 229
Answers to Multiple-choice Questions 229

11. **Computing Platforms 230**
    11.1 Introduction 230
    11.2 Exploring Cloud Management Products 231
    11.3 SOA and Cloud Computing 231
    11.4 Online Analytical Processing 232
    11.5 Business Intelligence 232
    11.6 Independent Software Vendor 234
    11.7 Cloud Performance Monitoring Tools 235

11.8 Quality of Service Issues in Clouds 235
11.9 Intercloud 236
11.10 Sky Computing 236
11.11 Xen Cloud Platforms 237
11.12 Tplatform 237
11.13 Force.com and Salesforce.com 238
11.14 Apache Virtual Computing Lab 238
11.15 Enomaly Elastic Computing Platform 239
11.16 MapReduce 239
11.17 Hadoop 240
11.18 Cloud Mashup 241
11.19 OpenNebula 241
11.20 Nimbus 242
11.21 Google App Engine 242
11.22 Microsoft Hyper-V 243
11.23 Microsoft Azure 244
11.24 AJAX 245
11.25 EMC 246
11.26 NETAPP 247
11.27 Cloud Service Suppliers and Threats 247
11.28 Service Level Agreement 248
11.29 Third-party Technology 249

Points to Remember 250
Key Terms 251
Multiple-choice Questions 252
Review Questions 253
References 253
Answers to Multiple-choice Questions 253

12. Advanced Technologies in Cloud Computing 254

12.1 Introduction 254
12.2 Cloud Computing Trends 254
12.3 Understanding Cloud Tools 256
12.4 Cloud with DiverseLook 256
12.5 Media Clouds 257
12.6 Security Clouds 258
12.7 App-specific Clouds 259
   12.7.1 Virtualized Desktop 259
12.8 Groupware Clouds 260
12.9 Mobile Cloud Computing 262
12.10 Cloud Computing Environment Open-Stack 264
12.11 Selection of Cloud Application 265
12.12 Cloud Descriptor Language 265
12.13 Green Computing 267
12.14 Workload Pattern for Clouds 268
12.15 Third-party Technology 270
12.16 Intercloud 271
12.17 Azure Cloud Services 272
12.18 Bigtable 273
   12.18.1 Chubby 275
   12.18.2 Development of Bigtable 276
12.19 Cloud Usage for Big Data Analytics and Internet of Things 276
   12.19.1 Different Aspects of IoT Systems 281
12.20 CometCloud 282
12.21 T-Systems 283

Points to Remember 284
Key Terms 284
Multiple-choice Questions 285
Review Questions 286
References 286
Answers to Multiple-choice Questions 286

Appendix-A 289
Appendix-B 292
Appendix-C 296
Appendix-D 299
Appendix-E 302
Appendix-F 305
Appendix-G 308
Appendix-H 310
Model Question Papers 315
Index 321
About The Author 327
Related Titles 328

CHAPTER 1

Overview of Cloud Computing

> **Learning Outcomes**
>
> After completing this chapter, students will be able to:
>
> - define cloud computing
> - describe need of cloud computing
> - describe history of cloud computing
> - explain historical evolution of cloud computing
> - describe benefits of cloud computing
> - understand limitations of cloud computing
> - explain elastic computing
> - differentiate various vendors of cloud computing
> - distinguish traditional data center and cloud data center

1.1 INTRODUCTION

Cloud computing is a technology which utilizes the Internet and central isolated servers in order to sustain applications and data. Users can access applications and data at any workstation through the Internet. This technology permits much more proficient computing by consolidating bandwidth, processing, and storage memory. Cloud offers robust memory administration, thus there is no necessity to sustain memory on a personal system. It alters the means by which the Internet and computer are used.

In this chapter, we will discuss the fundamental techniques and components in cloud computing, technologies from where cloud computing originated, and the various services provided by cloud computing to its users. Later in the chapter, the limitations of cloud computing and the important challenges, which prove to be obstacles in cloud computing, will be discussed. We will also discuss the difference between traditional data center and cloud data center.

1.2 ESSENTIALS OF CLOUD COMPUTING

Cloud computing is a type of computing that provides an off-premise computing facility like storing data on virtual resources using the Internet. The main component behind cloud computing is the data center. The data center refers to an on-premise hardware facility that is used for many purposes, for example, storing data on the local network.

The term 'cloud' is defined by NIST [10] as follows:

"Cloud computing is a model for enabling ubiquitous, convenient, on-demand network access to a shared pool of configurable computing resources (e.g., networks, servers, storage, applications, and services)

that can be rapidly provisioned and released with minimal management effort or service provider interaction. This cloud model is composed of five essential characteristics, three service models, and four deployment models."

Cloud computing offers services instead of a product, whereby shared software, information, and resources are supplied to computers and other tools efficiently over a network. Cloud users should not need to identify the site and other particulars such as infrastructure but cloud computing offers software applications, computation, storage resources, and data access and data administration facility.

End users access cloud-based applications via diverse interfaces such as a light-weight desktop, a web browser, or different mobile applications, whereas applications such as data and business software are saved on servers at an isolated site. Cloud application suppliers attempt to provide enhanced functioning and service than that provided if software programs were deployed locally on the end-user or on detached computers.

Cloud computing performs tasks at a faster rate to meet the demands of users. It permits the data center to allow enterprises to acquire applications and work on data quickly, and needs only simple administration and less upholding. Many unpredictable and uncertain company orders of IT resources, such as networking and servers, are effortlessly met with the cloud computing technology. The basic structure of cloud computing is shown in Fig. 1.1. As given in the figure, facilities and services are offered by cloud providers in a cloud computing environment and different users from various locations and devices can request for specific services that are offered.

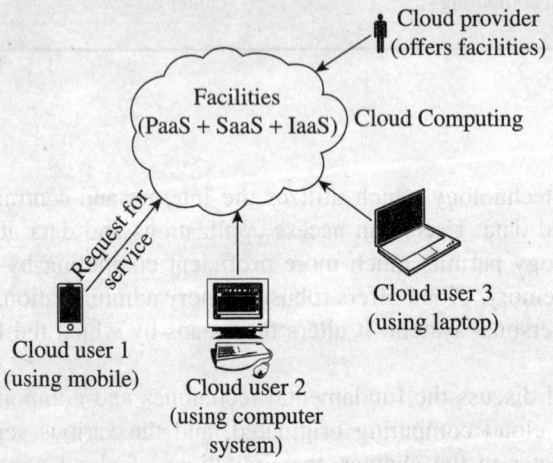

Fig. 1.1 Basic structure of cloud computing

As cloud computing is a recent technology, different people have different views about it. Cloud computing actually meets the overall software and hardware demand of an organization, user, or company.

Cloud computing is a novel approach and an important innovation in how we operate applications and save information. On the cloud, everything is hosted effortlessly. This is easier than managing data and programs on a personal desktop computer. You can access every application and any record from anywhere on the globe.

Associates working towards a similar goal may team up, irrespective of the positions they hold, and work in parallel. Cloud computing works to lessen the capital expenses involved in storing data. The IT division can concentrate on the actual coding and technical problems, rather than on maintaining

the data center. It reduces the total investment in hardware and software charges of a corporation. Some of the benefits of cloud computing are given here:
1. It improves parallelism and allocation of resources for fast accessing
2. One may acquire software services, networked storage space, computer resources, and various other services at a single place
3. An additional company hosts a set of applications, get software renewals (with no charge), and so on
4. It improves monetary burden such as operational expenses, renewing charge, and capital expenses

Hotmail, Gmail, Yahoo email, etc., are all simple illustrations of cloud computing. You do not need a server or software for using them. Customers would just require an Internet connection and then begin functioning with cloud services. The email administration software and server are on the cloud and are completely controlled by the cloud service suppliers, Google and Yahoo, among many others. The customer may use modernized software and have the advantages of cloud computing. Cloud computing is an array of network, hardware, storage, interfaces, and services which facilitate the various services. We can also say that the term 'cloud' is a set of hardware, network, storage, services, and interfaces that facilitate the service.

In cloud architecture, there are generally five main components of cloud infrastructure.
- Front-end interface for users for simple access and for using cloud resources
- Management for handling networking resources
- Storage for virtual machine
- Constant storage tool that may be organized within working virtual machines
- Monitoring tools for initiating virtual machines on the cloud

There are two types of a cloud environment:
1. The end user who has no idea about cloud complexity
2. The cloud service provider who has the liability of controlling the complete cloud environment and offer services to the consumer. One of the jobs of the supplier is safety, and it assures the consumers the degree to which their data is protected. The cloud service supplier is also accountable for IT resources, uploading, and other services offered to the user. Various services and resources are provided to users by the cloud provider, as suggested and managed by the cloud administrator, in the cloud environment, as shown in Fig. 1.2.

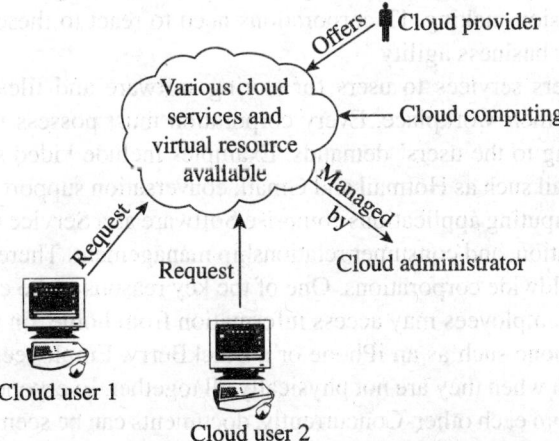

Fig. 1.2 Cloud resource management

Cloud computing gives users the option of accessing information from any place at any point of time. To access the conventional computer system, you should be in a similar physical position as your data storage tool. The cloud eradicates this barrier. Suppliers of clouds offer you the obligatory software and hardware for operating your company or home applications.

It is required to pay for storage space, hardware, and software for a business or corporation if they are using cloud resources provided by cloud providers. Small corporations as well may save their information on the cloud, which will lessen the price of buying hardware and memory tools. They only need to purchase a specific volume of storage space, as per the requirement.

You require an Internet connection to access the cloud. The benefit of this is that you can access that record from anywhere, by any tool that can access the Internet. Workers at distinct sites can access similar data on the cloud and any tool may be used (e.g., a laptop, desktop, mobile phone, or tablet). Cloud computing involves a cloud consumer, cloud provider, cloud auditor, cloud broker, and cloud carrier, as shown in Table 1.1.

Table 1.1 Terminology used in cloud computing

Cloud consumer	An individual person or organization that sustains a business relationship with cloud providers and avails the services offered by the provider
Cloud provider	An individual person or organization who offers a service and is liable for the services of cloud computing to the parties that demand it
Cloud auditor	A party that conducts evaluation of cloud services, such as performance, operation on various systems, and security, among others
Cloud broker	The management between cloud providers and cloud consumers, like presentation and delivery of various services
Cloud carrier	The mediator responsible for connectivity and transport of cloud services from service providers to cloud consumers

1.3 NEED OF CLOUD COMPUTING

Every corporation desires to provide workers with a comfortable platform for working. In a corporation, there are top-level professionals who are always in the pursuit of more elasticity, heavier workload at lower fees, and the use of information as a competitive benefit to recognize the most appropriate information and data for decision-making. IT corporations need to react to these changes by converting IT into a domain with better business agility.

Cloud computing offers services to users for storing software and files distantly, instead of on a server or a hard drive at their workplace. Every corporation must possess its own personal cloud that may be adapted according to the users' demands. Examples include video sites such as Facebook and YouTube, web-based email such as Hotmail and Gmail, conversation support tools like Skype, and many others. Certain cloud computing applications comprise Software as a Service (SaaS), file storage, and file back-up, file synchronization, and consumer relationship management. There are many benefits of using cloud computing for worldwide corporations. One of the key reasons is the elasticity provided by it.

Through the Internet, employees may access information from home, on the way, from a customer's office, or from a smartphone such as an iPhone or a BlackBerry. Employees may also jointly work on documents and files, even when they are not physically all together. Everyone can work mutually even if they are physically far from each other. Concurrently, documents can be seen and proofread even though they are in remote areas.

Cloud computing may be extremely fast and simple to operate. Since downloading and deploying of software needs time, clouds maintain everything up to date. Cloud computing is cheaper as well. There is no requirement of purchasing and deploying costly software as it is already deployed online and you operate it from there. Cloud computing provides agility and it may be easily and swiftly scaled up and down as per the requirement.

One of the chief benefits of using cloud computing for various corporations is that it provides nearly infinite storage, in contrast to a server, and takes into consideration the limits of a hard drive as it is online. There is no requirement to pay for enormous disk space and devices. There are many challenges associated with a conventional infrastructure:

Software licensing and support For every application and data center, licensing is needed. However, in cloud computing, for allocated data centers, only a single licence is needed for the application.

Scalability Conventional infrastructure cannot extend easily at a particular instance of time, and scalability requires variation with time. It has to regularly improve in order to face the challenges.

Accountability The application in conventional infrastructure never has vital liability and power.

Modifiability When alteration is needed, the application constantly needs and sustains extra charge.

Physical security It is tough to uphold security, and therefore, security is still a serious issues related to cloud computing.

Cost-effective management To make the application significantly accessible, the replication of data is required from time to time, which is very cost effective for a organization.

After many years of data center augmentation and development of IT, various companies are left with overgrown, complex computing platforms. Cloud computing is a new trend in computing due to its many benefits, which are discussed in the following sections in detail:

1.3.1 Reduced Costs

Cloud technique is rewarded incrementally, thus helping in the reduction of expenditure to an organization. With the help of cloud computing, IT expenses can be minimized. For example, if you are offered a business application over the Internet, you need not deploy and set up any resource at your own risk or cost.

Cloud computing services can minimize the updating requirement of software and hardware because expenses of maintenance and upgradation are handled by the cloud provider.

Though outsourcing IT trade requires extra concentration, the cloud provider handles complexity of technical proficiency, permitting users to concentrate on their main business. IT cloud computing follows a pay-as-you-go approach, where only a low preliminary investment is needed. The main cause of companies to use cloud computing is to save funds. The technology behind the cloud eliminates the servers' cost, maintenance fees, data center space, software licences, etc. Hence, asset expenses are minimized and substituted by scalable and convenient operating costs.

Another aspect that should be taken into account while selecting the cloud is that customer organizational support and maintenance expenses are minimized drastically as these costs are shifted to the cloud supplier, comprising 24/7 support. The requirement for extremely trained and costly IT recruits is minimized as well. In cloud computing, resources are used more effectively, resulting in considerable support and saving of energy expenses.

In practice, it has been discovered that companies spend almost double on server energy expenses than on hardware. An option has been provided by cloud computing for these costs. With cloud computing, corporations need not purchase and deploy costly platforms and software in order to host the software. Apart from many cloud computing applications being provided cost-free, end users are just needed to subscribe to services desired by them, rather than purchasing necessary software. According to requirements, you may scale up or down.

1.3.2 Scalability

With cloud technology, more information can be saved, when compared to personal computer systems by companies. Some of the important advantages of scalability are as follows:

1. One of the biggest advantages of cloud computing is that a business pays only for the services it avails. In a conventional infrastructure and technology, businesses should invest in advanced storage tools and servers which normally occurs at fixed prices. Cloud computing is exclusively scalable and flexible, functioning on the basis of usefulness and permitting businesses to pay as per work and the resources they use.
2. Since cloud computing is based on virtualized technology, RAM space, storage, etc., are simple and swift to use and append. The requirements of a business can be accomplished in hours rather than days.
3. In a cloud environment, scalability is a benefit. With the expansion of the business, further resources are included already to support the progress of the business. In association with SaaS, businesses have to pay according to their demand, that is, pay more for more demand and less for less demand.
4. As business requirements go up and down, instead of buying and making costly advances by yourself, your cloud service supplier may deal with it for you. As this service frees up your time, you may focus more on the functioning of your company.

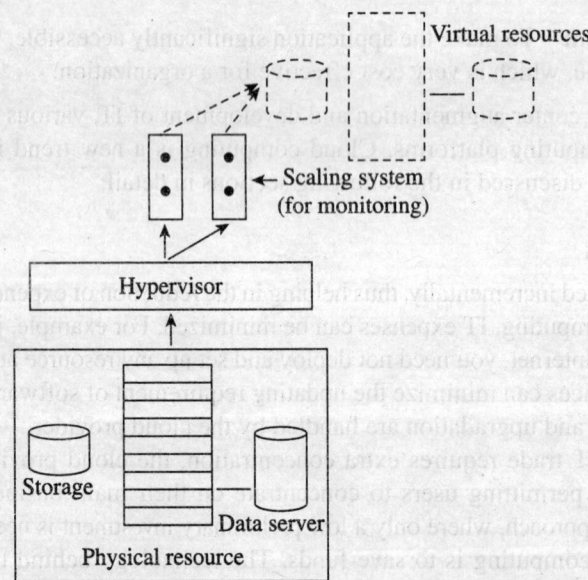

Fig. 1.3 Scaling management in cloud computing

As shown in Fig. 1.3, the scaling system in a cloud environment will maintain a record of the virtual resource requirements of cloud users, and resources' requirement can be kept up to date.

1.3.3 Remote Access

Through cloud computing, it becomes very easy to synchronize data access between international offices. Once data is virtually stored, it can be shared effortlessly between offices that are far from each other through isolated access. The advantages of isolated access are that any tool can be used, any time and at any place.

Anytime, access to Viewpoint V6 Software is offered by Viewpoint Cloud Computing and it is the top incorporated comprehension software solution of the industry that can be accessible from any place with an Internet connection.

Regardless of place, users would have access to their software, attributing the newest information and data on any venture. Users can do the following:
1. Access project reports and data, alter orders, etc.
2. Sense the 'always on' benefit of being capable of giving up one zone and carry on even on your smart cell phone.
3. Expand your trade and support your cell phone sales strength as everybody has 24 × 7 access to the cloud any time, from any mobile tool or desktop.

The advantages of cloud computing and web-based business cooperation applications all emphasize on the advantages of isolated access. Cooperating on shared records expands the speed upon which people may complete complex jobs collectively. Accessing private files from any isolated desktop connection signifies that a person is certainly not coupled to a machine or site in order to use software and files that are vital to them, whether for personal or business use. Web and cloud computing are as good as the extent to which they facilitate people to share and access; isolated access is the chief advantage of these technologies.

Isolated access functions in three fundamental methods. The first is the streaming of data from one machine to another; this occurs when a person online listens to a radio station or watches a movie. The second one is when web applications exhibit an interface which permits the web user to interact with an application such as an online store or a search engine. The third one is when files are made comprehensible on an isolated desktop computer through desktop sharing and isolated control software, and are cloned to the PC of the end user to be controlled and cloned back to the initial site. For the third use, users download isolated PC access software, a petite yet precious piece of software for small ventures and also for large- and middle-sized businesses.

1.3.4 Disaster Relief

Natural calamities such as earthquakes, floods, internal troubles, and wars might result not only in the loss of data of e-governance applications but also in unavailability of services. In a different geographical locality, multiple set-ups along with total backup and retrieval explanations should survive. Disaster recovery control measures should be put in place and exercised from time to time. Data and applications should be surplus and must be accessible at short notice to switch from one data center to another. Cloud virtualization techniques permit restoration and backup. As compared to a conventional data center, it provides flawless migration of applications.

1.3.5 Ease of Implementation

Over the last several years, cloud computing has become very popular, as now-a-days, workplaces and homes have access to broadband Internet. Cloud computing has many benefits over other conventional ways of hosting and networking. These benefits are particularly noticeable for small ventures which require the strength of business services, but the finances are unavailable for purchasing computers, paying workers, and executing the technology.

For those who do not have the knowledge of modern technology, executing cloud computing services might tend to be a little inconvenient on home networks. However, this can be accomplished easily with an Internet connection and a cloud computing host. With this benefit, it becomes easy for small-scale company owners to set up services even if they are unaware of the execution of modern technology.

With the help of these benefits, anybody can get started on cloud computing. The benefits are particularly useful for small enterprises; nevertheless big corporations may also benefit from cloud computing. Cloud applications do not need to be upgraded, fixed, or downloaded. It is easy to learn and use applications and several of these are accessible at a cost-free trial, to check if it suits some small enterprises or not. For small enterprises, various cloud-based software and applications are offered, which are beneficial for smooth running of businesses.

1.3.6 Skilled Vendors

Cloud computing business models need suppliers to appoint, teach, and maintain highly talented workers to maintain the quality of service. Cloud computing suppliers maintain a professional's requirements at their end.

1.3.7 Response Time

Cloud computing achieves an improved response, compared to other types of computing. The response time, is faster when compared to normal hardware and server.

At present, cloud computing is growing in a totally new manner, as businesses of every range and form are getting used to this recent technology. Cloud computing is used for data storage services and software applications which are sent in real time over networks, generally, the Internet. These services principally comprise everything you may perform on a PC—data storage, email, and productivity and conversion applications. The advantages of cloud computing can comprise improved cooperation, cheaper rates, and better mobility.

Cloud computing has significantly lower costs than the equivalent user licences and desktop software. The subscription services provide the best features and priority consumer support although they are paid as per usage.

Possessing such kind of productivity applications and storage 'in the cloud' facilitates access to your files anywhere and anytime. It makes it easier to work on projects regardless of locality and time zones.

Industrial cloud service suppliers must have very strong data backup systems. Through cloud computing, it is improbable that your data will be lost since service suppliers will usually have data retrieval systems in place. Nevertheless, accessibility is a more common drawback. Round-the-clock access is one of the assurances of cloud computing, but the truth is that it is not possible every time. Even chief suppliers own services that can go offline owing to system maintenance or failures from time to time. You would require steady Internet access at your end so as to ascertain your access to the existing services.

Box.net is an online workspace service meant for file grouping and sharing, and QuickBooks Online is a multi-user accounting software.

1.3.8 Easy to Customize

Customization may be possible for easy access of resources to some degree, as per our need. Physical servers or virtual servers may be customized to distinct schemes via a control panel.

Other than these, there are various other benefits of cloud hosting over isolated hosting:
1. Pre-configured operating system—A variety of famous Linux allocations (Debian, Red Hat, Ubuntu, Arch, Fedora Enterprise Linux, and several editions of Windows-based servers)
2. Committed IP addresses for cloud servers
3. Conversion amid servers in the similar cloud, free of conversion expenses and at high speed
4. Allocation or replication over many remote sites

1.3.9 Virtual Provisioning

A novel technology used in storage is the fact that storage space is allocated on demand to various devices on the virtual storage network. There is a virtualized environment for controlling, monitoring, and maintaining a physical disk storage that is connected with virtual machines.

Thin provisioning is another term used for virtual provisioning. Virtual provisioning is mainly used in a virtual environment, whereas thin provisioning is generally used in a physical computing environment. Virtual provisioning does not ensure the assigning of a higher storage capacity to VMs. It offers physical storage to each unit of virtual memory, based on the demands of the user.

1.3.10 Fully Automated Storage Tiering—FAST

Fully automated storage tiering (FAST) mechanically shifts active data to storage tiers with high-performance computing and stationary data to different storage spaces at low cost. It is useful to increase the performance of the applications, compared to other traditional technologies like Serial Advanced Technology Attachment (SATA). It is difficult to do the same optimization in data storage with a manual system. By continuously monitoring FAST, one can easily identify active or inactive data. On the basis of set principles, the administrator can control and manage systems automatically. It is an optimized method that does not add any extra expenditure and burden on the system.

1.4 HISTORY OF CLOUD COMPUTING

Cloud computing is an Internet-based service that has evolved after going through a number of phases, for example, grid and utility computing, SaaS, etc.

In 1999, Salesforce.com came into the market. This was a pioneer of cloud computing. After that, Amazon Web Services was launched in 2002, which provided customized cloud-based services including storage, computation, etc., to the cloud users. Another big invention in cloud computing was in 2009, as Web 2.0 and Google services, through Google Apps.

The following sections show the historical evolution of computing.

1.4.1 Client-Server Technology

Client-Server is the technology behind cloud computing. Client-Server technology is shown in Fig. 1.4. In this, multiple computers perform collectively to augment computing power.

The server is the prime regulator wherein software applications and data are kept for access. If a user requires to operate a program or access precise data, he/she needs to connect to the server, to get suitable access and to perform various operations whilst renting the data or program from the server.

The client may request to be associated to the server, to which the server replies appropriately. This is known as dumb terminal as it does not have high processing power, storage space, or memory. The client is simply a tool which is associated with the user for facilitation.

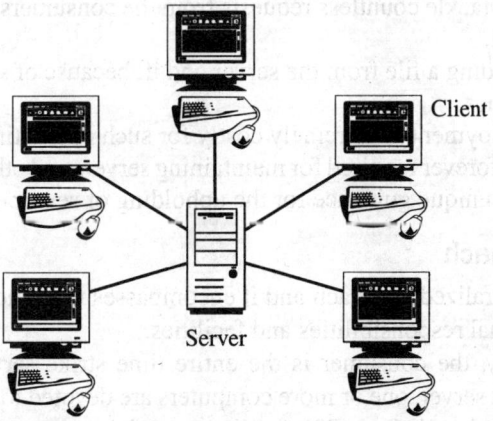

Fig. 1.4 Client-Server technology

The user needs to obtain consent until and unless it does not get approval to access the processor. Due to inadequate processing power, IT employees neither acquire instant access nor can two users access similar data concurrently in client–server technology.

You are required to wait for your number, in case lots of populace is sharing a single computer, even though that computer is an enormous processor. Thus, in a client server, instant access is not probable all the time. Thus, the client server also has a centralized storage, divergent from cloud computing in which it does not have a user-centric converge. Thin clients and fat clients are also used at times, which is a little different from client–server technology.

Fat clients refer to a computer in a client–server technology that is independent of the central server for performing various computations. Fat clients make periodic connections with the server, for performing large functions. Without synchronous connections, it easily performs computations, when compared to thin clients.

A thin client is a computer that is used to create a virtual environment. It depends on the server for performing computation. It shares a desktop, data, and file storage. The advantage of using thin clients for hardware optimal utilization is to reduce software maintenance cost and maintain security of data.

Advantages of Client–Server Networks

Centralized control There is a centralized power used in the client-server model. Servers assist in controlling the complete system. Access acceptance of distinct users and resource allotment is made by servers.

Administration managed File administration turns out to be trouble-free since every file is saved at a single place.

Replication for backup Since complete data is saved on the server, it is easy to create a back-up of it. During the time of recovering the missing data, it performs a vital role.

Easy updating possible Variations may be made simply by mere advancement of the server.

Remote service Access of distant server is possible to accomplish the needs of consumers and support distinct network.

Secure and safe For any computing, safety is a vital feature. Safety convention and access privileges may be termed at the time of association of server.

Disadvantages of Client–Server Networks
1. If the server is unable to tackle countless requests from the consumers, it might lead to congestion with data getting missed.
2. In case you are downloading a file from the server and if, because of some fault, it gets discarded, download too discontinues.
3. Administration and deployment is extremely costly for such computing.
4. Expert IT populaces are forever required for maintaining servers and other technological particulars of the network. It needs unique guidance for the upholding of server.

1.4.2 Peer-to-Peer Approach

Peer-to-Peer (P2P) is a decentralized approach and it encompasses no principal server. It is a design in which every computer has equal responsibilities and facilities.

In client–server technology, the consumer is the entire time strike server for diverse requests. In conventional design of a client server, one or more computers are devoted to serving the others. In a P2P setting, there is no master (boss) and slave. P2P facilitates straight swap of services and resources. No one lingers on for others to react since all are masters (boss) and there is no need for a principal server as any of the computers may perform in that capability, when called on to do so. This kind of network is not simple to manage.

Disadvantages of Peer-to-Peer Networks
1. It is not easy to administer this type of network.
2. Safety matters are forever on this network and it cannot be tackled appropriately.
3. Backup or data revival is not simple. Every computer must have its personal imitation system.

1.4.3 Distributed Computing
To amplify the throughput and for the utmost exploitation of the computing power of a system in a network, we may utilize distributed computing. A system is not completely busy all the time; several systems remain idle many times, so if the idle time of various systems is integrated and used for computation, which functions for the highest consumption, it is known as distributed computing. Distributed computing utilizes those idle resources that are not utilized for some reason or the other. Figure 1.5 shows distributed computing.

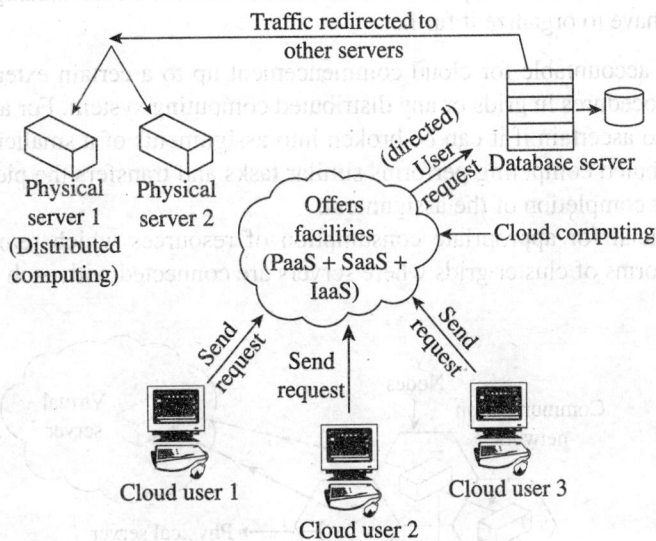

Fig. 1.5 Distributed computing

For highest consumption, free-time dispensation is occasionally uploaded in order to allocate a computing network and to unite with other PCs in the project. If sufficient computers are involved in the computing process, it replicates the dispensation power of bigger supercomputers and processors.

Disadvantages of Distributed Computing
There are several problems regarding transfer and allocation of IT resources. They are as follows:
1. Growing computing power at every data center
2. Growing storage facility
3. Under-consumption of the resources in various scattered data centers
4. Rise in maintenance expenses of data centers

1.4.4 Evolution of Cloud Computing from Grid Computing
Grid computing utilizes a network or group of computers for making computing resources like super computers, and performs large or complex operations and tasks over it. It is not necessary to have a

network of computers at one geographical location. Unused computing powers of many computers are used to perform complex scientific problems using grid computing.

When computers are united mutually for an application, they may be tightly coupled or loosely coupled. Tightly coupled systems via a system bus or some further speedy short-space network normally share memory and other system resources, along with the processors. A geographic discrete system is utilized in grid computing. Associates of grid computing communicate via networks; it does not matter where the computers are actually placed. Grid applications are frequently intended to acquire the benefits of unused CPU cycles accessible on every computer component. Grid computing is fairly distinct from cloud computing. It uses the resources of various computers in a network to perform.

Grid computing is attractive for several reasons:

1. Computer resources are not appropriately utilized; as a result it is profitable to employ a known sum of computer resources.
2. It accomplishes the need of high computing power.
3. The resources of various computers can be shared with an understanding, not requiring a single computer to have to organize it further.

Grid computing is accountable for cloud commencement up to a certain extent. There is a system of parent and child procedures in grids or any distributed computing system. For a specific assignment, an initial evaluation, to ascertain if it can be broken into assignments of a smaller range, is conducted. If it is feasible, distributed computing performs similar tasks and transfers the pieces of job into an additional computer for completion of the assignment.

It is also beneficial for appropriate consumption of resources which remain unused. Figure 1.6 shows the typical forms of cluster grids where servers are connected with each other in an organization

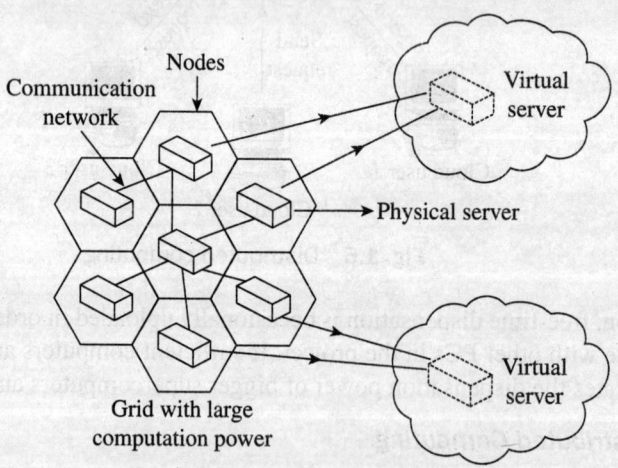

Fig. 1.6 Typical forms of cluster grids

network; there is one administrator to control the servers and so, services are accessed by the clients on the network.

There are numerous reasons as to why you could decide to perform an application on a grid instead of a high performance computing (HPC). Additional savings or money, and data accessibility—both kinds of resolution need enormous sums of computing strength.

Evolution of cloud computing from grid computing is shown in Table 1.2.

Table 1.2 Evolution of cloud computing from grid computing

Grid computing	Utility computing	Software as a Service	Cloud computing
Big crisis could be resolved with equivalent computing	Provided computing resources as metered services (disburses as per usage)	Beneficial in usage based payments to applications.	An Internet based computing offering services such as IaaS, PaaS, and SaaS.

Grid technology supports application-oriented inter domain business, so the purpose of grid security infrastructure is to protect shared resources from unintended users and also support fundamental feature of security like authentication and authorization. Authentication means that the entity has to prove that it is really what it claims to be and authorization means access permission of shared resources under different conditions given to different users.

Authentication Infrastructure

The generally used authentication infrastructure is public key infrastructure, which is based on public key cryptography. A third-party mediator is involved for this authentication process, that issues certificate to users as grid identity that allows users to use shared resource in the grid infrastructure. Another user authentication is done through Kerberos. Session key is issued to the users by the authentication servers for accessing resources in the grid. Security key means special token issued to the users.

A different method, Athens, is also used, which maintains separate user account for each resource they want to access and users' accounts are managed centrally by an account server. One level authentication technique is used, which is based on user name and password.

Authorization Infrastructure

Akeni authorization infrastructure method issues users' certificate to access a shared resource under different condition. A trusted entity is defined to gain access of shared resource. Use condition on resource is also defined for every stake holder, for keeping data safe and unreached from each other. Another method is privilege and role management, in which for accessing resource, users have to present role-based certificate that defines user role and attribute. One of the important methods is virtual organization membership service that maintains all information about users centrally through a virtual organization administrator. Certificate needs to be present for accessing a shared resource, and only after checking the validity of certificate users are allowed to access resources.

Other method of access control of user identity is grid map files. A distinguished list is prepared for shared resources used by particular user accounts and the list is shared on each resource. Generally, user mechanisms of security in grid computing are authentication and authorization and these are termed as hard security, whereas other method, trust management based system, is called as soft security.

Trust between two parties is a bidirectional relationship, which decides extent up to which one party depends or relies on the other. Trust management consists of a trustor and a trustee. Mutual trust relationship is of the following types:
1. Provision trust—It describes a user's trust on a service provider or service.
2. Access trust—It describes service provider trust in the user access on provided resource.
3. Identity trust—It describes trust on identity claimed by the user.
4. Delegation trust—It describes trust on someone which acts and makes decision on behalf of some other.

Goal of trust model is to support decision making for various interactions. Trust values are calculated for prediction of future possibilities. Depending upon application trust value, trust model is of three types:
1. Fuzzy logic model
2. Probability theory model
3. Mathematical method model

Fuzzy logic uses linguistic terms for calculating trust value that explains its believe on the other entity. In probability based model, trust is calculated on the basis of previous experience that determines future actions. In mathematical method, calculated index value determines the level of belief on the other entity.

1.4.5 Autonomic Computing

This is a system that supports computing to perform and work without any outer control or intervention. The phrase is on the basis of the autonomic nervous system of the human body that manages heart functioning, breathing, and many other functions. The aim of autonomic computing is to have the computer carry out versatile and critical functions without any interference by a user. Each task may be programmed, with orders given according to necessity, and evading user interference as per the need.

1.4.6 Platform Virtualization

Virtualization is a base for clouds, irrespective of whether you are heading towards constructing a mini-cloud in a prevailing data center or want to place your applications on a complete cloud.

A virtual picture offers an undefined number of hardware resources for strengthening the accessibility and functioning of an application; the choice on which resources to virtualize is normally handled down to a query of the resources previously being utilized on a variety of accessible servers. Each user acquires a service according to the requisites in virtualization.

The unused time of a server is involved in waiting for output or input, or is devoted to an assignment, working for lesser consumption of CPU and rotating its computational power for new assignment to be completed. Virtualization is a proficiency which conceals physical resources and emerges as virtual resources for users. Organizations have to carry out many steps in order to accept cloud computing. In a conventional data center, resources are devoted for every business application or entities. IBMS/360-67 supports up to four processors. It, in fact, supports dynamic address translation (DAT) to perform with competent paging.

Virtualization makes physical resources look like virtual resources in front of users. Virtualization is founded on the perception of a virtual machine working on a physical computing platform. Virtualization is managed by a Virtual Machine Monitor (VMM), called a hypervisor. An open-source hypervisor, Xen, is broadly utilized for cloud computing.

1.4.7 Service Oriented Architecture—SOA

A software allocation and installation module is that in which applications are offered to consumers as a service. The applications may work on the computing systems of users or the web servers of suppliers. A variety of software is easily accessible on the cloud and instantaneously accessed by several users.

An array of services can communicate with one another. Cloud computing is Internet-based computing, where mutual information, software, and resources are offered to consumers on-need, for example, a public utility.

In cloud computing, service level agreements (SLAs) are mandatory to manage the usage of resources. In the negotiation process, a joint decision is made between the parties, service provider, and service consumer in the context of cloud computing. Quality of service (QoS) is the ability to offer various priorities to dependents based on applications and consumers, and guarantees a certain level of performance. QoS norms are rich and are extremely dependent on the application.

The general service arrangement is as follows:
1. Loss—Chance that a flow's data is missing
2. Delay—Time it acquires a package's flow in order to find it from source to target
3. Bandwidth—Greatest speed at which the source may transmit data

Service condition in the cloud relies on the SLAs which represent a contract made between the customer and the service provided as well as non-functional necessities of the service, in particular, QoS. SLA considers its responsibility, service charge, and fine in case of violations of the agreement.

1.4.8 Utility Computing

Utility computing disburses resources as a metered service when required. The aim is to utilize services resourcefully and efficiently, which lessens related expenses as well. The expression 'utility' is used to evaluate such a computing resource consumption and imbursement to utilities such as natural gas suppliers or electricity suppliers for appropriate consumption of resources.

Utility computing is the procedure of offering computing services via an on-demand, pay-per-use invoicing system. It is a computing enterprise module where the supplier possesses, works, and controls the computing resources and infrastructure, and is accessed by subscribers as and when needed on a metered and leasing basis.

Utility computing is one among the most famous IT services' modules, basically due to the economy and elasticity offered by it. This module is based on the one used by traditional utilities such as gas, electricity, and telephonic services. The customer has access to a virtually infinite delivery of computing resolutions over the virtual private network or the Internet that may be sourced; supply is managed by the service providers. Utility computing may offer virtual software, virtual storage, virtual servers, and other IT resolutions. Managed IT services, grid computing, and cloud computing are based on the idea of utility computing. Like other kinds of on-demand computing, for example, grid computing, the utility module looks to raise the effective use of resources or/and reduce related prices.

The word utility is used to create a likeness to other services like electrical power, which looks at meeting the changeable demands of consumers, and to pay for the resources based on usage. This approach is becoming even more usual in business computing and is occasionally used for the customer market, for website access, Internet services, and other applications.

1.4.9 Web 2.0

Web 2.0 represents a change in technology in the world of the World Wide Web. It is usually designed to increase data security and customization of application as per the requirement with improved functionality.

Web-based service hosting, main social networking, sharing videos, etc., are important provisions provided by Web 2.0. In Web 2.0, the world wide web (WWW) puts stress to generate content by the user, and easy access and other operations on the content.

The important features of Web 2.0 are as follows:
1. Easy to access
2. User interaction and participation
3. Rich customization features
4. Easy communication through video chatting, instant messaging facilities, etc.
5. User-friendly writing tools and applications
6. Data management and analysis
7. Multimedia supporting tools
8. Web application and hosting

1.4.10 Parallel Computing

Parallel computing supports a type of computation which is helpful for carrying out computation of a program simultaneously. It is based on the principle that a single large problem is divided into small parts and parallely runs different parts on different machines. Distributed or grid computing is also a special type of parallel computing in which computers are connected on a network. Geographically dispersed computer resources are used for a common purpose. Different parts of the same problem run in parallel for faster and easy processing. It is cost effective to run a program on a super computer. Grid infrastructure supports different parts of the same problem to be run on multiple machines at the same time. This is also helpful in removing complications related with many instances of the same program sharing memory and space at the same time.

Parallel computing simultaneously uses various computing resources for solving a computational problem:
1. Discrete parts of a broken problem can be solved in parallel
2. Further, every part is broken down into a series of instructions
3. Different processors are used to execute the instructions in parallel
4. Coordination method works behind parallel computing

Parallel computing supports applications that require processing of a large problem in a sophisticated way. Some of the examples are:
- Big data problem
- Data mining
- Search engines
- Medical diagnosis
- Virtual reality
- Multimedia

1.5 BUSINESS AND INFORMATION TECHNOLOGY PERSPECTIVE

Cloud computing technology is valuable to both end users and developers. Cloud computing offers the developer an augmented quantity of storage and added strength. It is simple for them to operate the application. It is a creative method for accessing information, and for processing and evaluating data. It unites resources and people from any place. Users are no more constrained by physical restrictions.

Cloud computing proposes various advantages to the user. An individual using a web-based application is not physically compelled to one PC, network, or location. Users can record and applications can be accessed from anywhere, at any time. There is no problem of losing data in case a computer collapses. Records hosted on the cloud remain forever, so there is no issue even if something happens to the machine of the user. If the machine of a user collapses, even then, the user may log in with an additional machine and data can be accessed and stored. After that, there is the advantage of pool partnership. Users from all around may group resources on similar projects, applications, and records, in actual time.

Cloud computing proposes amenities at the lowest rate, since the cloud allows more competent resource sharing than that of conventional network computing. Users do not have to be worried about software or hardware installation or updating, as it is for the cloud provider. With cloud computing, the hardware needs to be physically adjacent to an office of the data center or company. Cloud computing infrastructure may be situated at any place. As extra cloud resources are forever ready, corporations need not buy resources for irregular and rigorous computing assignments. Cloud resources are available on a charge basis.

Cloud service providers propose a number of advantages over and above those provided by remote hosting:
1. Accessibility of data all over
2. Physical servers or virtual servers
3. Servers' interaction within similar clouds
4. Allocation or imitation of resources at numerous physical regions
5. Strength offered by different cloud storage capacities

Other services provided by cloud computing are discussed in the following sections.

1.5.1 Electronic Faxing

Secure faxes are transmitted to specific telephone number and are directed to an e-mail address as PDF attachments. Outgoing messages are transmitted through e-mail and conveyed to fax machines all around the world.

1.5.2 Voice on Clouds

Cloud-founded Google Voice can deal with calls, in case the call is made by an user on a published phone number. The call can be acknowledged from any telephone number associated to Google voice.

1.5.3 Commerce on Clouds

Businesses can be tackled via clouds, for example, the sale and purchase of items. A few books are accessible for sale as downloadable e-books on websites. The numerous sites interrelate flawlessly. Online buying, screening of items, and entire transactions may be handled effortlessly.

1.5.4 Distributed Hosting on Clouds

Godaddy.com is faultlessly hosted and provides services in this context. You might have utilized Rack space, Amazon, and many other websites for availing services.

1.5.5 Accounting and Online Banking

The online banking system offers convenient banking, encompassing numerous characteristics such as amount transfer and balance enquiry, among others. You might have applied on CapitalOne bank instead of Quickbooks; or NetSuite Small Business or other new excellent cloud-based alternatives. Consequently, the web-based, bill-paying application of banks is dealt by a different cloud-based dealer which interfaces with the cloud-based Automated Clearing House (ACH) system for delivering and disbursing dues.

The cloud provides complete safety of data in the bank. The complete SaaS application is accessible to banks for invoice imbursement and similar services. Similarly, in many organizations, salaries are is also accepted electronically as direct deposit payments. Cloud computing may be used not only for business-to-personal communication, but also for business-to-business communication.

1.6 NEWS ON CLOUDS

Some of the news available on the cloud are as follows:
1. A mobile phone can be used to access services related to news.
2. Google Apps or Gmail is capable of seeking information via e-mail, rapidly from any tool. We can talk and work with partners or consumers without any language barrier.
3. Distribution and editing of data with trouble-free collaboration using Google items Docs and Sites. TripIt is a private travel that assists in arranging tours. Data is gathered from consumers and colleagues by using Google types. There is joint work on a general venture.

4. Through Force.com, you may construct a scalable business application on the cloud platform. Both Google's cloud and salesforce.com computing platforms are employed to generate business and web applications.
5. Using online patterns for presentations, spreadsheets, and records
6. Functioning steady, safe, and quick Web apps
7. Easily and firmly distributing video in apps through Youtube for Google apps

1.7 BENEFITS OF CLOUD COMPUTING

Cloud computing technology offers various benefits to both cloud service consumers and cloud service providers. The main advantage of cloud computing systems and technologies is increased economical return due to reduced maintenance costs related to infrastructure and IT software. Capital costs are costs associated with assets that need to be paid in advance to start the business. Before the advent of cloud computing, software and IT infrastructure generated capital cost, since they were paid upfront to afford computing infrastructure and software for enabling the business activities of an organization. The revenue of the business is then utilized to compensate over time for these costs. In case of hardware, it is always associated with depreciable values. To make profit, the organizations have to also compensate this depreciation created by time, thus reducing the net gain obtained from the revenue. In this way, cloud computing technology transforms IT infrastructure and software into utilities. Cloud computing offers the following benefits:

Pay as per use   On demand access to pay-as-you-go computing resources on a short-term basis and ability to release these computing resources when they are no longer needed.

Reduced investment and proportional costs   The product wholesaler purchases goods in bulk at a low price. Public cloud providers base their business model on the mass acquisition of IT resources that are then made available to cloud consumers via attractive prices. This opens the door for organizations to gain access to powerful infrastructure without having to purchase it themselves.

The investment in cloud-based IT resources is in the reduction or outright elimination of up-front IT investments, namely hardware and software purchases, and ownership costs. The cloud measures operational expenditures (directly related to business performance) to replace anticipated capital expenditures. This is also referred to as proportional costs. The same rationale applies to operating systems, middleware or platform software, and application software.

Accessibility from anywhere   Resources can be accessed from anywhere, irrespective of location and device. This feature facilitates business continuity around the clock.

Increased scalability   The business load can be handled with scalability of the respective resources without much effort, time, and cost.

Increased availability and reliability   Resources provided as services are available all the time. Even if there is a failure in any of the components of a service, the provider immediately identifies, isolates, and replaces the failed components without any performance degradations.

Dynamic provisioning   It is the perception of having unlimited computing resources that are available on demand, thereby reducing the need to prepare for provisioning.

1.8 LIMITATIONS OF CLOUD COMPUTING

Cloud computing is broadly acknowledged as a revolutionary IT concept and along with customized assistance may suit the requirements of varied consumers, scaling from big ventures and small-beginners to end-users. Many cloud-based applications like Gmail have become very successful; however, in the information technology departments of organizations and corporations, the decision makers continue to refuse to use the cloud. Currently, companies mainly just contract applications which comprise less confidential data. The ones which become ready to move to the cloud still insist on third-party risk appraisal or enquire with cloud suppliers on the following:

1. By whom the applications and data will be accessed and how will that be scrutinized?
2. What security methods are used for storage and transmission of data?
3. How data and applications from diverse consumers are reserved separately?
4. Where will the data be stored in terms of geographical sites? Will the selection of the site influence us?
5. Can these details and channels be specified in a service-level contract?

Each of these consumer worries are the chief obstacles to the implementation and development of cloud computing. Some of the limitations of cloud computing are discussed next.

1.8.1 Availability of Services

Consumer administration interfaces of public clouds are only possible through the Internet. As services are a primary concern of consumers, they sometimes need to discard all the data from the cloud environment provided to them, while sometimes they may want to recover all the data. There is an augmented risk of disaster in this when compared to conventional services, as there are more ways to access the application or information over cloud computing.

1.8.2 Data Lock-in

SaaS permits the services to be interoperable on every cloud. However, shifting of data and applications from one platform to another is a challenge to the cloud provider for a big organization handling high volumes of data. Google is the single cloud supplier to attain a more typical environment and they also have a scheme, known as Data Liberation Front, to support user shifting applications and data in and out of their platform.

1.8.3 Data Segregation

It is not simple to isolate cloud users from each other. A straight effect of the multitenant control mode, where virtual machines of distinct consumers are co-located on a single server or data on single hard disks, is the main concern related to privacy. This set of risks comprises matters regarding the breakdown of mechanisms to separate memory or storage among distinct users.

Amazon EC2 service measured this as a real threat and rectified this attack by effectively overcoming the following:

1. Finding out where a particular virtual machine command is positioned in the cloud infrastructure
2. To determine whether two instances are resident in a similar physical machine
3. The secrecy of the data should be guaranteed, whether or not it is in transit. It should be required to offer a closed box implementation environment where the secrecy and reliability of the data must be confirmed by its possessor.
4. In a majority of circumstances, data should be encrypted at a certain time when it is within the cloud. Several procedures are unfeasible to perform with encoded data, and moreover performing computation with the encoded data must utilize more computing resources.
5. The user encodes the data earlier to upload it to the cloud. When specific data is needed, the token creator is used by the user to produce a token as well as decryption key. The token is transmitted to the cloud, the chosen encoded file(s) are downloaded, and after that these files are confirmed locally and decrypted using the key. Sharing is facilitated by transmitting the decryption key and token to the other user with whom you wish to cooperate.

1.8.4 Privilege Neglect

Companies sometimes take advantage of the liberty given to them. They disclose sensitive data of their company to others for some benefits. The threat of a malicious insider with access to confidential data is a concern for any outsourced computation model. Miscreants might affect and harm the consumer's fame and brand or openly harm the consumer. Mistreatment of opportunity not only spoils brand name, but may also place protected data in the hand of competitive attackers. It must be observed that similar kinds of attacks may be taken out by in-house workers in a conventional infrastructure too.

1.8.5 Scaling Resources

A web application designer who hosts its service on a cloud can view how the reply time gradually increases when usage of the application rises since the cloud does not scale up resources rapidly enough. The capability of scaling resources up and down to meet workload is one of the chief benefits of cloud computing. Resource pooling through multitenancy is also an important element that is managed by the cloud provider.

Separate storage devices are provided to every client on the cloud network, called a single tenant; and in a multi-tenant environment, a single storage device is shared by more than one cloud user as shown in Fig. 1.8. In the figure, there are two consumers 1 and 2, who are sharing a single shared storage for storing data, so there is the risk of interchanging or risk related to mismatch of data if proper arrangement is not carried out.

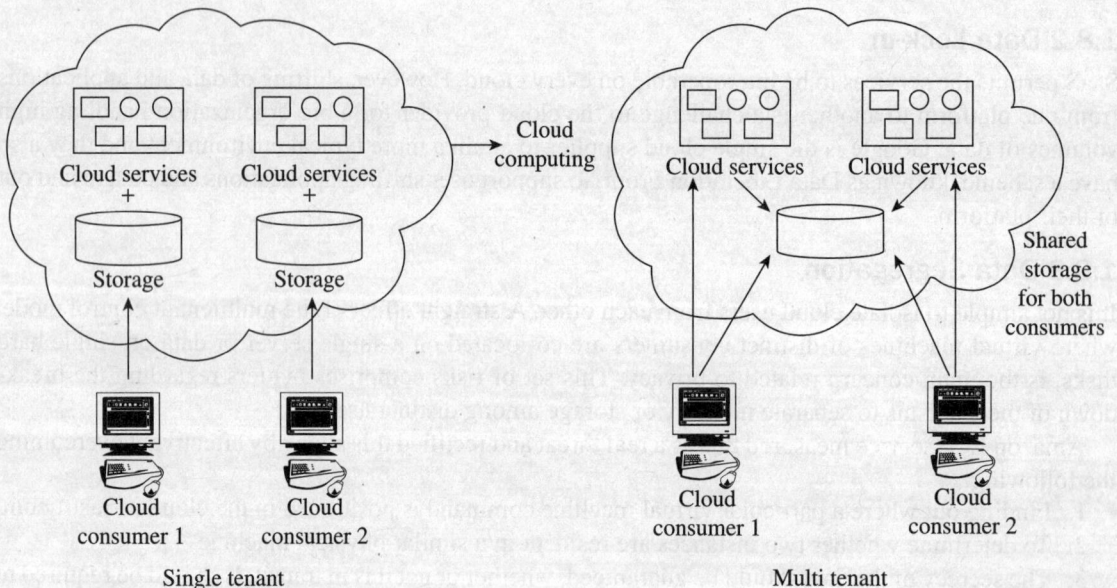

Fig. 1.8 Multi-tenancy in cloud computing

1.8.6 Data Location

The geographical site of the data also counts as a challenge. Being aware of the geographical site of data is essential to protect it, since there could be significant differences amid rigid strategies in various countries. The route followed by the data is also important. It may be difficult for an application operator to install applications at the smallest 'distance' from the users.

At present, there are cloud suppliers who leave the alternative of the data center site to the user. For example, Amazon proposes one site in Europe and two in other countries. It is expected that other suppliers will follow Amazon's region option proposal as the site of data is a rising and significant requirement of promising consumers.

1.8.7 Deletion of Data

Public cloud users might need their data to be removed, that is, totally erased from the cloud.

Sometimes, one company migrates its data to another cloud provider. In that case, they want complete deletion of the data or complete migration of data; if this is not done, the benefit of the data might be used by the malicious user later. Various security agencies have been advised to use cipher text form of data for high security.

1.8.8 Recovery and Backup

For safety purpose, keeping the data of a consumer safe at different locations, for easy recovery and backup, if there is any failure, is a big challenge. A proposal of data backup must be proposed to cloud suppliers in of the event of a disaster. This can be achieved by the replication of data diagonally on various sites and the proposal should be referred in the service level contract.

1.8.9 Offline Clouds

For several users who require an application to be accessible the whole time through, becoming entirely dependent on the Internet could prove to be highly risky or unfeasible. This generates greater trouble in case the user is shuffling and there is a change in the connection quality. Thus in several cases, trusting the Internet service supplier is not an alternative. At present, a web browser is a widely used software application and all applications can be easily accessed through the interactive web browser. Locally, it is not necessary to maintain a hard disk with a strong processor because customized services are available on the cloud.

Google launched Gears, a free-of-cost add-on for the browser, which allows data to be saved locally in a complete searchable database while surfing the Internet. Gears resolved the 'offline problem' permitting web applications to resume their working while offline and subsequently coordinating when the link was accessible again. The latest edition of the HTML protocol tackles the offline matters with a pair of constituents—database and AppCache.
1. Canavas—Offers an influential and clear-cut meaning to depict arbitrary graphics on a web page using Javascript
2. Video—Aims to assemble a simple video on a web page as it is to establish images nowadays
3. Web workers—A novel method to take on gear jobs which should hold up the web browser

1.8.10 Unpredictable Performance

The cloud-end consumer would not even know the number of physical machines on which their application was functioning. The single source of information which the user has regarding these servers is the hardware specification offered by the cloud supplier for every kind of service. Further, these metrics do not have a similar significance in the cloud server as they had in a conventional server, since in the cloud server, some users can share I/O resources and compute on a specified case of a physical processor. A similar performance at similar financial levels has been expected by the user, but this might not be simply accurate, since the performance depends on several aspects and the end user has no control over many of them.

1.9 HOW TO DEVELOP CLOUD INFRASTRUCTURE

Infrastructure should meet the following vital features for assisting users to access data proficiently and efficiently at any occasion:

Accessibility It is the major responsibility of every central origin that data is accessible, on order, to users.

Functioning Optimal service and functioning should be offered by the data center.

Supple High-priority business needs may be under the control of the prevailing infrastructure, without any disruption of accessibility and with the least charge and least variation.

Safety Data must be protected from illegal and malevolent users.

Manageability Corporations try to reduce IT expenses on the data center and increase the consumption of prevailing resources.

In today's competitive world, a corporation should be flexible and capable of reacting quickly, and this should be achieved with the least investments in costs. Cloud computing is a completely automatic request accomplishment procedure which is dedicated to flexibility, quicker access, and cost savings.

For the development of cloud infrastructure, the following are needed:
1. Understanding the prevailing conventional data center
2. Computing resources that will be virtualized
3. Installing service administration devices

An infrastructure must accomplish the necessary uniqueness to support cloud services. It may be assembled by using a shared group of computing resources such as network, storage, and compute so as to accomplish cloud services. The infrastructure must be flexible for meeting the numerous demands of its customers. It also permits them to provision resources on order over a network. Cloud services facilitate optimization by managing and scrutinizing resource usage and by preservation of energy.

Along with the virtualization feature in cloud computing, it is possible to offer flexible physical infrastructure to cloud users. Largely, virtualizations offer us the ability to give continuous services to consumers. Cloud infrastructure may be built in several stages:
1. The first starts with thoroughly recognizing the prevailing physical infrastructure with its procedures and constituents.
2. The next step is to concentrate on accumulating the prevailing infrastructure resources by using virtualization technologies. Therefore, the accessible resource allows centralized administration of resources and permits quicker resource provisioning.
3. Then comes the step to install service administration devices, which allow mechanization of procedures and administration to reduce human interference. Service administration devices comprise purposeful services as well as those that permit utilization-based metering so that customers have to pay for just what is utilized by them. Through service administration, on-order provisioning of IT resources turns out to be livelier and permits IT to be sent as a service.

Core Components of Traditional Data Centers

A conventional data center is the prevailing infrastructure which processes data using IT resources. The core components of a traditional data center are as follows:

Application Program employed to carry out numerous computing functions. It may be an operating system, DBMS, and many more.

DBMS It is an administration system which offers the ability to save or get data from rationally prepared tables.

Compute Resources which work numerous applications using various elements

Storage This is used to save data for often use

Network It is the ability to communicate among systems. It assists us to share data and resources.

All the core elements of a traditional data center work together, to complete a task.

1.10 VENDORS OF CLOUD COMPUTING

With the migration of various organizations to the cloud-based technology, there are many vendors who have come into existence with incredible facilities, that not only easily offer customization as per user requirements but also have distinct features. Some of them are explained here:

1.10.1 Amazon Web Services—IaaS

The cloud computing corporation of Amazon.com—Amazon Web Service (AWS)—offers Infrastructure as a Service (IaaS) on the cloud for associations needing computing storage, power, and further services.

Elastic Compute Cloud Elastic Compute Cloud (EC2) is a web service which permits resizable computing ability on the cloud. The consumers may generate virtual machines (VMs), that is, server cases known as Amazon Machine Image (AMI), on which the consumer may put in any software of his/her preference. A pay-by-the hour system is followed.

Simple Storage Service (S3) S3 offers a web service interface which may be used to regain and store an infinite quantity of data, from any place, at any time, via the Internet.

Amazon SimpleDB is integrated for providing AWS services such as Amazon S3 and EC2, which provide the infrastructure for creating various web applications.

1.10.2 Google—SaaS, PaaS

Google App Engine is Google's Platform as a Service (Paas) that provides hosting and produces web applications on the Google Infrastructure. Presently, Java and Python are the supported programming languages. Up to a specific level, the resource-used App Engine is without any charge. Payment is charged for further bandwidth, CPU cycles, and storage needed by the application. Software as a Service (SaaS) provides business agreements and email. It is similar to conventional office suits, comprising Sites, Talk, Docs, Calendar, and Gmail.

In fact, the Google cloud is something which will entirely alter how people access data they look for. The Google Cloud is powered by thousands, possibly millions of unique services and servers which accommodate a surprising quantity of information. These are situated at various sites on the globe and maintain many clones of the information which are available on the Internet. Relevant information of the users is replicated on various servers.

Basically, Google Cloud is a 'reference' to the information which has been stored and made clear by Google. Services of cloud computing may be used from any site to access information which has been saved by Google. Services are provided by Search Docs, Google Maps, etc.

1.10.3 Microsoft Azure Service Platform—PaaS

Azure Service Platform is the proposal of Microsoft PaaS, an operating system known as Windows Azure, which performs as a runtime for the application and offers a set of services such as SQL Services, Live Services, and NET Services.

Windows Azure is a Microsoft Cloud computing platform used to develop, launch, and control applications via a universal network of Microsoft-controlled data centers. Windows Azure permits applications to be developed using various distinct languages, frameworks, or devices and makes it potential for designers to amalgamate communal cloud applications within their accessible IT environment. Windows Azure offers both IaaS and PaaS services and is categorized as the 'public cloud' in cloud computing policy of Microsoft, with its SaaS offering, Microsoft Online Services.

The following new characteristics were released by Windows Azure:

1. Websites permit designers to develop sites using PHP, Node.js, or ASP.NET and may be installed using TFS, FTP, etc.
2. Virtual machines permit designers to drift infrastructure and applications without altering the existing code and may operate both Linux virtual machines and the Windows Server.
3. Cloud services is a platform of Microsoft as a Service environment which is used to generate scalable services and applications. Supports automated installations and multi-tier states.
4. Data management, an SQL database once recognized as SQL Azure Database, performs to generate, scale, and expand applications into the cloud by using Microsoft SQL Server techniques. It amalgamates with System Center and Active Directory.
5. Media service is a PaaS-based service that may be used for content security, encoding, analytics and/or streaming.

The Windows Azure platform, which became available in the market in 2010, offers an API developed on XML, REST, and HTTP, which facilitates a designer to interrelate with the services offered by Windows Azure. Microsoft also offers a consumer-side operated class library which summarizes and customizes interrelating services as per user requirement. It also amalgamates with Eclipse, GIT, and Microsoft Visual Studio as it may be used as the integrated development environment (IDE) to build and print Azure-hosted applications.

1.10.4 Rackspace—Cloud Hosting

Rackspace is the service head in Cloud Computing and an initiator of OpenStack, an open source cloud platform. The San Antonio-based vendor, which operates around more than thousand enterprises, offers dedicated support to its consumers, athwart a variety of IT services, comprising cloud computing and managed hosting. Their exclusive consumer service policy has benefited them in getting the faith of their customers. Rackspace has been identified by Bloomberg Business Week as a 'Top Hundred Functioning Technology Corporations' and was highlighted in the list of Fortune. The corporation was also placed in the Leaders for Cloud Infrastructure under Service and Web Hosting.

1.10.5 Salesforce.com—SaaS, PaaS

Salesforce is a supplier of SaaS-based goods, along with having a PaaS offering, Force.com. It is a universal venture software corporation with headquarters in San Francisco, United States, California. Salesforce is best identified for its consumer relationship management (CRM). It was in graded position in Fortune's 100 Best Corporations.

1.11 ELASTIC COMPUTING

Elastic computing is offered by cloud computing where computing resources may be scaled up and down by the cloud service supplier. Elastic computing is the capability of a cloud service supplier to provision flexible computing strength when and where required. The elasticity of such resources may be in terms of bandwidth, storage, processing power, etc. Cloud computing pertains to provisioning on-demand computing resources at the click of a mouse. The quantity of resources that may be sourced via cloud computing integrates nearly all the aspects of computing from basic processing power to enormous storage space.

On a small scale, it can be done manually but for huge deployments, there is automatic scaling. For instance, a better supplier of online videos might set up a system so that the number of web servers online are scaled all through peak performance hours.

In cloud computing, elasticity is described as the level to which a system is capable of adapting to workload variation by offering and taking back resources the autonomic way; at every point in time the accessible resources meet the present need. It is a vital feature, which distinguishes it from earlier computing paradigms, like grid computing. This dynamic difference, so as to meet an unreliable workload, is known as elastic computing.

1.12 SOCIAL NETWORKING

The Internet-based social media programs are used to build connections with family, friends, classmates, clients, and customers. Social networking may be done for business purposes, social purposes, or both. The programs show the connections among people and ease the ability of new links. Examples of social networking include LinkedIn, Facebook, etc. A social networking website is an online podium which permits customers to build a public profile and interact with other users on the website. Generally, social networking websites have a new record of people with whom they share a link and then permit the people in the record to verify or reject the link. After the establishment, the new customers may explore the networks of their links for making further links.

Social networking sites have various rules for setting links, but they frequently permit customers to examine the links of a confirmed link and even advise further links on the basis of an established network of a person. Some social networking websites like LinkedIn are used for creating professional links, whereas sites such as Facebook are on both sides of the line (i.e., professional and private). There are also networks that are created for a particular customer base, like political or cultural groups within a specified region or even dealers in economic markets.

1.13 ENTERPRISE CLOUD COMPUTING

Enterprise cloud computing is the process of using cloud computing for saving cost and for business innovation by getting extraordinary speed and agility, and improved collaboration among customers and business partners. Enterprise cloud computing is important because:
1. Cost of accessing data can be reduced to a great extent by linking it directly with the usage. Customers are charged on a pay-per-use basis.
2. Start-ups can test out new business ideas risk-free and at low cost, due to enormous scalability. Since there is no upfront capital expense involved, in case a new project takes off, it can be scaled up instantly, and vice versa.
3. Enterprise cloud computing allows a company to create a shared workspace in order to collaborate with its trading partners and work together as a 'virtual enterprise network'. In this way, they can share the information and communication resources, without actually owning it all. This also helps in lowering costs.

As shown in Fig. 1.9, an enterprise with n numbers of hosts can connect through cloud services and different types of services supported by cloud network such as database, servers, and various applications.

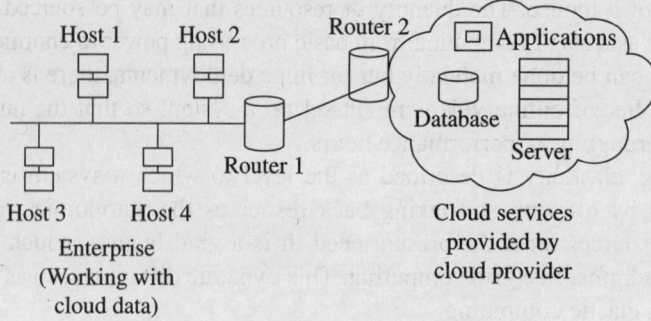

Fig. 1.9 Enterprise cloud computing

 Points to Remember

1. Cloud computing is a technology which uses the Internet and central remote servers (data center) to maintain data, software, storage, and applications. It offers the following:
   (a) On-demand self-sufficient services
   (b) Omnipresent network access
   (c) Location-independent resource (access from anywhere)
   (d) Speedy elasticity
2. Cloud application doesn't need software or a server to use it and does not call for software updation.
3. Cloud computing allows users to use any application without installation and access their files at any computer with Internet access any time.
4. Cloud computing is becoming a progressively more attractive alternative for many organizations.
5. Cloud computing promises to reduce operational and capital costs.
6. Peer-to-peer is a decentralized approach having no center server.
7. Cloud computing is essential as it helps in reducing costs; offers scalability, remote access, disaster relief, ease of implementation, and better response time; and provides a virtual environment.
8. Grid is the application of multiple computers working on a single problem at the same time.
9. In utility computing, computing resources are disbursed as per usage.
10. Software as a Service is beneficial in usage based payments to applications.
11. Virtualization means the logical partitioning of physical computing resources into multiple execution environments, including servers, applications, and operating systems.
12. Building the cloud infrastructure involves the following:
    (a) Understanding the existing traditional data center
    (b) Virtualizing the computing resources
    (c) Deploying service management tools
13. Cloud computing has the ability to increase the usage level of the infrastructure through multi-tenancy.
14. Windows Azure is a Microsoft Cloud computing platform used to build, deploy, and manage applications through a global network of Microsoft-managed data centers.
15. Major challenges with traditional infrastructure software licensing and support, scalability, accountability, modifiability, physical security, and cost management.
16. The limitations of cloud computing are availability of service, data lock-in, data segregation, privilege neglect, scaling resources, data location, deletion of data, recovery and backup, offline cloud, and unpredictable performance.

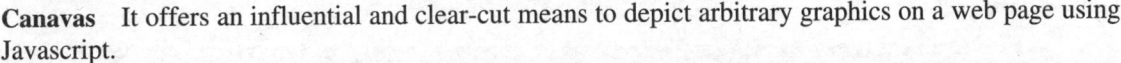
Key Terms

Canvas It offers an influential and clear-cut means to depict arbitrary graphics on a web page using Javascript.

Cloud computing Cloud computing is the dynamic delivery of information technology resources and capabilities as a service over the Internet. Cloud computing is dynamically scalable and often transmits virtualized resources over the Internet. It provides services such as Infrastructure as a Service (IaaS), Platform as a Service (PaaS), and Software as a Service (SaaS).

DBMS A type of system of managing databases for providing facilities like storing or retrieving information from organized tables.

Distributed computing A distributed system consists of multiple computers that communicate through a computer network to achieve a common goal.

Grid computing The application of the processing power of multiple networked computing resources to solve a specific problem.

Hyper text markup language (HTML) A language mainly used for static web page designing

IP addresses A unique address provided to each computer in a network

Lock in Cloud vendor lock-in is a problem without a villain, according to Tom Hughes-Croucher, a technical evangelist at Yahoo. It makes a customer dependent on a vendor for products and services, unable to use another vendor without substantial switching costs.

Media services A PaaS offering that can be used for encoding, content protection, streaming, etc.

Network It is a facility to communicate between systems.

Peer-to-peer A different type of architecture in which each computer in the network has equivalent capabilities and responsibilities. It is not a centralized approach.

Remote access A distinct technology that allows logging into a system as an authentic user into a remote location without being physically present at the system. This technology is commonly used on corporate sectors but can also be utilized on home networks.

Replication Creation of different copies at various locations.

Scalability Change as per the demands.

Service level agreement (SLA) It is a type of agreement or contract between the cloud provider and cloud users for availing services from the cloud system.

Service oriented architectures (SOA) A set of services that communicate with each other, whose interfaces are known and described, whose functions are loosely coupled, and whose use can be incorporated by multiple organizations.

Service provider Those who are responsible for IT assets and maintenance services provided to users

Software as a Service (SaaS) Among the various services of a cloud, SaaS is a deployment model in which applications are provided to customers as a service.

Structured query language (SQL) SQL is a special-purpose programming language designed for managing and handling data in a relational database management system (RDBMS).

Trojans A Trojan is a non-self-replicating type of malware which performs an enviable function but instead facilitates unauthorized access to the user's computer system.

Utility computing The packaging and delivery of computing resources to a customer who pays for the resources as a metered-based service when needed. Customers have to pay on the basis of how much they have used.

Web workers A novel method to take on gear jobs which should hold up the web browser

Multiple-choice Questions

1. Which of the following is an example of a cloud computing application?
   (a) Facebook
   (b) Twitter
   (c) Skype
   (d) Salesforce.com and Googleapp
   (e) All the above

2. The logical partitioning of physical computing resources into multiple execution environments is called:
   (a) Grid computing
   (b) Platform virtualization
   (c) Distributed computing
   (d) None of these

3. The term used to describe a hypervisor running multiple operating systems simultaneously is:
   (a) Full virtualization
   (b) Para virtualization
   (c) Partial virtualization
   (d) Nested virtualization

4. Which among these best describes the difference between SOA and cloud computing?
   (a) Metered service
   (b) Shared resources
   (c) SOA existing within a firewall
   (d) Leveraging IT resource on demand

5. Cloud is a set of _____ that provide the service.
   (a) Hardware
   (b) Networks
   (c) Storage and services interfaces
   (d) All the above

6. The participants in cloud computing are _____.
   (a) The end user
   (b) The business management which has the responsibility of managing the overall cloud governance and provide services to the customer
   (c) The cloud service provider who are responsible for IT assets and maintenance
   (d) All the above

7. The core elements of a traditional data center is/are_____.
   (a) DBMS
   (b) Compute
   (c) Network
   (d) All the above

8. Peer-to-peer is a _____.
   (a) Decentralized approach
   (b) Centralized approach
   (c) Distributed approach
   (d) None of these

9. The advantages of client server networks is/are_____.
   (a) Centralization
   (b) Proper management
   (c) Backup and recovery possible
   (d) All the above

10. The objective of autonomic computing is to have the computer perform _____.
    (a) Critical and complex functions
    (b) Virtualization
    (c) On-demand services
    (d) None of these

11. Security is enhanced by which services in the cloud infrastructure?
    (a) Intrusion prevention
    (b) Hardware (intelligent switch)
    (c) Isolation of virtual network
    (d) File providing different permissions
    (e) DHCP used to track the IP address

12. What is cloud computing replacing?
    (a) Expenses of computer hardware
    (b) Software upgrades expenses
    (c) Data centers
    (d) All the above

13. What is the prime concern about cloud computing?
    (a) Security concerns
    (b) Too many platforms
    (c) Accessibility
    (d) Too expensive
14. Which of these is not the leader of cloud computing?
    (a) Google
    (b) Amazon
    (c) Blackboard
    (d) Microsoft
15. Which of the following is not a major cloud computing platform?
    (a) Google 101
    (b) IBM Deep blue
    (c) Microsoft
    (d) Azure
16. What represents the 'cloud' in cloud computing?
    (a) Wireless
    (b) Wireless LAN
    (c) Crowd of people
    (d) The Internet
17. Which of these should a company consider before implementing cloud computing technology?
    (a) Employee satisfaction
    (b) Cost reduction
    (c) Sensitivity of information
    (d) All the above
18. The challenges with traditional infrastructure include:
    (a) Software licensing and support
    (b) Scalability
    (c) Accountability and modifiability
    (d) All the above
19. The advantage of cloud over remote hosting is _____.
    (a) Virtual servers or physical servers that can be customized to different plans through a control panel
    (b) Dedicated IP addresses for cloud servers
    (c) Replication or distribution over various distant locations
    (d) All the above
20. Which of these are the challenges of cloud computing?
    (a) Safeguarding data security
    (b) Managing the contractual relationship
    (c) Managing the cloud
    (d) All the above

Review Questions

1. What is cloud computing and how is it different from the Internet?
2. What is the need of cloud computing?
3. Explain the different elements responsible for the origination of cloud computing.
4. What are the core elements of a traditional data center?
5. What is virtualization? What are its various benefits?
6. What is distributed computing? Explain.
7. What is grid computing? How is it different from cloud computing?
8. How is a traditional data center different from a cloud data center?
9. What are the various services provided by cloud computing?
10. What are the advantages of peer-to-peer networking?
11. What are the various challenges of cloud computing?
12. How is cloud computing beneficial?
13. How can you say that security is one of the major challenges for cloud users?
14. Why is data segregation a limitation for cloud users?
15. What do you understand by remote access?
16. How can you say that interoperability and portability are the challenges of cloud computing?
17. What are the various vendors of cloud computing?
18. How can we use Windows Azure in the application platform of a public cloud?

19. What do you understand by customization? How can we use it in cloud computing?
20. What are the applications of utility computing with reference to cloud computing?
21. What is the need of elastic computing?

References

1. *Cloud Security A Comprehensive Guide to Secure Cloud Computing*, Ronald L. Krutz and Russell Dean Vines, ISBN: 978-0-470-58987-8, Wiley Publication, 2010
2. *Cloud Computing for Dummies*, Judith Hurwitz, Robin Bloor, Marcia Kaufman, and Dr Fern Halper, ISBN-10: 0470484705, Wiley Publication, 1st edition, November 16, 2009
3. *Cloud Computing Technologies and Strategies*, Brian J.S. Chee and Curtis Franklin, Jr, ISBN 9781439806128, CRC Press, April 16, 2010
4. *Cloud Computing: A Practical Approach,* Anthony T. Velte, Toby J. Velte, Ph.D., Robert Elsenpeter, ISBN-10: 0071626948, McGraw-Hill, 1st edition, November 1, 2009
5. *Grid and Cloud Computing*, Katarina StanoevskaSlabeva, Thomas Wozniak, and Santi Ristol, ISBN-10: 3642051928, Springer, 2010 edition, November 19, 2009
6. *Implementing and Developing Cloud Applications*, David E.Y.Sarna, ISBN-10: 1439830827, Auerbach Publications, November 26, 2010
7. *Market-oriented Cloud computing: Vision, Hype, and Reality for Delivering It Services as Computing Utilities. In High Performance Computing and Communications*, R. Buyya, C.S. Yeo, and S. Venugopal., 2008. HPCC'08. 10th IEEE International Conference, pp. 4–13 IEEE, 2008
8. *Mastering Cloud Computing*, Rajkumar Buyya, Christian Vecchhiola, S. Thamarai Selvi, Tata McGraw Hill Education Private Limited, 2008
9. *Cloud Computing and Virtualization*, V. Rajeswara Rao, V. ShubbaRamaiah, ISBN-10: 9383635045, BS Publications/BSP Books, 2014
10. National Institute of Standards and Technologies (NIST) http://csrc.nist.gov/publications/nistpubs/800-145/SP800-145.pdf, last accessed in January 2015

Answers to Multiple-choice Questions

1. (e)	5. (d)	9. (d)	13. (a)	17. (d)
2. (b)	6. (d)	10. (a)	14. (c)	18. (d)
3. (d)	7. (d)	11. (a) and (c)	15. (b)	19. (d)
4. (d)	8. (a)	12. (d)	16. (d)	20. (d)

CHAPTER 2
Factors that Affect Cloud Computing

Learning Outcomes

After completing this chapter, students will be able to:

- understand cloud data center requirements
- describe architectural, technological, and operational influences on cloud computing
- enlist issues in scalability of cloud architecture and applications
- understand influences of cloud on various businesses
- define autonomic computing
- explain IT service management

2.1 INTRODUCTION

Cloud computing is a technique that helps all IT functions. It eliminates the technical obstacles which organizations have to deal with so as to be information-rich and information-centric. The business world is expected to concentrate further on optimizing their information designs by using IT services and on-demand IT services instead of interior performances and infrastructure. In this chapter, we will discuss the data center requirement with its various aspects, its influence on cloud computing (including technical influence), what open-source software is, the basics of virtualization, information technology service management, and the effects of cloud computing on various businesses.

2.2 CLOUD DATA CENTER REQUIREMENTS

A cloud data center consists of computer systems and related components, for example, networking, storage, etc., which are kept at one place. The data center is a highly sensitive area with very strict environmental control, and entry is restricted for unauthorized users; safety measures are also designed in a way that protect any type of physical hazard in the data center. A data center comprises the following areas:

1. The first distribution area consists of various network equipment such as switches, routers, multiplexers, and firewalls.
2. The second distribution area consists of network, storage, etc.
3. The third area is that place where the actual rack cabinet is kept for computing and storage.

A supportive control system is also present for proper maintenance such as air conditioning, ventilation, heating, etc. The control system also works for maintaining the threshold temperature in the room.

The power supply in the data center is also not easy to install, as it requires a high level of expertise. In cloud data center, various IT and non-IT equipment are kept at one place; this needs a proper power backup facility in case of a power cut or any other problem. The energy consumption at various data centers tends to exceed the average limit. In fact, this is an area of research for scientists right now. For calculating power consumption, power usage effectiveness (PUE) is calculated.

Appropriate instructions and management of information design and information possession is vital. For good management, high-quality content is necessary to achieve organizational cloud computing. Appropriate management techniques, along with high-content quality, will raise the importance of information possession in both the long-term and short-term period. Control panel-oriented applications and business aptitude are important to the business society, are precise to execute, have assessable advantages, need iterative and attentive growth procedures, are read-only applications, and have lesser risk. Cloud computing provides the business world a chance to influence, discover, and develop the information possessions of the company to make actionable and informed assessments as well as measure achievement.

Flexibility, agility, and low price are the factors that make the cloud computing module reliable, particularly for business intelligence and control panel enterprise applications. This chapter discusses various architectural, technological, and operational influences on cloud computing in detail.

2.2.1 Architectural Influences

Cloud computing has been backed by architectural growth. The effects vary from progress in high-functioning computing to parallelism and scaling progress, discussed in the following sections.

High-performance Computing

Due to high-functioning computers and the Internet, fast development has taken place in computing. This development is the transfer from jobs which are computationally precise to those that are data concentrated. This development has led to several kinds of cloud computing applications that are convenient to operate due to high-functioning computers.

An attractive feature, besides the growth of supercomputers, was the thought of linking low-price, commercially accessible personal computers in a network group to make a high-functioning computing system. This concept was invented by NASA in 1993. They used open-source operating systems such as Linux or Solaris so that all the linked machines seemed like one resource to the user.

Utility and Enterprise Grid Computing

It is a kind of distributed and parallel system which facilitates the selection and sharing of geographically spread resources. A business net can supply a virtual or conventional relationship, which may use loosely coupled resources situated in a number of geographic sites under various managements.

A business net also supplies a vast variety of IT services such as computers, printers, databases, storage, and applications as required by business. The business net controls provision and registration, bills, and offers safety for these kinds of services, as shown in Fig. 2.1. As seen in the figure, various cloud users (such as 1 and 2) can request for services provided by the cloud service provider and there is a monitoring system to monitor cloud user activity. Database log files are managed to keep track of each and every type of activity in the network, and as per the service provided, the user has to pay.

Utility computing and business networks are executed using virtualization and values that may offer the basis for offering SaaS services to consumers. The accessible and existing practices and languages which support utility computing and business are—extensible markup language (XML), open grid services interface (OGSI), simple object access protocol (SOAP), web services description language (WSDL), and universal description discovery and integration (UDDI).

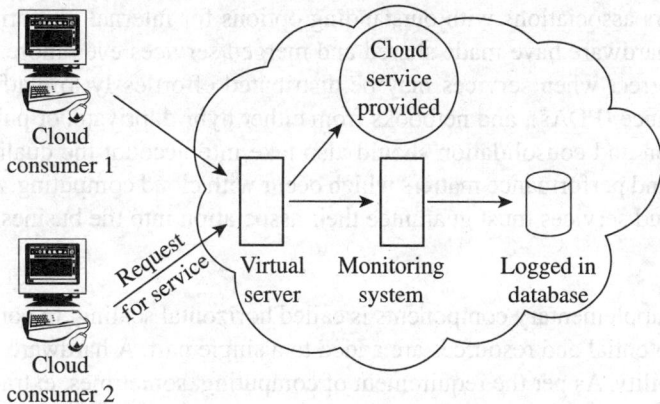

Fig. 2.1 Monitoring system of cloud computing

Utility computing and business networks, if operated and executed properly, offer the following advantages:
1. Improved efficiency
2. Increased productivity
3. Increased collaboration and improved communication
4. Improved flexibility
5. Shared resources
6. Rapid and increased access to a variety of computing resources
7. Reduction in effort required to manage multiple, non-integrated systems
8. Increased security

Autonomic Computing

Autonomic computing is a computing model with self-managing capabilities without the need of any external intervention. It works like a human body's nervous system. A self-management-based computing works without human involvement, and in case of failure, the computing does not stop but automatically migrates to another computer in the network. The rising connectivity and complexity of computing resources, which are needed to execute the cloud, call for a novel means to control, work, and maintain the cloud infrastructure. IBM built the idea of autonomic computing. They refer to it as an approach to self-managed computing with least human interference. The aim of autonomic computing is to offer complex systems with self-optimizing, self-healing, and self-diagnosis abilities.

The advantages of autonomic computing are as follows:
1. Running systems without employees' participation
2. Expanding the abilities of systems
3. Supervising complexity of systems
4. Administrating complex systems at minimum price
5. Familiarizing yourself with the latest technologies
6. Understanding and running drivers for numerous systems' applications

Service Consolidation

Sharing and consolidation of services built up as a profitable tie-up to supply such services over a network, as required, is known as service consolidation. Virtualization supports a dynamic group of resources such as storage and servers. Amalgamation of services like SaaS into the cloud pattern on a pay-per-use basis offers associations with outstanding options for internal platform. The low prices of the cloud computing hardware have made shared and merged services even more desirable nowadays. This is specifically correct when services may be distributed effortlessly to platforms such as iPods, personal digital assistance (PDAs), and netbooks from either hybrid, private, or public clouds.

Service consumption and consolidation should also take into account the quality of service (QoS), safety, exit approach, and performance matters which occur with cloud computing. At the business level, the access of outer cloud services must guarantee their association into the business network.

Horizontal Scaling

A system built using supplementary components is called horizontal scaling. In contract to this, vertical scaling means extra potential and resources are added to a single part. A hardware server is an example of both kinds of scalability. As per the requirement of computing, sometimes, extra memory or processing power is added to enhance the capability of the server. Horizontal scaling is an attractive feature in IT and is supported by cloud computing as it is required at the time of redundant data storage to reduce the chances of entire or partial system failure as shown in Fig. 2.2. Scaling permits users to increase or decrease IT resources as per the requirement.

The two types of scaling are given here:
1. Horizontal scaling—It includes scaling out and scaling in
2. Vertical scaling—It includes scaling up and scaling down

Horizontal scaling is mostly used in cloud computing (compared to vertical scaling) as it requires downtime when replacement is taking place. The differences are listed in Table 2.1.

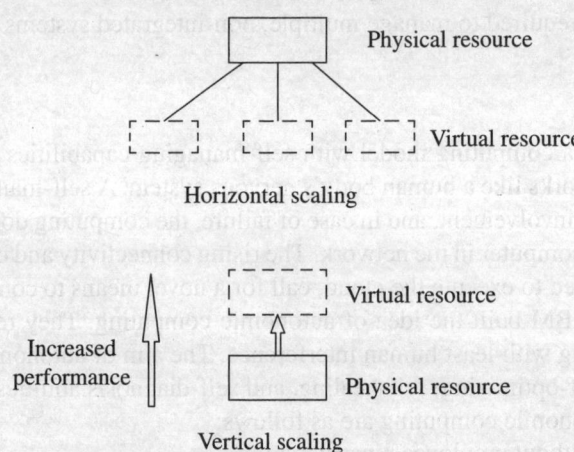

Fig. 2.2 Horizontal and vertical scaling

Table 2.1 Differences between horizontal scaling and vertical scaling

Horizontal scaling	Vertical scaling
Less expensive	More expensive
Does not require extra downtime	More downtime required for replacement
Extra set-up not required	Extra set-up required
Supplementary IT resources required	Supplementary IT resources not required
Not restricted by hardware power	Restricted by hardware power

Scaling may be executed in both distributed and centralized systems. In centralized systems, scaling up or vertical scaling is realized by raising the capacity of accessible resources.

In addition to offering enhanced functioning, horizontal scaling is used to execute consistency and idleness of loosely coupled systems. Hence, distributed systems are more flexible and allow breakdown of several resource divisions. This capability to consistently cause horizontal scaling is a vital aspect in the achievement of cloud computing. Normally, vertical scaling is simpler to execute, but it is more costly. Besides, there is a probability of malfunctioning. Horizontal scaling is generally less expensive and more flexible, but it is a little tougher to execute than vertical scaling.

Vertical scaling uses superior and larger functioning hardware to scale. The horizontal scaling method relies on using additional machines rather than more effective machines. Horizontal scaling is mainly valid for Web 2.0, in which, as applications increase, there is an equivalent reduction in working. As the majority of applications are data concentrated in cloud computing, considerable progress in functioning may be attained by horizontally scaling the database. Scaling includes replicating the database diagonally on various servers. Some of the strategies used are as follows:

1. Caching—Reduces response time to operate memory
2. Table-level partitioning—It is useful in handling databases efficiently
3. Shading—Managing applications by separating datasets into smaller components diagonally across various physical servers

Web Services

A web service is defined by the World Web Consortium as a software system designed to support interoperable machine-to-machine interactions over a network.

The web service can be defined by the SOAP as well. For exchanging information, it acts as a lightweight protocol. It is an XML-based protocol which consists of three sections:

1. It works like a wrapper that defines a framework for describing what is in a message and how it is processed. It also consists of a set of encoding rules for expressing instances of application-defined data types and has a convention for representing remote procedure calls and responses.
2. SOAP has the potential to work with a combination of other protocols. However, the only requirement is to define the document and describe how SOAP is used in combination with HTTP and the HTTP Extension Framework.
3. A web service is defined by NIST as 'self-describing and stateless module that performs discrete units of work and is available over the network'. A usual interface used by a web service has been described in web service definition language (WSDL) to offer conversion among computing platforms operating distinct applications, with the SOAP XML-based procedure supporting this switch of data over HTTP.

High-scalability Architecture

The scalability of a cloud computing system guarantees that the cloud may support augmented loads. Hence, every cloud platform design must be constructed with greater scalability, facilitating augmented capability in a linear style in accordance with the workload. Numerous options are accessible in order to support superior scalability.

2.2.2 Issues in Scalability of Cloud Architecture and Applications

'Scalability' means the number of sessions, consumers, operations, and transactions which can be held by the entire system. In simple words, scalability means doing what a person does in a bigger way. Scaling a web application means permitting more people to make use of application by developing it to meet increasing demand, without making a change in the code or sacrificing the affinity of data and levels of service to the demand of your users. Many companies make a muddle of applications which do not fit in the set standards and do not reveal a unified implemented arrangement. This decreases their capability to repeat on product growth and hence generates a falter in business. The solution to solve this problem is to adopt a scalable platform architecture which secures all applications.

Building a scalable, flexible architecture for a service or application might be a significant challenge. It is difficult to recognize the pressure points in your application until it actually fails. However, more and more organizations are developing applications which need greater up-time and high-load tolerance. In addition, businesses are required to be capable to develop their user base with a least of effort that puts more pressure on applications and drives them to deal with escalating demand.

For such applications, a scalable and solid platform architecture is necessary. Each feature of the design of application needs concern, including the concern of means in which the runtime of hard-hit fields should be minimized, or of the means in which caching might be made little bit smaller to simplify the memory footprint. From this point of view, making a scalable platform architecture is truly much an art than a science, so smart businesses frequently turn to dealers who can supply and control a scalable architecture which fulfills their requirements.

A scalable platform permits businesses to deal with large-scale business issues via the high-performance processing of huge data volumes. By accomplishing a service-oriented architecture (SOA) architecture which each application might acquire, you can confirm that each of your application has a competently scalable architecture and can be efficiently upgraded and managed.

Challenges faced by an Application Developer in Developing Cloud Applications

Some of the challenges are:

Lack of standardization As every cloud provider supports different programming languages and interfaces, there is a requirement of standardizing them.

Lack of extra programming support As applications hosted on cloud can be mirrored on different machines, on demand access of such applications faces delays as latency decreases. Automation of serving such kind of applications is a regular task of cloud platform service providers. To make this process seamless, a good number of state variables of the application need to be stored when application context switches from one place to another and requires cloud environment changes. Cloud providers use datastore to store the state of such applications with lot of restrictions like prohibition to install third-party libraries.

Debugging and development kits For ease of development environment, good integrated development environments (IDEs) are helpful for cloud programming. However, until now there is no good IDE with debugging and testing experience to do cloud programming because of vivid nature of cloud application programming interfaces (APIs), for example, Rackspace, Amazon, Google, etc. have their own set of APIs to access cloud services. Many developers are facing problems when moving the code from local environment to the cloud environment because of behavioral inconsistencies in the local environment.

Metrics and best practices Since cloud is a business model, consumers have to pay the usage of almost every CPU cycle so that presenting a metrics on usage of memory and processing time of application is very useful for the developer to do programming on the optimum use of processing power. One of the best practices for the cloud provider is to keep common code patterns into the libraries so that users can run the most optimal code for a certain operation.

Factors that Affect Cloud Computing

Table 2.2 Summary of different cloud service models

Service Model	Provider	Usage Target
SaaS	Google Gmail	Email
	XDrive	Storage
	Salesforce.com	CRM
	Smugmug	Data sharing
	MuxCLoud	Data processing
PaaS	Google App Engine	Web applications
	Azure	Enterprise applications, Web applications
	Heroku	Web applications
	Aneka	.Net Enterprise applications, Web applications
	Force.com	Enterprise applications
IaaS	GoGrid	Compute, Memory, Storage
	Amazon EC2	Compute, Memory, Storage
	Flexiscale	Compute, Memory, Storage
	Rockspace	Compute, Memory, Storage
	Eucaliptus	Compute, Memory, Storage

For cloud service models and their providers, refer to Table 2.2.

Design Patterns for Key Issues of Cloud Application Development

The design patterns include:

Scalability Scalability is defined as dynamically increasing and decreasing the load according to the requirement. Scalability in cloud perspective can be addressed as follows:

- Stateless—The maintenance of cloud based applications may further deteriorate the important issue like scalability involving persistence of applications. Hence, it is highly suggested to use RESTful state of applications.
- Parallelization—MapReduce and SPDY are mainly used for parallelizing applications on clouds. Here, it can be observed that the parallel processing model widely deviates from the typical request-reply paradigm as the task is being performed in parallel by multiple processing units controlled by a standard application delivery controller.
- Load Sharing—As good numbers of load balancing algorithms are provided by different middleware, the major task of the developer is to plug the application to existing APIs.
- Partitioning—Partitioning involves intelligent load distribution among different nodes considering many other issues such as data availability, efficiency, and performance. Figure 2.3 indicates an illustration of how application switches from one pool of resources to another using better node selection algorithms.
  - Vertical Partitioning—In this scheme, partitioning is done with many processing units and the application routing requests associated with an URI are carried out by a separate function.
  - Horizontal Partitioning—In this scheme, a partitioning key is used and persistence-based load balancing is adopted.
- Relaxing of data constraints—This deals with algorithms related to immediate processing of data along with storage and access, which requires intelligent usage and partitioning of contents.

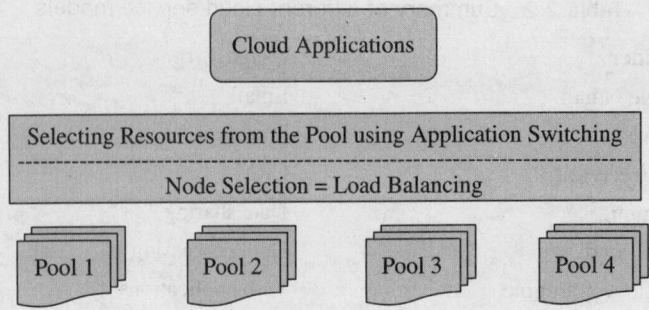

Fig. 2.3 Grouping instances in to task specific pools

To achieve this, application developers need some time to be relaxed on the constraints around access times for some types of data.
- At last, application developers also need to architect solutions that separate data reads from writes.

Availability Cloud applications should be designed in a way to handle situations when any resource fails to cope with the need to provide the required data. To guarantee high availability under such failed conditions, the application architecture needs to be accustomed to enable redundancy and fault-tolerant structures. Usually, the availability is measured in terms of uptime and down time.

$$\text{Availability} = 1 - (\text{downtime}/\text{uptime})$$

Multi-Tenacity A tenant is a customer or application which shares a common access with specific privileges to once instance. The customers are allowed to share computing resources in either public or private cloud with the help of cloud computing architecture called multi tenant. Every customer data is separated from other, which means it is invisible to other in the public cloud environment. In a private cloud, the customers can have different parts of divisions inside the same organization. In a public cloud, the customers are from different companies. So, most public clouds use the multi-tenancy architectural model. Cost wise, it is less expensive because it allows them to run with one server instance and makes it easier to give updates to a large number of customers.

High Performance MapReduce is a parallel programming model developed at Google with the objective of implementing large-scale search and for text processing on massively scalable web data stored using Big Table and distributed file system (DFS). MapReduce is designed for processing and generating large volumes of data via massively parallel computations and utilizing tens of thousands of processors at a time. Ensure progress of computation even if processors and networks fail is called fault tolerant.

For example, Hadoop is an open source implementation of MapReduce available on pre-packaged AMIs on Amazon EC2 cloud platform.

Rapid Elasticity Capabilities can be elastically provisioned and released, in some cases automatically, to scale rapidly outward and inward commensurate with demand. To the consumer, the capabilities available for provisioning often appear to be unlimited and can be appropriated in any quantity at any time.

2.2.3 Technological Influences

Technology helps in keeping corporations' transaction and financial matters (income and profits), finances, and personal functional metrics up to date. It permits the corporations to make enhanced decisions and take proper action. The 'big deal' is to expand the sales, profits, and enterprise ability of the delivery sequence along with the final result that makes the consumer happy. The kinds of computing tools used by experts may be laptops, smartphones, desktops, etc. Every novel tool that is available generally has abilities associated with rich data, conversions, content, and applications.

SaaS, along with cloud computing, signifies that information is not attentive on personal machines in a permanent site. It is united into a single digital 'cloud' accessible at the click of a mouse from thousands of distinct tools. Technology corporations have transferred numerous software applications which enterprises normally control for themselves over the cloud, although various more still have to be swapped over. With architectural impacts, progress in technology has apparently had an effect on the expansion and execution of the cloud computing pattern. Several of the main technological impacts are discussed in the following sections.

Universal Connectivity

Cloud computing needs global access and connectivity to the Internet in order to be successful. It assists associations and customers by providing connectivity anywhere among consumers, government companies, and enterprises via ways like peer-to-peer exchanges, Web 2.0, and web services. Such global connectivity must be achieved via high-speed, broadband networks. The continuous development of broadband links is important to the development and universal expansion of cloud computing. A vital matter regarding global connectivity is net impartiality. Net impartiality maintains the position of the Internet, whereby users are under the influence of the content and applications, and the whole network traffic is handled uniformly.

Commoditization

Before the 1980s, computer systems were defensive and had their individual software, hardware, and set of rules. After 1980, with advancement in personal computers (PCs), several hardware and software elements became compatible and consistent among platforms. Later, emphasis on wide area networks (WANs) and local area networks (LANs) led to consistency in conversion rules and ultimately the Internet, which further speedened up commoditization.

Corporations such as Prodigy and CompuServe with proprietary techniques provide direction to the declining price of bandwidths, and the convenience and suppleness offered by the World Wide Web. Powerful drivers, in the way towards commoditization, include open-source software such as OpenOffice and FireFox, and the swiftly declining prices of PDAs, servers, multifunctional cellular goods, and PCs.

Matters of such commoditization are relevant to cloud computing as well. With the advent of new cloud computing technology and the associated trend of outsourcing in many industries, the commoditization of IT services has become more significant. In case of failure for providing services to the users, it is very important for service providers to make alternative options to the users on demand.

Cloud services have five basic features such as on-demand self-service, broadband network access, resource pooling, elasticity, and the ability to monitor services. As part of the approach to cloud computing, businesses will merge one or two measures which support exchange and interoperability of services among cloud dealers. These measures may be de facto, open, or formal. De facto measures could appear from use by leading dealers such as VMware or Amazon.

Open-source Software

Open-source software in cloud computing may draw distinct views. The open-source software used in cloud computing may offer the following benefits:
1. Access and availability to source code
2. Easy amalgamation and growth of latest applications

3. Capability to expand, alter, and reallocate software
4. Easily available upgrades and patches
5. Open file arrangements
6. Minimal obstacles for new users to test the software
7. Avoidance of vendor lock-in
8. Low barriers for new users to try the software

Open-source software like Linux is used by several cloud suppliers so as to access and occasionally alter the code of source in order to offer customized services. This directs to proprietary technology in several cases. An added alternative for executing cloud computing services is the use of open-source computing platforms. For open-source cloud software to grow up, open norms and regulations need to be built to support interoperability of services.

Virtualization

Conventionally, virtualization of server was observed as a price-saving process. The chief advantages of virtualization, which are intrinsic to cloud computing, are as follows:
1. Invoicing based on usage
2. Quick installation of extra servers
3. Support of economies of scale
4. Division of the consumer from physical server sites
5. Usage according to the service-level arrangements
6. Optional sourcing support
7. Application mobility among data centers and servers

Various cloud services, operational tools, and cloud resources are available for cloud users and the service management system handles the requirement of various resources in the network. Various types of devices can be used to take services from the cloud network, such as computer, laptop, and mobile, as shown in Fig. 2.4.

2.2.4 Operational Influences

Operations' discussions have a considerable influence on the installation, operation, protection, and a variety of matters related to cloud computing. From the viewpoint of both the supplier and the consumer of cloud computing services, the chief operational impacts are discussed in the following sections.

Consolidation

Consolidation refers to the fact that a physical resource or server can be shared by many users and also made accessible by a variety of applications at the same time. The aim behind consolidation is to make proper utilization of underutilized resources and make efficient usage of existing resources. As cloud computing is based on the concept of virtualization, the same instance of a physical resource is shared by multiple users at the same time and that is why it changes the meaning of consolidation as well.

Basically, there are two types of consolidation—server consolidation and storage consolidation. Storage consolidation is a system of centralizing data storage between multiple servers. It is helpful to facilitate data backup at various levels and minimizes the time required for accessing and storing data. The supported features of storage consolidation include simplified storage infrastructure, efficient management, and optimized resource utilization with low cost. Common storage consolidation architectures are network-attached storage (NAS), redundant array of independent disks (RAID), and storage area network (SAN).

Server consolidation can be done in several ways. One of the options is to use blade servers, which consists of modular circuits within a card. Server virtualization makes a single physical server available to others by creating virtual instances of the server. The complexity involved is the need to handle

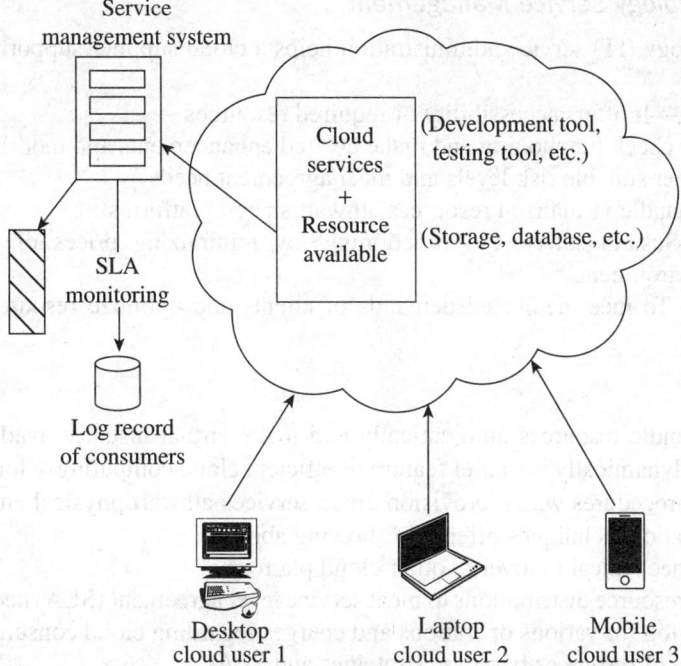

Fig. 2.4 Cloud management systems

instances in keeping the data hidden from the users. Server consolidation reduces physical resources on a location by proper utilization of the resource that leads to energy conservation. Server consolidation can be achieved by any architecture as follows:

1. Network attached storage (NAS)—Better hard drives with good processing power are used for storing data.
2. Redundant array of independent disks (RAID)—A single logical device is shown to the user, apart from which data is also kept on various disks.
3. Storage area network (SAN)—A fibre channel technology for providing services over a large geographical area is used.

Outsourcing

Cloud computing offers flexible billing alternatives and price savings via outsourcing. The huge investments of cloud suppliers in emergent high-capacity infrastructures eliminate the requirement for consumers to make huge additional or initial open expenditures for internal IT systems. With outsourcing, cloud computing can provide the following benefits:

1. Disaster recovery
2. Economy of scale
3. Security
4. Automatic and continuous hardware and software upgrades
5. Libraries of applications
6. Performance monitoring and management
7. Rapid capability expansion
8. Significant energy savings
9. Better throughput
10. Availability
11. Flexibility

Information Technology Service Management

Information technology (IT) service administration helps a cloud supplier support the following functions:
1. Error handling—It offers accessibility of required resources
2. Visibility—To check functioning and make desired enhancements and modifications
3. Safety—To offer suitable risk levels and meet agreement needs
4. Control—To handle virtualized resources athwart shared platforms
5. Automation—Sustain safety and functioning, by minimizing prices of sustaining complex computing environments
6. Performance—To meet dedicated demands of clients and optimize resources at low operating prices

Automation

The capability to handle resources automatically and make virtual instance available by transferring virtual applications dynamically is a chief feature of efficient cloud computing. Cloud automation offers measures to set up procedures which provision cloud services athwart physical and virtual cloud platforms. Cloud automation techniques offer the following abilities:
1. Elasticity by mechanical failover to other cloud platforms
2. Amend cloud resource distributions to meet service level agreement (SLA) needs and performance
3. Maintaining a log for various operations and charges regarding cloud consumers
4. Administration of resources based on strategies and SLAs
5. Observation of virtual machine-associated data, such as consumption history, file system access history, owner, and storage usage
6. Enforcement of safety limitations concerning directories and configuration components
7. Observing secrecy and safety rules

2.3 INFLUENCE OF CLOUD COMPUTING ON BUSINESS COMPANIES

Many enterprises have by now effectively outsourced numerous IT services and performances to concentrate resources on their main company. Cloud computing is coming up as a means to outsource IT, even more in the coming years, as companies will continue to move their in-house technological infrastructure to the cloud. With enterprises' technological IT infrastructure moving to the cloud, they will be capable of concentrating more on the business-centric features of IT. Most remarkably, they will expend more time defining information design instead of technical design and will expend more time handling their information benefits instead of their technology benefits.

Appropriately handling of information benefits inside a cloud computing module is particularly vital for front-end IT service regions and applications such as business performance management (BPM), business intelligence (BI), and functioning metrics console where the enterprise society conventionally has a more significant relationship with IT teams than other back-end service regions. Console applications and enterprise intelligence are the subject regions of IT and these come as part of cloud services. These applications are simple to execute, are inclined to be business oriented, have assessable advantages, are greatly observable to trade society, need active and iterative growth procedures, are somewhat less risky, and are read-only applications.

Cloud computing provides corporations the alternative to discover self-service or on-demand IT services offered by cloud providers. As technology advances, corporations will move their IT concentration towards information design and towards setting up the control and instruction features for administrating their information benefits. Inside the cloud computing module, a conventional, in-house IT team will go through an alteration to turn it into more governance-oriented, business-associated, content-conscious, and less technology oriented. IT teams will become more trade confident as IT service and on-demand IT services augment.

Enterprise policy and IT policy are connected to each other. Since a technologist's job is outsourced in the cloud computing module, in-house IT team arrangement will utilize their time in understanding enterprise data and regulations handling the data, and in comprehending enterprise policies and aims. They will become the drivers of information design. Therefore, stress on information design and the increasing IT team of enterprise-oriented informationists will help in expanding managerial policies, which will take enterprise decision-making to the limits of forever enhancing and extending managerial information benefits.

Cloud computing applications at the business level, business-unit, or departmental levels will permit the enterprise society and IT teams to work together closely in order to appropriately handle their content quality, information policy, and governance procedures in the modern world of outsourced Software as a Service (SaaS), Information as a service, Infrastructure as a Service (IaaS), and Platform as a Service (PaaS) IT module. Cloud computing with various advantages and tools affect many companies' working style and this is discussed in detail in the following parameters.

2.3.1 Business Alignment

A business alliance of all IT self-service applications, particularly console applications and enterprise intelligence, is vital for sustaining information quality, and is significant in the modern world of IT self-service. The concentration of the IT team of a corporation will transfer from running hardware assets and data center functions to handling the following responsibilities:

1. Recognizing enterprise policies, functioning metrics, drivers, market dynamics, purposes, and many more
2. Classifying trade definitions (business unit, department-level, etc.) and trade regulations
3. Forming a value-added information collection which links to the purposes and aims of a corporation
4. Assessing and predicting the realistic advantage of cloud computing applications
5. Recognizing modern challenges of risk administration in on-demand IT self-service

From a business viewpoint, the actual skill is that it may enhance the relationship among business and IT. The conventional IT module comprises a major component of fixed price in the yearly budget, without the capability to bend prices up and down. Occasionally, nearly 20 per cent of the IT budget is accessible to fund novel enterprise plans which raise revenue, lessen price, with flexible hardware and software options, and may be adjusted up and down depending on the requirements of the business. This permits more expenses to be concentrated on technology which directly carries the value of businesses.

Second, enhancing the availability of resource is another chief enterprise benefit of cloud computing. Cloud computing considerably minimizes or eliminates the up-front expenditure on hardware, software, and project execution. Owing to the low cost, corporations using cloud computing may benefit with IT being more accessible to the enterprise.

As cloud computing uses a 'pay-as-you-go' backing module, it is essential for the enterprise to ascertain the exact value of the money spent. It makes no meaning for the corporation to pay for data, applications, and services which do not ever fetch any value to the enterprise. It is the compulsion of the corporation to be attentive and eliminate or regulate such data, services, or applications which are not accumulating value as calculated by the corporation.

2.3.2 Governance

To acquire a great level of value administration of information assets, it is essential to set up and maintain good control of data, content, business regulations, system functioning, modules, usage, information, and much more. Another expression for good control is suitable 'command and control' of

information assets. In a cloud computing module, having suitable and efficient command and control is vital and can be a major problem for the corporation. The following points are important to know how cloud computing affects control and governance on data stored, when you are a cloud user:
- Process controls and process observation
- Content secrecy and safety
- Content consistency and master data management
- Cloud computing capability maturity model (CMM)
- Incorporating and running rising cloud computing IT models—SaaS, IaaS, and PaaS

The cloud maturity module comprises 60 abilities which encapsulate the finest practices. Such abilities offer the feature mandatory to actually assess and direct the development of cloud proposals. There are six spheres in the maturity model:

Business and strategy Organizations accept to migrate to cloud while keeping in mind points that are better for a business organization and the strategy to be followed. This includes expected profits, expected expenses, business inspiration, funding models, guiding principles, etc.

Architecture This refers to controlling abilities regarding the description of the entire architecture and strategies such as interoperability, self-service, and resource pooling which are measured in the module.

Infrastructure This refers to controlling abilities regarding the service infrastructure and devices offered in the proposal. Provisioning, module covering, and shared services are mainly essential in cloud infrastructure.

Information This refers to controlling features regarding the information of the cloud, such as metadata administration, data strength, and consumer powers.

Projects, portfolios, and services This refers to controlling abilities regarding the setting up and construction of cloud services and administration of selection of services.

Operations, administration, and management This refers to controlling abilities regarding the post-installation features of cloud services, that is, the administration, management, and operation features of the cloud environment. This comprises abilities for the release of self-service performance and modifies administration.

Points to Remember

1. A cloud data center comprises computer systems and related components such as storage, networking, etc.
2. Cloud computing is affected by architectural, technological, and operational influences.
3. A scalable platform permits businesses to deal with large-scale business issues via the high performance processing of huge data volumes.
4. There are many advantages linked to utility and automatic computing.
5. Two types of scaling include horizontal scaling and vertical scaling.
6. The scalability of a cloud computing system guarantees that the cloud may support argumented loads.
7. The continuous development of broadband links is important to the development and universal expansion of cloud computing.
8. What drives commoditization is open-source software such as OpenOffice and Firefox, and the declining prices of PDAs, servers, multifunctional cellular goods, and PCs.

9. Open-source software like Linux is used by cloud suppliers to access and sometimes modify the code of source to offer customized services to clients.
10. Virtualization of server is a price-saving process.
11. Consolidation, outsourcing, information technology service management, and automation are the few operational influences on cloud computing.
12. Cloud computing minimizes the up-front expenditure on hardware, software, and project execution.
13. It maintains data secrecy, master data, data consistency, handles incorporating and running of cloud computing IT models—SaaS, IaaS, and PaaS.

Key Terms

Caching It involves lowering the application response times by performing memory caching of heavily accessed data using horizontally scaled, dedicated cache servers to reduce the load on application servers.

Cloud computing capability maturity model (CMM) It includes 60 capabilities that capture the best practices that Oracle has collected over the years working with a wide variety of companies. These capabilities provide the details necessary to truly measure and guide the progress of a cloud initiative.

Extensible markup language (XML) It is a type of markup language used to define and support a set of rules of encoding documents in such a format that it is understandable by a human as well as a machine.

Master data management (MDM) It comprises a set of processes, governance, policies, standards, and tools that consistently define and manage the master data of an organization.

Network attached storage (NAS) It is a type of computer storage server in a network for giving a variety of file-level data access services to the clients. It has good processing power.

Open grid services initiative (OGSI) It is a framework that supports Java and is used to develop software modules and libraries.

Redundant array of independent disks (RAID) A single logical device is shown to the user, but apart from that, data is also kept on various disks.

Shading It refers to managing a growing number of applications by dividing data sets into smaller elements across many physical servers and segregating the transactional bandwidth across these servers.

Simple object access protocol (SOAP) Simple object access protocol (SOAP) defines the messaging protocol XML.

Storage area network (SAN) A fibre channel technology for providing services over a large geographical area.

Table-level partitioning It involves slicing data horizontally and distributing the data across database instances.

Web services description language (WSDL) It is a language written in XML used to define web services and specify the parameters to access a service.

Web 2.0 A new technology supported by the World Wide Web that supports user teamwork, generates content, and is used for social networking, among others

Multiple-choice Questions

1. One of the advantages of grid computing is:
   (a) Improved flexibility
   (b) Cost
   (c) Speed
   (d) None of these

2. Autonomic computing helps in:
   (a) Extending system capabilities
   (b) Adapting new technologies
   (c) Managing complexity of system
   (d) All the above

3. An important issue related to universal connectivity is:
   (a) Broadband network
   (b) Quality of service
   (c) Net neutrality
   (d) None of these

4. One of the advantages of open-source software is:
   (a) Improved flexibility
   (b) Cost
   (c) Speed
   (d) None of these

5. The benefits of virtualization is/are:
   (a) Fault tolerance
   (b) Speed
   (c) Separation of duties
   (d) All of these

6. The function of IT service management is/are:
   (a) Security
   (b) Performance
   (c) Control
   (d) All the above

7. The number of domains in maturity model are:
   (a) Four
   (b) Six
   (c) Eight
   (d) None of these

8. The key benefits of outsourcing that can be provided by clouds are as follows:
   (a) Resiliency
   (b) Disaster recovery
   (c) Economy of scale and security
   (d) All the above

9. Utility computing, if implemented and managed properly, can result in:
   (a) Increased productivity
   (b) Increased collaboration and improved communications
   (c) Improved flexibility
   (d) All the above

10. Managing a growing number of applications by dividing data sets into smaller elements across many physical servers is called _____.
    (a) Shading
    (b) Caching
    (c) Filtering
    (d) None of these

11. Simple Object Access Protocol (SOAP) is used to define:
    (a) Messaging protocol XML
    (b) Protocols for web pages
    (c) Both (a) and (b)
    (d) None of these

Review Questions

1. What are the various architectural influences on cloud computing?
2. How are operation influences associated with cloud computing?
3. How does cloud computing influence business and governance?
4. How is data quantity important for cloud computing?
5. What do you understand by enterprise grid computing?
6. What is horizontal scaling?
7. What is open-source software?
8. How can outsourcing be done keeping the operational influences in mind?

9. What is IT service management?
10. What are the different domains in the maturity model?
11. How is horizontal scaling different from vertical scaling?
12. How can businesses grow with the help of cloud computing tools? Discuss in detail.
13. What are the challenges faced by an application developer in developing cloud?

References

1. *Cloud Security A Comprehensive Guide to Secure Cloud Computing*, Ronald L. Krutz and Russell Dean Vines, ISBN: 978-0-470-58987-8, Wiley Publication, 2010
2. *Cloud computing for Dummies*, Judith Hurwitz, Robin Bloor, Marcia Kaufman, and Dr. Fern Halper, ISBN-10: 0470484705, Wiley Publication, 1st edition, November 16, 2009
3. *Cloud Computing Technologies and Strategies*, Brian J.S. Chee and Curtis Franklin, Jr, ISBN 9781439806128, CRC Press, April 7, 2010
4. *Cloud Computing: A Practical Approach*, Anthony T. Velte, Toby J. Velte, Ph.D., Robert Elsenpeter, ISBN-10: 0071626948, McGraw-Hill, 1st edition, November 1, 2009
5. *Grid and Cloud Computing*, Katarina StanoevskaSlabeva, Thomas Wozniak, and Santi Ristol, ISBN-10: 3642051928, Springer, 2010 edition, November 19, 2009
6. *Implementing and Developing Cloud Applications*, David E.Y. Sarna, ISBN-10: 1439830827, Auerbach Publications, November 26, 2010
7. *Market-oriented Cloud Computing: Vision, Hype, and Reality for Delivering IT Services as Computing Utilities. In High Performance Computing and Communications*, R. Buyya, C.S. Yeo, and S. Venugopal, 2008. HPCC'08. 10th IEEE International Conference on pp. 4–13 IEEE, 2008
8. *Mastering Cloud Computing*, By Rajkumar Buyya, Christian Vecchhiola, S. Thamarai Selvi, Tata McGraw Hill Education Private Limited, 2008
9. *Cloud Computing and Virtualization*, V. Rajeswara Rao, V. Shubba Ramaiah, BS Publication, ISBN-10: 9383635045, BS Publications / BSP Books, 2014
10. André B. Bondi, 'Characteristics of scalability and their impact on performance', *Proceedings of the 2nd international workshop on Software and performance,* Ottawa, Ontario, Canada, 2000, ISBN 1-58113-195-X, pages 195–203
11. Lu, W. and Jackson, J. and Barga, R (2010), *Azureblast: a case study of developing science applications on the cloud*, Proceedings of the 19th ACM International Symposium on High Performance Distributed Computing
12. *Load balancing and MapReduce* (2011), http://www.ibm.com/developerworks/cloud/library/cl-mapreduce, last accessed in May 2018

Answers to Multiple-choice Questions

1. (a)   4. (a)   7. (c)   10. (a)
2. (d)   5. (a)   8. (d)   11. (a)
3. (c)   6. (d)   9. (d)

Cloud Computing Architecture

Learning Outcomes

After completing this chapter, students will be able to:

- comprehend characteristics of cloud computing
- define grid computing
- explain important features of cloud and grid computing
- describe grid architecture and cloud computing architecture
- differentiate between grid and cloud computing

3.1 INTRODUCTION

Grid computing is the integration of computer resources for achieving similar objective. The grid may be a dispersed system along with non-interactive workloads which comprise a huge number of files. What differentiates grid computing from conventional, unnecessary functioning computing systems like group computing is that grids are loosely attached and geographically distributed. Although one grid may be dedicated to a specific application, it is utilized for a diversity of objectives. Grids are frequently created with middleware software libraries of a common grid. In this chapter, we will discuss grid computing, with its application and advantage, how cloud computing is different from grid computing, important features of cloud computing, and cloud architecture.

3.2 GRID FRAMEWORK OVERVIEW

Grids are a type of dispersed computing system, whereas a virtualized super computer is made from various networked, loosely attached computers temporarily joined for performing huge tasks. 'Grid' or 'disseminated' computing, for several applications, may be distinguished as an exceptional kind of equivalent computing which relies on whole computers connected to a network (public, private, or the Internet) through a conventional network interface, like the ethernet.

Computing grids are not distinct electrical grids. In an electrical grid, wall channels permit us to link to an infrastructure of resources. After getting connected to the electrical grid, you never require recognizing where the power plant is situated or how are you receiving the current. Middleware is used in grid computing in order to synchronize various IT resources in a network and making them work as a virtual intact. The objective of grid computing is to offer users access to the resources as per the requirement. Grids focus on two different but associated objectives—supplying isolated access to IT resources and building up processing control. The most understandable resource comprised in a grid is a mainframe, but grids too include data-storage systems, sensors, applications, and additional resources. The grid is a technology which controls two factors—allocation and trust.

Grid computing is a versatile technology which has its base in e-science and has progressed from previous expansions in parallel and high-performance computing (HPC). Before 1990, it appeared when high functioning computers were linked with rapid data communication along with the purpose to assist calculation and data-concentrated scientific applications. At that point in time, this was indicated as hyper computing or meta computing and the stress was on synchronized use of accessible computing resources meant for high functioning applications.

On the basis of the illustration of cluster computing and hyper computing, it became apparent that sharing of resource could be applicable for other application regions as well. Accordingly, it became apparent that resource sharing must be offered in a standard mode and should not be aimed merely for particular high-functioning applications.

A grid system is a system that:
1. Synchronizes resources which are not subject to centralized power
2. Employs customary, open, common-function interfaces, and protocols
3. Conveys nontrivial behaviour of service

The main resources that can be shared in a grid are:
1. Processing and computing power
2. Networked file and data storage systems
3. Bandwidth and communications
4. Application software
5. Tools used for scientific purpose

The distinct definitions broadcast by intellectual, forecasters, and business resulted in a huge terminological confusion in the market over the suggestion of the expressions for grid and grid computing. Some are given below:

Grid middleware is exclusive software that offers the essential functionality needed to facilitate sharing of various resources and setting up of virtual businesses. Grid middleware is exclusive software that is incorporated into the infrastructure of the concerned corporation. Grid middleware offers a unique virtualization and sharing layer which is positioned among the various infrastructures and the particular user applications using it.

Grid computing is fundamentally the installed Grid middleware or the computing permitted by grid middleware based on synchronized, safe, flexible resource sharing among a collection of resources, people, and organizations. Grid computing means that mixed groups of storage systems, servers, and networks are grouped jointly in a virtualized system which is displayed as the only computing unit to the user. On the other hand, working style and instructions are similar to grid applications and infrastructure.

Grid infrastructure refers to the union of grid middleware and hardware which converts single portions of data resources and hardware into an incorporated virtualized infrastructure that is displayed to the user as the only computer in spite of heterogeneity of the fundamental infrastructure.

Utility computing is a type of computing that provides customized applications of grid and computing as a service. It is based on pay-as-per-utilization business modules.

3.3 GRID ARCHITECTURE

The grid design offers an outline of the grid constituents, describes the objective and operations of its constituents, and shows how the constituents interrelate with each other. The chief concentration of a grid design is on the protocols and interoperability among users and suppliers of resources in order to establish the sharing relationships. Various layers of the grid architecture are described below.

1. The *Fabric layer* includes the physical resources that are shared inside the grid. This comprises network resources, computational resources, storage systems, sensors, software modules, and additional system resources.
2. The *Connectivity layer* facilitates the switch of data among the fabric layer resources. The most significant functionalities at the connectivity layer comprise identification, transfer, navigation, and support for a safe conversation. The most crucial requirements for security support involve support for login, support for designation as per which a program may perform and access resources according to the user's authority, and support for interoperability in combination with regional security resolutions and regulations.
3. The *Resource layer* provides the protection and interaction activity as distinguished by the connectivity layer, which is used for many applications such as accounting, scrutinizing, etc., and computes whole expense for using individual resource. It incorporates mainly information and management practices. Information practices are employed for finish information concerning the creation and state of clear resources. Management practices are employed for consulting access to resources and provide a 'strategy application point' by making certain that the resources' usage is consistent with the method under which the resource is to be shared.
4. The *Collective layer* is liable for the whole worldwide resource management and for interaction with collection of resources. Collective layer methods carry out a plentiful range of sharing ways. The most vital facilities of this layer are directory services, co-allotment, scrutinizing, investigative services, data imitation services, and setting up and collaborating services. The collective layer services are generally cited by programming devices and models such as grid-permitted programming systems, workflow systems, cooperation services, and software detection services. This layer also tackles society support mutually with accounting and imbursement services.
5. The *Application layer* involves user applications which are installed on the grid. It is significant to observe that no user application can be installed on a grid, just a grid-permitted or gratified application, that is, an application which utilizes various processors of a grid setting or which may be implemented on various machines.

The five layers of grid computing are interconnected to one another. Every following layer utilizes the interfaces of the fundamental layer. Mutually, they generate the grid middleware and offer a complete collection of functionalities essential for facilitating dependable, competent, and safe resources' sharing like data. The key functionalities of a grid middleware are as follows:

1. Integration and virtualization of various independent resources
2. Requirement of information concerning resources and their accessibility
3. Lively and flexible resource administration and allotment
4. Brokerage of resources based on open markets or corporation strategies
5. Safety comprising agreement and confirmation of users and accountability
6. Licenses administration
7. Expense and invoicing
8. Transport of non-insignificant 'Quality of Service'

Grid is a versatile system and no particular technology comprises a grid. Constructing and offering a grid needs a performance system of similar services from suppliers of software.

3.3.1 Advantages of Grid Computing

The chief possible return of grid computing for an enhanced IT administration in corporations may be summarized as follows:

1. Grids control combines systems mutually into one big computer, and thus, has better computational control to an assignment and allows better consumption of accessible infrastructure. With grid computing, under-consumed resources can be utilized better.

2. Grid computing allows price savings in the IT branches of corporations because of pointed whole charge of tenure (TCO). As an alternative of investing in fresh resources, larger order may be met by getting benefit of utility computing or by higher consumption of existing resources.
3. Grid computing facilitates better scalability of infrastructure by eliminating restriction essential in the false IT limitations prevailing among sections or separate pools.
4. Grid computing also results in enhanced effectiveness of computing, data, and storage resources because of equivalent CPU ability, load balancing, and access to supplementary resources. Since computing and resources can be balanced as per requirements, grid computing results in reliability and increased robustness. Failing resources may be restored quicker and simpler along with other resources accessible in the grid.
5. Grid computing permits a more proficient business administration of spread IT resources. With virtualization, resources may be enhanced and consistently controlled. This makes it possible to centrally set priority and allocate spread resources to assignments.
6. Grid computing, in amalgamation with utility computing, permits the alteration of capital expenses for IT infrastructure into operational expenses and offers the chance for augmented flexibility and scalability. On the other hand, the utility computing usage results in higher safety and secrecy risks. In general, grid computing has the prospective to enhance charge for performance of IT in companies. The augmented scalability and suppleness of IT resources and the capability to quickly regulate business procedures to novel business requires results in benefits on the business level.

Probable certain gains on the business level are listed as follows:
(a) Improved performance and time-to-market
(b) Lesser costs and improved revenues due to enhanced processes
(c) Improved group effort abilities
(d) Improved sharing

3.3.2 Challenges of Grid Computing

The main challenges of grid computing could be explained in the following way:
1. It is not enough to just change the prevailing spread IT infrastructure into a grid. In majority of instances, investments are required for making the existing applications to work on a grid infrastructure.
2. Lack of values for grid computing make resources' findings for grid technology difficult and risky.
3. Grid computing is a versatile technology and the launching of grid computing in a corporation is characteristically a long-standing plan that needs time until the visibility of first results. The beginning of grid computing could need consistency of physical resources. Even if grids would essentially be capable to handle heterogeneity of resources that are accessible, advanced heterogeneity of resources might need advanced savings in terms of money and time and hence increase the downfall risk.

3.4 CLOUD COMPUTING ARCHITECTURE

The three developments that assure the present awareness of grid computing are as follows:
1. Service Oriented Computing
2. Software as as Service (SaaS)
3. Cloud Computing

The incorporation of mixed physical resources into single virtualized and centrally accessible computing entity has turned out to be potential with grid computing. Grid technology is developed to make the functioning of utility computing easy. Utility computing offers various computing models on a disburse-per-utilization basis. Although the growth in grid technology is fundamentally pushed by system software and hardware suppliers like IBM and Sun, there is advancement in the software industry towards SaaS pushed by software dealers, as for instance, SAP and Microsoft. Both advancements, SaaS and utility computing, demonstrate the rising tendency towards outer installation and sourcing of applications and computing.

SaaS and utility computing are two corresponding movements. SaaS desires a flexible, scalable, and effortlessly accessible infrastructure on which it may perform. With the aim of fulfilling market requirements, the subsequent usual step in advancement is the amalgamation of these two movements into a novel method which offers:

1. Flexible, scalable, dependable, and robust physical infrastructure
2. Platform services which facilitate programming access to physical infrastructure via conceptual interfaces
3. SaaS installed, progressed, and workable on a scalable and flexible physical infrastructure

This novel online platform is said to be cloud. Cloud computing results from the union of grid computing, SaaS, and utility computing. It fundamentally symbolizes the growing tendency towards the external installation of IT resources, such as computational storage, control or business applications.

In cloud computing environment, physical resources are made available to cloud users with the help of virtualization software in the form of virtual resources. Request of client is evenly distributed among the servers for maintaining proper load balancing. Cloud computing architecture is not fixed as other computing architectures, but it is different on the basis of different jobs, resource distribution, etc.

Basic cloud computing environment is shown in the Fig. 3.1 in which various services such as available servers, virtual desktop, system software, application software, database, etc. are available for cloud users. Users can avail the services using any device such as desktop system, laptop, mobile, tablet, etc.

The architecture is discussed based on different criteria in the following sub sections.

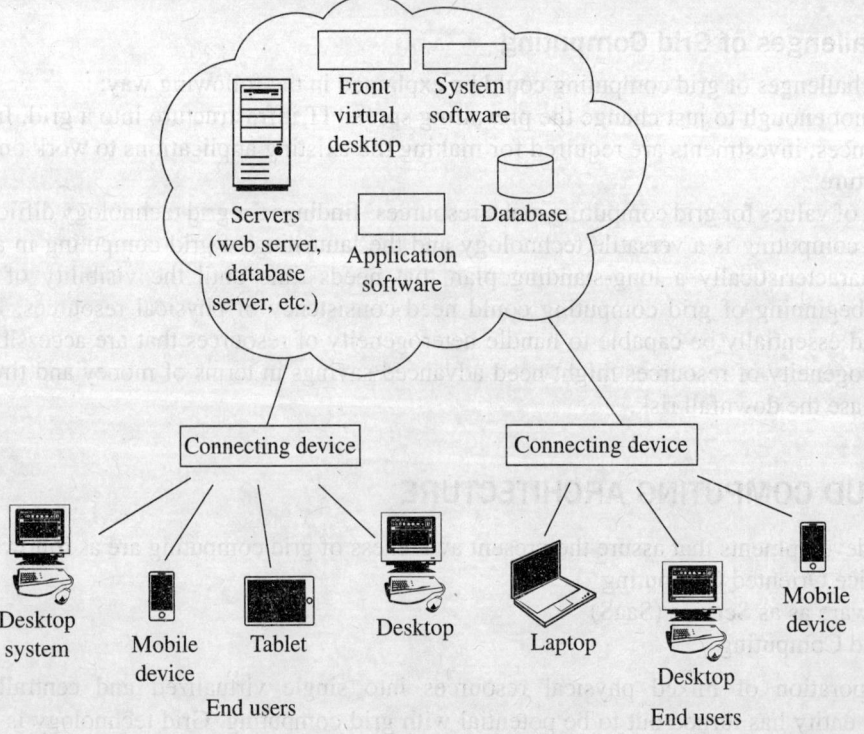

Fig. 3.1 Cloud architecture

3.4.1 On the Basis of Load Balancing

Workload distribution maintains both IT resource overutilization and under-utilization up to a certain extent. At the time of dynamic workload distribution, it is important to know the type and geographical location of the IT resource. Monitoring of runtime workload tracking and data processing is also necessary for proper load balancing.

Load balancing is the technique which is responsible to distribute load, that is, number of requests, number of users, etc. across one or additional servers, network interfaces, hard drives, or other computing resources. Many reasons to use load balancing include improved performance, reliability, elasticity, scalability, and availability. Load balancing in cloud computing is totally different from the conventional architecture of load balancing.

For proper load balancing across various IT resources and to increase performance, there is a load balancer mechanism which handles runtime distribution.

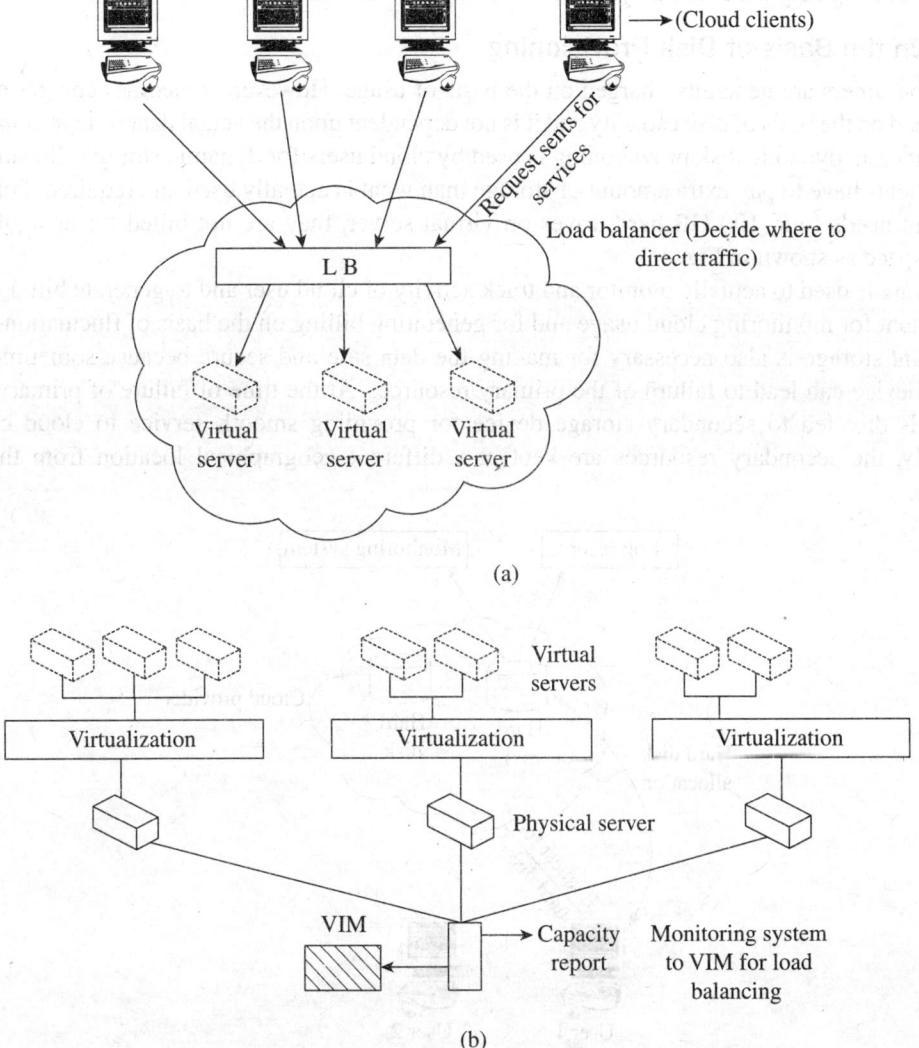

Fig. 3.2 (a) Load balancing management (b) Monitoring system for load balancing

The distribution function includes:
1. A high-power resource for handling workload that requires more processing power.
2. Providing services on the basis of priority.
3. Directing traffic to a particular IT resource as per the requirement by cloud users.

Load balancer is able to perform functions such as optimizing resource utilization, better throughput, maintaining quality of services, etc. It can be a hardware or software. It can be a dedicated hardware device, dedicated software for handling traffic, or software that can be handled by cloud management software. It is not visible to cloud users, as it acts between user request and IT resource allocation. Distribution of workload is on the basis of user demand.

As shown in Fig. 3.2(a), if a cloud user requests for a server, load balancer acts as resource allocator between user and cloud service that is hidden from the user. As shown in Fig. 3.2(b), resource is replicated to generate new instances of virtualized IT resource by the virtual infrastructure manager (VIM) for providing proper load balancing and runtime distribution of client demands. VIM gets various reports from capacity monitoring system for making new instance.

3.4.2 On the Basis of Disk Provisioning

Cloud consumers are generally charged on the basis of usage. However, sometimes charges are already determined on the basis of disk capacity and it is not dependent upon the actual data storage consumptions.

In that case, dynamic disk provisioning is used by cloud users for dynamic storage allocation, due to which clients have to pay extra amount of storage than what is actually used and required. For example, if a client needs four, 100 GB hard drives on virtual server, they are not billed for using 400 GB of storage space as shown in Fig. 3.3.

Software is used to actually monitor and track activity of cloud user and to generate bill. Log storage is important for monitoring cloud usage and for generating billing on the basis of fluctuations of usage. Redundant storage is also necessary for making the data safe and secure because sometimes a cloud storage device can lead to failure of the primary resource. At the time of failure of primary resource, request is directed to secondary storage device for providing smooth service to cloud consumers. Generally, the secondary resources are kept at a different geographical location from the primary resource.

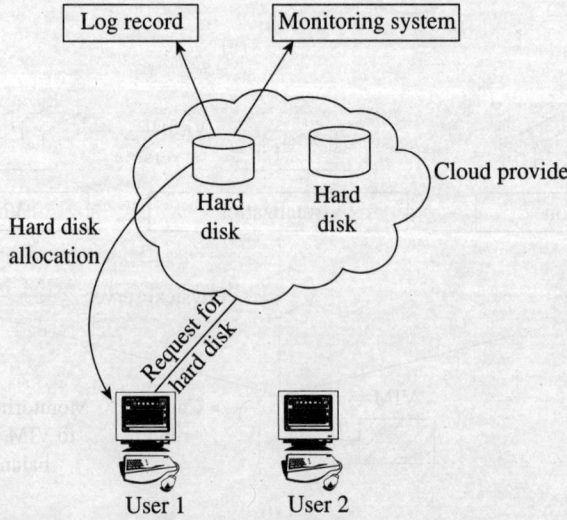

Fig. 3.3 Disk provisioning

3.4.3 On the Basis of Storage Management

Storage device with dual array is also used by some cloud providers for better data redundancy, which means placing secondary storage device at some different geographical location for making data recovery at the time of disaster. Third-party network connection is required for proper data replication. Over utilization of storage device causes performance degradation. Therefore, underutilized resource, where storage potential is not used, is used further by evenly distributing the resource among the storage system. In the given Fig. 3.4(a), data is saved as Logical unit number (LUN) and various LUNs can be saved in a storage device as per the requirement. Storage 1 is overloaded as compared to storage 2 and storage 3, and this is not the even distribution of workload and better potential utilization of the resource is not in the distribution. So, storage is redistributed among all the three storage resources in Fig. 3.4(b).

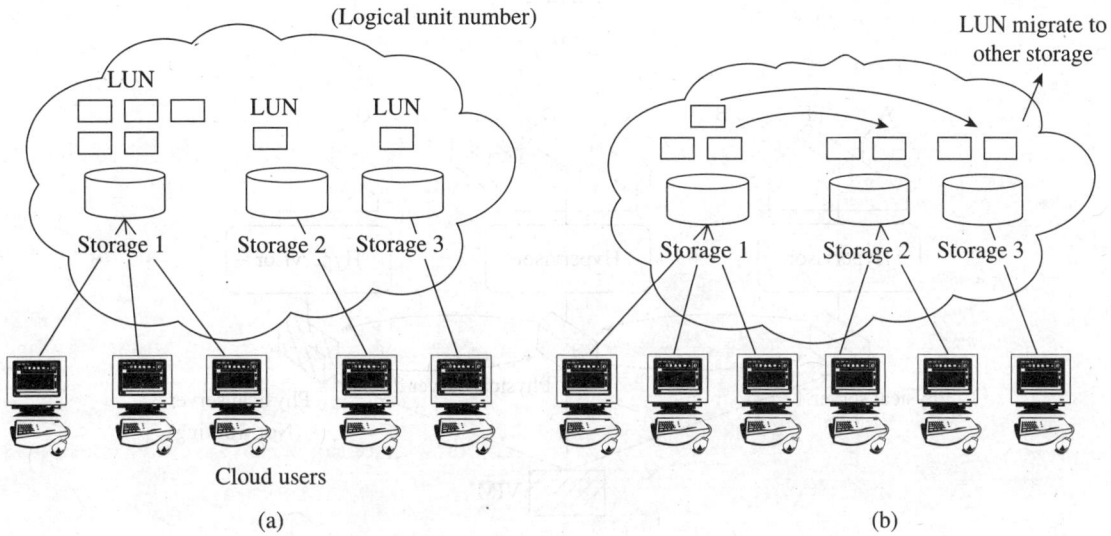

Fig. 3.4 (a) Uneven distribution of storage (b) Even distribution of storage

3.4.4 On the Basis of Hypervisor Installed

A hypervisor is responsible for creating many virtual servers from one physical server, but if the physical server fails due to any reason, then the virtual server fails as well. For handling and maintaining runtime operations, if hypervisor and its underlying physical server fail, then hosted virtual server migrates to another physical server or hypervisor. A virtual infrastructure manager (VIM) is responsible for maintaining and continuously monitoring a group of hypervisors. VIM initiates live migration of affected virtual machine in case of any failure.

Physical servers A, B, and C are working properly in Fig. 3.5(a). Here, as per the given Fig. 3.5(b), physical server C is not working properly and so the other server is not receiving any response. At this situation, virtual instances F and G are migrated to some other server dynamically without any disturbance to the cloud users by VIM.

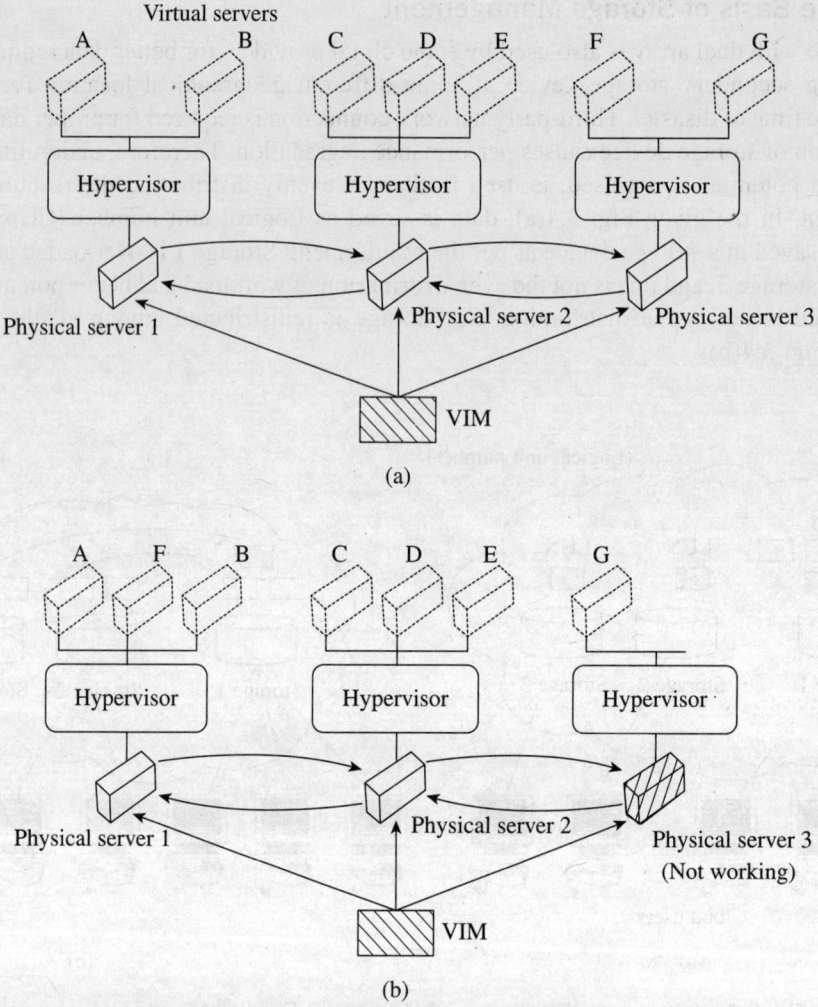

Fig. 3.5 (a) Working of hypervisor (b) Migration of virtual server

3.4.5 On the Basis of Migration

A mechanism that supports runtime transfer of virtual servers, from one to another is called Live Migration of a virtual machine. In Fig. 3.6, there are physical servers with name A and B. Virtualization software is used to make physical resource (server) available for the end users of cloud as virtual server.

Auto-scaling is possible in virtual server if the workload increases. If at run time there is need of migration, then the following steps have to be followed:

1. In the given Fig. 3.6, work is overloaded on virtual server of physical server A, so VIM commands the hypervisor to suspend the execution of the busy physical server and migrate load to some other server.
2. The VIM instructs the instantiation of virtual server on an idle physical server. State information of busy server is getting synchronized with the idle server and now VIM instructs hypervisor to resume the virtual server processing without disturbing the cloud user data processing.

For even distribution of workload, some time there is a need to migrate data from one storage device to another storage device. If the monitoring system in the cloud environment discovers uneven distribution of workload or if storage capacity of a storing device reaches to some threshold value as seen in Fig. 3.7(a), then LUN will be migrated to some other storage device as shown in Fig. 3.7(b).

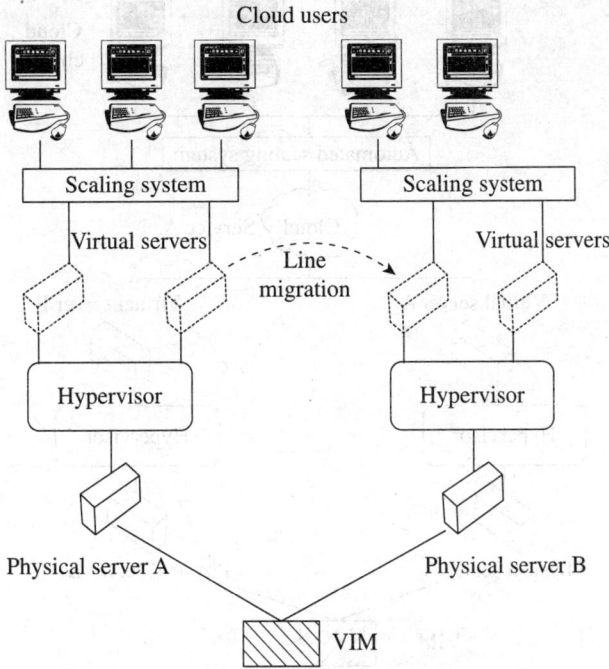

Fig. 3.6 Live Migration

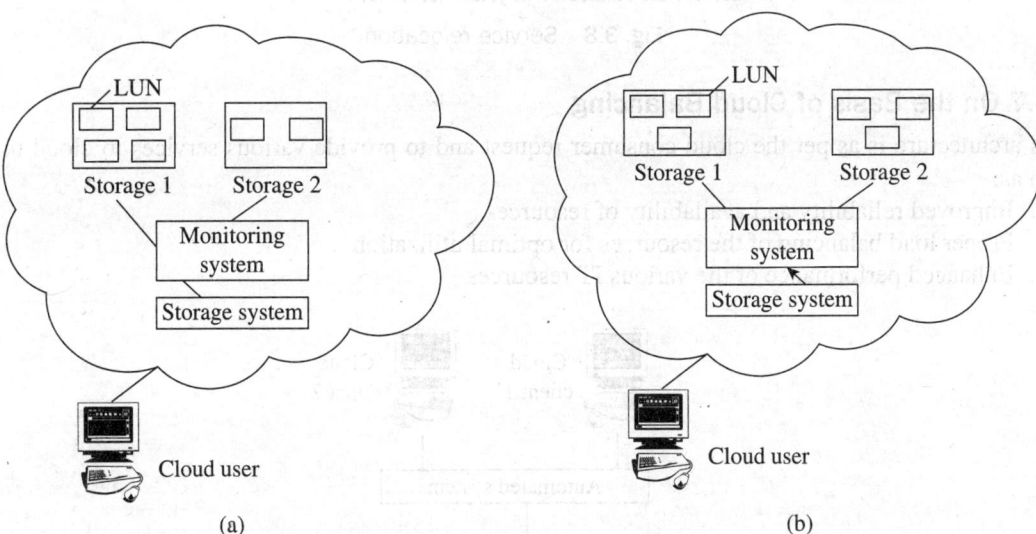

Fig. 3.7 (a) Uneven distribution of workload (b) Even distribution of workload

3.4.6 On the Basis of Service Relocation

Due to many reasons, some time for a particular instance of time, services of cloud are made unavailable to the cloud user. Some of the reasons are as follows:
1. Maintenance required due to any problem such as hardware failure, updating required, etc.
2. Migration of data and services from one machine to another
3. Processing capacity required by the cloud user exceeds the threshold value

As in the given Fig. 3.8, virtual servers A and its various hosted services of physical server A are initiated and migrated on physical server B.

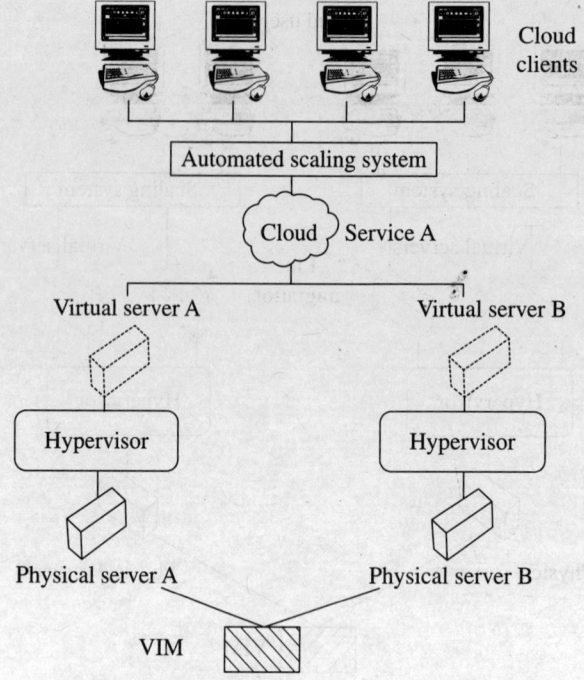

(Replication of virtual server A and its hosted
service are created on physical server B)

Fig. 3.8 Service relocation

3.4.7 On the Basis of Cloud Balancing

This architecture is as per the cloud consumer request and to provide various services to cloud users, such as:
1. Improved reliability and availability of resources
2. Proper load balancing of the resources for optimal utilization
3. Enhanced performance of the various IT resources

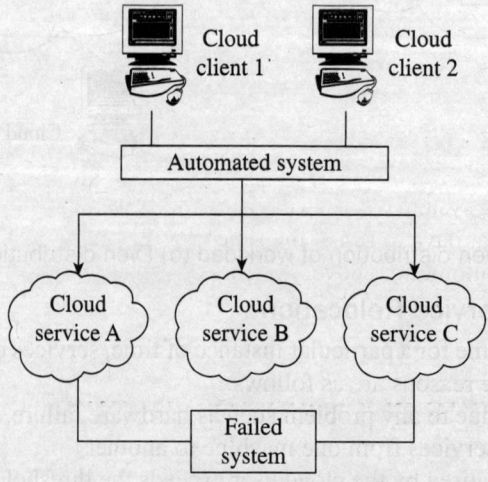

Fig. 3.9 Cloud balancing

For providing various services to cloud users and keeping record of redundant IT resource, there is an automated scaling listener and failover system. On the basis of performance, cloud clients forward cloud service request to the redundant IT resource. Scaling listeners are aware about all redundant array of resources and failover system works at the time of failure in the cloud environment or IT resource as shown in Fig. 3.9.

3.4.8 On the Basis of Virtual Switches Load Balancing

With the help of virtual switches, virtual resources are made available to the cloud user. A physical uplink acts as an interface for cloud consumers and virtual resources. Physical uplink monitors the traffic in the cloud network and all clients send requests through this link. As the number of users and service requests increase after crossing a threshold value, performance of the network goes down causing sensitive packet loss and many other problems in the network.

To overcome the above problem, multiple uplinks are added for proper balancing. Multiple and redundant path with multiple uplinks can easily handle network traffic and improve performance of the network. Traffic shaping policies are used to reconfigure virtual switches as per the multiple physical links shown in Fig. 3.10.

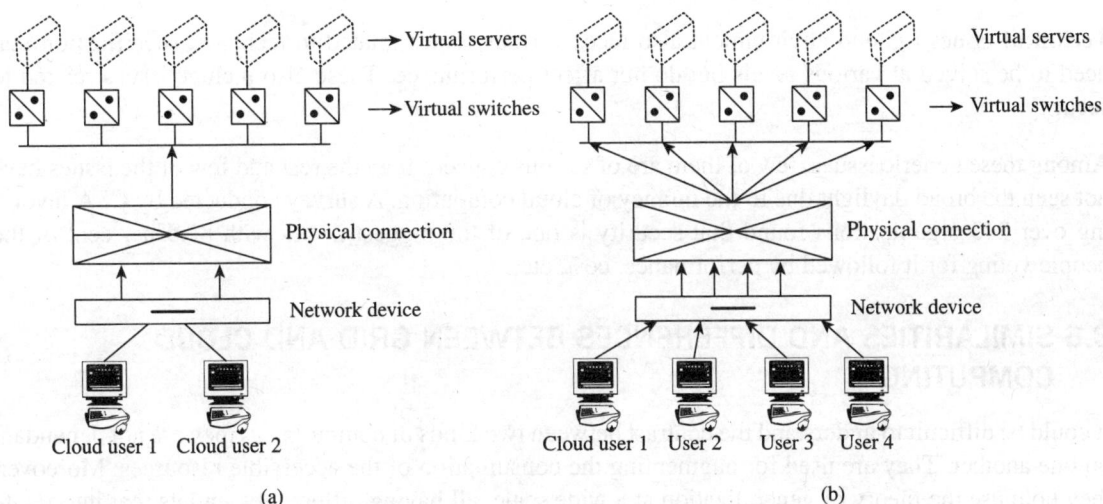

Fig. 3.10 (a) Single connection between network device and switches (b) Multiple connection between network device and switches

3.4.9 On the Basis of Failure Detection and Recovery

The problem of failure of an IT resource at run time can be solved by redirecting traffic with some other available option. A monitoring system works in the network to monitor activities in the network and it has some predefined functions that have to run at the time of a particular event. Recovery policies are also defined in the system when automatic recovery occurs due to any failure. Due to failure of data center, new instances will be made available at another data center for proper cloud management and virtual images of resources are kept in the physical storage device.

3.5 KEY DESIGN ASPECTS OF CLOUD ARCHITECTURE, CLOUD SERVICES, AND CLOUD APPLICATIONS

Apart from various advantages of cloud computing, it also has various issues related to its architecture.

Issues at Design Level

The key issues related to create an open architecture and the development of heterogeneous platforms:

Issues of Architectural of Cloud Computing Cloud computing architecture needs to support essential features such as separation, scalability, and reusability with flexibility. However, for the development of this type of architecture, developers face many challenges due to the new technologies and various industry requirements.

Platform Related Issues With the increasing demand of cloud computing, there are various issues related to platform and infrastructure development of cloud computing as per the user requirement.

Issues Related to the Implementation

At the time of implementation of cloud services there are still some issues, such as

Issues related to Business Organizations are sometimes interested to adopt cloud services for their various needs of IT industry but the cost and security concern on growing datacenter not only increases cost but saves energy as well.

Technical Issues Cloud environment also faces various issues related to technical specification that need to be solved at various levels but do not affect performance. These also include issues related to security.

Among these generic issues, few of them are of serious concern than the rest and few of the issues have not seen the broad daylight due to the infancy of cloud computing. A survey conducted by CSA involving over 240 organizations found that security is one of the biggest issues with 87.5 per cent of the people voting for it followed by performance, cost, etc.

3.6 SIMILARITIES AND DIFFERENCES BETWEEN GRID AND CLOUD COMPUTING

It could be difficult to understand the contrast between two kinds of computing as they are not dependant on one another. They are used for augmenting the consumption of the accessible resources. Moreover, they both use the theory of generalization at a wide scale, all having different essentials that interrelate with one another.

The single selective aspect among the two is the technique used by it for computing the responsibilities inside their personal surroundings. In grid computing, a large assignment is divided into minor responsibilities that are spread across diverse computing machines. After finishing these minor responsibilities, they are pushed back to the main machine, which in response, proposes one output.

A cloud computing design is planned to facilitate users to utilize distinct services without investing in the original design. Although grid proposes similar provision for computing control, cloud computing is not limited to merely that since cloud users may gain different services like website hosting.

Cloud Computing

Corporations with cloud computing may scale up their business without spending in new infrastructure or certify new software. Cloud computing is of specific advantage to small and medium-sized companies which desire to entirely outsource their data-center infrastructure or big corporations which desire to acquire peak load ability bearing the charge of constructing big data center. In both cases, service customers use what they require on the Internet and spend only for what they utilize.

It is not necessary for the service customer to be at a PC, utilize an application from the PC, or buy a particular edition which is constructed for PDAs, smart phones, and other tools. The customer does not possess the software, platform, or infrastructure in the cloud. They need not be bothered about how networks and servers are reserved in the cloud. Customers can access various servers everywhere in the world.

Grid Computing

Cloud computing develops from grid computing and offers on-demand resource provisioning. Grid computing might or might not belong to the cloud, depending on the kinds of users using it. If the users are systems' integrators and managers, they are concerned about how things are sustained in the cloud. They promote, virtualize, and deploy applications and servers.

Grid computing needs the use of software which may separate and pass on parts of a program as single big system picture to numerous computers. One worry regarding grid is that if single part of the software on a joint crashes, other parts of the software on other joints might crash too. This is relaxed in case that constituent has a failover constituent on another joint, but trouble may yet take place if constituents rely on other parts of software to achieve one or more grid computing responsibilities. Big system pictures and related hardware to run and sustain them can donate to huge assets and functioning costs.

Similarities and Differences

Grid computing and cloud computing are scalable. Scalability is proficient via load balancing of application cases operating independently on a diversity of operating systems and associated via web services. Network bandwidth and CPU are assigned and de-assigned on order. The storage capability of system goes up and down on the basis of number of users, cases, and the quantity of data shifted at a specified time.

Both practices involve multitask and multitenancy, implicating that numerous consumers may carry out diverse responsibilities, accessing one or multiple application cases. Sharing resources among a big group of users helps in lessening expenses of infrastructure and peak load ability. Grid and cloud computing offer service-level agreements (SLAs) for uptime accessibility of around 99 per cent. If the service slides below the definite uptime service level, the service credit for receiving data to the customer gets delayed.

The Amazon S3 offers a web services' interface for the recovery and storage of data in the cloud. Regulating limits the number of items you may save in S3. You may save an item as minute as 1 byte and as big as 5 GB or even some terabytes. S3 uses the beginning of buckets as containers for every storage position of your items. The data is saved firmly using the similar data storage infrastructure which is used by Amazon for its e-commerce websites.

While the grid storage computing is well suitable for data-concentrated storage, it is not economically suitable for collecting items as minute as 1 byte. In a data grid, the quantities of distributed data should be big for highest profit. A computational grid concentrates on computationally determined functions. Amazon Web Services in cloud computing proposes two sorts of cases—high and standard CPU.

Cloud computing is where you acquire access to the resources of a self-governing third party over the internet.

Common examples include:
- Web-based email
- Web-based accounting systems
- Web-based credit card software

Cloud computing offers 'Software as a Service' or SaaS applications. These software are installed on your server, but perform each of their heavy tasks using infrastructures of somebody else. Several general illustrations comprise:
- VOIP phones
- Online backup
- Video games with online play capability

However, grid computing is used when the processing authority of service or an application is distributed across multiple systems. This is usually done to augment processing capability or enhance flexibility of system.

Grid computing too has unique applications inside the business area. For instance, a company might choose to virtualize their database system so as the application might be hosted across various data centers. In the occasion that any one of these systems crashes, the application might continue working without any disturbance.

Along with cloud computing, your corporation acquires feasibility and expense-savings. With grid computing, your corporation acquires suppleness and authority. While raising your IT policy, the profits of both strategies must be judged. When functional with the suitable planned direction, all of these plans may be effectual devices in meeting your expense, safety, quality, and competence goals.

By separating the logical from the physical resource, virtualization determines a few of the challenges met by grid computing. While grid computing attains high consumption via the allotment of numerous servers on a particular job or assignment, the virtualization of servers in cloud computing attains high consumption by permitting single server to compute numerous responsibilities concurrently.

3.7 CHARACTERISTICS OF CLOUD COMPUTING

Cloud computing could be of many types, as the cloud could be hybrid, public, or personal. As the beginning of information technology, it has performed a vital share in making certain that businesses and corporations work efficiently. Information technology offers services that are consistent, accessible, and protected consistently. To attain the greatest quality cloud computing, business possessors have turned to its features and uniqueness for attaining this service. Cloud computing attracts end users and consumers due to the peculiar exceptional uniqueness.

Fast scalability is the main feature of cloud computing. Alterations and improvements to the services are done effortlessly and instantly, facilitating the cloud computing service to be flexible. A business possessor may simply demand processing speed, data storage, other bandwidth, and further licenses or users. There is no necessity to do project execution and project estimate as the system simply desires the business possessor to put an order to the cloud computing dealer.

With the cloud computing service, it is possible to assess everything. The business owner might complete a precise number of user license per software, a continuing network bandwidth, and data space which fulfils the demands of the business. Due to this characteristic, the price of cloud computing becomes conventional. It also characterizes the inclusions in the service accurately. If the business proprietor avails these services, staff might become updated with distinct services online with huge data spaces, a variety of new software, multi-value added services, various processing techniques, and ease of accessibility to a competent and rich network.

The capability of cloud computing to allow the business holder to choose his existing and future requirements is its vital characteristic. In case the company expands, it may simply require further services that may match the requirements. Cloud computing also makes accessible various software or hardware resources. A business holder may access these resources on order. Cloud hosting is consistent and controls the entire cloud, thus providing more bandwidth, data spaces, and resources on the basis of the requirements of the location. Websites' resources that are not accessed at present are freed and transferred to locations that require further data space, bandwidth, and other resources.

For cloud computing, safety is one of the concerns. Since data is shared inside a server, the supplier should make sure that every account is protected that could be accessed by authorized users having one account. Data loss is to be avoided as the provider should make certain that each software or hardware resource is high end since there are lots of customers depending on the service. In cloud computing, backup is too complicated. A business holder is not required to be anxious regarding backup dependability as the dealer has made steps in order to provide a great backup system. Server fall down or disk breakdown should not make a great deal trouble as the provider may effortlessly restore the newest backup.

Cloud hosting is meant for company units that strongly use the resources. Small-and medium-scale companies may too be adapted but only large corporations could take benefit of the power, flexibility, and accessibility of cloud computing. Big companies move their applications that use up resources in large amounts to the cloud so as to free up their previous devoted servers to reduce operation charge.

The definition of cloud computing by NIST [10] has five important features which propose a solid test for everyone in conflict to provide a cloud computing service or ask to execute a cloud computing on site.

The features are as follows:
1. On-demand self-service: This implies that the customers, comprising non-IT persons, may unilaterally provision the service and scale it up or down by them.
2. Broad network access: This implies the service is uninterruptedly accessible by using the standard selection of tools comprising conventional mobile tools, PCs, and portable computers.
3. Resource pooling: This implies customers share a universal multi-occupant situation where virtual and physical resources can be dynamically allotted.
4. Quick elasticity: This implies the service may be swiftly scaled and frequently mechanically, such that to the customer, the facility seems infinite.
5. Calculated service: This implies the service and its required resources are metered for the consumer.

Apart from the vital features précised by NIST, other features which should also be considered are discussed in the sections below.

3.7.1 On Demand Self Services

Computer services such as applications, email, server, or network service may be offered without the requirement of any human interface with every service supplier. Cloud service suppliers offering on-demand self-services comprise Salesforce.com, Microsoft, Amazon Web Services (AWS), IBM, and Google. NASDAQ and New York Times are corporations that use AWS.

A customer's requirements can alter from time to time due to which it is known as 'on-demand'. The important factor is that all the provisioning procedures do not require human interference.

3.7.2 Broad Network Access

Cloud applications and facilities are available over the network and can be used by means of standard procedures which encourage use by various thick or thin customer platforms such as PDAs, laptops, and mobile phones.

By use of cloud, you have the alternative to load the laptop of end users or not. Thick customers are users who download files of big size to their workplace before using the characteristics. Thin customers, on the other hand, are users who download a file of small size and may access all the accessible aspects and resources. In other words, it is regarding how much you trust the workplace and cloud.

3.7.3 Resource Pooling

The computing resources of the supplier are grouped together to cater to numerous customers using a multiple-renter module, along with distinct virtual and physical resources vigorously allocated and reallocated in accordance with the requirement. The resources include memory, storage, processing, network bandwidth, various mail services, and virtual machines. The joint grouping of the resource makes scale economies.

Resource grouping is regarding forcefully conveying computing resources to numerous consumers. It may modify from time to time according to the needs of users.

3.7.4 Quick Elasticity

Cloud services may be flexibly and swiftly provisioned, in a few instances mechanically, to rapidly scale out and swiftly release to rapidly scale in. The facilities accessible for provisioning to the customer frequently seem to be infinite and may be bought in any amount at any time. Imagine that you are hosting a website and you get 1000 hits per day on an average. All of a sudden, you are deploying a project and for a specific day, lots of users will be logging in online at the similar time. At that particular instant, there may be 10, 0000 hits in a day. For such a situation, during a usual day, the cloud will allocate you one server but in peak time, it will go up to seven servers and back to one server in usual hour. The finest feature is that you simply pay as per the usage. If you yourself are hosting it, then you will be required to buy five servers to get ready for the peak hours that are not excessively used at a time. Throughout the remaining time, the other servers will simply relax doing nothing.

3.7.5 Calculated Service

Usage of cloud computing resource may be controlled and reported while providing transparency to both the customer and provider of the used service. Cloud computing services use a metering facility, which allows optimizing and managing resource use. This means as for electricity, IT services are also charged for each usage metrics, that is, pay for every use. The more you consume, the more the bill. Simply as utility corporations sell electricity to subscribers and telephone corporations sell data and voice services, IT services like data center hosting, network security management, or even departmental invoicing can nowadays be effortlessly sent as a contractual service.

At last, cloud computing is usage-focused. Customers pay for simply the resources used by them and are thus charged on a utilization-based module. Cloud computing platforms should offer means to shut in usage data, which allows chargeback reporting and incorporation with invoicing systems.

From the viewpoint of user, it is the facility to pay just for the resources used by them, eventually supporting them to reduce their expenses. From the viewpoint of supplier, it permits them to follow usage for billing and charge-back reasons.

In summary, each of these describing features is essential in making a business personal cloud able to attain powerful value that comprises investments on capital things and operating expenses, lessened support expenses, and considerably improved business flexibility. Each of these facilitates is used by the companies to develop their earnings margins and competitiveness in the markets where they work. As cloud is a pay-as-you-go service, you will be charged according to the quantity of resources used by you.

3.7.6 Multi-persistence

It refers to the desire for strategy-focused segmentation, enforcement, control, separation, invoicing modules, and service levels for distinct customer areas. Customers could consume public cloud service offerings of supplier or in fact be from the similar company, like discrete business entities instead of different managerial units, but would yet share infrastructure.

3.7.7 Dynamic Computing Infrastructure

Cloud computing needs a dynamic computing infrastructure. The basis for the vibrant infrastructure is a scalable, safe, and consistent physical infrastructure. There must be unemployment levels to guarantee high level of accessibility, but mainly it should be simple to expand as demand by usage growth, with no requirement of design reworking. Subsequently, it should be virtualized.

Nowadays, virtualized situations force server virtualization as the foundation for operating services. Such services require simple provisioning and de-provisioning through automation of software. These service workloads are required to be shifted from one physical server to another as the ability needs to reduce or increase. Ultimately, this infrastructure must be consumed exceedingly, whether offered by an in-house IT branch or an outer cloud supplier. The infrastructure should carry business value above and over the asset.

A lively computing infrastructure is vital to efficiently support the flexible nature of service provisioning and de-provisioning as demanded by users whilst satisfying high levels of safety and honesty. The consolidation offered by virtualization, attached with provisioning mechanization, generates a high level of recycling and consumption, finally producing an incredibly effectual use of capital belongings.

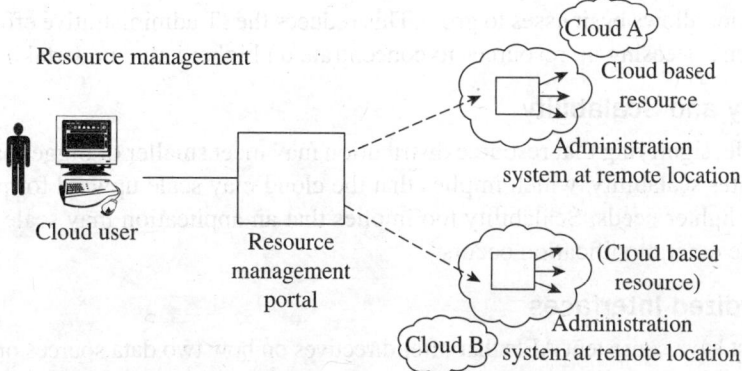

Fig. 3.11 Resource management

As shown in Fig. 3.11 if a single cloud user is taking services from more than one cloud provider such as A and B, then a separate administration system provides services to remote users and resource management portal manages resource of both the clouds.

3.7.8 IT Service-centric Approach

Cloud computing is IT service-centric. Usually, cloud users wish to operate a few business applications or services for a particular, appropriate objective. They would desire to effortlessly and quickly access a committed case of a service or an application. By summarizing the server-centric outlook of the infrastructure, system users may effortlessly access strong, pre-defined computing situations designed particularly around their service.

The IT service centric method allows user acceptance and business flexibility. The quicker and simpler a user may operate a managerial assignment, the more the business grows, providing heavy returns or lessening expenses.

3.7.9 Self-service Based Usage Model

Self-service offers users the ability to assemble, upload, plan, install, control, and report on their company services on demand. A self-service cloud offers simple-to-use, normal user interfaces which allow users to effectively control the lifecycle of service delivery.

The self-service advantage from the user's viewpoint is of independence and empowerment level which generates important business flexibility. One advantage frequently ignored from the viewpoint of IT team or service supplier is that the more self-service is allotted to users, the less managerial participation is required. It saves money and time, and permits managerial employees to concentrate on more planned, high-valued jobs.

Cloud consumers may provision cloud services by skipping the long procedure. Services such as storage, computing, process, software, and many more are provided.

3.7.10 Self-managed Platform

For a service supplier or an IT team to capably supply a cloud for its components, they should power a technology platform that is self-controlled. Clouds facilitate self-administration through software automation, influencing the following capabilities:
1. Reserving and planning resource capability
2. Abilities for managing, configuring, and reporting to make sure resources may be assigned and re-assigned to various users
3. Devices for managing access to resources and strategies for how resources could be used or functions could be carried out

Each of these abilities allows businesses to grow. This reduces the IT administrative effort level and lowers functioning costs, releasing up resources to concentrate on higher value undertaking.

3.7.11 Elasticity and Scalability

The cloud is flexible, signifying that resource distribution may meet smaller or bigger based on the need. Suppleness facilitates scalability, which implies that the cloud may scale upward for peak requirement and downward for lighter needs. Scalability too implies that an application may scale while adding up users or when some other modification occurs.

3.7.12 Standardized Interfaces

Cloud services must have consistent APIs that offer directives on how two data sources or applications can function with one another. A consistent interface allows the consumer to connect to cloud services together.

Cloud computing services can be used by the customer on order without any human interference or long executions. These services are accessed commonly and scaled up or down according to requirement, providing a factual efficiency method for utilization.

3.8 CLOUD AND DYNAMIC INFRASTRUCTURE

Cloud service characteristics include reduced cost, high scalability, pay-as-you-grow facility, guaranteed data center and network uptime, better resource utilization, and lesser implementation time since resources are available on demand.

Cloud services are exclusive as they permit you to see, amend, and share files saved on the cloud. At the same time, as no two cloud services are alike, all of the services offer almost similar basic functionality and features.

The finest cloud computing services are those which permit you to store and upload any sort of file you would keep on your local hard drive, from word documents to music files. Several services even let you store contacts, calendar, and your email in the cloud. Every cloud service you consider should too let you to see, amend, and share your matter in spite of what tool or computer is used. Security issues can be solved by file encryption, and password sharing is restricted to protect your data.

Points to consider while selecting a cloud provider as per the requirement are given below:
1. Ease of use: It is vital to choose a cloud service which is spontaneous and unambiguous, bearing in mind how frequently you will be expected to access your substance in the cloud. The interface and devices of service should be simple to guide and suitable to use.
2. Help and support: Receiving assistance as per requirement is essential when using any sort of technology comprising cloud services. Accessible support alternatives must comprise technical support through email, live chat, and telephone. As resources, the service must also offer a knowledge base and user forums.
3. Packaged software: This is the largest region of the SaaS market. Packet software comes in many distinct flavours for supply chain administration, customer relationship management, human resources and financial management, in order to name the most universal. These include concentration on a particular procedure, such as managing wages, advantages, and annual performance assessments of staff. These goods are likely to have some feature in common. They are intended with particular business procedures developed in which consumers may amend. They have moved in huge numbers to the cloud since consumers were finding it to be too tough to control the platforms.
4. Shared software: This gradually is the more dynamic region of the market, which is determined by the universal accessibility of the internet, united with the reality that teams are positioned all over the globe. This region is dominated by software which meets all kinds of mutual attempts comprising document cooperation, project scheduling, email, web conferencing, and even instant messaging. In a manner, it was expected that such platforms should shift to the cloud. These jobs arise all through the company and are required to be simply accessed from various positions.
5. Tool management: It means managing tools to sustain the installation and progress of SaaS. Imagine the advance devices which designers require while generating and expanding a SaaS platform, as well as for monitoring, measuring, and testing which is required by the designer and a consumer. Management tools must be decided in service agreement associated to the use of this sort of software in the real world.
6. Mobile access: Widespread access is perhaps one of the major promotion points of cloud computing services. Whether you are working from home on your iPad or computer at the office, cloud services permit you to access your substance anytime, wherever, and on any one of your tools. You can search for services which propose the maximum series of mobile access, comprising apps for famous smart phones and the facility to sign into your account from every mobile browser.

The facility to perform in the cloud from a mobile tool is the main constituent of Software plus Services. However, what do you require to set on the cloud? It actually depends on your company. There are various free applications which can be used by you on the cloud. For example, look for free apps of Google. You may begin a record at your PC and after that share it with others or keep on functioning on it on your mobile tool. This is a simplistic illustration, however, it explains the way by which you could utilize the cloud to your benefit, particularly with mobile users.

Instead of using Google Docs or Microsoft Live to work together on credentials, perhaps your corporation wants a unique application in service medium. In these instances, you merely require to refer to a service such as Force.com and perceive if anybody has already formed the application required by you. Google Android is one means to make your programmers active.

Google Android—A wide combination of foremost technology and wireless corporations required creating Android, a complete and an open platform for mobile tools. T-Mobile, Google Inc., HTC, Motorola, Qualcomm, and others worked together for developing Android via the Open Handset Alliance, an international combination of technology and mobile business leaders. This association shares a universal aim of promotion innovation on mobile tools for providing customers an opportunity to experience functioning enhancements over existing mobile platforms. By supplying programmers with a fresh level of directness, which permits them to work jointly, Android offers fast services.

7. Line of business services: These are platform provided to enterprises and corporations. They are sold through a payment service. Applications enclosed under this class comprise business procedures, such as consumer relations applications, supply-chain administration applications, and business-oriented devices.
8. Customer-oriented services: These services are provided to the common public on a payment basis. However, more frequently than not, they are provided for free and are supported by marketing. Illustrations in this class comprise online gaming, consumer banking, and web mail services, among others.

3.9 IMPEDIMENTS TO CLOUD ADOPTION

Businesses must vigilantly think about five chief barriers for prosperous implementation of cloud computing. These are as follows:

1. Security—Marketable cloud suppliers propose wide access to end users and, therefore, functions and access agreements are less convenient. Virtualization significantly appends to the complication of this procedure and offers relief through hypervisors and virtual switches.
2. Privacy—Subjects related to secrecy comprise authority of information, access and management, the accessibility of review tracks and agreement with business, and lawful rules and values.
3. Irresponsibility of vendors—Public cloud IaaS suppliers have yet to build up a strong track record at the bottom of huge creation or business systems.
4. Risk improvement—It is hard to decide how fine a supplier is justifying data position, loss, or safety oriented risks. Therefore, necessities for data security must be firmly administered via the use of contractual service level agreement.
5. Inheritance of applications—Chief business applications are frequently extremely twisted, customized, and complicated.

Points to Remember

1. Cloud computing services use a metering capability, which enables to control and optimize resource use.
2. Cloud computing is IT service-centric.
3. Self-service provides users the ability to upload, build, deploy, schedule, manage, and report on their business services on demand.
4. The cloud is elastic, meaning that resource allocation can get bigger or smaller depending on demand.
5. Grid computing is the amalgamation of computer resources from multiple administrative domains to reach a common goal.
6. Grids are a form of distributed computing whereby a 'super virtual computer' is composed of many networked loosely coupled computers acting together to perform large tasks.
7. Grid middleware is specific software, which provides the necessary functionality required to enable sharing of heterogeneous resources and establishing of virtual organizations.
8. Utility computing is the provision of Grid Computing and Applications as a Service.
9. Characteristics of cloud computing are:
    (a) On-demand self service
    (b) Broad network access
    (c) Resource pooling
    (d) Rapid elasticity
    (e) Measured service
    (f) Elasticity and scalability
    (g) IT service-centric approach
    (h) Standardized Interfaces

10. The main resources that can be shared in a Grid are:
    (a) Computing/processing power
    (b) Data storage/networked file systems
    (c) Communications and bandwidth
    (d) Application software
    (e) Scientific instruments
11. Points to consider while selecting a cloud provider as per the requirements are ease of use, help and support, packaged software, shared software, tool management, mobile access, line of business services, customer-oriented services.

Key Terms

Collective layer It is responsible for all global resource management and for interaction with collections of resources.

Fabric layer It comprises the physical resources which are shared within the grid.

High performance computing (HPC) An advanced computing technology to support collective computing power for higher performance.

Resource pooling This means consumers share a common multi-tenant environment where physical and virtual resources may be dynamically allocated.

Service level agreements (SLA) Agreement signed between cloud provider and cloud users regarding various service related parameters.

Voice over internet protocol (VOIP) It is a methodology and group of technologies for the delivery of voice communications and multimedia sessions over Internet Protocol (IP) networks such as the Internet.

Multiple-choice Questions

1. What is an example of a single purpose environment?
   (a) Any application on any server
   (b) Interface to large computer
   (c) Interface to large storage
   (d) Mainframe

2. Which is an important feature for the customer in multi-tenant environments?
   (a) Availability
   (b) Network bandwidth
   (c) Network latency
   (d) Security

3. What is an important feature for assessing cloud applications in the cloud?
   (a) The application should be compatible with the browser of the user's computer.
   (b) The application should use the same programming language as the clients.
   (c) The user should know on which server the application is located.
   (d) The user's identity should be known by the application.

4. What explains keypoint relationship between provider and customer in cloud computing?
   (a) Increased focus on SLAs
   (b) Less compliance to standards
   (c) Less focus on SLAs
   (d) More focus on training

5. How can confidentiality of information be achieved?
   (a) By ensuring enough resources to make information available for all users
   (b) By preventing unauthorized changes
   (c) By regularly backing up the information
   (d) By restricting access to information

6. Which among the following is not a rationalize measure against data loss?
   (a) Audits
   (b) Authentication and authorization
   (c) Encryption
   (d) Storage area network (SAN)
7. Self-service provides users the ability to _____ on their business services on demand.
   (a) Upload and build
   (b) Deploy and schedule
   (c) Manage and report
   (d) All the above
8. The main resources that can be shared in a Grid are _____ .
   (a) Computing/processing power
   (b) Data storage/networked file systems
   (c) Communications and bandwidth
   (d) All the above
9. Facilities provided by cloud computing are _____ .
   (a) World class data center facilities
   (b) Better resource utilization
   (c) Lesser Implementation time
   (d) All the above
10. _____ means cloud can scale upward for peak demand and downward for lighter demand.
    (a) Elasticity
    (b) Scalability
    (c) On Demand
    (d) All the above

Review Questions

1. What is grid computing?
2. How grid computing is different from cloud computing?
3. What are the various characteristics of cloud computing?
4. What are the different services provided by cloud computing?
5. What are the various advantage of grid computing?
6. What are the different application areas of grid computing?
7. What are the different impediments of cloud adoption?
8. Explain the architecture of grid computing?
9. What are the various challenges for grid computing?
10. What do you understand by elasticity and scalability?
11. What are the application area that is fully as per the requirement of grid computing?
12. How can we customize grid computing as per the requirement of applications?

References

1. Cloud Security A Comprehensive Guide to Secure Cloud Computing Ronald L. Krutz and Russell Dean Vines, ISBN: 978-0-470-58987-8, Wiley Publication, 2010
2. Cloud computing for dummies By Judith Hurwitz, Robin Bloor, Marcia Kaufman, and Dr Fern Halper, ISBN-10: 0470484705,Wiley Publication, 1 edition, November 16, 2009
3. Cloud Computing Technologies and Strategies, Brian J.S. Chee and Curtis Franklin, Jr, ISBN 9781439806128, CRC Press, April 7, 2010
4. Cloud Computing: A Practical Approach Anthony T. Velte, Toby J. Velte, Ph.D., Robert Elsenpeter, ISBN-10: 0071626948, Publisher: McGraw-Hill, 1 edition, November 1, 2009
5. Grid and Cloud Computing, Katarina StanoevskaSlabeva, Thomas Wozniak, and Santi Ristol, ISBN-10: 3642051928, Springer; 2010 edition, November 19, 2009

6. Implementing and Developing cloud applications by David E.Y.Sarna, ISBN-10: 1439830827, Publisher: Auerbach Publications, November 26, 2010
7. R. Buyya, C.S. Yeo, and S. Venugopal. Market-oriented cloud computing: Vision, hype, and reality for delivering it services as computing utilities. In High Performance Computing and Communications, 2008. HPCC'08. 10th IEEE International Conference on pages 4–13 IEEE, 2008
8. Mastering Cloud Computing, By Rajkumar Buyya, Christian Vecchhiola, S. Thamarai Selvi, Published by Tata McGraw Hill Education Private Limited, 2008
9. Cloud computing and Virtualization, By V. Rajeswara Rao, V. Shubba Ramaiah, BS Publication, ISBN-10: 9383635045, Publisher: BS Publications / BSP Books (2014)
10. Features of cloud computing: http://csrc.nist.gov/publications/nistpubs/800-145/SP800-145.pdf, last accessed in May 2018

Answers to Multiple-choice Questions

1. (d) 3. (a) 5. (d) 7. (d) 9. (d)
2. (d) 4. (a) 6. (d) 8. (d) 10. (b)

CHAPTER 4

Models of Cloud Computing

> **Learning Outcomes**
>
> After completing this chapter, students will be able to:
>
> - comprehend service models of cloud computing
> - describe cloud services provided by SaaS, IaaS, and PaaS
> - describe cloud stack and cloud storage
> - differentiate various deployment models
> - list the benefits of service models

4.1 INTRODUCTION

In this chapter, we first present a user's picture of each of the models. Next, we consider the economics of the cloud computing model. The cloud computing system is composed of a set of layers upon which distributed applications are built. These layers include *infrastructure, platform,* and *software.* Based on these three layers, we can devise three cloud computing models are devised.

1. Infrastructure as a Service (IaaS) model provides infrastructure-related services and is responsible for handling hardware-related issues, power, and cool management in data centers.
2. Platform as a Service (PaaS) model takes the responsibilities of operating system, database management, server, and programming language.
3. Software as a Service (SaaS) model handles software-related issues and provides amenities to the cloud users.

In each cloud model, the cloud service provider facilitates consumers of cloud services to actually focus more on the business requirements; they need not to worry about the underlying technologies. Computer resources are provided on demand to the cloud users as per requirements, for example, the supply of water and electricity.

4.2 CLOUD SERVICE MODELS

In this section, the various services provided by cloud computing are discussed. The suppliers of cloud computing offer services on the basis of IaaS, PaaS, and SaaS models.

As shown in Fig. 4.1, layer-1 is the bottom layer, that is, IaaS; layer-2 is the middle layer, that is, PaaS; and layer-3 is the top layer, that is, SaaS. On the basis of allocation of resources, cloud computing offers their services.

1. Bottom layer (layer-1)—IaaS—accommodates memory, CPU, and additional hardware resources
2. Middle layer (layer-2)—PaaS—accommodates diverse settings for consumer-particular services
3. Top layer (layer-3)—SaaS—cloud service accessing occurs via web browsers and web services

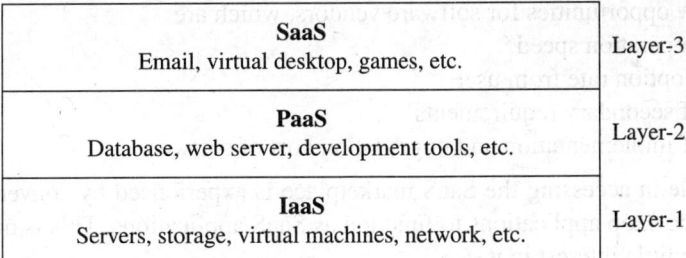

Fig. 4.1 Services provided by cloud computing

4.2.1 Software as a Service

Software as a Service (SaaS) is a software distribution model in which applications are hosted by a vendor or service provider and made available to customers over the Internet. Cloud suppliers manage and control the application software in the cloud. The software is accessed by cloud users from the site of cloud customers. The cloud users do not administer the cloud platform and infrastructure on which the application is operating. This reduces the requirement to deploy and operate the application on the personal computers of a cloud user. A cloud application is different from additional applications because of its flexibility. This may be attained by copying responsibilities on various virtual machines at operate-time to meet altering work needs. The work is allocated by load balancers over the array of virtual machines. To regulate a huge number of cloud users, cloud applications may be multitenant, that is, one machine can serve many cloud users easily.

Examples of SaaS are Quickbooks Online, Google Apps, Netflix, Salesforce.com, Microsoft Office 365, Photoshop.com, Gmail, Acrobat.com, Google Docs, and Intuit QuickBooks Online.

National Institute of Standards and Technologies (NIST) defines cloud SaaS as follows:

> *The capability provided to the consumer is to use the provider's applications running on a cloud infrastructure. The applications are accessible from various client devices through either a thin client interface, such as a web browser (e.g., web-based email), or a program interface. The consumer does not manage or control the underlying cloud infrastructure including network, servers, operating systems, storage, or even individual application capabilities, with the possible exception of limited user-specific application configuration settings.*

As a service, software offers network-based access for commercial accessible software. SaaS symbolizes the prospect of lesser price for businesses to utilize the software using it on need instead of getting a licence for each computer. Despite getting many licences for a user, a company can acquire a licence for using it over a lifetime and can accumulate more capital by doing this.

Some of the applications of SaaS are given here:
- Complaint resolution system
- Employee management system
- Attendance resolutions system
- E-police, E-court
- Municipal maintenance
- Water board, billing, payment systems
- District management solutions
- Service desk

SaaS presents new opportunities for software vendors, which are:
- Augmented operation speed
- Improved adoption rate from user
- Reduction of secondary requirements
- Reduction of implementation and upgradation cost of software

The major obstacle in accessing the SaaS marketplace is experienced by conventional software firms, while permitting desktop applications to function as SaaS applications. This is one of the main reasons cloud movers take little interest in it.

You may find many resemblances between cloud technology and the client–server technology. The client makes a request for a service to the server and the server in turn provides the service to the client as shown in Fig. 4.2. As in cloud technology, the cloud client makes a request to the cloud server and the cloud server provides the service requested by the client. This has been shown in Fig. 4.3. For businesses, this sort of computing technique succeeded effectively, as IT departments were able to renew the versions and it was done faultlessly on an iterative base.

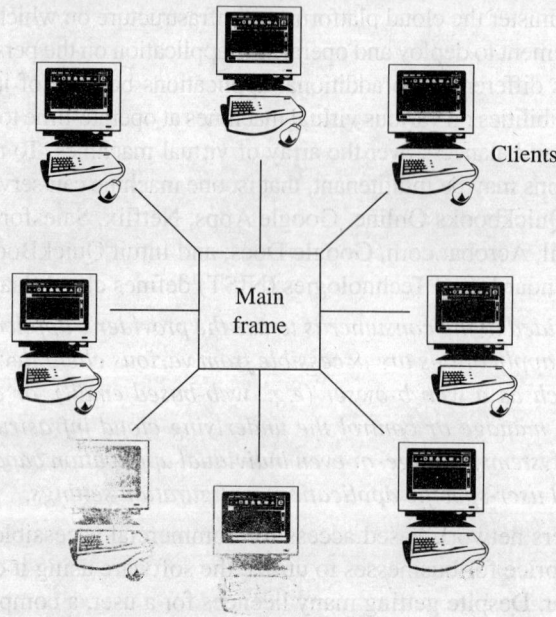

Fig. 4.2 Client–Server Technology

The size of a SaaS infrastructure is large in contrast to that of a client–server technology and in the number of customers to whom it should be capable of serving. Figure 4.3 shows the relationship of a client to the cloud in SaaS. The cloud consists of various diverse computer resources and tools to operate various software and applications needed by customers. Many clients can simultaneously operate services provided by various cloud service providers.

SaaS software is easily accessible by cloud users. Cloud users have to pay very low cost for these facilities. Figure 4.4 shows SaaS provided by cloud computing. The varieties of business models for SaaS are very exciting, having different features as per user requirements. For instance, Intuit proposes QuickBooks Online as a SaaS with a monthly service rate.

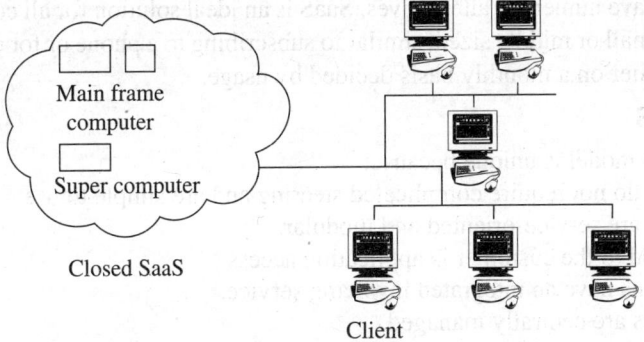

Fig. 4.3 Cloud technology

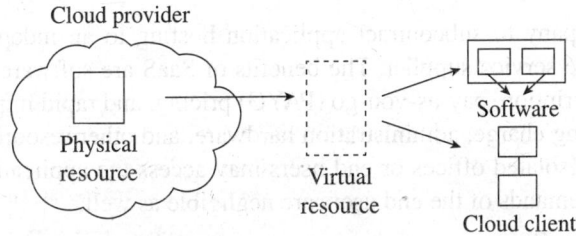

Fig. 4.4 Software as a Service

However, if a program has been constructed for performing on Windows 7, it has to be compatible with Windows XP. Hence, we must be very alert about the functionalities and attributes that should be capable of functioning on both editions. This sometimes disturbs the financial status of the company, when it comes to updating the platform as per the application requirement. In such a situation, the SaaS software is economical for corporations that reduce the charge of upgradation and execution.

Importance of SaaS

The advantage of the SaaS model is that the applications serve a wide range of users and these can be adapted to specific needs with little customization. SaaS is a one-to-many software delivery model, where an application is shared across multiple users. The following are some of the reasons SaaS services are required:

1. Straightforward expenses are nil.
2. You only need a web browser to access the application. It doesn't require other hardware purchase or software installation.
3. It provides quick operation service.
4. SaaS is extremely scalable.
5. Since the source code is the same for each customer, it is a multi-tenant design that makes it extremely proficient.
6. SaaS can endure every demand, because of easy arrangement; this is usually not simple with conventional applications.
7. Any noble technical modernization is effortlessly incorporated by the supplier that is accessible to all subscribers because, usually, all the consumers use a similar code base.

In the conventional model, the consumer has many concerns. Some of these include the following:
- Compatibility with hardware, additional software, and operating systems
- Licensing and compliance issues

As large companies have numerous alternatives, SaaS is an ideal solution for all companies, irrespective of whether they are small or middle sized, similar to subscribing to a phone or for electricity and making payments to the supplier on a monthly basis decided by usage.

Uniqueness in SaaS

Software as a Service model is unique because:
1. Its applications do not require complicated steering and are simple to use.
2. Its applications are service-oriented and modular.
3. The product sold to the customer is application access.
4. SaaS applications have an integrated invoicing service.
5. The applications are centrally managed.
6. Its applications ensure that the data of every consumer is saved and protected.
7. Its applications require offering complicated business procedure arrangements for consumers.
8. Its applications are required to continually offer swift releases of noble potential and traits.

SaaS facilitates the company to subcontract application hosting to an independent software vendor (ISV) or another software service supplier. The benefits of SaaS are software cost reduction, service-level improvement, subscription, pay-as-you-go (PAYG) pricing, and rapid implementation. This, at all times, lessens the licensing charge, administration hardware, and other resources needed by the inside host for the application. Isolated offices or end users may access the application more willingly via a browser. The hardware demands of the end users are negligible as well.

Various Providers of SaaS

- NetSuite
- Intuit
- Intacct
- Financial Force.com
- Coupa Software
- AT & T

4.2.2 Platform as a Service

As you are aware, a platform in computer software is nothing but the computing platform, which means a certain hardware architecture, an operating system (OS), and runtime libraries. All together, it can be said to be the stage on which computer programs can run. The Platform as a Service (PaaS) model makes all of the facilities required to support the complete life cycle of building and delivering web applications and services available from the Internet. Cloud computing has evolved to include platforms for building and running web-based applications, a concept known as PaaS. Cloud suppliers, in the PaaS model, carry a computing platform characteristically comprising a database, operating system, web server and programming language implementation, as shown in Fig. 4.5. Application designers may build and operate their software resolutions on a cloud platform devoid of the expense and complexity of purchasing and running the basic software and hardware layers. Examples of PaaS include Heroku, Amazon Elastic Beanstalk, Google App Engine, Microsoft Azure Mendix, and Engine Yard.

National Institute of Standards and Technologies (NIST) defines cloud PaaS as follows:

> The capability provided to the consumer is to deploy onto the cloud infrastructure consumer-created or acquired applications created using programming languages, libraries, services, and tools supported by the provider. The consumer does not manage or control the underlying cloud infrastructure including network, servers, operating systems, or storage, but has control over the deployed applications and possibly configuration settings for the application-hosting environment.

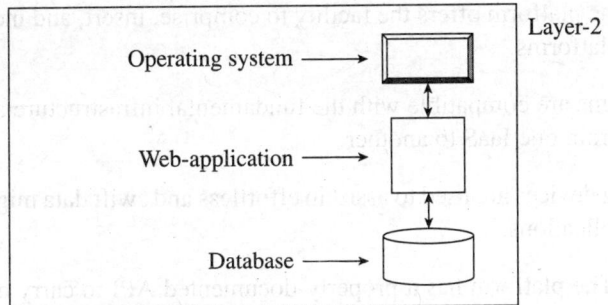

Fig. 4.5 Platform as a Service

The cloud proposes standard platforms for facilitating a variety of systems. A number of standard platforms they offer are as follows:
1. Multiple operating system support
2. Platform for accessing database
3. Act as middleware

PaaS allows users to manage various resources of the cloud infrastructure. Developing a web application is not an easy task for the development team. Even in leading corporations, there is characteristically only one network manager resource allotted to a number of development groups. The following has to be performed in the PaaS:
- Attain and install the server.
- Organize the operating system, operate time settings, and source manage depository and other middleware to work efficiently.
- Organize the operating system, operating time settings, warehouse, and supplementary middleware
- Copy data for further reference.
- The best way to comprehend PaaS is to split it separately into its major constituents—service and platform.

Uniqueness in PaaS

Platform as a Service has unique features which make it different from other services provided by the cloud providers, such as the following:

Application expansion structure A vital application expansion structure developed on technology is extensively used. The cloud user can customize the application as per the requirement.

Simplicity of use PaaS uses a user-friendly approach. Devices which have drag-and-drop options to support several average integrated development environments (IDEs) are available. It helps to quicken application development.

Accessibility An alternative platform is reachable and available anywhere, anytime.

Scalability The platform is adequately elegant to control the flexible ability of a fundamental infrastructure to manage application loads.

Safety The platform deals with items such as SQL operation, cross-site drafting, traffic encryption, and service rejection and formulates it into intrinsic application advancements. Besides, cloud provides platform support for only log-on facilities, for you to be capable of incorporating it within the on-premise applications or any other cloud applications.

Comprehensiveness The platform offers the facility to comprise, insert, and incorporate other applications set up on similar platforms.

Portability The platforms are compatible with the fundamental infrastructure and permit corporations to shift the application from one IaaS to another.

Porting devices Porting devices are used to assist in effortless and swift data migration from on-premise applications to other applications.

Properly documented The platform has a properly-documented API to carry out assignments such as user verification, recovery, saving of files, and occasionally even making straightforward calls to a database. This will permit your company to have the flexibility of customizing and generating a software application to interface with the platform which meets the particular requirements of a company.

PaaS is a platform that supports software construction and installation like services. Service support is provided to the users as per requirement and some are dedicated to application designers, software testing, etc. PaaS also supports services such as development setting and compilers; users can download the services and easily use them as a tool for various purposes. Google Apps Engine (GAE) supports these types of services through any browser. Your concentration should only be on developing the application and the platform can be handled by cloud providers.

Google App Engine

Google App Engine allows users to build and run applications on Google's infrastructure. These applications are very easy to create and maintain with the facility of scaling up and down. You need not worry about maintaining the complexity of servers; you only need to upload your application and move further. Google App Engine is a platform for providing users various built-in services and API. You can build your own web applications and mobile tools. As per the traffic, it automatically handles applications and you need not pay more for services you have not used. You are free to upload your code; the rest is managed by Google. Other tools and built-in services are also available, such as load balancing and application logging for users. Google App Engine also automatically offers instant scaling feature to your application. Security features are also associated with your web application that is provided by Google App Engine free of cost.

Python is the language support by Google App Engine. You can run Google App Engine software development Kit (SDk) on the Windows operating system to simulate the run time environment. If you want to install Python, you can use the following link: http://www.python.org/download/releases/2.5.4/

Download

Google App Engine is available at http://code.google.com/appengine/downloads.html

You can use this address to download any package. Download the installer on any folder, for example, a folder on the desktop with the name myGAE. After double clicking, you can install Google Application Engine in the folder.

Using GoogleApp (First Application) to Make Application

You can create a simple application using the '+' option already provided.
1. First of all you have to make a folder, for example, Myapp, and then make a subfolder within it.
2. By using text editor, you can make your file and save it into the subfolder with a .yaml extension.
3. Make another file with a .py extension and save it in the same folder
4. Move ahead by starting GoogleAppEngineLauncher given in application
5. Go to file and select AddExistingApplication and locate the folder and subfolder you have created. After selecting your application, click Run.

6. The application will start soon and you get an icon to move ahead
7. After pressing Browse you get your application at http://localhost
8. You can edit and make changes in your application with the given tools
9. For shuting down the server, select your application and click the stop button

PaaS Selected as per Requirement

Google Apps Engine (GAE) is more well-liked among individuals using Python, Java developers, etc. Microsoft Windows Azure is aiming its enterprise class users group. ASP.Net (C#, VB.Net) developers will discover that it is easy to accept it. Amazon has also stimulated a group to propose it's PaaS—Beanstalk (an additional alternative for Java developers).

Some of the Indian-based PaaS suppliers such as Wolf frameworks and OrangeScape are creating impression for their 4G visual PaaS. OrangeScape apps may operate on all the main cloud platforms, such as Microsoft Azure, Google App Engine, Amazon EC2, and IBMSmartCloud, without redrafting applications. Heroku and Engine Yard is the foremost cloud PaaS provider. Heroku (attained by saleforce.com) is a desired PaaS for Facebook applications' formation. DotCloud should be searched for a multi-language application platform.

For cloud telephony service, KooKooPaaS has been proposed by India-based OzonetelSystems. Figure 4.6 shows Platform as a Service provided by cloud computing. Physical resources are made available to cloud clients by using various virtualization tools. Virtual resource of PaaS provides development tools, ready platform for various applications, etc., to cloud users.

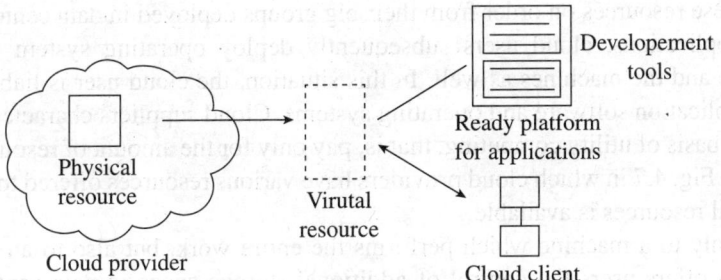

Fig. 4.6 Platform as a Service provided by cloud computing

PaaS is analogous to SaaS, but the service is a complete application improvement environment, and not merely the utilization of an application. Services provided by PaaS are different from SaaS services in which they offer a cloud-hosted virtual platform, available through a web browser.

Both the computing platform and the solution loads are delivered by PaaS suppliers. This speeds up the installing process and development of software applications. Software designers may create web applications without having to worry about setting up software tools on their personal computer, and then conveniently install or assign their application to the cloud. PaaS summarizes a software layer and offers it as a service which could be used to construct sophisticated services.

Features of PaaS for Application Developers

The following are the important features of PaaS for application developers:
1. A virtual development environment
2. Application principles generally based on the developers' necessities
3. An interface with tools 'virtual development'
4. A ready-to-use tool for public application developers

The PaaS model offers a minimum charge to application developers by supporting the entire software development life cycle (SDLC) of the web application.

Various Service Providers of PaaS

- Terremark
- Engine Yard
- AT & T
- Atlassian
- PivotalLab
- AppScale
- Engine Yard
- Flexiscale

4.2.3 Infrastructure as a Service

Infrastructure as a Service (IaaS) is the delivery of computer infrastructure as a service. In this most fundamental cloud service model, cloud suppliers propose computers, as physical or more frequently as virtual machines, and further resources. The virtual machines operate as visitors by a hypervisor, such as KVM or Xen. Administration of groups of hypervisors by the cloud operational support system directs to the facility to support a huge number of virtual machines. Additional resources in IaaS clouds comprise images in virtual machine image history, file-based and unprocessed (block) storage, software collections, firewalls, IP addresses, load balancers, and virtual local area networks (VLANs). IaaS cloud suppliers provide these resources on order from their big groups deployed in data centers.

To install the applications, cloud users subsequently deploy operating system images on their application software and the machines as well. In this situation, the cloud user is liable for sustaining and patching the application software and operating systems. Cloud suppliers characteristically invoice IaaS services on the basis of utility computing, that is, pay only for the amount of resources allotted and utilized, as shown in Fig. 4.7 in which cloud providers have various resources offered to the user and the virtual instance of all resources is available.

IaaS refers not only to a machine which performs the entire work, but also to an ability specified to companies which offers users the control of additional storage space in data centers and servers. Examples of IaaS include Rackspace Cloud, RightScale, Amazon CloudFormation (fundamental services like Amazon EC2), and Google Compute Engine.

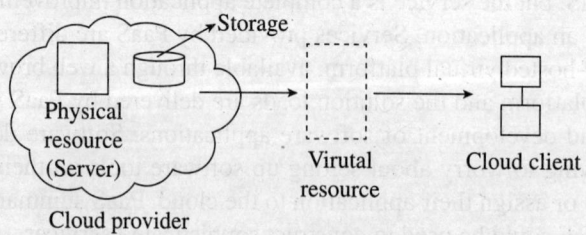

Fig. 4.7 Infrastructure as a Service

National Institute of Standards and Technologies (NIST) defines cloud IaaS as follows:

The capability provided to the consumer is to provision processing, storage, networks, and other fundamental computing resources where the consumer is able to deploy and run arbitrary software, which can include operating systems and applications. The consumer does not manage or control the underlying cloud infrastructure but has control over operating systems, storage, and deployed applications; and possibly limited control of select networking components (e.g., host firewalls).

IaaS provides tools to access a fully virtualized infrastructure. The entire three layers of services can also be combined and used to fully utilize IT resources. Companies can fully avail the facilities provided by the cloud provider by paying a very little amount to cloud providers as companies never want to invest in supplementary expenditure.

PaaS is dedicated to the application developer, whereas SaaS is for the end user. IaaS offers applications and middleware support to the application developer.

Primary Facets of IaaS

Cloud users can avail and enjoy the facilities provided by cloud providers. Instead of looking at the Internet as only a universal cloud, it is possibly more correct to look at it as a system of numerous clouds. There is scarcity of norms in cloud computing which clearly shows service norms and agreements about the facilities taken by the cloud users. Possibly, someday, the Internet actually will be the only, unified cloud where VMs might be transmitted smoothly to 'the cloud' without worrying about file set-up, and unified groups of VMs might be run. The foremost significant aspect of IaaS is flexibility. Grouping of physical servers to develop a virtual cloud is a perception known as cloud clustering.

Machine Virtualization

At present, it is predicted that Google has more than 1 million x86 servers in 12 major data centers and about 20 smaller centers on distinct continents—a big cloud. Google is persistent about using inexpensive x86 parts in place of the much more costly enterprise server constituents discovered in numerous commercial data centers. Second, idleness, failover, grouping, scrutinizing, and other infrastructure administration assignments are controlled by a virtualization system which performs under the operating system level instead of using different hardware like load balancers to control these assignments. The relationship between hypervisor, VMs, and computer has been shown in Fig. 4.8. Various virtual machines are supported by the hypervisor for providing services to many users.

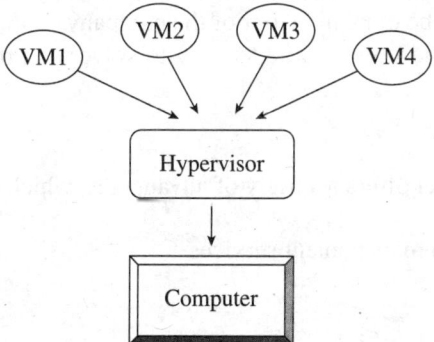

Fig. 4.8 Relationship among VMs, hypervisor, and computer

It is easy to recognize IaaS, as it is usually platform-free. It consists of an amalgamation of software and hardware resources. IaaS software is a low-stage code which runs independent of an operating system known as a hypervisor and is responsible for keeping record of hardware resources and distributing those resources on the basis of order. This process is termed as resource pooling.

A hypervisor, also known as virtual machine manager (VMM), is one among the several hardware virtualization practices which authorizes various operating systems, labelled guests, in order to work concurrently on the computer of a host. It is given such a name as it is conceptually a single level superior to an administrative program. The hypervisor offers to the guest operating systems a virtual operating platform and controls the implementation of the guest operating systems. Multiple cases of a collection of operating systems might share the virtualized hardware resources. Hypervisors are very normally organized on server hardware, along with the purpose of managing guest operating systems, which themselves perform as servers.

With IaaS, you have the ability to use networks, storage, and further computing resources, where you may install and operate subjective software such as applications and operating systems. The majority uses instances for cloud computing to pursue a similar elementary layering arrangement you are already familiar with. A software load or platform is installed on a network infrastructure and applications are operated ahead of the platform.

Various Service Providers of IaaS

Amazon is the pioneer of IaaS. In India, IaaS providers include NetMagicSolutions and InstaCompute (from Tata Communications). The other leading providers are:
- Rackspace
- Joyent
- Rightscale
- Terremark
- GoGrid
- Elastic Hosts
- Symetriq

The range of IaaS dealers is incredibly vast, as several propose big complete data-center-style infrastructure imitation (e.g., Oracle, IBM, Sun, Joyent, Terremark), whereas others propose further end-user-centric services, like simple data storage (e.g., Dropbox Amazon Simple Storage Service S3).

Computing systems infrastructure has conventionally been an incredibly huge part of a company's expenditure. Buying or taking rental software, hardware, etc., are the points that companies are always not sure about, that is, what has to be done in favour of the company. IaaS clearly mentions the services provided by the cloud provider, and utilizes a better way to solve the problem of a company, up to a certain extent.

Benefits of Service Models

The cloud computing service model offers a variety of advantages, which are listed here:
1. Global accessibility
2. Automated update and patch management services
3. Seamless integration
4. Scale easily
5. Maximize uptime
6. High availability
7. Cost saving
8. Flexibility

4.2.4 Cluster as a Service

Cluster computing has gained popularity in industry and academia. For various distributed applications, such as data analysis, simulation, web services, etc., commodity server clusters are being used. All distributed applications do not work on one framework.

Cluster computing gains popularity in industry and academia. Commodity servers' clusters are used for various distributed applications such as data analysis, simulation, web services, etc. Not one particular framework can fit every distributed application, not even the Openstack cloud framework. For example, some researchers desire to install Hadoop clusters on bear metal servers. To this problem, one solution is to assign a layer below the IaaS/PaaS layer with the job of handling cluster deployment. This idea is known as the Cluster as a Service (CaaS) layer for allocating servers.

In an academic institution, researchers, for their individual research projects, had been using their own computing resources. It was fine till power shortages became a problem. The institution's director asked a cloud research group to create a research cloud where each researcher could move their computer clusters. HPC clusters are used by some research groups whereas Hadoop clusters by others. Only a few groups offer web services to the public. Each cluster usage pattern is different and as per need of time vary from each other. Thus, in case of critical power consumption, the resource has to be dynamically allocated to each cluster.

Design Issue Needs

Design requirements for CaaS are:
- For every cluster, dynamic resource allocation is required
- It is important to secure isolation among clusters
- Sufficient capacity and performance for every cluster

Design Description
- Between IaaS/PaaS layer and CaaS layer, there is a separation
- Efficiently handling of CaaS layer machine images using containers
- CaaS layer is a web service
- Isolation of Network through tagged VLAN
- Automatic package installation

4.3 CLOUD COMPUTING SUB SERVICE MODELS

Apart from the three main service models of cloud computing, the following are some of the sub-service models, which are also providing services to cloud users.

4.3.1 Everything as a Service

Everything as a Service (XaaS) cloud computing provides various services to users on the basis of user demand. XaaS in cloud computing is a term that is used for the wide variety of services and applications emerging for users to access on demand over the Internet.

XaaS supports various services such as SaaS, IaaS, desktop as a service, disaster recovery as a service, marketing as a service, and many others. It provides facilities and flexibility to users for customizing the computing environments as per requirements. Apart from the necessary services, various other services are also available on the cloud environment so it is the essence of cloud computing that provides and delivers services to users, online, over the Internet, rather than providing service on site.

4.3.2 Compliance as a Service

Compliance as a Service offers compliance collection and facilitates your cloud applications as per corporate policies or organization requirements. Issues of cloud compliance occur when you make use of cloud storage or any type of backup services. Customer data is moving from internal storage to the cloud environment so it is the vital responsibility of the cloud provider to maintain a service-level agreement for compliance. Customers are always concerned about cloud security—what information should be put on a public cloud and what on a private cloud. Security of cloud and cloud compliance is actually the responsibility of both the cloud vendor and cloud customers. Certificates for security compliances are provided by cloud vendors (e.g., azure, amazon, etc.).

4.3.3 Identity as a Service

Identity as a Service (IdaaS) refers to identity services by cloud service providers for providing on-site or off-site services to customers. Services may include directory management, or the operation of a single sign-on service (SSO). IdaaS is actually an authentication infrastructure that IdaaS refers to identity services by cloud service provider for providing on-site or off-site services to customers. Services may include directory management or the operation of a SSO. IdaaS is actually an authentication infrastructure that is managed and hosted by a third party. The cloud service provider hosts the application and rent is collected on usage basis. Access to specific applications is on a role-base access and whole virtualized desktops can also be accessed through a secure portal. IdaaS is a tremendously wide term, including software, platform, and infrastructure services for both private and public clouds. Enterprises can guarantee consistency in authentication, authorization, administration, and auditing. In IdaaS development and implementation, there are a number of challenges. Security depends on the type of identity.

- SaaS—Customers using IdaaS with SaaS get services on the basis of types of user, such as internal users, external users, or others.
- PaaS—Customers using IdaaS with PaaS handle issues regarding web service.
- IaaS—Management of privileged access to virtual machines is handled in IdaaS with IaaS.

4.3.4 IaaS: DataBase as a Service (DBaaS)

DBaaS permits the access and utilization of a database administration system as a service.

4.3.5 Paas: Storage as a Service (STaaS)

It is accountable for the transfer of data storage as a service, comprising database services, often owed on a utility computing base.

4.3.6 SaaS: Communications as a Service (CaaS)

It offers a business relations' resolution, such as video conferencing, instant messaging, voice over Internet protocol (VOIP), and many more.

4.3.7 SaaS: Security as a Service (SECaaS)

It offers the safety of corporation networks and mobile networks via the Internet for different dealings, databases, applications, events, and system proceedings.

4.3.8 SaaS: Monitoring as a Service (MaaS)

It offers services for the transfer of second-level infrastructure such as asset tracking, log management as a service, etc.

4.3.9 PaaS: Desktop as a Service (DTaaS)

It is a service or platform provided by the cloud provider by which back end of the virtual desktop infrastructure is hosted.

4.3.10 IaaS: Compute Capacity as a Service (CCaaS)

CCaaS is the condition of 'unprocessed' computing resources, characteristically used in the implementation of mathematically versatile models from either a 'supercomputer' resource or a great number of distributed computing resources anywhere that the assignment is carried out correctly.

4.4 CLOUD DEPLOYMENT MODELS

The cloud model is invented with four deployment models—public cloud, private cloud, hybrid cloud, and community cloud. Deployment is, in fact, an operational model. Different cloud deployment models are shown in Fig. 4.9.

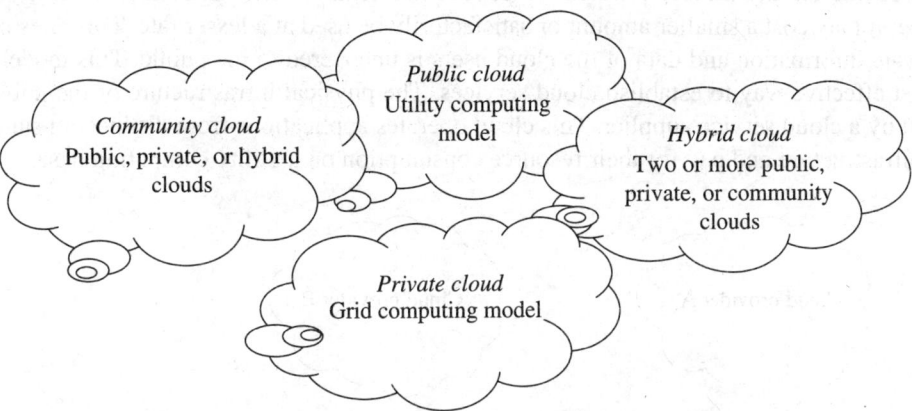

Fig. 4.9 Various cloud deployment models

A majority of the companies concentrate on controlling the cloud so as to reduce capital expenses and manage operating expenses. Models have been suggested by the National Institute of Standards and Technology (NIST). As per NIST, the following are the deployment models:

Private cloud Cloud infrastructure is provisioned for exclusive use by a single organization comprising multiple consumers (e.g., business units). It may be owned, managed, and operated by the organization, a third party, or a combination of them. It may exist on or off premises.

Community cloud The cloud infrastructure is provisioned for exclusive use by a specific community of consumers from organizations that have shared concerns (e.g., mission, security requirements, policy, and compliance considerations). It may be owned, managed, and operated by one or more of the organizations in the community, a third party, or a combination of them. It may exist on or off premises.

Public cloud The cloud infrastructure is provisioned for open use by the general public. It may be owned, managed, and operated by a business, academic, or government organization, or some combination of them. It exists on the premises of the cloud provider.

Hybrid cloud The cloud infrastructure is a composition of two or more distinct cloud infrastructures (private, community, or public) that remain unique entities, but are bound together by standardized or proprietary technologies that enable data and application portability (e.g., cloud bursting for load balancing between clouds).

Though the cloud may convey protection, security issues are still associated with the cloud. It is not easy for a company to enforce security parameters at various levels. It is also not cost effective for a company. Thus, it is vital for companies to recognize their needs before selecting different installment models accessible on the cloud.

The diverse infrastructure deployment models are distinctive by their design, the position of the data center, and the needs of the consumers from the cloud supplier. Clouds could also be categorized on the basis of the fundamental infrastructure installment model as private, public, and hybrid or community clouds.

4.4.1 Public Clouds

The public cloud is the first deployment model (Fig. 4.10). In this model, users have many options to opt for and decide on any service provider as per requirement. 'Public' does not constantly indicate that it is free; it may cost a smaller amount or satisfactorily be used at a lesser rate. This does not mean that the private information and data of the cloud users is uncovered to the public. This model offers a flexible, cost effective way to establish cloud services. The physical infrastructure of the public cloud is possessed by a cloud service supplier. This cloud operates applications from distinct consumers who share this infrastructure and pay for their resource consumption on a utility computing base.

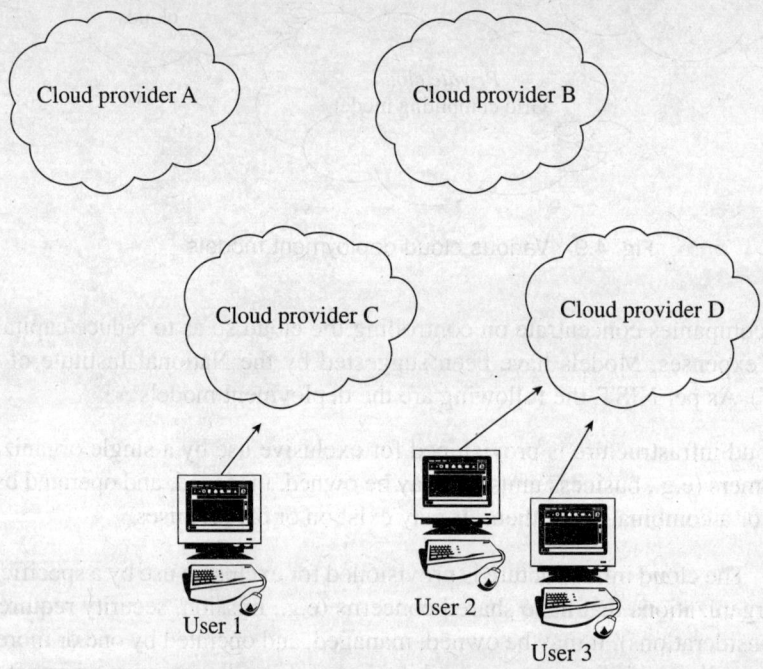

Fig. 4.10 Public cloud computing

In a public cloud, computing resources are available for all. No initial investment is required for availing any services from the cloud. Examples of public cloud vendors include Google, Amazon Elastic Compute Cloud, Windows Azure Services Platform, Microsoft, etc. The cloud infrastructure is made accessible to the common community or a big business pool. Various infrastructure as well as services are offered to users who request for the services of cloud computing. Google is an example of public cloud services offered to the users. Users avail various services offered by the cloud provider on a pay-per-user basis.

This model is best matched for company necessities in which it is needed to administer load run through host SaaS applications, consume provisional infrastructure for rising and experimenting applications, and administer applications which are utilized by various users that would need high investment in infrastructure from companies. This model assists in the reduction of capital expenses and removes equipped IT expenses. Figure 4.11 shows the working of cloud providers. Different clients can easily access collection of services provided by cloud providers.

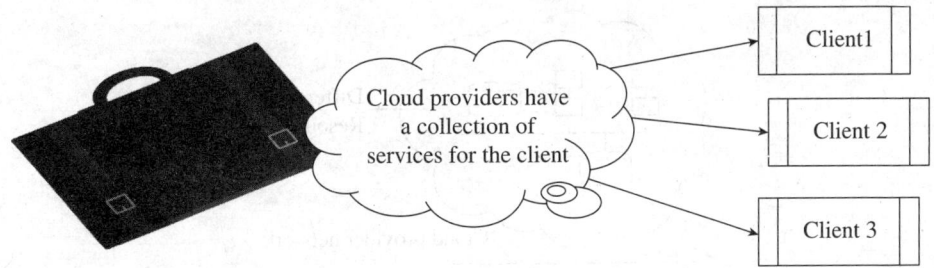

Fig. 4.11 Working of cloud providers

Public Cloud—Azure

Azure has a wide range of operating systems, various programming languages, frameworks, tools, databases, etc. It supports to build apps with JavaScript, Python, .NET, Java, etc. It also provides support to make back-ends for Android.

Azure has an efficient IT environment with the largest network of secure private network, databases, and storage with various security features. Azure supports flexibility of user demands by providing a scale up or down feature and accordingly pay-as-you-go service is supported. Billing is done on a per-minute basis and provides users with infrastructure services such as compute, storage, and bandwidth with very good performance. Azure has a large network at the data center across several countries.

To the common community, public cloud storage, applications, and additional resources are made accessible by a service supplier. These services are free or proposed on a pay-per-use model. Usually, public cloud service suppliers such as Google, Microsoft, and Amazon AWS take possession of and run the infrastructure, and propose access via the Internet (direct connectivity is not proposed).

The common community is classified under personal companies or users. The public cloud infrastructure used is in the possession of a cloud services dealer association. Characteristically, the cloud is functioned and handled at a data center possessed by a service dealer who hosts numerous customers and uses the exciting provisioning.

Execution of scalable services platform and pay-as-you-go licensing is also a striking constituent of public cloud computing. Such are the benefits of shared hardware infrastructure, software infrastructure, preservation, advances, modernization, and improvement. Reasonably, using a public cloud could offer approximately instant price savings to a corporation. Isolated hosting, shared infrastructure, and vibrant provisioning and licensing are robust attractions for a corporation.

Depending on particular requirement of a corporation, like customized arrangement necessities and service-level agreements (SLAs) concerning up-time necessities, a corporation should cautiously think of transferring vital applications to a public cloud dealer. Safety is the most significant of these necessities to be taken care of.

Besides every day operational assignments, this third-party administration comprises safety responsibilities like scrutinizing, execution, and sorting of controls. This usually reduces the control on data by company or cloud users as the entire data is kept on a cloud environment. Users should be careful about data that requires continuous scrutiny. Examples of public cloud vendors are Google, Amazon Elastic Compute Cloud, Windows Azure Services Platform, Microsoft, etc.

4.4.2 Private Clouds

The private cloud is the second deployment model. The private cloud offers several advantages of an open cloud computing setting that comprises its service support and flexibility. The difference

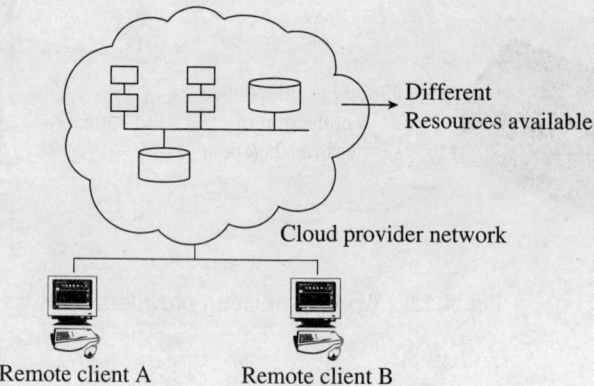

Fig. 4.12 Private cloud

comprising a private cloud and a public cloud is perceived in several services or applications proposed by a private cloud service. The growth and information are managed inside the cluster without the restrictions of the system bandwidth, authorized requirements, and security procedures disclosure. Private cloud is displayed in Fig. 4.12. Furthermore, private cloud services offer the user control over cloud infrastructure.

Private clouds allow infrastructure to be accessed only by the members of the organization and granted by third parties. Private cloud is hosted in the data center of the company and offers services only to users within the company. The major drawback with a private cloud is higher cost as compared to a public cloud. Examples of private cloud include Eucalyptus cloud computing infrastructure with Ubuntu Server, Elastra private-cloud, Vmware, Microsoft, etc.

Private cloud is cloud infrastructure controlled exclusively for a solo corporation, whether controlled within or by a third-party and hosted internally or externally. Commencing a private cloud plan needs a big stage and amount to virtualize the company setting. It will need the corporation to re-examine judgments regarding accessible resources. Private cloud is more sensitive about security as various sensible and private matters are kept on the cloud by cloud users, so safety plans are discussed in detail while moving towards a private cloud.

> "The cloud infrastructure is provisioned for exclusive use by a single organization comprising multiple consumers (e.g., business units). It may be owned, managed, and operated by the organization, a third party, or some combination of them, and it may exist on or off premises"[9].

A pure private cloud is constructed for the best use of a single customer, who possesses and completely manages this cloud. Furthermore, there are deviations of this in expressions of function, possession, etc. The truth that the cloud is used by a particular consumer is the unique feature of every private cloud. A private cloud could be possessed by the consumer, but constructed, deployed, and directed by a third party instead of the consumer. The physical servers could or could not be positioned at the location of the consumer. A 'virtual private cloud' is a freshly launched option to a private cloud. In virtual private cloud, a consumer is allotted a private cloud inside the public cloud's physical infrastructure. Because of the allotment of particular resources inside the cloud, the consumer may be guaranteed that their data is saved and privilege is completed on devoted servers. By means of virtualization, several corporations are setting up private cloud computing situations intended to be simply used by their staff or selected partners.

Generally, private clouds are owned by bigger corporations and governmental organizations, instead of end users or small corporations. The difference introduced in expenses is a chief cause for this. A private cloud needs an infrastructure expense as in IT infrastructure, as an organization has to be moderately big to obtain advantages from the private cloud model. A bigger corporation generally demands complete control and access to the in-house firewalls and virtualized situation needed to set up the private cloud. However, several smaller corporations have the want for such power, and they might subscribe to a private cloud dealer.

In a private cloud installment, safety is stricter than on a public cloud. A business which has safety concerns might desire to use the power a private cloud can provide as the business possesses the infrastructure and has control over how applications are installed on it. Safety worries are handled by the firewall system of a consumer.

In addition to safety causes, this model is accepted by corporations in circumstances when applications or data are needed to agree with various rigid paradigms that might need data in order to administer for secrecy and reviews which manage the company.

Some SaaS applications, like SugarCRM, offer alternatives to their customers to maintain their data with security on the private cloud environment. Amazon also supports services of the virtual private cloud. Examples of private cloud include Eucalyptus cloud computing infrastructure with Ubuntu Server, Elastra private-cloud, Vmware, Microsoft, etc.

4.4.3 Community Clouds

Community cloud is the third model. The community cloud is limited and consumed by means of a group or cluster which includes universal significances and reason, such as a general task. The associates of the society assign contact to the application and information on the cloud. This variety will possibly provide a better power of protection and segregation.

A community cloud falls between public and private clouds category. The drawback related to a community cloud is that of having costs higher than a public cloud. Examples of community cloud include Google's 'Gov Cloud', NASA Nebula cloud, etc.

Community Cloud—OpenNebula

OpenNebula is a cloud computing tool for running various distributed data center infrastructures. The OpenNebula tool controls a virtual infrastructure of the data center to construct hybrid, public, and private executions of infrastructure as a service. OpenNebula is free and open-source software, put through the necessities of the Apache Licence edition 2. It coordinates network, storage, virtualization, security, and scrutinizing technologies to install multi-layer services as virtual machines on distributed infrastructures, merging both isolated resources and data center cloud resources, as per allotment strategies.

The tool includes characteristics for administration, amalgamation, scalability, accounting, and safety. It also declares consistency, portability, and interoperability, offering managers and cloud users with a number of cloud interfaces (e.g., vCloud, OGF Open Cloud Computing Interface, Amazon EC2 Query) and hypervisors (e.g., VMware, KVM, and Xen) and may put up manifold software and hardware amalgamations in a data center.

OpenNebula was a guiding corporation in Google Summer of Code 2010. It is subsidized by C12G. OpenNebula is utilized by telecom operators, hosting suppliers, IT services suppliers, supercomputing centers, international research plans, and research labs. A number of other cloud resolutions employ OpenNebula as the kernel service or cloud engine.

Infrastructure has been shared by community cloud among some associations from a particular society with familiar fear (i.e., acquiescence, safety, influence, and many more), whether controlled inside or by a third party and hosted inside or outwardly. Community cloud is sometimes more expensive when compared to private cloud.

When numerous consumers have similar requirements and necessities, they may share an infrastructure and could share the administration and arrangement of the cloud. This administration could be made by third parties or by themselves.

A cloud deployment model, which is being swiftly executed, is known as a community cloud. Conceptually, from anywhere among a public cloud and a private cloud, community cloud represents a shared infrastructure which is occupied and supported by numerous corporations. This shared cloud resource can be consumed by groups which have interconnected aim, like combined acceptance necessities, non-competitive company objectives, or group safety resources. Though the physical maintenance of the shared cloud might exist on any location or may on a third-party location, running the community cloud might turn out to be difficult, because of the changing or undefined responsibility and control, creating it fairly technically demanding to handle resource secrecy, administration, flexibility, safety, and latency necessities. Community cloud is displayed in Fig. 4.13.

> Corporations that share the cloud infrastructure support a particular community which has shared apprehensions (e.g., safety necessities, assignment, and acquiescence and strategy consideration). It can be controlled by the corporations or a third party and might exist off-premise or on-premise.

In the community deployment model, numerous corporations share the cloud infrastructure with similar strategy and agreement consideration. This assists in the reduction of expenses (in contrast to a private cloud), since it is shared by a bigger group or cluster.

Many state-level government sectors that require access to data concerning the regional population or information associated to infrastructure such as roads, hospitals, electrical stations, and more, may employ a community cloud to run data and applications. Examples of community cloud include Google's 'Gov Cloud', NASA Nebula cloud, etc.

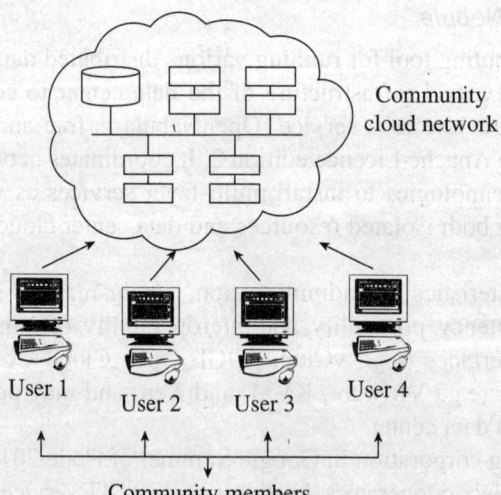

Fig. 4.13 Community cloud

4.4.4 Hybrid Clouds

The last model is the hybrid cloud. The hybrid cloud is a combination of a private and public cloud which is mutually dependent on one another. In this model, cloud users are supplied with information on the public cloud, in spite of the reality that the cloud supplier has to maintain the company-significant services and information in a few instructions.

Hybrid cloud is a constitution of two or more clouds (i.e., community, public, or private) which remain exceptional units but are bound mutually, providing the advantages of various deployment models. By means of employing 'hybrid cloud' design, individuals and corporations are capable of acquiring levels of error tolerance combined with regionally instant usability. Hybrid cloud design needs both on-premise resources and off-place (isolated) server-based cloud infrastructure. Hybrid cloud is shown in Fig. 4.14.

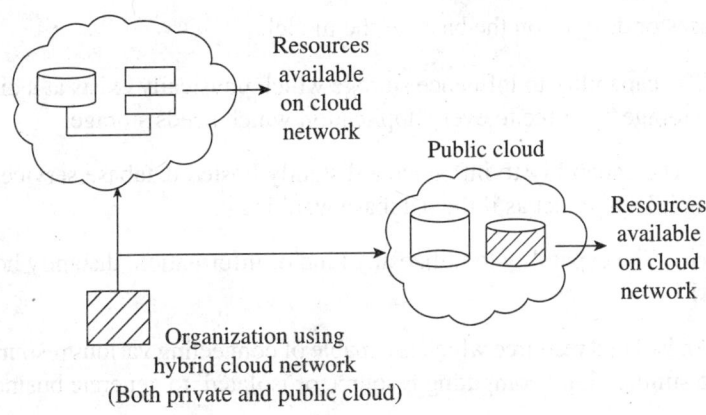

Fig. 4.14 Hybrid cloud

Hybrid clouds do not have the confidence, safety, and flexibility of internal applications. Hybrid cloud offers the flexibility of internal applications along with the scalability and error tolerance of cloud-based services.

A hybrid cloud is a combination of the public, private, and community cloud. It is defined by NIST as follows:

> *"The cloud infrastructure is a composition of two or more distinct cloud infrastructures (private, community, or public) that remain unique entities, but are bound together by standardized or proprietary technology that enables data and application portability (e.g., cloud bursting for load balancing between clouds)"* [9].

An illustration of hybrid cloud deployment might consist of a corporation installing non-critical software applications within the public cloud, whereas holding perceptive or significant applications in a private cloud, on the location.

One characteristic of hybrid clouds which makes them distinguishable from the other kinds of cloud deployment is 'cloudburst'. Most general hybrid clouds are an amalgamation of both public and private cloud computing settings that are installed, employed, and perform constantly.

Independent software vendors (ISVs) propose virtual applications which may offer a 'cloudburst' self-service means. A fine source to explore numerous virtual applications is VMware's Virtual Appliance.

The deployment model assists companies to seize the benefit of protected applications and data hosting on a private cloud, and benefits from expenditure profits by maintaining shared applications and data on the public cloud. This model is also well used for managing the cloud, which is meant for circumstances where the prevailing private cloud infrastructure is enabled to deal with the load and needs an emergency choice for supporting the load. Therefore, the cloud handles workloads among private and public hosting without any trouble to the users.

Moreover, any constitution of clouds, whether they are public or private, might form a hybrid cloud and be administered as the only unit, provided there is a sufficiently standard structure used by the component clouds.

4.5 ALTERNATIVE DEPLOYMENT MODELS

A completely dissimilar outlook of the cloud computing design is within the Jericho cloud cube model and the Linthicum model.

4.5.1 Linthicum Model

There are 10 main classes or designs on the basis of the model:

Storage as a Service   The capability to influence storage which physically exists at a different location, but is logically a local storage resource to every application which needs storage.

Database as a Service   The capability to influence a distantly hosted database service, sharing it with other users, and keeping it local to act as if the database were local.

Information as a Service   The capability to utilize any kind of information, distantly hosted, via a definite interface like an API.

Process as a Service   An isolated resource which is capable of connecting various resources collectively, either hosted inside the similar cloud computing resource or isolated, to generate business procedures.

Application as a Service   Any application conveyed over the web platform to an end user, characteristically controlling the application via a browser.

Platform as a Service   An absolute platform, comprising interface improvement, application expansion, investigation, database expansion, and storage, conveyed via a distantly hosted platform to subscribers.

Integration as a Service   The capability to transport a whole amalgamation load from the cloud, together with interfacing with applications, flow control, semantic negotiation, and amalgamation intend.

Security as a Service   The capability to carry principal safety services distantly over the Internet.

Management as a Service   Any on-command service which offers the capability to control one or more cloud services, characteristically uncomplicated things such as topology, resource consumption, virtualization, and uptime administration.

Testing as a Service   The capability to analyse regional or cloud-carried systems by using testing services and software which are distantly hosted.

4.5.2 Jericho Cloud Cube Model

In January 2004, the IT safety association of corporations, government clusters, and dealers, intellectuals 'dedicated to advancing secure business in a global open-network environment' created the Jericho Forum under the sponsorship of the Open Group. Initially generating to tackle network issues, the medium has dealt with the trouble of protecting corporation deals via the Internet. In February 2009, they carried a realistic structure towards generating the true partnership-oriented design. Subsequently, the medium published the Jericho Cloud Cube Model version1.0 in April 2009.

The objective of the Cloud Cube Model is to:
1. Indicate that not all that is executed in the clouds is good; it might be best to run some corporation tasks by using a conventional non-cloud approach.

2. Describe the diverse cloud configurations which have been identified by the Jericho Forum.
3. Explain chief aspects, threats, and advantages of every cloud configuration.
4. Offer a structure for discovering in further detail the character of various cloud configurations and the matters which require building them securely and to protect the areas to work in.

The model for cloud computing is explained by the Jericho Cloud Cube Model as encompassing four 'dimensions':

Internal or external   This describes the physical position of the data. If it is inside your individual physical periphery, in-house, or exterior, which means it is not inside your individual physical periphery.

Proprietary or open   Proprietary denotes that the corporation offering the service is holding the resources of condition under their possession. Open clouds are using technology which is not proprietary.

Perimeterized or de-perimeterized architectures   Within your conventional IT perimeter, de-perimeterization has forever been associated with the fixed removal, breakdown, or decrease of the conventional IT perimeter.

Outsourced or insourced   Outsourced means the service is offered by a third party, whereas insourced is the service offered by personal employees under your power.

4.6 CLOUDSTACK

CloudStack is cloud software which assists users to alter the cloud according to their requirements. It is an open-source platform for developing hybrid, public, and private infrastructure as service clouds. It controls and supports the network, storage, and compute joints in a cloud infrastructure. It is used to arrange, control, and systematize situations in cloud computing.

CloudStack is used to generate flexible cloud services. It is, in fact, an Infrastructure as a Service which carries some infrastructure or associated technique for service hosting for the developer. This is specifically why cloud stack is known as 'do it yourself'. It supports various hypervisors along with manifold hardware into an only virtual access. It has a clear interface which assists by displaying elements. First, cloud stack was possessed by Cloud.com which was a freeware. It was later followed by Apache Software Foundation. With CloudStack, you are capable of the following:
1. Establishing an on-command, flexible cloud computing service. Service suppliers may offer self-service virtual machines, networking arrangements, and storage sizes over the Internet.
2. CloudStack may be used to construct an on-command cloud computing service along with flexibility. Service supplier provides storage and virtual machines, and much more on the Internet.
3. An organization or worker could establish an on-premise private cloud along with CloudStack.

4.7 CLOUD STORAGE

Cloud storage is a service model wherein data is maintained, controlled, and backed up distantly and made accessible to users over a network (characteristically the Internet). Figure 4.15 explains the remote services provided to the cloud consumer.

There are three major cloud storage models which are as follows:
1. Public cloud storage services, like Amazon's Simple Storage Service (S3), offers a multi-occupant storage appropriate for data.
2. Private cloud storage services offer a dedicated storage restricted behind the firewall of a corporation. Private clouds are suitable for users who require customization and more power on their data.

3. Hybrid cloud storage is an amalgamation of the other two models, which comprise no less than a single public cloud and a single private cloud infrastructure. A corporation could, for instance, collect forcefully used and prepared data on a private cloud and sharable data on a public cloud.

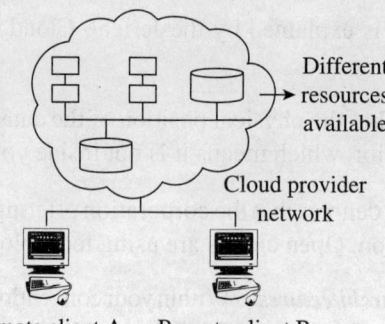

Fig. 4.15 Remote services provided to cloud consumer

Cloud storage is a module of networked online storage in which data is saved in virtualized groups of storage that are normally hosted by third parties. Hosting corporations control big data centers and common people who need their data to be hosted generally take storage space on a rental basis from them. In the background, the data center workers virtualize resources as per the necessities of the consumer and interprets them as storage groups that the consumers can themselves use to save data objects or files. Actually, the resource can link diagonally with numerous servers.

Cloud storage services can be accessed via a web service application programming interface (API), or via a web-based user interface.

Points to Remember

1. 'SaaS' is used for both 'Security as a Service' as well as the more common 'Software as a Service'.
2. PaaS is a common platform that supports software development, testing, and organization. The whole software life cycle can be controlled on a PaaS. More than one user can work simultaneously on the same platform or software very easily.
3. Amazon EC2 is a well-known example of IaaS. Google App engine is an example of PaaS and Salesforce.com is an example of SaaS.
4. The layer below the IaaS/PaaS layer that performs the job of handling cluster deployment is called Cluster as a Service (CaaS).
5. A hybrid cloud is a mixture of a public and private cloud that are interdependent on each other.
6. A type of cloud which is accessed and utilized by a limited group of people having a common mission or interest is known as community cloud.
7. Amazon is the pioneer of IaaS.
8. The virtual machines are run as guests by a hypervisor, such as Xen or KVM.
9. A public cloud is a cloud computing deployment scheme that is generally open for use by the general public.
10. Alternative deployment models include Linthicum model and Jericho Cloud Cube model.
11. CloudStack is an open-source platform to build public, private, and hybrid infrastructure as service clouds.
12. Cloud Storage is a service model wherein data is maintained, controlled, and backed up distantly and made accessible to users over a network.

Key Terms

CaaS Communications as a Service delivers a Session Initiated Protocol (SIP)-based audio collaboration and on-net web conferencing over a virtual private network (VPN) using a hosted model.

CcaaS Compute Capacity as a Service means that the resource runs applications with the assistance of basic computing components. Compute basically consists of physical and logical components. By physical components, we mean hardware devices, whereas logical refers to software and protocols used.

Cloud Compliance as a Service This offers compliance collection and facilitates your cloud applications as per corporate policies or organization requirements.

DbaaS Database as a Service provides the following services to users: combine and shared platform for accessing databases, flexibility to access database resources according to the user need, charges on the basis of database usage.

DtaaS Desktop as a Service is an efficient desktop infrastructure provided by the service provider to reduce the complexity and cost of your desktop infrastructure. Services can be availed by taking an Internet connection on a rental basis.

Hybrid cloud The cloud infrastructure is a composition of two or more distinct cloud infrastructures (private, community, or public) that remain unique entities, but are bound together by standardized or proprietary technology that enables data and application portability (e.g., cloud bursting for load balancing between clouds).

Private cloud The cloud infrastructure is provisioned for exclusive use by a single organization comprising multiple consumers (e.g., business units). It may be owned, managed, and operated by the organization, a third party, or some combination of them, and it may exist on or off premises.

SaaS The capability provided to the consumer is to use the provider's applications running on a cloud infrastructure. The applications are accessible from various client devices through a thin client interface such as a web browser (e.g., web-based e-mail). The consumer does not manage or control the underlying cloud infrastructure, including network, servers, operating systems, storage, or even individual application capabilities, with the possible exception of limited user-specific application configuration settings.

SECaaS Security as a Service is a platform in which the service provider amalgamates the security services into a business infrastructure. Services are cost efficient as compared to the services provided by the individual organization.

StaaS Storage as a Service is a platform provided by the cloud provider for data storage for cloud users.

Multiple-choice Questions

1. Which property of a private cloud be considered for the delivery model of highly regulated workloads?
   (a) System development testing
   (b) Awareness of data location
   (c) Throughput of batch processing
   (d) System monitoring (production)

2. Which cloud deployment model does an enterprise retain to complete control over the construction and delivery of all cloud services?
   (a) Hybrid cloud
   (b) Private cloud
   (c) Community cloud
   (d) Public cloud

3. A cloud environment in which multiple users share and access cloud services, while infrastructure resides off premise is a _____.
   (a) Hybrid cloud
   (b) Private cloud
   (c) Community cloud
   (d) Public cloud
4. Which characteristics of cloud computing may prohibit a company from utilizing a public cloud offering?
   (a) Metering
   (b) Flexibility
   (c) Self service
   (d) Resource pooling
5. What are the two important characteristics of a cloud delivery model?
   (a) Service based
   (b) Share to all
   (c) Both (a) and (b)
   (d) Security
6. Among the given attributes, which is incorporated in public cloud computing?
   (a) Metering
   (b) Scalability
   (c) Multi-tenancy
   (d) Rapid provisioning
7. What is the function of hypervisor in a cloud solution?
   (a) It imitates a system call.
   (b) It provides virtualization.
   (c) It optimizes I/O performance.
   (d) It shares one CPU with multiple operating systems.
8. _____ is/are cloud PaaS providers.
   (a) Engine yard
   (b) Heroku
   (c) Terremark
   (d) All the above
9. _____ is the delivery of an enterprise communications solution, such as voice over IP, instant messaging, and video conferencing applications as a service.
   (a) CaaS
   (b) PaaS
   (c) IaaS
   (d) SaaS
10. Who is/are the leading IaaS providers?
    (a) Rackspace
    (b) Joyent
    (c) Rightscale
    (d) All the above

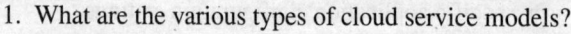

Review Questions

1. What are the various types of cloud service models?
2. What are the various advantages of PaaS over SaaS?
3. Explain the characteristics of SaaS.
4. What are the various points to be considered when a client opts for SaaS?
5. Explain the services provided to an application developer by cloud providers.
6. What are the different types of deployment models?
7. How is the community model different from a hybrid model?
8. Explain in detail about the Jericho cloud cube model.
9. Explain the various services offered by IaaS.
10. Explain Linthicum Model in detail.
11. Why is CloudStack called 'do it yourself'?
12. What is the requirement of compliance as a service in cloud computing?
13. How is identity as a service handled in SaaS, PaaS, and IaaS?

References

1. *Cloud Security A Comprehensive Guide to Secure Cloud Computing*, Ronald L. Krutz and Russell Dean Vines, ISBN: 978-0-470-58987-8, Wiley Publication, 2010
2. *Cloud Computing for Dummies*, Judith Hurwitz, Robin Bloor, Marcia Kaufman, and Dr. Fern Halper, ISBN-10: 0470484705, Wiley Publication, 1st edition, November 16, 2009
3. *Cloud Computing Technologies and Strategies*, Brian J.S. Chee and Curtis Franklin, Jr, ISBN 9781439806128, CRC Press, April 7, 2010
4. *Cloud Computing: A Practical Approach*, Anthony T. Velte, Toby J. Velte, Ph.D., Robert Elsenpeter, ISBN-10: 0071626948, McGraw-Hill, 1st edition, November 1, 2009
5. *Grid and Cloud Computing*, Katarina StanoevskaSlabeva, Thomas Wozniak, and Santi Ristol, ISBN-10: 3642051928, Springer; 2010 edition
6. *Implementing and Developing Cloud Applications*, David E.Y.Sarna, ISBN-10: 1439830827, Auerbach Publications, November 26, 2010
7. *Market-oriented cloud computing: Vision, Hype, and Reality for Delivering IT services as Computing Utilities. In High Performance Computing and Communications*, R. Buyya, C.S. Yeo, and S. Venugopal., HPCC'08. 10th IEEE International Conference on pp. 4–13 IEEE, 2008
8. Cloud Service Models, http://cloud.ebrc.com/Cloud-service-models, last accessed in January 2015
9. National Institute of Standards and Technologies (NIST) http://csrc.nist.gov/publications nistpubs/800-145/SP800-145.pdf, January 2015
10. *Mastering Cloud Computing*, Rajkumar Buyya, Christian Vecchhiola, S. Thamarai Selvi, Tata McGraw Hill Education Private Limited, 2008
11. Infrastructure-as-a-service, Amazon EC2: https://aws.amazon.com/, last accessed in February 2015
12. *Cloud Computing and Virtualization*, V. Rajeswara Rao, V. ShubbaRamaiah, BS Publication, ISBN-10: 9383635045, BS Publications / BSP Books, 2014 Platform-as-a-service, GoogleAppEngine: https://cloud.google.com/appengine
13. Cloud Computing Concepts, Technology and Architecture by Thomas Erl, ZaighamMahmood, Ricardo Puttini, ISBN-10: 0133387526, Pearson publication,1st edition 10, May 2013
14. Software as a Service, SalesForce.com:https://cloud.google.com/appengine/February 2015

Answers to Multiple-choice Questions

1. (b)	3. (d)	5. (c)	7. (a)	9. (a)
2. (b)	4. (d)	6. (a)	8. (d)	10. (d)

CHAPTER 5

Cloud Data Center

Learning Outcomes

After completing this chapter, students will be able to:

- comprehend the core elements of cloud data center
- describe the different storage options
- describe RAID technology and its advantages
- understand database and its management
- understand the various technologies of backup and recovery
- discuss replication technologies
- describe life cycle management
- describe cloud analytics
- understand traditional data center management

5.1 INTRODUCTION

Before cloud computing, traditional computing methods were used. In this chapter, we will discuss the differences between cloud computing and traditional computing, the various devices used for storage, storage network technologies, and virtualization. In the last part of the chapter, we will discuss the recovery and backup of data in a cloud computing environment and the information management technique used in computing.

5.2 CLOUD DATA CENTER CORE ELEMENTS

The key component of cloud computing is virtualization, which provides a different environment to the user with specific customization features. Cloud services have three distinct characteristics which differentiate them from traditional hosting—it is sold on demand (i.e., on the basis of a time period such as hours and minutes), it is elastic, and the service is fully managed by the provider.

The important cloud elements are as follows:
1. Clients (i.e., mobile, thin, or thick)
2. Data center (i.e., collection of servers, IT, and non-IT equipment)
3. Distributed servers (geographically distributed)
4. Storage

A data center (sometimes called a server farm) is a centralized ordnance for the storage, administration, and distribution of information and data. Characteristically, a data center maintains the entire

infrastructure and makes computer systems and related elements, such as storage systems and telecommunications, familiar with each other. The principal components of a cloud data center (CDC) comprise:
1. Application: It is a computer program which has the ability of computing operations. Applications can use a DBMS that uses operating system services in order to work on, retrieve, and store functions on storage tools.
2. DBMS: It offers planned means to save data in rationally prepared tables which are unified. DBMS optimizes the retrieval and storage of data.
3. Compute: It is a physical computing machine which controls applications, databases, and operating systems.
4. Storage: It refers to a tool which constantly saves data for subsequent use. The distinct necessities of storage are dependent on the sum of data to be saved and for the period it is to be saved.
5. Network: It is a connecting path which allows communication among compute systems and customers or among storage and compute systems.

These principal constituents are characteristically observed and administered as different units. However, to deal with data processing constraints, each of these constituents should work collectively. The other constituents of a cloud data center are ecological controls and power supplies, such as fire repression and air conditioning.

5.2.1 Application

An application offers an interface between the host and the user, and among multiple hosts. Classic business applications employ databases which contain a three-layered design—the application user interface is the front-end layer, the computing sense or the application itself is the middle layer, and the fundamental database which systematizes the data is the back-end layer, as shown in Fig. 5.1. Data is saved on the server so when the consumer makes a demand, the server replies. The application transmits demands to the fundamental operating system to carry out read/write (R/W) functions on the storage tools. Applications may be tiered upon the database that sequentially uses OS services in order to carry out R/W functions to storage tools. These R/W functions (I/O functions) allow communication between the back-end and front-end layers. Application input/output (I/O) trait is a vital structure that manipulates the whole functioning of the fundamental IT system. Applications perform a vital task to manage the conditions of demand and reply.

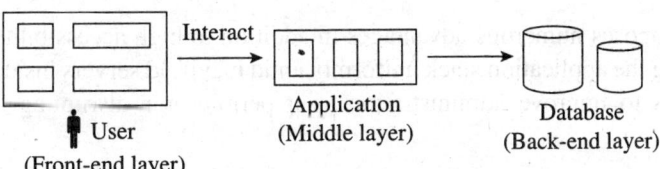

Fig. 5.1 Three-layered design

5.2.2 Database Management Systems

A database is a planned mode to save data in rationally ordered tables which are unified. A database assists to optimize the recovery and storage of data. A database management system (DBMS) is a compilation of computer programs which manage the preservation, formation, and employment of a database. The DBMS handles demand of an application for data and instructs the operating system to access suitable data. The DBMS controls incoming data, arranges, and allows the data to be extorted or customized by users or further programs. Some of the well-known tools of DBMS are SQL Server, Oracle, MySQL, among others.

5.2.3 Compute

Compute consists of physical components (hardware devices) that communicate with one another using logical component (software and protocols). It has three chief physical constituents—memory, central processing unit (CPU), and input/output (I/O) tools. Memory is used to save data, either provisionally or eternally. Read-only memory (ROM) and random access memory (RAM) are the two kinds of memory normally present in a compute system. I/O tools facilitate distribution and acquiring of data from and to the compute system. Despite physical constituents, it possesses a set of regulations known as protocols and compilation of programs known as software.

Communication may be one of the following types:
1. User to compute interactions: Controlled by fundamental input–output tools.
2. Compute to storage/compute interactions: Controlled by the host adapter or host regulator which unites a compute system to other compute storage/system tools. Host bus adaptor (HBA) is an illustration of a host regulator which unites compute systems to fibre channel storage tools.

Compute systems might be separate servers/blade servers, plain laptops, processor computers, and many more. Blade servers were constructed in response to the growing need of a computing authority which never utilizes a huge ground space. Blade servers combine system level and control operations into one, incorporate framework, and facilitate the adding of server units as hot pluggable constituents. Blade server technology significantly augments server compactness, and lesser power and cooling expenses improve server extension and reduce data center administration.

Server grouping is a way of assembling two or more servers and creating them to work collectively as a solo system. When a malfunction happens on one joint in a group, resources are readdressed and the workload is shifted to other nodes in the group. The group service is the software which unites the joints in the group and offers a solo-system vision to consumers who are using the group.

Multiple servers are fetched mutually in a group in order to enhance accessibility and functioning. These joints communicate with one another over a personal network. Communication among the joints of a group facilitates the group service to identify joint crashes and grade variations, and controls the group as one unit.

Server grouping proposes numerous advantages in addition to high accessibility. It also offers load balancing by allocating the application stack uniformly amid manifold servers inside the group. Another benefit of grouping is to improve administration as it permits non-disrupting upholding of server resources.

5.2.4 Storage

Data generated by companies or individuals should be saved so that it is effortlessly available when required. Tools intended for saving data are known as storage tools or merely storage. The sort of storage used differs on the basis of the kind of data and the point at which it is generated and used. Tools like memory in a digital camera or cell phone, CDROMs, DVDs, and disk drives in private computers are illustrations of storage tools. A storage tool utilizes optic, solid, or magnetic medium. DVD/ CD utilizes optical media, whereas diskettes, tapes, and disks use magnetic medium for storage.

Storage Device Options

A popular storage alternative for backup is the tape, because of its transportability and comparatively low price. Data is saved on the tape linearly all along the length of the tape. Recovery and exploration of data is consecutively made, exiting numerous seconds for accessing the data. On a tape drive, the read/write top strokes the surface of the tape that instigates the tape to debase or tire out after using repetitively. Further, the overhead allied with administrating tape media is noteworthy. A comparison of various storage devices is shown in Table 5.1. Optical disk storage is accepted in small, solo-user computing situations. Optical disks have a restricted pace and ability that confines the optical media use as a company data storage resolution.

Table 5.1 Comparison between various storage devices

Storage devices/Drives	Functions/Features
Tape drive	• Low-cost solution for long-term data storage • Sequential data access, physical wear and tear, and storage and retrieval overheads
Optical disk	• Write once and read many times • Limited in capacity and speed • Popular in small, single-user environments
Disk drive	• Random read and write access • Uses mechanical parts for data access • Most popular storage device with large storage capacity
Solid state drive	• Provides ultra-high performance required by mission- critical applications • Very low latency per input output, low power requirements, and very high throughput drive

A benefit of optical disk storage is the facility to write once and read many (WORM). To some extent, optical disks assure that the content has not been modified. Therefore, they may be used as low-price options for long-term storage of small quantities of fixed contents.

Disk drives are the most accepted storage means for accessing and saving data for concentrated functioning and online applications. A disk drive utilizes a swiftly stirring arm to read and write data diagonally, an even platter covered with magnetic elements. Data is shifted from the magnetic platter via the R/W head to the computer. Some platters are accumulated collectively with the R/W head and regulator, and this is termed a disk drive. Disks support swift access to arbitrary data positions. This indicates that data could be written or regained rapidly for a large number of synchronized applications or users. Besides, disk drives offer huge storage facility.

Solid state drives (SSDs), also known as flash drives, belong to the current generation. Flash drives employ semiconductor-based, solid-state memory (flash memory) in order to recover and save data.

Redundant Array of Inexpensive Disks and its Levels

Redundant array of inexpensive disks (RAID) is a means of saving the same data on diverse sites. Since the same data is saved, it is referred to as redundant. The data is saved on manifold disks to enhance functioning. An illustration of RAID is given in Fig. 5.2. The storage drive is separated into entities extending from a division (512 bytes) up to numerous megabytes. This is referred to as disk stripping, which is the procedure of separating a fraction of data into blocks and scattering the blocks athwart some panels on some hard disks. Every stripe is the dimension of the least panel.

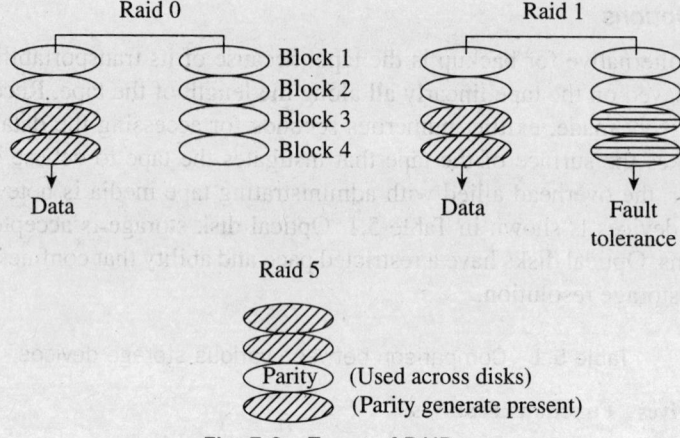

Fig. 5.2 Types of RAID

Disk drives are prone to collapses due to automatic deterioration and other ecological aspects. A disk drive crash might result in loss of data. At present, thousands of disk drives are employed by data centers in their storage infrastructures. Larger the number of disk drives in a storage collection, bigger the possibility of a disk crash in the range. RAID technology was built to improve this problem. RAID is a facilitating technology which controls manifold disks as components of an array. The definitions of various RAID levels are shown in Table 5.2. The technology offers data security against drive collapses. It concurrently also enhances storage system functioning by helping input/output from manifold disks.

Storage systems along with flash drives are profited in terms of security and functioning by executing RAID. Parity, mirroring, and striping are RAID techniques which materialize the basis for describing a variety of RAID levels. These techniques decide the accessibility of data and working of a RAID collection. The RAID regulator assists in executing these RAID techniques.

Table 5.2 Definition of various RAID levels

Raid levels	Definition
RAID 0	Striping with no fault tolerance
RAID 1	Disk mirroring
Nested	Combinations of RAID levels
RAID 3	Parity RAID with dedicated parity disk
RAID 5	Parity RAID with distributed parity across all the disks in the set
RAID 6	Distributed parity RAID with dual parity

Intelligent Storage System

High levels of accessibility, working, scalability, and safety are required by applications. A disk drive is a principal constituent of storage which manages the working of every storage system. A few of the older disk range technologies might not beat working chains because of the restrictions of a disk drive and its automatic constituents. A vital contribution has been made by RAID technology in order to augment storage dependability and working but disk drives, regardless of a RAID execution, might not meet functioning necessities.

A novel raise in storage, recognized as an intelligent storage system, has been developed along with advances in technology. Such intelligent storage systems are wealthy RAID ranges which offer exceedingly optimized input–output processing facilities. These storage systems are arranged with a huge sum of memory (known as cache) and manifold I/O trails, and utilizes complicated algorithms to meet the requisites of function-perceptive applications. These ranges include an operating situation which optimally and intelligently controls the allotment, consumption, and administration of storage resources.

An intelligent storage system consists of four main elements—physical disks, cache, front-end, and back-end. An I/O demand obtained from the compute system at the front-end port is developed via cache and the back-end in order to permit recovery and storage of data from the physical disk. A read demand may be serviced in a straightforward manner from cache in case the demanded data is discovered in cache.

5.2.5 Network

In cloud computing, for various computing communication, TCP/IP protocol is used for wide area network (WAN) and metropolitan area network (MAN), and Ethernet is used for local area network (LAN). Every compute system is associated with the network via a network interface card (NIC). Every NIC card has an exclusive address known as media access control (MAC) address that exclusively ascertains joints in the network.

Routers and switches are the usually used interconnect tools. A router is a tool or software which decides the subsequent network spot to which a package should be dispatched to arrive at its target. Router permits distinct networks to converse with one another. Switches permit diverse joints of a network to communicate reliably with one another and to offer scalability to the network. Co-axial cables, twisted pairs, optical fibres, etc., are the commonly used physical cables/media. Compute-to-storage communication is allowed by a variety of hardware constituents such as NIC, CNA, HBA, router, switch, protocols, and cables.

- Host bus adaptor (HBA): It is an application-specific integrated circuit (ASCI) board which carries out I/O interface operations amid the storage and the host, alleviating the CPU from added I/O dispensation workload.
- Converged network adaptor (CNA): It is a multi-function adapter that merges the functionality of a fibre channel HBA and an NIC card on only one adapter.

Compute systems converse with storage tools by using network or channel technologies. Channel technologies offer permanent associations amid compute systems and their tangential tools and support communication over small distances. While using channels, static associations are assigned to the operating system in advance. Rigid amalgamation between protocol transmission and the physical interface reduces the overhead needed for setting up communication and for transferring great quantities of data to the statically defined tools.

Network technologies are suppler than channel technologies and offer better detachment facilities. Network communication involves sharing bandwidth among numerous systems. Network and channel technologies employ different hardware constituents, such as interlock tools, buses, ports, cables, and many more procedures for communication. Routers, switches, modems, etc., are a few of the normally used interlock tools. Port permits connectivity between a device and other peripheral tools. Cables connect the compute systems to in-house or outside storage tools using fibre or copper optic media. Coaxial, twisted pair, optical fibre, etc., are a few of the normally used cables.

Peripheral component interconnect (PCI) is a condition which normalizes how PCI extension cards, like modems or network cards, switch information with the CPU. PCI offers the interconnection between the CPU and the connected tools. PCI's plug-and-play functionality allows the compute system to simply arrange and identify novel tools and cards.

5.3 STORAGE NETWORK TECHNOLOGIES AND VIRTUALIZATION

Cloud computing offers virtualization to provide services to more than one user at a time. So, proper communication is important between storage and virtualization devices. It is very essential to save data in a proficient way so that every time it is needed, it is effortlessly accessible with genuineness of data. Waiting too long for the repossession of data can lead to crash of the system. Simultaneously, the complete charge of running the information should also be low.

Just-in-time information for business users It is the information ought to be accessible to company users at the time they require it. The volatile expansion in online storage, break out of novel applications and servers, extending of mission-vital data all through businesses, and order for 24×7 data accessibility need to be addressed.

Resilient and flexible storage architecture The storage infrastructure should offer pliability and suppleness which changes with the varying necessities of the company. Storage must be scaled without negotiating the working necessities of the applications. Simultaneously, the entire charge of organizing information should be low.

Fibre channel storage area network (FC SAN) This is a high-pace, devoted network of compute systems and shared storage tools. FC SAN employs small computer system interface (SCSI) over FC protocol for transferring data between storage tools and compute systems. FC SAN guarantees high accessibility of vital applications by offering manifold connectivity trails amid storage tools and the compute system. Hot-plugging facilities are offered by FC SAN which allows corporations to deploy, organize, and fetch storage online without going through downtime of the server. FC offers a sequential data shift interface which may function over optical fibre (for front-end connectivity) and/or copper wire (for back-end connectivity).

Channel interface facilitates data speeds up to 16 Gbps and proposes throughput of 3200 MBps. FC communication employs fibre channel protocol (FCP), which is SCSI data, summarized and transferred inside fibre channel frames.

5.3.1 Components of Fibre Channel SAN

The following are the components of a Fibre Channel SAN:
- Node ports
- Cables
- Connectors
- Interconnecting devices
- Storage arrays
- SAN management software

The fibre channel fabric is a rational space wherein every joint converses with each other via an FC switch or manifold unified FC switches. If an FC fabric involves manifold switches, they are associated mutually via an FC cable. In a switched fabric, the association between any two switches is known as inter switch link (ISL). ISLs permit for two or more fibre channel switches to be allied collectively in order to develop a bigger fabric. ISLs are accustomed to shift from servers to storage ranges and the fabric administration traffic from one switch to another. Using inter-switch associations, a switched fabric may be extended to unite a proliferation of joints.

Compute systems converse with storage tools via specific vents known as ports. Ports are the fundamental construction blocks of an FC network. In the network, ports may be of different kinds as follows:
- **N_ port** It is an end point in the fabric. It is also called the node port. Characteristically, it is a compute system port host bus adaptor (HBA) or a storage range port which is associated to a switch within a switched fabric.
- **E_ port** It is an FC port which develops the association between two FC switches. This port is called the expansion port. The E_port on an FC switch unites to the E_port of other FC switches in the fabric via an ISL.
- **F_ port** It is a port on a switch which unites an N_port. It is also defined as a fabric port.
- **G_ port** It is a standard port which may function as an F_port or an E_port and decides its functionality mechanically all through initialization.

World wide name and channel address are the two kinds of addresses which are used for communication in an FC SAN situation. A fibre channel address is dynamically allotted when a joint port logs on to FC SAN. The FC address is a 24-bit processing plan along with three divisions. The first area in the FC address restrains the domain ID of the switch. A domain ID is an exclusive recognition number offered to every switch in FC SAN. The area ID is employed to recognize a cluster of switch ports employed to unite joints. An illustration of a cluster of ports along with a universal area ID could be a port card on the switch. The last field recognizes the port inside the cluster.

In FC, every tool is allocated a 64-bit unique identifier known as the world wide name (WWN). The fibre channel employs two kinds of WWNs—world wide port name (WWPN) and world wide node name (WWNN). Unlike an FC address, which is vigorously allocated, a WWN is a static term for every tool on an FC network. WWNs are like the MAC addresses employed in IP networking. WWNs are allocated via software or burned onto the hardware. A number of pattern descriptions in a SAN utilize WWN for recognizing HBAs and storage tools.

Zoning is an FC switch operation which allows joints inside the fabric to be rationally divided into pools which may converse with one another. When a tool (storage assortment or compute system) logs on a fabric, it is recorded through the name server. While a port logs on the fabric, it moves via a tool detection procedure with other tools recorded in the name server. The zoning operation manages this procedure by only permitting the members in a similar zone to set up these link-level services. Zoning can be classified into three kinds as described here:
1. Port zoning: In order to characterize zones, it utilizes the FC addresses of the physical ports. In port zoning, data access is decided by the physical switch port to which a joint is associated. Port zoning is known as hard zoning as well.
2. WWN zoning: In order to characterize zones, it utilizes world wide names. WWN zoning is also termed soft zoning. The main benefit of WWN zoning is its elasticity. It permits the SAN to be reflexed without having to rearrange the information of the zone.
3. Mixed zoning: It merges the traits of both port zoning and WWN zoning. Using mixed zoning allows a specific port to be united to the WWN of a joint. Zoning is used in combination with logical unit number (LUN) masking for controlling server access to storage.

5.4 OBJECT-BASED STORAGE TECHNOLOGIES

Object-based storage merges data with rich metadata in order to create an 'object'. Object-based storage saves data in a flat address space. There are no nested directories or hierarchies. Therefore, there are no restrictions on the files numbers which can be saved. The storage capability could be simply scaled from terabytes to petabytes. Every object in object storage is recognized through a distinctive ID known as object ID. This ID is created by using a disorder operation and assurances that each object is exclusively recognized. It also serves up as a unique pointer to an object similar to URLs that point to unique files on the Internet. HTTP communication has been employed by object storage as its typical interface. This makes it perfect for communicating data shifts along with storage sites via the Internet and the intranet.

Simple object access protocol (SOAP) is a means of switching messages between associates on a disseminated network, like the Internet. SOAP offers an array of XML aspects and components that are utilized to build a 'SOAP' message. The REST protocol is employed to recover information from a website by interpretation of web pages which comprise the XML file. XML reports depict information which is accessible on a web page. This information may subsequently be accessed by typing the uniform resource locator (URL) of the web page. Both REST and SOAP put their messages inside an HTTP message before conveying them.

Unstructured data is data which has no exact structure or plan which states how it is designed, saved, systematized, or accessed inside the system. Illustrations are contracts, text documents, movies, pictures, blogs, music, etc.

The design of SAN is extremely scalable, but is not a suggested alternative for applications that require sharing of data. Traditionally, unstructured data has been saved in NAS file systems. File systems systematize data into a hierarichal arrangement of files and folders or directories. For smaller data arrays, this system is fine but happens to be expensive and becomes difficult with the growth in the amount of data. These were the major causes for the materialization of object-based storage technologies. They have an extremely scalable design along with fine data sharing abilities.

Object-based storage has an even address space that fulfils the want for controlling RAID and LUN groups. A disorder performance is used to create an object ID for every object that serves as an influential means for review capability.

Rather than RAID systems used for backup strengthening, storage managers can force object-based storage to simply generate multiple copies, as required, with every copy recognized with a similar object storage ID. These copies may further be allocated geologically, increasing the defence offered by replication. By using an even address space, object-based storage facilitates elastic scalability in terms of statistics and capability of objects. Object-based storage systems which might expansively be used, include cloud, multimedia substance-rich web applications, documentation, among others.

5.5 UNIFIED STORAGE

Unified storage merges SAN-based, object-based, and NAS-based access inside a single amalgamated platform. It supports NAS protocols (i.e., NFS for UNIX or Linux and CIFS for Windows) fibre channel, iSCSI, REST, SOAP, and FCoE protocols. The capability to assist multiple protocols from a similar storage system aids to liberally merge and counterpart workloads to really enhance consumption. Possessing a one-data model and toolset for amalgamated storage facilitates a reliable administration structure athwart various workloads and applications. This significantly reduces management and generates a hierarchy of standards from administration of physical storage to application-level incorporation. Amalgamated storage has been offered by storage consolidation. This lessens the storage necessities of the corporation which, sequentially, lessens the charge of attaining storage benefits, space power, and cooling. Amalgamated storage offers an exceedingly scalable design which may be scaled from workgroup to complete enterprise systems.

5.6 BUSINESS CONTINUITY

At present, constant information access is compulsory for smooth performance of corporation functions. The charge of inaccessibility of information is bigger than ever; the outages in reputed companies are estimated at millions of dollars per hour.

Business continuity (BC) is a significant procedure for classifying and executing. BC is an incorporated and business-ample procedure which comprises each activity (in-house and peripheral to IT) that a corporation should carry out in order to alleviate the effect of intended and unintended downtime. BC involves arranging for, responding to, and improving from a system outage which unfavorably influences corporation functions. The aim of a corporation permanence resolution is to guarantee the 'information accessibility' needed to perform essential company functions. There are synchronized procedures of reinstating the infrastructure, systems, and data, mandatory to support chief ongoing corporation functions in danger. It is a procedure of reinstating or recommencing corporation operations from a reliable replica of the data. After completion of all the retrievals, the data is authorized to guarantee its accuracy.

Hot site It is a site where functions of businesses may be stimulated, in the event of a catastrophe. It is a site prepared with all the necessary operating systems, hardware, network, and application support which help carry out corporation functions and where the tool is accessible and operating at all times.

Cold site It is a site where functions of businesses may be stimulated, in the event of a catastrophe. It has least IT infrastructure and ecological amenities in place, but is inactivated.

Cluster A set of servers and other essential resources are united to function as a solo system. Clusters guarantee high load balancing and accessibility. Characteristically, in failover clusters, single server works on an application and modernizes the data, and the other is reserved on stand-in to take over entirely, whenever requisite. In more complicated clusters, manifold servers may access data, whilst usually one server is reserved on stand-in.

5.7 CLOUD BACKUP

Backup is a replica of the manufactured data, generated and maintained for the only intention of improving corrupted or deleted data. With mounting business and rigid orders for data storage, accessibility, and preservation, corporations are dealing with the assignment of backing up data.

Corporations require backup data at a cheaper price with the least number of resources. Corporations should guarantee that true data is in the correct place at the correct time. Backup technologies, maintenance, and revival necessities for applications and data are a vital step to guarantee successful execution of the revival and backup solution. The resolution should allow effortless recovery and revival from backups, as required by the corporations.

Backups are carried out for three key reasons—documentation, operational restores, and disaster recovery. Disaster recovery tackles the condition to be capable to reinstate all, or a great part, of an IT infrastructure in case of a major catastrophe. The backup replicas are used for reinstating data at an alternating location when the primary location is harmed because of a catastrophe.

Based on necessities, corporations use diverse backup approaches for catastrophe recovery. Data in the construction situation alters with each industry deal and function. Operational backup is a backup of data at a point in time and is used to reinstate data in the occurrence of data loss or rational corruptions which can happen during routine procedures. The reinstatement needed in most corporations falls in this class.

Documentation is a general prerequisite used to protect contract report, email, and other corporation work goods for rigid approval. The rules could be in-house, governmental, or may result from particular business necessities. Backups are also carried out to tackle archival necessities.

The majority of corporations use an amalgamation of these three kinds of backup to meet the backup and recovery necessities. Full backup is a backup of the total data on the manufactured amounts at some point in time and is generated by replication of the data on the manufacture amounts to a secondary storage tool. This is much quicker, but takes longer to reinstate. Cumulative backup imitates data which has been distorted since the last full backup. This technique takes more time than incremental backup, but is quicker to reinstate.

Synthetic full backup is another kind of backup which is employed in executions where the construction amount resources cannot be entirely set aside for a backup procedure for expanded phases. It is generally generated from the freshest full backup and all the incremental backups worked subsequently. A synthetic full backup facilitates a full backup copy to be generated offline devoid of distracting the input–output operation on the manufacture amount. This also frees up network resources from the backup process, making them accessible for other construction uses. A backup system uses client server design with a backup server and multiple backup consumers. The backup server controls the backup functions and sustains the backup list that restrains information regarding the backup metadata and backup procedure. The backup server relies on the backup consumers for collecting the data to be backed up. The backup consumers may be native to the server or may occupy an additional server, apparently to back up the data perceptible to that server.

The backup metadata has been obtained by the backup server from the backup consumers to carry out its actions. The metadata is saved either locally inside the backup server or outwardly in a storage range. The storage joint is accountable for writing data to the backup tool. Characteristically, the storage joint is incorporated through the backup server and both are hosted on a similar physical platform. The storage node is directly connected to a backup device. Some backup architecture refers to the storage node as the media server because it connects to the storage device.

5.8 CLOUD AND DISASTER RECOVERY

The backup server commences the backup procedure for distinct consumers according to the backup program organized for them. The backup server synchronizes the backup procedure with all the constituents in a backup arrangement. The backup server sustains the information regarding the backup consumers to be dealt with and the storage joints to be employed in a backup function. The backup server recovers the backup-concerned information from the backup list and, on the basis of this information, initiates a suitable storage joint to put in the backup media into the backup tools.

Concurrently, it initiates the backup consumers to transmit their metadata to the backup server and to back up the data to a suitable storage joint. On getting this demand, the backup consumer transmits trailing information to the backup server. The backup server inscribes this metadata on its backup list. The backup consumer transmits the data to the storage joint, and the storage joint inscribes the data to the storage tool. The storage joint transmits trailing information to the backup server as well in order to maintain it updated regarding the media being employed in the backup procedure. A reinstate procedure is manually commenced by the backup consumer. Upon getting a restore demand, the user unlocks the reinstate application in order to analyse the consumer's record which has been backed up. Whilst choosing the consumer for which a reinstate demand has been made, the user also requires recognizing the consumer who will obtain the reinstated data. Data may be reinstated on a similar consumer or on another consumer, given the appropriate consents, and then the user chooses the data which is to be reinstated. Since the total information arrives from the backup list, the reinstated application should communicate with the backup server as well. The backup server recognizes the backup media needed for the reinstate and informs the storage joint to put in the backup media. Then, the data is interpreted and transmitted to the consumer which has been recognized to obtain the reinstated data.

Tape drives, a low-priced alternative, is used for backup. Tape drives are termed for sequential or linear access tools as the data is printed or interpreted consecutively. A physical tape library supplies lodging and authority for a number of tape cartridges and tape drives. Disks have now restored tapes as the primary tool for saving backup data, due to their functioning benefits. Backup-to-disk systems propose simplicity of execution, reduced price, and enhanced importance of service.

Apart from functioning advantages in words of data shift charge, disks too propose quicker revival in contrast to tapes. Backing up disk storage systems proposes lucid benefits, owing to their essential random access and RAID security facilities. Several types of backup permit for backup descriptions to remain on the disk for a period of time even after they have been staged. This facilitates a much quicker reinstate.

A virtual tape library (VTL) also has the same components as that of a physical tape library. As for backup software, both physical tape library and virtual tape library are the same. Virtual tape uses disks for backup. In emulation software, each virtual tape is assigned a portion of a LUN on the disk with the database having a list of virtual tapes. A virtual tape can span multiple LUNs, if required. File system awareness is not required while using backup to disk due to virtual tape solutions. Virtual tape supports instantaneous support, which is distinct from physical tape library, and has mechanical delays.

5.9 REPLICATION TECHNOLOGIES

The procedure of generating an accurate/similar replica of data is known as replication. The accurate copy of data that is generated is known as replica. Such replicas may be used for revival and resurrect functions in the occurrence of data loss. The main aim of replication is to allow users to have the chosen data at the correct place, in a condition suitable to the needs of revival. This permits reviving industry functions by using the replicas. Replicas may be used to address a number of business permanence performances, such as those given here:

1. Offering an alternating source for backup to enhance the effect on construction
2. Offering a source for rapid revival
3. Facilitating judgment support actions, like reporting
4. Mounting and analysing projected modification to an application or an operating situation
5. Reviving an application from the copy in the occurrence of a malfunction in the source level

Key Factors to Consider with Replicas

Replicas may be continuous or point-in-time (PIT).
- Continuous replica: The data on the replica is matched with the manufacture data during the entire period.
- PIT: The data on the replica is a copied picture of the manufacture at a certain timestamp.

A reliable replica guarantees that the data lessened in the compute system is appropriately detained on the disk at the time the replica is generated. Guaranteeing control is the chief necessity of every replication technology. Local replication is the procedure of replicating data inside a similar range or similar data center. Local replication technologies may be categorized on the basis of the site where the replication is carried out.

1. Compute-based: Replication is carried out using the resources of the CPU of the compute system through software which is working on the compute system. Compute-based regional replication may be more classified as file system snapshot and logical volume management (LVM)-based mirroring.
2. Storage array-based: Replication is carried out on the storage range by using the resources of the CPU of the range via the operating environment of range.

For every business function, the replica may be accessed by an alternating server. In such replications, the requisite number of replica tools must be chosen from a similar group and then the data must be replicated amid the source–replica pair. Storage group-based regional replication may be classified as follows:
- Pointer-based virtual replication
- Pointer-based complete degree replication
- Complete degree mirroring

Remote replication is the procedure of generating replicas of data to be kept in isolated places for safety. Remote replicas assist corporations to improve the threats associated with regionally determined disasters. Similar to regional replicas, they may also be employed for further business functions. The infrastructure where the data is saved at the chief location is known as source. The infrastructure where the replica is saved at the isolated location is called target. Data has to be shifted from the source location to the target location over several networks. The two fundamental manners of remote replications are as follows—synchronous and asynchronous replication.

For improvement of threats recognized in two-site replication, three-site replication is employed. In a three-site replication, data from the source location is replicated to two remote locations. Replication might be synchronous or asynchronous. SAN-based isolated replication permits the data replication among assorted dealer storage groups. Data is moved from one group to the other. The technology makes application and server operating system autonomous, as the replication functions are carried out by one of the storage groups. There is no effect on the manufacturer servers or the LAN as replication is made by the group and the data is moved over the SAN.

5.10 TRADITIONAL DATA CENTER MANAGEMENT

A traditional data center is different from cloud data center as shown in Figs 5.3 and 5.4. The chief administration actions in a conventional or traditional data center are as follows:
1. Vigilance and scrutinizing
2. Reporting
3. Accessibility administration
4. Capability administration
5. Functioning administration
6. Safety administration

Scrutinizing helps in investigating the condition and consumption of constituents of different storage infrastructure. Compute systems, storage, and networks are the chief constituents which should be observed for accessibility, capacity, functioning, and safety. Accessibility means the availability of a constituent to carry out a preferred function. Scrutinizing software constituents or hardware constituents for convenience comprises inspecting their accessibility condition by listening to prearranged signals from tools.

Cloud Data Center 111

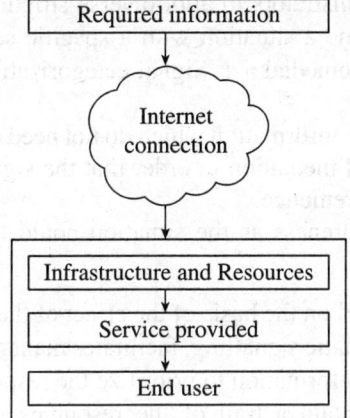

Fig. 5.3 Services provided by traditional data center

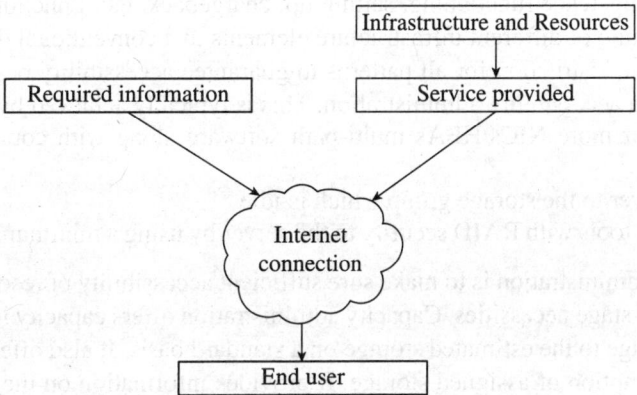

Fig. 5.4 Services provided by cloud data center

Capacity refers to the sum of storage infrastructure accessible resources. Scarce capacity might lead to tainted functioning or even accessibility of service/application. Capacity scrutinizing guarantees continuous data scalability and accessibility by preventing outages prior to their occurrence. Capacity scrutinizing is predictive and precautionary, and generally controlled with superior investigative devices.

Functioning scrutinizing assesses how proficiently constituents of distinct storage infrastructure are working and assists in recognizing blockage. Functioning scrutinizing generally determines and evaluates actions in terms of reply period or in terms of the capability to act upon at some predefined stage. It also deals with consumption of resources that influence the manner in which the resources act and react.

Scrutinizing cloud data center resources for safety assists to trail and prevent illegal access and login crashes, whether malevolent or unintentional. Safety scrutinizing also assists in tracking illegal arrangements and modifications of storage infrastructure constituents. Physical safety of a storage infrastructure is also persistently scrutinized by using video cameras, biometric scans, or badge readers.

Signalling of procedures is an essential part of scrutinizing. There are some situations viewed by scrutinizing, like failure of switches, power, memory, or disks that might affect the accessibility of services which need instant managerial concentration.

Scrutinizing devices facilitate administrators to allot diverse strictness stages for diverse situations in the storage infrastructure. Every time a situation with a specific severity stage occurs, a signal is forwarded to the manager to begin a remedial act. Signal categorizations may vary from information alarms to serious alarms.

1. Information signals offer valuable information which do not need any interference by the manager.
2. Warning signals need managerial mediation in order that the signalled situation is restricted and does not come in the way of convenience.
3. Serious signals need instant awareness as the situation could have an influence on the entire working system or accessibility.

Signals may be allocated a severity level on the basis of the effect of the signalled situation. Continuous scrutinizing, in combination with automatic signalling, facilitates managers to react to malfunctions proactively and rapidly. Signalling offers information to prioritize the response of managers to procedures.

It is hard for corporations to maintain a trail of the resources which they encompass in their conventional data center (e.g., the number of storage groups, the group dealers, means of usage of the storage groups, and the applications). Reporting on conventional data center resources comprises maintenance track and collecting information from diverse elements. This information is accumulated to create news for competence functioning, setting up, chargeback, etc. Functioning reports offer facts regarding the functioning of different infrastructure elements in a conventional data center.

Setting up a suitable instruction for all patterns to guarantee accessibility based on service levels is the vital assignment in accessibility administration. This is typically achieved by:

1. Installing two or more NICs/HBAs multi-path software along with course failover ability and server grouping
2. Linking the server to the storage group which is idle
3. Gaining storage tools with RAID security to the server by using a minimum of two front-end ports

The aim of capacity administration is to make sure sufficient accessibility of resources for every service based on their service-stage necessities. Capacity administration offers capacity investigation and evaluates the assigned storage to the estimated storage on a standard basis. It also offers a trend investigation of the genuine consumption of assigned storage. It provides information on the speed of utilization as well, which should be streamlined alongside storage achievement and installment schedules. Capacity administration takes into consideration the future wants of resources and origin of observation and problem-solving to collect such information.

Functioning administration makes certain the most favourable functional competence of each constituent. Functioning analysis is a vital action which assists in the recognition of the functioning of storage infrastructure components. This study offers information on whether a constituent is congregating the probable functioning levels. Some functioning management actions are commenced for the installment of a server or application in the existing storage infrastructure. Each constituent should be validated for functioning abilities, as described by the service levels.

Safety administration avoids illegal access and arrangement of storage infrastructure constituents. The safety administration assignments in a SAN situation comprise arrangement of zoning to confine unauthorized access to the specific storage group ports. Masking prevents data corruption on the storage cluster by restricting compute access to a specific compilation of consistent devices.

5.11 INFORMATION LIFE CYCLE MANAGEMENT

Data, when first generated, often has the highest cost and is used persistently. As data gets older, it is not accessed very often and is of less worth for the corporation. Comprehension of the information life cycle assists in the installation of suitable storage infrastructure, consistent with the varying importance of information. For instance, in an application of sales order, the importance of the information varies from the time the order is placed till the time the contract becomes void. The importance of the information is highest when a corporation gets a new sales order and processes it to distribute the goods. After the fulfillment of order, the order or consumer data is not required to be accessible for concurrent access. This data may be shifted by the corporation to a less exclusive secondary storage along with lesser availability and accessibility necessities.

Information life cycle management (ILM) is a procedure for organizing information via its life cycle, from beginning to its clearance. The key assessments required to be made as division of the ILM strategy for the business are as follows:

When is it important to record the business data from live or transactional databases to archived databases?

and

Up to what phase will the data be saved in the operational databases before they may be set out forever?

The vital features are as follows:
1. Insignificant or surplus information slows application functioning and augments the time needed to advance applications and backup databases.
2. In-house features will principally be determined during negotiations, which refers to how valuable the information will be to the corporation in its business dealings.
3. Peripheral aspects will be principally directed by authorized and inflexible necessities; in particular, the least sum of time information enclosed by that legislation must be reserved.

After the cancellation of the contract, the corporation may record or set out the data to generate space for further high-worth information. Nowadays, businesses need data to be guarded and accessible 24×7. Data centers may achieve this with suitable and best use of storage infrastructure. An effectual information administration strategy is needed to support this infrastructure and control its profits. Information life cycle management (ILM) is a practical approach which permits an IT corporation to efficiently control data all through its life cycle, on the basis of predefined business strategies. This permits the corporations to optimize the storage infrastructure for highest return on assets. An ILM policy must comprise the following features:

Business-centric It must be incorporated with chief applications, plans and procedures, of the corporation to meet both the present and future augmentation in information.

Centrally managed Information and other resources of a company must be centrally managed by the ILM policies.

Policy-based The execution of ILM must not be limited to only some sections. ILM should be executed as a strategy and must include all business resources, procedures, and applications.

Heterogeneous An ILM policy must take into consideration all kinds of operating systems and storage platforms.

Optimized While the importance of information changes, an ILM policy must be able to accommodate diverse storage necessities and allot storage resources on the basis of the importance of information to the corporation.

Tiered storage Tiered storage is an approach to describe distinct storage layers to lessen the overall storage charge. Every layer has diverse levels of functioning, security, data access regularity, and other negotiations. Information is saved and moved among distinct layers on the basis of its importance over time.

Data accessed reasonably and other vital data are saved on tier 2 storage that can be a less costly media proposing modest security and functioning. Occasion-precise or not, often, accessed information can be saved on subordinate tiers of storage.

5.12 CLOUD ANALYTICS

Cloud analytics is a sort of cloud service module where exploration of data and associated services are carried out on a private or public cloud. Cloud investigatives may mention to any business aptitude procedure or data investigative which is performed in association with a cloud service supplier. Cloud analytics is also called SaaS-based business intelligence (BI).

Cloud analytics is chiefly a cloud-facilitated resolution which permits a corporation or person to work intelligence measures or business studies. Such services and resolutions are distributed via cloud modules, such as hosted data storehouses, SaaS BI and social media investigative goods controlled by the cloud. Cloud analytics services act like a characteristic data investigative service, offering analogous facilities and traits. The single dissimilarity is that cloud investigation incorporates all or some of the service modules of cloud computing in distributing that resolution.

Though cloud analytics is chiefly a SaaS-based resolution, it may also be a hybrid cloud solution. For instance, cloud or hosted data storehouses not only offer the infrastructure to save enormous sums of data, but also permit business intelligence/data investigative software to recover valuable information where and when it is needed. Furthermore, several resolutions may also be distributed via PaaS, wherever the corporation/end users may generate proprietary data investigative software to work on the cloud storage infrastructure.

Cloud analytics is a service module wherein constituents of the data investigative procedure are offered via a private or public cloud. Cloud analytics services and applications are characteristically proposed underneath a contribution-based or utility (pay per use) costing model. The six chief constituents of analytics are described by Gartner [9] as data models, data sources, computing power, processing applications, sharing or storage of results, and analytic models. In its observation, any investigative proposal 'in which one or more of these elements is implemented in the cloud', is certified as cloud analytics. Gartner forecaster Bill Gassman remarked that dealers providing cloud-based technologies intended to support a one-component mention to themselves as cloud analytics corporations that may trigger mystification for prospective users.

Illustrations of cloud analytics services and goods comprise cloud-based social media investigative, SaaS BI and hosted data storehouses. SaaS business intelligence can transfer BI applications to end users from a hosted site. This module is scalable and makes set-up simpler and is less costly. However, it might not propose similar attributes as an internal application.

Cloud-based social media analytics involves the isolated provisioning of devices which comprise applications for choosing social media sites which serve your intentions, divide applications for gathering data, data investigative software, and storage services.

A hosted data storehouse is a centralized depository for business data which is made accessible to users from an isolated site controlled by the service supplier, instead of being positioned on the personal systems of corporations.

Before spending in cloud analytics, a corporation requires to completely grab the amount of what is occupied. Spending on cloud analytics may be rewarding for a corporation but appropriate preparation is necessary to make sure that all six investigative components are concealed.

5.13 COMPUTING ON DEMAND

On-demand computing (ODC) is a model of computing at enterprise level. In this technology, resources are offered on a pay-per-use basis. ODC accomplishes computing resources such as software applications, storage ability, and computational speed accessible to consumers when and as required for particular provisional projects, known or unanticipated workloads, regular work, or permanent computing and technological necessities.

ODC is recognized as utility computing or on-demand computing too. The main benefit of ODC is its low basic price, since computational resources are substantially hired when they are needed. This gives price savings over buying them completely. The idea of ODC is not very new. Before 1970, at the Massachusetts Institute of Technology (MIT), a visionary and perceptive statement had been made by John McCarthy that one day computing might be planned to offer services much as public utilities do. Over the next two decades, IBM and other mainframe suppliers made database storage and computing power accessible to several banks and other large associations around the world. Later, the business model was reformed since low-priced computers became omnipresent in the world of business.

During the 1990s, computer data centers were crammed with thousands of servers and utility computing appeared. Cloud computing, SaaS, and on-request computing—each one is a model for repackaging computational network services and software applications. The real and notional technologies, which permit these companies to build up ODC services comprise computer clusters, supercomputers, virtualization, and distributed computing.

The on-request model was established to overcome the general confront to a business enterprise of being able to fulfill changeable requirements competently. Since a business enterprise's requirement on computing resources may fluctuate severely, sustaining adequate resources to fulfil peak necessities may be expensive. On the other hand, if the business enterprise reduces prices by merely sustaining nominal computing resources, there will not be adequate resources to fulfil peak needs.

On-request computing goods are swiftly becoming common in the market. HP, Microsoft, Computer Associates, Sun Microsystems, and IBM are among the more famous on-request sellers. These companies mention to their on-request services and goods by various names. IBM names it as 'On Demand Computing'. Ideas such as adaptive management, utility computing, autonomic computing, and grid computing appear very similar to the idea of on-request computing. Senior analyst with ZapThink, Jason Bloombergutter says that on-request computing is a wide class which comprises all the other expressions, each one of which indicates something different. Utility computing, for instance, is an on-request tactic which merges infrastructure management and outsourced computing resources with a usage-based compensation arrangement (this tactic is occasionally called metered services).

Points to Remember

1. The core elements of a cloud data center consist of compute (server), storage, network, application, and DBMS.
2. DBMS consists of an organized form of data for fetching required information.
3. Compute is a physical computing device that acts as an interface between the operating system, application, and stored database.

4. Storage is a device used for physically storing data.
5. Object-oriented storage merges data with rich metadata in order to create an object.
6. Unified storage merges SAN-based, object-based, and NAS-based access inside a single amalgamated platform.
7. Different types of backup are—full backup, cumulative backup, and synthetic full backup.
8. The backup server recovers the backup-concerned information from the backup list and, on the basis of this data, initiates a suitable storage joint to put in the backup media into the backup tools.
9. The procedure of generating an accurate/similar replica of data is known as replication. Replicas may be continuous or point in time.
10. An application is a computer program dedicated for a particular type of application that supports applications with various computing operations.
11. Networking refers to the physical connection between various computers for sharing of resources and data.
12. The key management activities in a traditional date center are as follows:
    (a) Monitoring and alerting
    (b) Reporting
    (c) Availability management
    (d) Capacity management
    (e) Performance management
    (f) Security management
13. Cloud service has diverse characteristics due to which it is different from traditional hosting, as it is sold on demand and offers flexible services fully managed by the providers.
14. The information Life Cycle Management policy should be business-centric, centrally managed, policy-based, heterogeneous, optimized and with tiered storage.

Key Terms

Converged network adaptor (CAN) It is a multi-function adapter which consolidates the functionality of an NIC card and a fibre channel.

E_port It is an FC port that forms the connection between two FC switches.

F_port It is a port on a switch that connects an N_port.

G_port This port can operate both as E-port or F-port and at the time of initialization, its functionality is automatically set.

Host bus adapter (HBA) It is a type of application-dedicated service board that works as an interface between the host and storage, that makes the CPU free from additional workload.

N_port It is an end point in the fabric.

Point-in-time (PIT) At a particular instant of time, replica (a separate copy) of the data is created for future reference.

RAID It is a method that supports storing the same data at different locations.

SOAP (simple object access protocol) It is a way of exchanging messages between peers on a distributed network, such as the Internet.

Solid state drives (SSDs) An SSD is a storage device that stores constant data on solid-state flash memory.

Tiered storage Tiered storage is an approach to define different storage levels so as to reduce the total storage cost.

Unified storage Unified storage is a storage system that provides facility for managing files and applications with single device in a customized and manageable form.

Multiple-choice Questions

1. The essential cloud components are:
   (a) Clients
   (b) Data center
   (c) Distributed servers
   (d) All the above

2. The disadvantage of an optical disk is/are:
   (a) Limited capacity
   (b) Limited speed
   (c) Single user environment
   (d) All the above

3. Disk mirroring is used in:
   (a) RAID 0
   (b) RAID 1
   (c) RAID 3
   (d) RAID 6

4. F port is also known as:
   (a) N port
   (b) E port
   (c) Fabric port
   (d) C port

5. Soft zoning is referred as:
   (a) Port zoning
   (b) WWN zoning
   (c) Mixed zoning
   (d) None of these

6. The key management activity in a traditional data center is/are:
   (a) Application
   (b) Reporting
   (c) Storage
   (d) None of these

7. _____ is a way of exchanging messages between peers on a distributed network.
   (a) SOAP
   (b) HTTP
   (c) REST Protocol
   (d) None of these

8. Sequential data access is found in:
   (a) Tape drives
   (b) Optical disks
   (c) Disk drives
   (d) None of these

9. Physical security of a storage infrastructure is continuously monitored using _____.
   (a) Badge readers
   (b) Biometric scans
   (c) Video cameras
   (d) All the above

10. Alert classifications can start from _____.
    (a) Information alerts
    (b) Warning alerts
    (c) Fatal alerts
    (d) All the above

Review Questions

1. What are the core components of cloud computing?
2. What do you understand by information life cycle management?
3. What are the different ways to manage traditional data centers?
4. What are the various storage devices used in cloud data centers?
5. What is the advantage of redundant array of inexpensive disks?
6. How many types of RAID are present? Explain in detail.
7. Explain the key management activities of a traditional data center.
8. What are the various replication technologies? Explain in detail.
9. What is the application of intelligent storage systems?

10. What are the components of fibre channel SAN?
11. How are object-based storage technologies different from other storage technologies?
12. What are cloud analytics?

References

1. *Cloud Security A Comprehensive Guide to Secure Cloud Computing*, Ronald L. Krutz and Russell Dean Vines, ISBN: 978-0-470-58987-8, Wiley Publication, 2010
2. *Cloud Computing for Dummies*, Judith Hurwitz, Robin Bloor, Marcia Kaufman, and Dr. Fern Halper, ISBN-10: 0470484705, Wiley Publication, 1st edition, November 16, 2009
3. *Cloud Computing Technologies and Strategies*, Brian J.S. Chee and Curtis Franklin, Jr, ISBN 9781439806128, CRC Press, April 7, 2010
4. *Cloud Computing: A Practical Approach*, Anthony T. Velte, Toby J. Velte, Ph.D., Robert Elsenpeter, ISBN-10: 0071626948, McGraw-Hill, 1st edition, November 1, 2009
5. *Grid and Cloud Computing*, Katarina StanoevskaSlabeva, Thomas Wozniak, and Santi Ristol, ISBN-10: 3642051928, Springer, 2010 edition, November 19, 2009
6. *Implementing and Developing Cloud Applications*, David E.Y. Sarna, ISBN-10: 1439830827, Publisher: Auerbach Publications, November 26, 2010
7. Market-oriented cloud Computing: Vision, Hype, and Reality for Delivering IT Services as Computing Utilities, In High Performance Computing and Communications, R. Buyya, C.S. Yeo, and S. Venugopal, 2008. HPCC'08. 10th IEEE International Conference on pp. 4–13 IEEE, 2008
8. *Mastering Cloud Computing*, Rajkumar Buyya, Christian Vecchhiola, S. ThamaraiSelvi, Tata McGraw Hill Education Private Limited, 2008
9. *Cloud Computing and Virtualization*, V. Rajeswara Rao, V. Shubba Ramaiah, ISBN-10: 938363504, BS Publications/BSP Books, 2014

Answers to Multiple-choice Questions

1. (d)	3. (b)	5. (b)	7. (a)	9. (d)
2. (d)	4. (c)	6. (b)	8. (a)	10. (d)

CHAPTER 6

Virtualization Technology (At Server)

Learning Outcomes

After completing this chapter, students will be able to:

- comprehend virtualization
- explain need of compute virtualization
- understand virtual clusters
- apply various techniques used for computing virtualization
- describe various resource management tools
- describe application of virtual machine
- describe hypervisor taxonomy
- appreciate the concept of virtual machine
- explain data center virtualization

6.1 INTRODUCTION

Virtualization refers to a technology that is used to make physical resources available as virtual resources. Many IT resources can be virtualized, for example, server/compute, storage device, network, etc. Cloud computing technologies use a set of techniques to create virtual servers, virtual storage, virtual networks, and perhaps virtual applications as well. Virtualization software is used to make a physical server like a virtual server. The physical server on which virtualization software runs is called host. Many virtual servers can be handled by one physical server. Each virtual machine has its own operating system which we call a guest operating system. System software and application software running on a virtual machine are not aware of the virtualization software running on a physical server.

Operating system-level virtualization can be achieved by installing virtualization software on already installed operating systems. For achieving hardware-based virtualization, tools are directly installed on a physical host machine. Virtualization tools like hypervisor are generally used for this purpose. In this chapter, we will discuss server virtualization in detail.

6.2 VIRTUALIZATION REFERENCE MODEL

The virtualization model consists of a host or physical resources in the first layer, virtualization tool in the second layer, and a guest in the third layer (application as well as virtual image) as shown in Fig. 6.1. Virtual hardware is used by a virtual machine (VM). In this virtualization model, the physical machine can be virtualized as virtual machines, that is, virtual machine 1, application 1, and application 2. Each virtual machine has its own operating system and applications. These virtual machines can be managed by the virtual machine manager. Virtual machines are configured with many virtual hardware tools, which can be added at the time of VM creation.

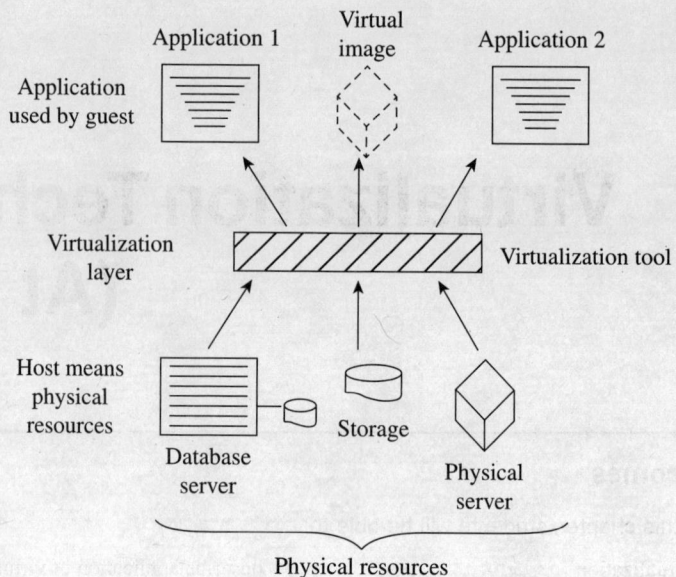

Fig. 6.1 Virtualization reference model

6.3 ADVANTAGES OF VIRTUALIZATION

The advantages of virtualization include the following:

1. It allows any network-enabled device to access any network application over any network.
2. It maintains isolation of one workload from another application to enhance security in the environment.
3. Virtualization of an application allows users to be comfortable with different versions of the operating system.
4. It can support and allow application with multiple instances to run on various machines concurrently.
5. It optimizes the use of a single system.
6. It enhances the reliability or availability of an application through redundancy.

6.4 SERVER/COMPUTE VIRTUALIZATION

Server/Compute virtualization in cloud computing refers to making a virtual edition of a device or resource, such as a server, storage device, network, or an operating system where the structure splits the resources as one or more environments for execution. Partitioning of the hard drive is also considered virtualization. Virtualized resources can interact with users and act as a single logical resource, and permits you to achieve more with your prevailing resources. Lack of virtualization hardware is dedicated to a particular objective, whether or not it is used vigorously; the whole configuration has to be reconstructed in case of failure of the hardware. It offers us the provision to work on various platforms.

A number of hardware tools assign as much place as required at any instant of time. This scalability permits you to pay only for what has been used by you and, if your needs change, new requirements are instantaneously met accordingly. In a cloud environment, there is a load balancer to monitor various available hardware tools to enhance services and consistency of services provided to the cloud users. With cloud computing and virtualization, you can enhance consistency by removing the particular point of failure. You can better consume the resources so that you may use what you require and make a payment for only what you use.

The following are the advantages of server/compute virtualization:
1. Consistency
2. Energy efficiency
3. Enhanced disaster recovery
4. Cost savings

A virtual machine is a reasonable computing system like a physical machine which governs an application and operating system (OS). An OS which operates within a virtual machine is known as guest operating system. Only one supported guest operating system can operate a single virtual machine at a time. Every virtual machine is autonomous and operates its application on its own.

Before Virtualization
- The infrastructure was expensive.
- Software and hardware were tightly coupled.
- There was a single operating system.
- There used to be underutilized accessible resources.
- Various applications were supported by the same machine.

Virtual Components in a Virtual Machine

Some of the virtual components used in a virtual machine are as follows:

Virtual central processing unit (vCPU) One or more vCPUs are used at the time of virtual machine configuration. The number of vCPUs may be increased or decreased according to the needs.

Virtual random access memory (vRAM) vRAM is the quantity of memory assigned to a virtual machine and it is clear to a guest operating system. This memory range may be altered according to the needs.

Virtual disk A virtual disk saves the virtual machine's operating system, application data, program files, and other data related to the virtual machine. A virtual machine must have at least a single virtual disk.

Virtual network adaptor (vNIC) It provides a similarity between virtual machine and physical machines, and between virtual machines on the same computer system and between virtual machines on different computer systems. vNIC performs specifically like a physical NIC.

Virtual DVD/CD-ROM and floppy drives These tools facilitate in plotting the virtual machines drive either to the image file on the storage or the physical drive.

Virtual SCSI (Small Computer System Interface) controller In order to retrieve virtual disks, virtual SCSI controllers are used by a virtual machine.

Virtual USB controllers These facilitate a virtual machine to associate to the physical USB controller and to retrieve the associated USB tool.

Virtual machine console A VM console provides the screen functionalities, the mouse, and keyboard to establish an OS, for which a virtual machine console is used.

The virtual machine console permits access to the BIOS of the virtual machine. It proposes the skill to power the virtual machine on/off and to reorganize it. Figure 6.2 shows virtualization management.

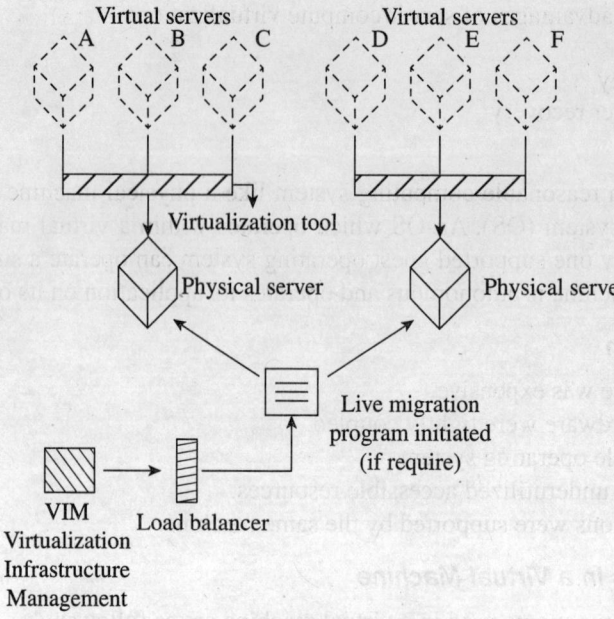

Fig. 6.2 Compute virtualization

With the help of virtualized software, various instances of physical servers are made available to cloud users. Load balancer works at the virtualization environment to keep track of various requirements and resource allotment to the users. Sometime, dynamic migration of resources is initiated due to many reasons—proper load balancing, for providing resource to other clients, for energy saving, etc. The virtual machine console is usually not used to associate to the virtual machine for everyday assignments. It is used for assignments such as troubleshooting matters and virtual hardware configuration.

6.4.1 Server/Compute Components

Compute refers to the resource-run applications with the assistance of basic computing components. Compute basically consists of physical and logical components. Physical components refer to the hardware devices, whereas logical refers to the software and protocols used. Two types of communication made easy by I/O devices include user-to-compute and compute-to-compute or storage. The first communication, user-to-compute is handled by I/O devices and the second one allows using the host controller or host adapter that helps to connect a compute system to another compute system or storage device.

Memory is used to store data either persistently or temporarily. Random access memory (RAM) and read-only memory (ROM) are the types of memory normally used in a compute system.

Host bus adapter (HBA) is an application-specific integrated circuit (ASIC) board that provides interface functions between the compute system and the storage. It also offers connectivity options known as ports to connect the compute systems to the storage device. Compute systems can be a simple laptop, servers, or blade servers. Blade servers support the growing need of computing power. Blade servers merge power and functions into a particular, integrated framework and allow the addition of server modules. Blade server technology significantly enhances server density and reduces the power and costs of cooling.

The logical components of a server/compute system comprise the following:

File system A file is a collection of related records or data stored data. Various access permissions can be given to the files by the owner.

Operating system Application and physical components of the compute system are handled by the operating system. Hardware resources allocation and management is also handled by the OS. Basic storage management tasks are also provided by the operating system. Fundamental components, such as the file system, volume manager, and device drivers, are under the control of the OS.

Volume manager Logical volume managers (LVMs) initiate a logical layer among the operating system and physical storage. Logical storage structures become visible adjacent to the operating system and applications. The LVM supports tools, for example, a set of operating system commands, library subroutines, etc., to allow creation and control of logical storage.

Device drivers Specific driver means special software that allows an operating system to interrelate with devices like printer, etc. With the help of device driver, the operating system can recognize various devices.

Compute to compute communication normally uses ethernet for local area network (LAN) and TCP/IP protocol for metropolitan area network (MAN) and wide area network (WAN). Compute to storage communication is facilitated by hardware components such as HBA, converged network adapter (CNA), NIC, switch, router, cables, and protocols.

External storage devices can also be directly connected to the compute systems or connected with the help of a storage network. It supports data access over the network in two different manners—block-level or file-level.

In block-level access, the file system is formed on a compute system, whereas in a file-level access, the file system is created on a network or at the storage side. File-level access method has higher overhead, compared to the data accessed at the block level, as shown in Fig. 6.3.

Storage is connected directly to compute systems in direct attached storage (DAS) architecture. Data from DAS can be accessed at a block level. On the basis of location of the storage device, DAS is classified as internal or external. In internal DAS, the storage device is positioned within the compute system and is linked to the compute system by a serial or parallel bus.

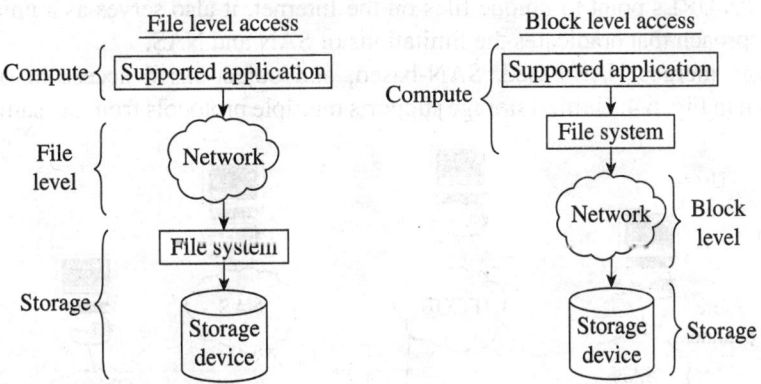

Fig. 6.3 Data access over network (file-level access and block-level access)

If the storage device is located outside the compute, it is an external DAS storage. External DAS beat the limitations of internal DAS. Compared to other storage networking technologies, DAS is a little cheaper. Its configuration and management is also very easy. There is very less requirement of hardware and software for operating DAS over a network. DAS has some limitations, for example, it has a limited number of ports for connecting the compute system to the storage. It also has a bandwidth limitation.

Proper management for resource utilization is not in DAS, due to which, some resources are over utilized and some underutilized.

As DAS is not sufficient to fulfill the need of a storage network, many storage network technologies have come into existence:
- Fibre channel storage area network (FC SAN)
- Network attached storage (NAS)
- Internet protocol SAN (IP SAN)
- Fibre channel over ethernet (FCoE)
- Object-based storage
- Unified storage

FC SAN is a high-speed, devoted network of compute systems and shared storage devices. It offers block-level access to storage devices. It allows a storage system to be shared by numerous compute systems. It is an improved form of storage resources and reduces the overall capital investment by the organization. It supports a centralized storage management system. It also provides numerous ways of connectivity between the compute system and storage device, and so is helpful to improve the reliability and availability of data. It has a serial data transfer interface that can function over a copper wire or optical fiber.

IP SAN technology supports block-level data transfer over the IP network. It reduces cost investment and management and makes it easy. IP network is robust in nature because it has the provision of disaster recovery and the security aspect is also high. FCoE facilitates SAN traffic transported over ethernet networks. FCoE makes use of a new version of the ethernet to make it more reliable. 'Enhanced' ethernet is known as converged enhanced ethernet (CEE). It merges LAN and SAN traffic over a single 10 GB ethernet connection. It reduces server cable numbers, adapters, and ports used in the data center, making the physical infrastructure simple. It also decreases overhead and complexity related to supervising the data center.

Object-based storage merges data with wealthy metadata for creating an 'object'. Flat address space is supported by object-based storage. Hierarchies or nested directories are not used in object-based storage. It supports unlimited file storage. A storage capacity ranging from terabytes to petabytes is supported by this technology. Each object has a unique ID called object ID and the ID is generated using a hash function. As URLs point to unique files on the Internet, it also serves as a unique pointer to an object. It is an approach that eradicates the limitations of SAN and NAS.

Unified storage merges NAS-based, SAN-based, and object-based access in one amalgamated platform as shown in Fig. 6.4. Unified storage supports multiple protocols from the same storage system,

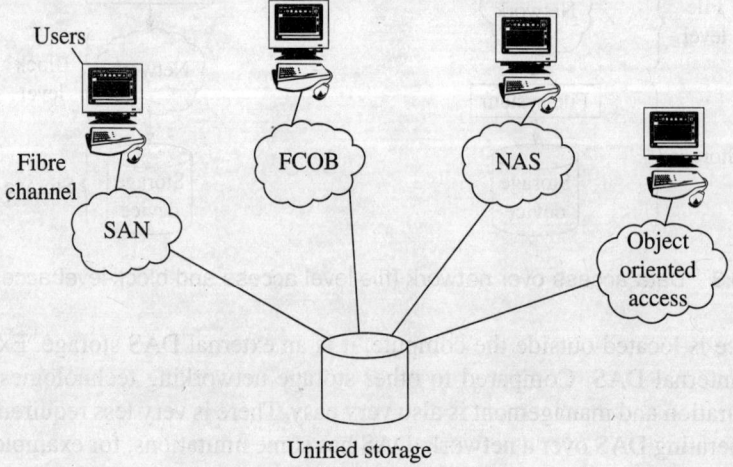

Fig. 6.4 Unified storage

which improves utilization of resources. Unified storage facilitates a reliable management frame across many applications with easy interface. Unified storage offers storage consolidation to support various applications. It helps to reduce the problem associated with storage of an organization, and to lessen the cost of buying storage, cooling, power, and space.

Storage is connected directly to compute systems in direct attached storage (DAS) architecture. Data from DAS can be accessed at the block level. On the basis of the location of the storage device, DAS is classified as internal or external. In internal DAS, the storage device is positioned within the compute system and is linked to the compute system by a serial or parallel bus.

Compute virtualization is a method of abstracting or concealing the physical hardware from the operating system and permitting various operating systems to manage simultaneously on one or more physical machine(s). An operating system and an application into a portable VM have been summarized through this method.

A virtual machine acts and seems like a physical machine. Every operating system manages on its personal virtual machines. In compute virtualization, virtualization layers act like an interface between virtual machine (on which an operating system is running) and the hardware. The virtualization layer is also called a hypervisor. For all virtual machines, standardized hardware has been given by the hypervisor.

6.5 NEED OF SERVER/COMPUTE VIRTUALIZATION

Usually, a single OS is installed per physical machine as the hardware and operating system are firmly coupled and cannot be split. For accessing resource utilization, a single application is installed per compute system. This initiates corporations into buying new physical machines for each installed application which results in rigid and costly infrastructure. In addition, these compute systems are underutilized and it is very common to discover compute systems operating at 15–20% consumption. Various machines in a traditional data center direct to the poor consumption of physical machines.

Compute virtualization facilitates and permits various applications and operating systems to function on a physical machine. This method considerably minimizes charge and enhanced consumption. Resource management is the allotment of a physical machine or clustered physical machines to VMs. It assists to enhance the consumption of resources since the requirement for resources keeps changing. It also permits the dynamic reallocation of resources to make effective use of the existing ability. Resource management provides support to prevent virtual machines from dominating resources and ensures conventional levels of services. Through resource management, resources are handed over as per the relative precedence of VMs.

A centrally controlled resource pool actually accumulates physical resources. Every physical machine and group has a parent resource pool which provides the resources of that physical machine or group. A child resource pool might be formed from the parent resource pool by the administrators. Each child resource pool possesses a few of the resources of their parents. A parent resource pool may include virtual machines, child resource pools, or both. The reservation and limit for every virtual machine and resource pool must be precise and used to direct the resources utilized by a virtual machine or resource pool.

Present CPUs are prepared with hyper-threading characteristics and multiple cores per CPU. A multi-core CPU is an incorporated circuit with which two or more processing units have been connected for improved functioning and more effective, synchronized processing of multiple resources. Hyper threading makes a physical CPU emerge as two or more CPUs. The job of the hypervisor scheduler is to meet system purposes such as consumption, throughput, and responsiveness.

A hypervisor augments and supports the CPU resources by use of modern CPU aspects such as hyper-threading and multicore. It also helps in the following ways:
1. Server consolidation
2. Improved security
3. Increased hardware consumption
4. Hardware independence and support portability
5. Decreased provisioning timing

6.6 VIRTUAL CLUSTERS

You have to adequately operate VMs working on a mass of physical computing nodes (also known as virtual clusters) in a high-performance virtualized computing environment. This includes virtual cluster arrangement, examining and handling over large-scale clusters. In addition, you will have to apply resource scheduling, server consolidation, load balancing, fault tolerance, and other methods. In a virtual cluster system, it is vital to store the big number of VM images competently.

There are common agreements for most applications or users, such as user-level or OS programming libraries. You may pre-install such software packages like templates (known as template VMs). By using these templates, users may develop their own software stacks. They can also copy new OS cases from the template VM. You can have user-specific elements like applications and programming libraries deployed to those cases in advance. The VMs (guest systems) and physical machines (host systems) may operate with different OSes. You can have every VM deployed on a remote server or imitated on multiple servers belonging to the different or same physical clusters. The virtual cluster boundary may vary with modifications.

The virtual environment design should be able to function quickly. In this case, deployment should be to build and allocate software stacks (i.e., applications, OS, and libraries) to a physical node within clusters as quick as possible and to instantly switch run time environments from one virtual cluster of user to another. In case one user completes using his system, the conforming virtual cluster should shut down or instantly append operations in order to save the resources to manage other VMs for other users. Recently, the 'green computing' concept has gained a lot of attention. Moreover, former approaches have aimed on energy cost savings at the single workstation level. They did not have a broader vision. Subsequently, they would not lessen the whole cluster's power utilization.

You can only execute cluster-wide energy-efficient methods to specific applications and homogeneous workstations. Live moving VMs permit you to deliver workloads from one node to other one. Moreover, it does not assure that those VMs can randomly move amid themselves. You cannot avoid the capability overhead created by VM live migrations. That overhead might have considerable negative effects on utilization of cluster, throughput, and quality of service issues. Hence, the challenge is to find how to design migration strategies for implementing green computing without affecting performance of cluster.

One more advantage for clustering carried by virtualization is load-balancing applications in a virtual cluster. You may use the frequency of user login and load index for achieving a load-balanced status. You may apply the automatic scale-up and scale-down mechanism of a virtual cluster based on this design. Consistently, you may increase utilization of mode resource and reduce response time of system. Mapping VMs to the most applicable physical node must boost performance. Dynamically altering loads amid nodes by live moving VMs is helpful in case the cluster node workloads become unbalanced.

6.7 ADVANTAGES OF SERVER/COMPUTE VIRTUALIZATION

Compute virtualization offers the following advantages:

Server consolidation Compute virtualization facilitates working of multiple virtual machines on a single physical server.

Segregation Though virtual machine may share the physical resources of a physical machine, they remain totally inaccessible to one another just as they were discrete physical machines. If we possess four virtual machines on one physical machine and any one of them fails, the remaining three virtual machines continue as they are without any alteration.

Encapsulation Encapsulation refers to a virtual machine which encloses an entire set of virtual hardware resources, applications, and an operating system. Encapsulation forms virtual machines portable and comfortable to handle.

Non-dependence on hardware A virtual machine is configured with virtual constituents such as network card, memory, SCSI controller, and CPU which are entirely independent of the core physical hardware. It gives us the liberty to shift a virtual machine from one x 86 machine to another without creating any alteration to applications, device drivers, or operating systems.

Reduction in cost Compute virtualization reduces charges, such as space (owned or hired) for physical machines, hardware and annual maintenance, power, and cooling.

6.8 TECHNIQUES OF SERVER/COMPUTE VIRTUALIZATION

The three methods which manage confidential commands to virtualize the CPU are discussed in the sections below.

Full Virtualization

In a complete virtualization, binary translation (BT) of OS commands is necessary. Binary translation refers to substituting guest operating system (an operating system functioning on a virtual machine) commands which cannot be virtualized with new commands having a similar importance on the virtual hardware.

Application requests run on a physical machine. Every virtual machine is allocated a virtual machine monitor (VMM), which executes BT and offers every VM all those services as of a physical compute, comprising virtual tools and virtual BIOS.

'Full virtualization' is offered by BT as the hypervisor does not combine the guest operating system from the principal hardware. The guest operating system is unaware of being virtualized and needs no alteration.

Para Virtualization

In para virtualization, guest operating systems (OS) are sensitive of being virtualized. In this method, the guest operating system kernel is altered to eliminate the requirement for BT.

Paravirtualization is feasible in an open-source operating system. A complete virtualization methodology should be accepted for original guest operating systems like Microsoft Windows Xen.

Hardware Assisted Virtualization

Hardware supported virtualization is achieved by creating hypervisor-aware CPU to deal with confidential commands. Virtualizing the x86 command set reduces the hypervisor overhead; it does increase the CPU overhead since the machine is generally bound by memory instead of processing power. These days, hardware-aided virtualization supports both memory virtualization and CPU.

6.9 VIRTUAL MACHINE AND HARDWARE COMPONENTS

A VM is a rational compute system similar to a physical machine which operates an application and an OS. An operating system which works within a virtual machine is known as a guest operating system. At a time, only single-supported guest operating may work on one virtual machine. Every virtual machine is autonomous and can operate its own application. According to a hypervisor prospect, a virtual machine is a distinct set of files. The set comprises virtual disk files, virtual machine swap file, virtual BIOS file, a log file, and a configuration file.

Network file system (NFS) and virtual machine file system (VMFS) are the file systems sustained by the hypervisor. The VMFS is a group of file systems augmented to preserve files of a virtual machine. Virtual machine file system can be deployed on Internet small computer system interface (iSCSI) storage and fibre channel, discretely from the local storage. The virtual disks are preserved on a VMFS as files. Network file system eases the preserving of virtual machine files on reserved file servers. NAS device recovered over an IP network and the network file system consumer built the protocol of network file system to communicate with the NAS tool.

Server virtualization is a physical server's setting into virtual servers to augment server resources. VM Ware is handled and managed by VMFS. Software is employed to allot the physical server into various virtual environments, recognized as virtual or private servers. The server resources are implied or hidden from consumers in a server virtualization method. This reduces the use of the server that is dedicated for one application or job. Server virtualization has numerous benefits. For example, it permits each virtual server to administrate its own operating system and each virtual server might be discretely rebooted. Server virtualization reduces rates since less hardware is required.

In a virtualization environment, if any of the physical servers does not work properly, virtual infrastructure management (VIM) is initiated to divert traffic to a new selected physical server. VIM is also responsible to access the capacity of other hypervisors in the network. As in Fig. 6.5, if E, F, and G virtual instances are not working, then live migration of these E, F, and G into a new destination will be carried out.

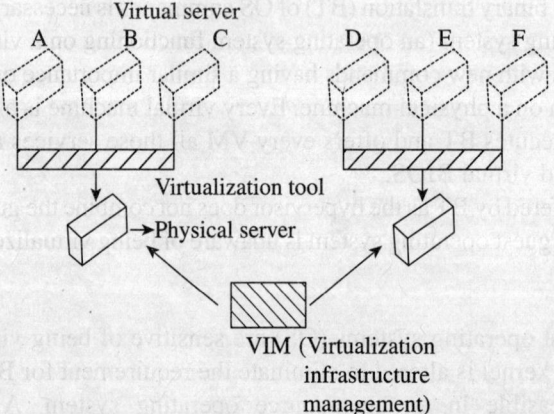

Fig. 6.5 Virtual machine management systems

6.10 HYPERVISOR TAXONOMY

A hypervisor, also known as a virtual machine manager, is a program that permits multiple operating systems to share one hardware host. Every operating system seems to have the host's memory, processor, and other resources entirely to itself. It is an administrating association that hosts resources and processors, assigning what is essential to every operating system one after the other and to make certain that the guest operating systems (known as virtual machines) may not disturb one another and the demand of all is served at every time.

Hypervisor is compute virtualization software which facilitates manifold operating systems to operate on physical machines simultaneously. The hypervisor directly interrelates with the physical resources of the x86-based compute system. The hypervisor is the main constituent of the data center consolidation. It permits multiple operating systems to stay on the same physical machine. Hypervisor has two main constituents—virtual machine monitor (VMM) and kernel.

1. A hypervisor kernel offers a similar utility as other operating systems such as file system management, process scheduling, and process creation. It is intended to specially support multiple virtual machines and to give core utilities such as I/O support, resources scheduling, and many more.
2. The VMM is accountable for really implementing instructions on the CPUs and carrying out BT. A VMM extracts hardware to emerge as a physical machine with its individual memory, I/O tools, CPU, and memory. Every virtual machine is allocated a VMM which has the share of I/O tools, memory, and CPU to effectively govern the virtual machine. When the virtual machine begins working, the control is shifted to the VMM, which consequently starts to accomplish commands from the virtual machine.

Hypervisors are categorized into two types:

Type 1 (Bare-metal hypervisor) The hypervisor is directly installed on the x86 supported hardware as shown in Fig. 6.6. Bare-metal hypervisor has straight access to hardware resources. Therefore, it is more proficient than a hosted hypervisor (e.g., Hyper-V, Xen, etc.)

Type 2 (Hosted hypervisor) The hypervisor is installed and operates as an application on the best operating system, as shown in Fig. 6.7. As it does not work on an operating system, it supports the broadest extent of hardware configurations. A hypervisor is the chief constituent of virtualization (e.g., Virtualbox (oracle), KVM). As type-1 hypervisors do not require host OS to fully utilize resources, they directly utilize the host hardware and resources.

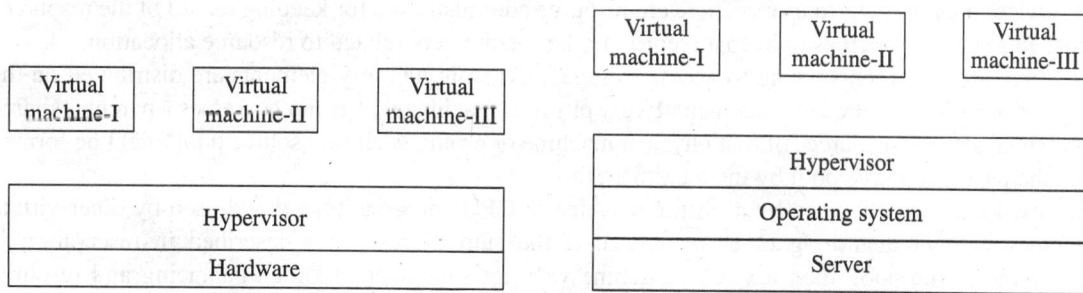

Fig. 6.6 Hypervisor Type 1   Fig. 6.7 Hypervisor Type 2

6.11 RESOURCE MANAGEMENT AND TOOLS

The framework of cloud computing is a complicated system consisting of shared resources (a large amount). These offer and support unpredictable needs and can be fully utilized by external events out of your control. Cloud resource management needs versatile judgments and policies for multi-objective optimization. It is extremely tough due to the complexity of the system that makes it unfeasible to have accurate full-state information.

The policies for cloud resource management associated with the three cloud delivery models, Software as a Service (SaaS), Platform as a Service (PaaS), and Infrastructure as a Service (IaaS) vary from each other. In all instances, the cloud services suppliers have to deal with large, variable loads which challenge the offer of cloud elasticity. In several instances, web services may be conditional.

For an unintended application, the condition is somewhat more complex. You can utilize auto scaling for unintended loads, given that there is a pool of resources you may release or allot as per requirement. Auto scaling is assisted by PaaS services like Google App Engine. Due to lack of standard auto scaling for IaaS, it is complex.

In cloud computing, where alterations are common and spontaneous, centralized control is not believable to offer a persistent service and performance assurances. Certainly, centralized control cannot offer sufficient services to the host of cloud management strategies you have to implement.

Autonomic strategies are of great attention because of the scale of the system, meaning the large amount of service demands by different cloud users. A vital goal is to reduce the charge of supplying the services of cloud computing. In particular, this also means reducing energy utilization. Rather than having the load equally distributed amid all servers, it is also responsible for reducing energy conservation. Resource management policies frequently mutually target power utilization and performance.

Dynamic voltage and frequency scaling (DVFS) methods like AMD PowerNow and Intel SpeedStep lower the frequency and the voltage to reduce power utilization. As an effect of lower frequencies and voltages, the performance of the processor reduces, though it does so at a significantly slower speed than energy utilization.

Resource management is the allotment of a physical machine or clustered physical machines to virtual machines. It assists to enhance the consumption of resources since the requirement for resources changes with time. It also permits the reallocation of resources to make more effective use of the existing ability.

Besides dominant resource consumption, resource management assists in the prevention of virtual machines from dominating resources and ensures conventional levels of services. By means of resource management, resources are assigned according to the relative precedence of virtual machines. For assigning resources, they should be shared and governed centrally.

A resource pool is a concept of collecting physical resources which are centrally controlled. Many resources are there with cloud providers to provide services to the cloud users. As per user requirements, the services are allocated to users. There are resource administrators for keeping record of the resources provided to users as well as to keep a record of other parameters related to resource allocation.

If there are five clients trying to access storage1, dynamic memory elements are distributed on the storage for proper resource management. Every physical machine and group possesses a parent resource pool which sets the resources of that physical machine or group. A child resource pool might be formed from the parent resource pool by the administrators.

Unused memory allocated by a virtual machine to CPU can be accessed and used by other virtual machines without disturbing other resources. If the sum of resources described in reservation is unavailable in the pool, then a virtual machine will not switch on. As load balancing and resource management is always a prime duty of the cloud environment, a resource administrator is present to keep a record of users and for providing various services and resources to the users instantly.

Present CPUs are prepared with hyper-threading characteristics and multiple cores per CPU. A multi-core CPU is incorporated with which two or more processing units have been connected for improved functioning and for more effective, synchronized processing of multiple resources.

A standard OS plans a thread or a process on a CPU, at the same time as the hypervisor arranges virtual CPUs of virtual machines on physical machines. A hypervisor augments and supports the CPU resources by use of modern CPU aspects like hyper-threading and multicore. During the functioning of multiple VMs, some of them may have the same sets of memory. This offers prospects for sharing memory among virtual machines.

Some virtual machines can enclose the same user data, administer the same guest operating system, or have the same applications. Through page sharing, the hypervisor may retrieve the surplus copies and keep only a single copy, which is to be shared by manifold virtual machines in the physical memory. Therefore, the total quantity of physical memory utilized by virtual machines is feasible. This is useful to improve consumption of energy.

A hypervisor recognizes surplus pages copied by their contents. This implies that pages having the same content may be shared despite where, when, and how those contents are created. In order to share, the content of the VM memory is scanned by the hypervisor.

When a write arises on the shared page, the standard copy-on-write (CoW) method is used to deal with these writes. Any effort to write on the shared pages will create a trivial page error. After the occurrence of a page error, the hypervisor will evidently generate a personal copy of the page for that virtual machine. It remaps the pointer to this personal copy of virtual machines. Thus, virtual machines may securely alter the shared pages without disturbing other virtual machines which are sharing that memory.

6.12 PHYSICAL MACHINE TO VIRTUAL MACHINE (P2V) CONVERSION

It is essential to understand the resemblance of virtual machines, particularly when it is regarding VM migrations in a virtualized cloud or to the data center. A VM maintains a relationship between various virtual machines, and between a hypervisor and a VM in a grouped server environment.

A relationship between virtual machines indicates whether the chosen virtual machine be positioned on a similar host or on diverse hosts. Holding virtual machines jointly can be valuable in terms of implementation, in case VMs are corresponding with each other strongly. On the contrary, anti-relationship needs certain VMs to be positioned on diverse hypervisors, possibly for accessibility or load assessment causes.

VM to hypervisor (or physical server) relationship instructed whether a virtual machine may be positioned simply on a specific physical server or it is permitted to travel on a discrete server, if needed. Virtual data center (VDC) may have some physical machines managing hypervisors. The resource management device offers the capability to direct these physical machines centrally. Resource management devices that work on a server of the management permit pooling of resources and allocate ability to VMs. It corresponds with the hypervisor to execute management functions.

Physical to VM exchange is a procedure via which a physical machine is transformed into a virtual machine. When transforming a physical machine, the 'converter application' (Converter) copies data on the hard disk of the source machine and shifts that data to the target virtual disk.

Copying is the procedure of generating a copied disk, where the copied disk is a virtual disk which is an exact clone of the source physical disk. After the completion of copying, steps of system configuration are executed to configure the target virtual machine. System configuration is the procedure of configuring the migrating operating systems to facilitate it to work on a virtual hardware. This configuration is executed on the destination virtual disk after copying and facilitates the destination virtual disk to work as a bootable disk in a virtual machine. After the completion of the conversion, migration of data can be done.

Advantages of P2V converters are:
1. Runs migration among heterogeneous hardware
2. Minimizes time required to set up a new virtual machine
3. Permits migration of machines to a new hardware without re-launching the application or operating system

6.12.1 Converter Components

The P2V 'converter application' comprises three constituents—converter server, converter agent, and converter boot CD.

A *converter server* is an application which is loaded on a discrete physical machine. It manages the conversion procedure in hot mode (when the source machine is managing its operating system). While running the conversation, the converter server propels and launches a converter agent on the source physical machine which requires conversion.

A *converter agent* is liable for running the physical to virtual machine conversion. This agent is deployed on the physical machine merely for hot conversions.

A *converter boot CD* is a bootable CD through which the operating system and converter application run and are used for cold conversion (when operating system is not running in source machine) when it is needed.

There are two means to shift from physical machine to virtual machine (VM). These are cold migration and hot migration.

Hot conversion comprises altering the source physical machine, at the same time, it is managing its OS. Since processes resume working on the source machine during conversion, the consequent virtual machine is not the carbon copy of the source physical machine. After the completion of the conversion, the target virtual machine is synchronized with the source machine.

Cold conversion, also known as offline conversion, is an alternative in which conversion of the source physical machine is executed when it is not managing its operating system. When executing cold conversion of a physical machine, the source machine is rebooted by using a converter boot CD which has its own converter and operating system. Cold conversation generates a reliable clone of the source physical machine since no variation happens on the source machine throughout the conversion.

6.12.2 Conversion Process

Hot conversion of physical machine to virtual machine comprises steps which are as follows:
1. The source machine is prepared by the converter for the conversion by installing the agent on the source physical machine.
2. A snapshot of the source has been taken by the agent.
3. The converter server constructs a virtual machine on the target machine.
4. The agent copies the physical disk of the source machine to the virtual disk of the target virtual machine.
5. The agent synchronizes the data and installs the vital drivers to permit the OS to boot from a VM and personalize the virtual machine (e.g., altering the machine name and IP address).
6. The virtual machine is prepared to work on the target server.

In cold conversation of a machine, the source physical machine is rebooted, having its own operating system. Conversion of physical machine to virtual machine is shown in Fig. 6.8. Cold conversion of a physical machine to virtual machine includes the following steps:
1. Converter software is running on the server.
2. Agent is installed on the physical machine (source) by the server.
3. Agent takes a snapshot of the data.
4. Virtual machine is created by the server on the physical machine (Destination)

5. Copy source disk to the virtual machine
6. Hypervisor is running on physical machine (Destination).

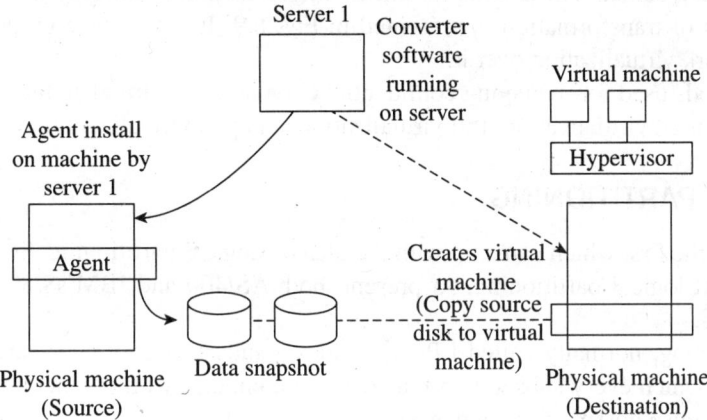

Fig. 6.8 Physical machines to virtual machine (P2V) conversion

While performing conversion of physical to virtual machine, you should consider the following points:
1. A virtual machine developed by the converter application encloses a duplicate of the disk state of the source physical machine.
2. Throughout this conversion, several hardware-dependent drivers and sometimes the mapped drive cannot be preserved.

The following configurations of source machine remain unaffected:
- Operating system configuration
- Data files and applications
- Section serial number for every disk partition

After conversion, the majority of the applications perform tasks accurately on the virtual machine as their data files and configurations have a position similar to that on the source machine. Still, the application can not run if it depends on particular features of the original hardware, such as the tool producer or series number.

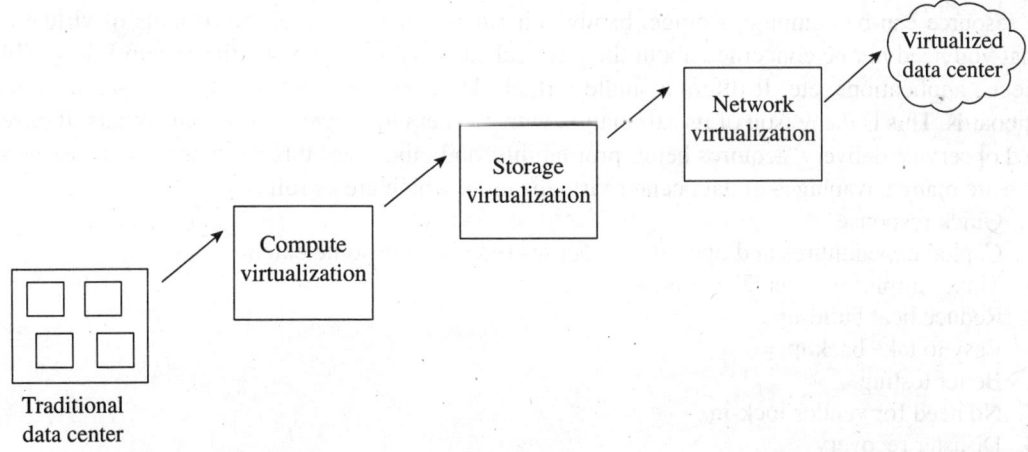

Fig. 6.9 Conversions from traditional data center to virtualized data center

Virtualization is the beginning in the direction of formation of cloud infrastructure. Changing a traditional data center (TDC) into a virtualized data center (VDC) needs the virtualization of the central essentials of the data center. Virtualizing an infrastructure facilitates an easy transition from TDC to VDC. The process of transformation is presented in Fig. 6.9. It takes place by performing compute, storage, and network virtualization over it.

The three methods used for managing confidential commands to virtualize the CPU on x86 designs are hardware supported virtualization, full virtualization, and paravirtualization.

6.13 LOGICAL PARTITIONING

In 1976, IBM was the first which came up with the idea of Logical partitioning. Sun Microsystems and Hitachi too support logical partitioning. At present, both AS/400 and IBM'sS/390 products continue logical partitioning.

Logical partitioning, normally called LPAR, divides a subset of computer hardware into multiple logical subsets, in which every subset is virtualized as a computer with distinct uniqueness. A distinct operating system is also hosted in every panel.

Computer resources, such as storage, processors, and memory, logically divide as multiple arrays of resources and every array can be managed independently. Formation of rational subsets depends upon the processor model that has been used by the system and accessible resources. Subset may be used for numerous reasons, such as database operation, client server operation, and many more.

6.14 TYPES OF VIRTUALIZATION

Different types of virtualization are discussed in the following sections.

6.14.1 Data Center Virtualization

Data centers consist of a wide variety of services which are offered through the Internet including SaaS, PaaS, web hosting, etc. The data center has various kinds of equipment to perform functions such as store, manage, process, etc. Data center is like a simple cage or rack that consists of equipment. Data centers' owners are generally large companies or government agencies. Physical infrastructure and IT equipment demands are going to increase day by day due to the rapid growth of data centers. Virtualization of the available equipment in the data center is called data center virtualization.

In data center virtualization, cloud infrastructure resources are kept as per the needs of a business. The resource can be compute, storage, bandwidth, and memory. One of the benefits of virtualization is that you need not be concerned about the physical capacity; you may get the resource accessible for projects, applications, etc. It offers a single virtual idea from the front end such as applications and dashboards. This is the reason of its association with business intelligence, ERP, and others. It raises the speed of service delivery, acquires better profitability, and minimizes threat for new enterprise as well. There are many advantages of data center virtualization, which are as follows:

1. Quick response
2. Capital expenditures and operating expenses reduce up to some extent
3. Make simpler various IT operations
4. Reduce heat build-up
5. Easy to take backup
6. Better testing
7. No need for vendor lock-in
8. Disaster recovery

6.14.2 Server Virtualization

Server virtualization actually hides the resources from users. It hides resources such as physical servers, operating system used, processor details, etc. Server manager, with the help of application software detaches one physical server to other remote virtual resources. Sometimes, the virtual environment is recognized as virtual private servers, containers, guests, etc.

Server virtualization has numerous benefits. For example, it permits each virtual server to administrate its own operating system and each virtual server might be discretely rebooted, independently of one another. Server virtualization reduces rates since less hardware is required. Server virtualization saves space by agreement since many machines may be merged into a single server managing various virtual environments. It reduces overall costs and investment for a company.

Mainly, three strategies are used for server virtualization—virtual machine model, paravirtual machine model, and virtualization supported by the operating system.

Solaris supports OS virtualization. Server virtualization may be observed as part of a whole virtualization tendency in business IT which comprises workload management, storage virtualization, and network virtualization. This tendency is one constituent in the expansion of autonomic computing, where the server environment will be capable to handle itself on apparent activities. Server virtualization may be used to eliminate server limit, help in catastrophe retrieval, unify server management, and improve server accessibility so as to make more effective use of server resources, and for development and testing.

6.14.3 Storage Virtualization

Storage virtualization means grouping of physical storage from numerous network storage devices, to perform like a single storage device. Cloud storage is also a frequently used term for storage virtualization. With the help of various management software, dispersed storage clusters, including multiple storage units, can also work as a unit. Data on cloud storage is integral and accessible by the users all the time; if any part is not working accurately, there are multiple storage facilities to provide uninterrupted services to the cloud users. More disks can also be added on the cloud storage, if required, any time.

Unstable growth of information is a giant problem for businesses today and storage virtualization offers the following advantages:
1. Change the data access as required
2. Easy and single interface is used for administering the storage
3. Data duplication becomes easy
4. Storage management efficiency can be optimized
5. Diminishes downtime

Storage management is time consuming, but storage virtualization makes creating backup easy, without having to spend much time. Actual complexity is hidden from the user. Storage virtualization can be easily implemented by applications software.

Functions such as physical storage, RAID, logical unit numbers (LUNs), LUN subdivisions, storage zones, logical volumes, etc., in various storage can be easily applied. The model of storage virtualization can be divided into four main layers—storage devices, block aggregation layer, file layer, and application layer.

Storage virtualization creates an abstraction layer between the operating system and physical disks. For efficient and better storage management, this technique is used. Logical space is created by virtualization software for managing physical devices. Various physical storage media are available for providing services to the users at the cloud data center. With the help of storage virtualization tools, the same physical devices can be made available to various cloud users as logical devices. Apart from this, cloud users do not know what they actually use as storage device—physical or virtual.

Virtual Provisioning

Novel technology used in storage means storage space is allocated on demand to various devices in the virtual storage network. There is a virtualized environment for controlling, monitoring, and maintaining physical disk storage that is connected with virtual machines.

Thin provisioning is another name used for virtual provisioning. Virtual provisioning is mainly used in a virtual environment, whereas thin provisioning is generally used in a physical computing environment. Virtual provisioning ensures to assign higher storage capacity to VMs. It offers physical storage to each virtual memory, based on the demands of the user.

Fully Automated Storage Tiering

Fully automated storage tiering (FAST) mechanically shifts active data to storage tiers with high-performance computing and stationary data to different storage with low cost. It is useful to increase performance of the applications, compared to other technologies that are traditionally used, for example, serial advanced technology attachment (SATA). It is difficult to do the same optimization in data storage with manual system. By continuously monitoring FAST, one can easily identify active or inactive data. On the basis of set principles, administrators control and manage systems automatically. It is an optimized method that does not add any extra expenditure and burden on the system.

6.14.4 Sensor Virtualization

In cloud computing, sensor virtualization means virtualization of a physical sensor as a virtual sensor by sensor cloud infrastructure. To provide services to the user when required, virtualized sensors are grouped dynamically.

As physical sensor devices have restricted resource and prospective, the sensor management handles IT infrastructure on cloud computing. The sensor actually converts physical quantities into signals. Today, sensors have many application areas. Physical sensors, which are in scattered form, are combined to create a group of sensors and are used in various applications. Users are concernd only with the status of virtual sensors; users actually do not know about the physical sensors that are virtualized and used by the concerned user.

Sensors' owners are not forced to register their wireless sensors. Wireless sensor network in association with the cloud provides quick response to users. It also allows high-speed processing of data. Easy sharing of data and resources over cloud sensor infrastructure provides resource optimization.

6.15 STORAGE AREA NETWORK

Storage area network (SAN) refers to the LAN design for managing huge amounts of data transfer. High-end servers, multiple disk arrays, etc. are used by SAN. It uses interconnection technology for supporting data storage, retrieval, and replication. NAS works on TCP/IP, whereas SAN for disk blocks transformation works on low-level network protocols.

SAN is also called system area network. Storage area networks are actually designed for data management. It is a rapid storage device network and can be connected with servers. SAN has block-level storage used by various applications. Direct attached storage (DAS) is not flexible as SAN. Figure 6.10 shows SAN. Storage from servers is used and placed in such a manner that these can be easily accessible by the applications. Extra investment on additional hardware storage is reduced in the organization and it also reduces spaces. SAN is helpful for transferring data from one storage device to another without disturbing other devices. SAN also supports fast backup as CPU cycles of server are not involved in the backup process. At the time of recovery, SAN plays an important role.

Virtualization Technology (At Server) | 137

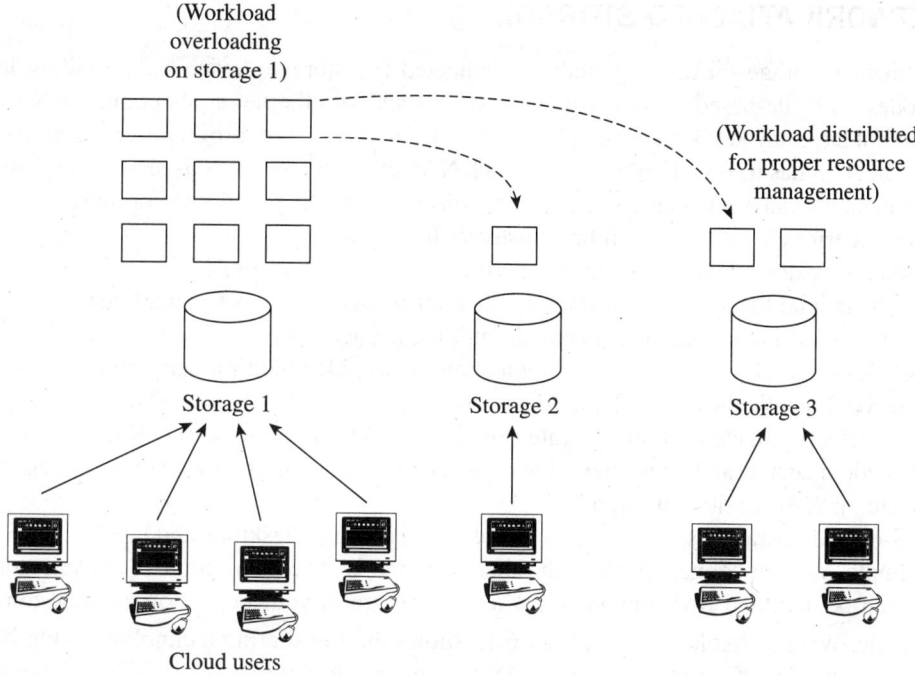

Fig. 6.10 Storage area network—SAN

As SAN also uses fibre channel technology or networking protocols to support networking, keeping data at remote locations is also very easily possible. Prior to SAN, many organizations were using direct attached storage (DAS) devices that reside on the server or work as a standalone device.

Figure 6.11 shows block-level storage virtualization. To store all the messages, contacts, and other data of mail application, SAN is used.

A logic fabric virtual SAN is created on physical FC SAN (fibre channel SAN). Communication among a group of nodes is facilitated by virtual SAN with few requirements in spite of what the physical location in the fabric is. VSAN also works like a VLAN. Each VSAN acts like an autonomous fabric and is handled independently.

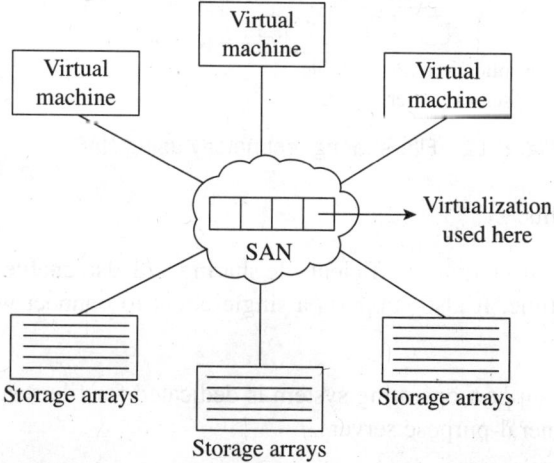

Fig. 6.11 Block-level storage virtualization

6.16 NETWORK ATTACHED STORAGE

Network-attached storage (NAS) is actually a dedicated file storage device for providing local area network nodes with file-based shared storage using a standard ethernet connection. As NAS devices normally do not have any keyboard or display device, web-based utility programs are used to configure and manage it. NAS has its own IP address and each NAS exists on the LAN as an independent network node. Several clients can work on the same file or project with the help of NAS. For more storage capacity, NAS is a superior choice because it has clustered disks.

Many cloud providers make NAS vendors partner for various purposes like backup of files. A NAS array is very beneficial for backup as well as for disaster recovery. Even in a small business, NAS has a server mode to perform functions such as email, multimedia, accessing databases, or print servers. NAS also supports RAID technology, where one logical unit is used for multiple hard disks. It was not easy to manage servers, handle the different platforms, security of data, etc., before NAS. Some examples of NAS devices include Seagate Central, Seagate Business Storage NAS, and 8-Bay Rackmounts. All NAS products provide a secure and centralized location for the files. Sharing of resources such as printer, smart TVs, etc., is also possible through NAS.

The NAS-owned operating system is very simple and is used in desktops and laptops. NAS set-up is also very simple. We can connect NAS with other peripherals. Accessing of NAS system storage data is easy—it can be accessed from anywhere, whether you are in your house, on another computer, or through mobile, Wi-fi technology, etc. Figure 6.12 shows the file sharing technology using NAS. You can easily connect your PC at office with a NAS system and do not need to manage a large computer system. You can even work while travelling, take backup, perform recovery, or download data.

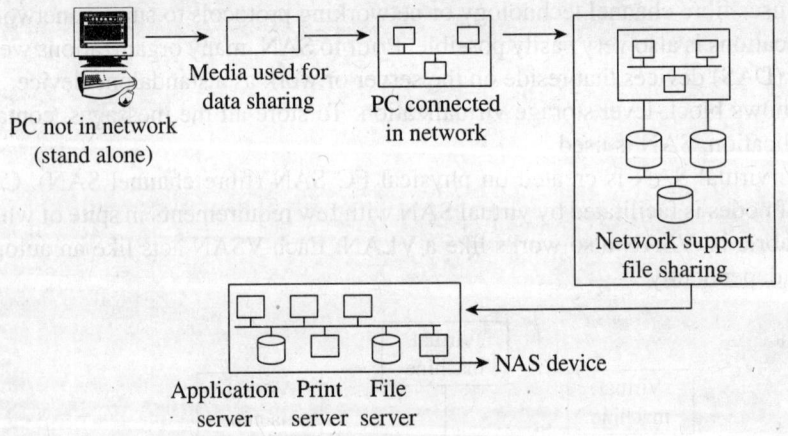

Fig. 6.12 File sharing technology using NAS

NAS has the following benefits:

Broad access to information It facilitates efficient file sharing and also enables a NAS device to serve various clients at the same time. It also supports a single client to connect with many NAS devices simultaneously.

Better efficiency The NAS support operating system is dedicated for file serving and so is helpful to improve the utilization of general-purpose servers.

Better flexibility Familiar for clients on both UNIX and Windows operating systems

Centralized storage Centralization of data storage minimizes replication of data on the client side.

Simplified management Due to a centralized system, it is possible to manage file systems very efficiently.

Scalability Supports various types of businesses as it is scalable

High availability NAS offers and uses clustering technology which is very helpful at the time of failover. It also has efficient replication and recovery techniques, which support high data availability.

Security As NAS support user authentication and file locking, it is a secure option.

NAS has the following components (refer to Fig. 6.13).

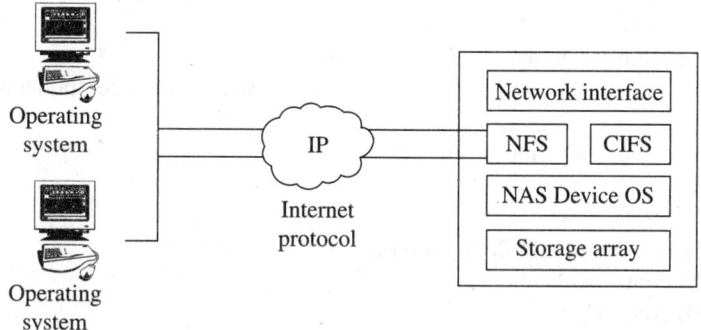

Fig. 6.13 Components used in NAS

- NAS head (CPU and memory)
- Network interface cards (NICs) for providing connectivity
- Operating system for handling NAS functionality
- Network file system (NFS) and common Internet file system (CIFS) protocols for file sharing. NFS mainly supports UNIX-based operating environments, whereas CIFS is supported by Microsoft Windows-based operating environments. Supported file sharing protocols facilitate users to share files with different operating platforms.
- Storage protocols to connect and manage physical disk resources
- Storage array

Comparison between SAN and NAS

Storage area network (SAN) supports networking, whereas network-attached storage (NAS) is a storage device, in a network. Operating systems consider SAN as a disk, whereas a NAS device is a file server. SAN supports block-level storage for servers, whereas NAS devices support file-level storage. For saving files such as word documents or MS Excel spreadsheets, NAS is generally used.

Points to Remember

1. Traditional data centers are labor-intensive, in terms of managing monitoring servers, storage, networks, applications, and provisioning.

2. Compute virtualization offers the following benefits:
   (a) Server consolidation
   (b) Segregation
   (c) Encapsulation
   (d) Hardware independence
   (e) Reduction in cost
3. Hypervisor is compute virtualization software that enables numerous operating systems to run on a physical machine.
4. 'Enhanced' ethernet is known as converged enhanced ethernet (or CEE).
5. Hypervisors are categorized into two: Type 1 (Bare-metal hypervisor), Type 2 (Hosted hypervisor)
6. Advantages of P2V (physical to virtual) converter:
   (a) Diminishes time required to set up a new virtual machine.
   (b) Migration of a virtual machine to a new hardware without reinstalling the operating system or application is easy.
   (c) Support migration crossways heterogeneous hardware.
7. A virtual machine (VM) can be configured with the following virtual components:
   (a) Virtual central processing unit (vCPU)
   (b) Virtual random access memory (vRAM)
   (c) Virtual disk
   (d) Virtual network adaptor
   (e) Virtual DVD/CD-ROM and floppy drives
   (f) Virtual SCSI controller
   (g) Virtual USB controllers
8. SAN is also called system area network.
9. SANs support block-level storage for servers, whereas NAS device supports file-level storage.

Key Terms

BIOS file (Virtual)   It saves the state of virtual machine BIOS.

Configuration file   It saves the configuration data selected during the formation of virtual machines.

Disk file (Virtual)   It saves the matter in the disk drive of the virtual machine.

Log file   This file holds a log of the activities of the virtual machine.

Paravirtualization   In this technology, guest operating systems can be recompiled earlier for installation inside a virtual machine, apart from the main operating system.

Swap file (virtual machine)   It is the virtual machine's paging file that backs up the RAM contents of the virtual machine.

Virtual central processing unit (vCPU)   It is also known as a virtual processor. It is actually a physical central processing unit (CPU) that is allocated to a virtual machine (VM). A virtual machine can be configured with one or more vCPUs when it is created.

Virtualized data center (VDC)   Collection of cloud infrastructure resources designed exclusively for enterprise business needs.

Virtual machine file system (VMFS)   Virtual machine file system (VMFS) consists of a group of very high performance file systems for hosting virtual machines (VMs) on a shared storage.

Virtual random access memory (vRAM)   vRAM is the amount of memory allocated to a virtual machine.

Multiple-choice Questions

1. A file that keeps a log of virtual machine activities is/are called:
   (a) BIOS file
   (b) Log file
   (c) Virtual disk file
   (d) None of these
2. The key benefits of virtualization is/are:
   (a) Cost saving
   (b) Energy efficiency
   (c) Reliability
   (d) All the above
3. A virtual disk stores:
   (a) A virtual operating system
   (b) Program files
   (c) Application data
   (d) All the above
4. _____ enables a virtual machine to connect to a physical USB controller.
   (a) Virtual USB controller
   (b) Virtual NIC
   (c) Virtual Disk
   (d) Virtual RAM
5. A hypervisor is used:
   (a) To increase hardware utilization
   (b) To improve security
   (c) For hardware portability
   (d) All the above
6. The benefits of compute virtualization is/are:
   (a) Isolation
   (b) Encapsulation
   (c) Hardware portability
   (d) All the above
7. The advantage of physical to virtual convertor is:
   (a) Reduction in set-up time
   (b) Enabling of migration (operating system)
   (c) Enabling migration (hardware)
   (d) All the above
8. _____ file backs up the virtual machine RAM contents.
   (a) Virtual BIOS file
   (b) Virtual swap file
   (c) Virtual Disk file
   (d) None of these
9. Cold conversion of a physical machine to virtual machine (VM) involves _____ .
   (a) Booting the source machine from the converter boot CD
   (b) The converter application creates a new virtual machine on the destination physical machine
   (c) The converter application copies volumes from the source machine to the destination machine.
   (d) All the above
10. A virtual machine (VM) can be configured with the following virtual components:
    (a) Virtual DVD/CD-ROM and floppy drives
    (b) Virtual SCSI controller
    (c) Virtual USB controllers
    (d) All the above

Review Questions

1. What do you understand by compute virtualization?
2. What is a virtual machine?
3. What are the advantages of compute virtualization?
4. What are the various components of a hypervisor?
5. What do you understand by resource management? Explain the different tools available for it.
6. How is a physical machine converted into a virtual machine using hot and cold process?
7. What are the various steps to convert a traditional data center to a virtualized data center?
8. What is a hypervisor? Explain the various categories of hypervisors in detail.
9. What are the various advantages and disadvantages of virtualization?

10. How is a traditional data center different from a cloud data center?
11. What is the need of data center virtualization?
12. How is server virtualization different from data center virtualization?
13. What do you understand by logical partitioning?

References

1. *Cloud Security A Comprehensive Guide to Secure Cloud Computing*, Ronald L. Krutz and Russell Dean Vines, ISBN: 978-0-470-58987-8, Wiley Publication, 2010
2. *Cloud Computing for Dummies*, Judith Hurwitz, Robin Bloor, Marcia Kaufman, and Dr. Fern Halper, ISBN-10: 0470484705, Wiley Publication, 1st edition, November 16, 2009
3. *Cloud Computing Technologies and Strategies*, Brian J.S. Chee and Curtis Franklin, Jr, ISBN 9781439806128, CRC Press, April 7, 2010
4. *Cloud Computing: A Practical Approach*, Anthony T. Velte, Toby J. Velte, Ph.D., Robert Elsenpeter, ISBN-10: 0071626948, McGraw-Hill, 1st edition, November 1, 2009
5. *Grid and Cloud Computing*, Katarina StanoevskaSlabeva, Thomas Wozniak, and Santi Ristol, ISBN-10: 3642051928, Springer, 2010 edition, November 19, 2009
6. *Implementing and Developing Cloud Applications*, David E.Y.Sarna, ISBN-10: 1439830827, Auerbach Publications, November 26, 2010
7. Market-oriented Cloud Computing: Vision, Hype, and Reality for Delivering IT Services as Computing Utilities. In High Performance Computing and Communications, R. Buyya, C.S. Yeo, and S. Venugopal, 2008, HPCC'08. 10th IEEE International Conference on pp. 4–13 IEEE, 2008
8. *Mastering Cloud Computing*, Rajkumar Buyya, Christian Vecchhiola, S. Thamarai Selvi, Tata McGraw Hill Education Private Limited, 2008
9. *Cloud Computing and Virtualization*, V. Rajeswara Rao, V. Shubba Ramaiah, ISBN-10: 9383635045, BS Publications/BSP Books, 2014
10. *Cloud Computing Concepts, Technology and Architecture*, Thomas Erl, Zaigham Mahmood, Ricardo Puttini, ISBN-10: 0133387526, Pearson publication, 1st edition, May 10, 2013

Answers to Multiple-choice Questions

1. (b)   3. (d)   5. (d)   7. (d)   9. (d)
2. (d)   4. (a)   6. (d)   8. (b)   10. (d)

CHAPTER 7

Virtualization Technology (At Network)

> **Learning Outcomes**
>
> After completing this chapter, students will be able to:
> - comprehend network virtualization
> - list the benefits of network virtualization
> - explain the benefits of virtualization
> - describe various network components
> - understand traffic management techniques
> - understand virtual machine migration services

7.1 INTRODUCTION

Nowadays, for better efficiency, price control, and operational optimization, centralization of all the scattered IT resources of a business is required. Multiple copies of the same resource (hardware and software) are provided to various users, and the data center manages multiple copies as per user requirement. The foremost approach of virtualization is to allow sensational swings in the manner the data center infrastructure is controlled, designed, distributed, and sourced. The rising tendency toward dynamic infrastructures, like call for elastic scaling, cloud, and automatic provisioning aspects requires challenging and new wants for the data center network.

In this chapter we will discuss network virtualization, network virtualization tools, benefits of network virtualization, various network components, traffic management between network components, and the various migration techniques used in networking.

7.2 EXPLORING NETWORK VIRTUALIZATION

Virtual machine (VM) is the new IT approach to use within the data center. The physical server platform is no more the fundamental constituent but is rather made up of various rational resources which are accumulated in the pool of virtual resources. Network designers can no more delay their design at the network interface card (NIC) level, but require allowing for the server platforms network particulars like virtual switches (vSwitches). In network virtualization, multiple virtual networks run with the help of a physical network as shown in Fig. 7.1.

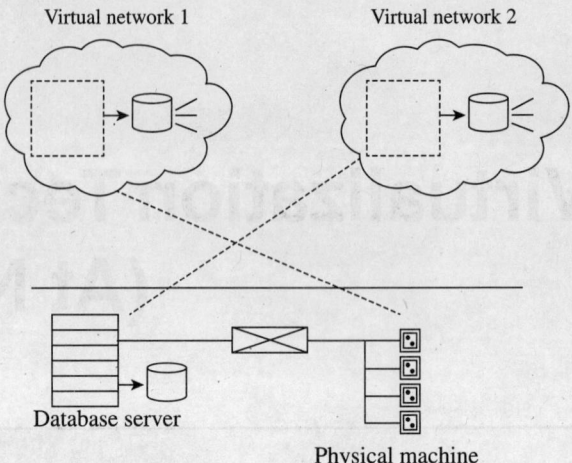

Fig. 7.1 Network virtualization

Infrastructure administration amalgamation turns out to be more significant in this environment as the inter-relations between functions and appliances are tougher to manage and control.

Network virtualization comprises rationally grouping and segmenting physical network(s) into distinct rational units known as 'virtual network(s)' and forming them to act as one or multiple separate network(s). It permits multiple virtual networks to share network resources.

A virtual network appears to be a physical network to the nodes connected to it. Two nodes connected to a virtual network may well communicate among themselves without navigating frames, although they are in discrete networks. Network traffic must be navigated when two nodes in discrete virtual networks are communicating, although they are connected to the same physical network. Network administration traffic, including 'network broadcast' within a virtual network, does not proliferate to any other nodes that belong to a different virtual network. This permits useful grouping of nodes by a normal set of needs in a virtual network, regardless of the geographic location of the nodes.

In virtual data center (VDC), network virtualization comprises virtualization of both VM and physical networks. The physical network may consist of network routers, hubs, switches, repeaters, adapters, and bridges.

The physical network provides connectivity
1. among physical servers,
2. between physical servers and clients, and
3. between physical servers and storage systems.

A VM network exists within a physical server. It comprises rational switches known as 'virtual switches', which perform in the same manner as that of physical switches. The VM network facilitates conversion among VMs inside a physical server.

A computer on which a hypervisor runs one or more virtual machines is called a host machine, and each virtual machine is called a guest machine. The hypervisor presents the guest operating systems with a virtual operating platform and manages the execution of the guest operating systems. Kernel-based virtual machine (KVM) is a virtualization infrastructure for the Linux *kernel* that turns it into a *hypervisor*.

Hypervisor kernels are associated with the VM network. Hypervisor kernels converse with the administration server and storage systems by using the VM hypervisor. The administration server should be a VM hosted in a physical server. In order to have conversion between two VMs existing in diverse physical servers and between VMs and its consumers, the VM traffic should pass through both physical networks and the VM. Hypervisor traffic is also needed to shift between physical networks and VM. Thus, the VM network should be linked to the physical network.

Network virtualization permits a manager to construct multiple virtual networks in the data center (DC). These virtual networks can bridge across both physical networks and VM, and share virtual and physical switches. A virtual network offers alignment of all the nodes which belong to a similar working unit in an enterprise.

7.3 TOOLS USED IN NETWORK VIRTUALIZATION

Network virtualization is operated by a physical switch operating system (OS) and hypervisor. These kinds of software permit an administrator to develop virtual networks on VM and physical networks. A physical switch controls an operating system that executes network traffic switching.

The operating system should have network virtualization functionality in order to develop a virtual network on the switch. Hypervisor has integral networking and network virtualization functionalities. A third-party software too offers these functionalities, which might be deployed on the hypervisor. Subsequently, the third-party software module substitutes the local networking functionality of the hypervisor.

7.4 BENEFITS OF NETWORK VIRTUALIZATION

Network virtualization offers better security by constraining access to nodes placed inside a virtual network from other virtual network. Thus, confidential data of one virtual network is isolated from other virtual networks. Network broadcast inside a virtual network is not permitted to propagate with another virtual network. Broadcast preserves network bandwidth that subsequently enhances virtual network working for common network traffic.

Virtual network permits alignment of nodes based on the necessity of a company. Whenever new necessities appear, a manager modifies the virtual network configuration by using administration software and rearranges nodes. The administration software offers an interface to configure virtual networks from a central administration workplace. The interface allows a manager to send configuration instructions to the hypervisor or physical switch operating system. As rearranging of nodes is not required for re-cabling and since physical transfer of tools is not required, administration of the network also becomes easy. Network virtualization permits multiple virtual networks to share a similar physical network. This enhances the consumption of network resources.

The other advantages of network virtualization are as follows:
1. *Reduction of hardware expense*. You may naturally save a great deal of funds by minimizing hardware expense using virtualization.
2. *Energy expenses*: Many businesses have discovered that virtualization has minimized the overall electricity utilization for server computers by around 80 per cent. This is the effect of using minimum computer hardware to perform more work.
3. *Recoverability*: One of the prevalent advantages of virtualization is not the saving of expense, but the capability to swiftly recover from hardware malfunctions.
4. *Disaster recuperation*: The most significant advantage of virtualization appears when an actual disaster recuperation condition occurs, and you have to reconstruct a single host computer and reorganize the hypervisor software. You may effortlessly reinstate the backup of virtual machines from the tape and after resuming the virtual machines, it will work.

7.5 FEATURES OF NETWORK COMPONENTS

Parallel to classic data center (CDC) networking, there are fundamental basic blocks to execute networking in a VDC. A VDC network infrastructure consists of both virtual and physical constituents. These constituents are linked to one another to allow the flow of network traffic. Network constituents such as virtual switch, virtual NIC, and virtual host bus adapter (HBA) are constructed within a physical server using a hypervisor. Virtual NICs permit VMs to link to the VM network. They remit and get VM traffic to and from the VM network.

7.5.1 Virtual Switches

Virtual switch is like a logical switching built into VMware so that a virtual machine network can be managed as per the requirement. Virtual switches act as an interface between virtual ethernet and the physical ethernet.

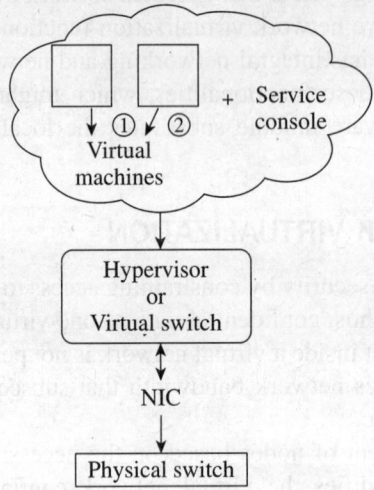

Fig. 7.2 Virtual switch

Virtual switches develop VM network and support the ethernet protocol as shown in Fig. 7.2. They offer association to virtual NICs and send VM traffic. They also manage storage, administration, and VM migration traffic to and from the hypervisor kernel. Physical adaptors like converged network adapter (CNA), NIC, and HBA facilitate physical servers to associate with physical networks. They send hypervisor and VM traffic to and from a physical network.

The physical network comprises physical routers and switches. Physical routers and switches offer associations among physical servers, between physical servers and consumers, and between physical servers and storage systems. On the basis of the network technology and supported protocol, these switches control fibre channel over ethernet (FCoE), ethernet, iSCSI, and fibre channel (FC) traffic.

The connectivity between VDC network constituents is based on the kind of protocol and the physical adapter used to allow physical server access to the storage system. A physical ethernet switch is used to associate the storage system with the physical servers.

Every physical server hosts multiple VMs which are associated with a virtual switch. Every VM at least has a single virtual NIC that receives or transfers VM input/output in the type of ethernet frames. Ethernet frames move through physical switches before reaching the final destination.

A hypervisor kernel is also associated with the virtual switch. Hypervisor kernel influences the physical and virtual switches to forward the IP management, storage, and VM migration traffic. A physical server has a single or more physical NICs. These NICs offer a connection between the physical and virtual switches and forward hypervisor kernel traffic among the switches.

A hypervisor kernel is instantly associated with the HBA. A fibre channel switch is also used for inspecting data packets where data packets are initiated and at the final destination of the packet, the HBA remits or gets storage traffic through an ethernet or FC switch.

A hypervisor kernel, however, uses a virtual switch to get or forward VM immigration traffic and management. A CNA card is used by a physical server in place of a distinct NIC and HBA. The CNA card offers association amid a physical FCoE switch and virtual switch. It has the capacity to unite both ethernet traffic and FC over an ethernet association. This enhances the hypervisor kernel in order to access IP and FC storage systems by using a network adapter.

The hypervisor kernel acknowledges CNA as an FC HBA and NIC. Hypervisor kernel, in order to access FC storage, instantly remits storage traffic to CNA. It remits traffic via the virtual switch to access the IP storage or for advanced management and VM immigration traffic.

Virtual switches control both VM traffic and hypervisor kernel traffic. Distinct kinds of ports are configured on a virtual switch for distinct kinds of traffic. Conversely, multiple virtual switches can be constructed, each with its own virtual port. Virtual ports are categorized as uplink port, hypervisor kernel port, and VM port:

1. Uplink ports join a virtual switch to physical NICs of the physical server where the virtual switch resides. A virtual switch may transport information to a physical network when one or more physical NICs are connected to its uplink port.
2. VM ports permit virtual NICs to link to a virtual port.
3. A hypervisor kernel port enhances the hypervisor kernel to link to a virtual switch.

A port group is a means for pertaining network policy settings to a group of VM ports and thus to a cluster of VM. This helps a manager to differentiate indistinguishable network policy settings across a cluster of VMs, instead of configuring the policies to VM ports personally.

The following are examples of network policies:
1. Security
2. Failover and load balancing across physical NICs
3. Preventive network bandwidth for VMs
4. Virtual LAN delegation to a VM port cluster in order to move the VM traffic

A virtual switch can have multiple port groups. VMs, which are linked to a VM port group, share a configuration pertaining to the port group. In a data center, server virtualization is directed autonomously from physical servers, requiring the union of storage, server, protection, and network supervisors.

Data center administrators are looking for reliable networking environments across physical and virtual environments, so that physical and virtual servers may use similar management devices, configurations, and policies. Network policies should drift automatically all along with mobile virtual machines to make sure that access, security, and implementation continue an integral manner since virtual machines shift from server to server.

For instance, the IBM system Networking Distributed Virtual Switch 5000V is a superior, feature-rich distributed virtual switch for VMware environments along with policy-based VM associatively. The IBM Distributed Virtual Switch (DVS) 5000V allows network managers accustomed with IBM System Networking Switches to control the IBM 5000V merely as IBM switches using superior management, networking, and troubleshooting characters so that the virtual switch is no more concealed and tough to control.

7.5.2 Virtual LAN

Virtual LAN (VLAN) permits you to have discrete LANs amongst ports on a similar switch. For example, we can organize a switch so that ports 1–32 are on VLAN A and ports 33–64 are on VLAN B.

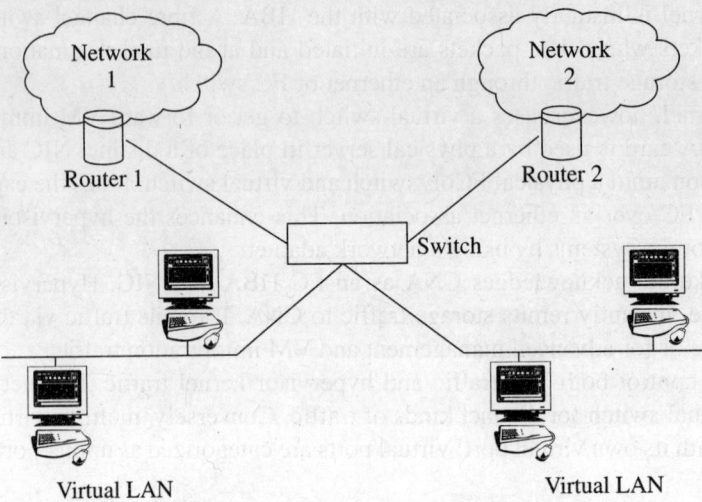

Fig. 7.3 Virtual LAN

A VLAN is a rational network constructed on a LAN or across multiple LANs consisting of virtual or physical switches. Every network is connected to a switch with the help of routers shown in Fig. 7.3. The VLAN skill may split a bulky LAN into lesser virtual LANs or merge divided LANs into one or more virtual LANs. A VLAN permits conversion among a cluster of nodes based on performing needs of a corporation, independent of the position of nodes in the network. All nodes in a VLAN can be linked to one LAN or distributed across multiple LANs. The advantages of a VLAN are given here:

1. Broadcast traffic inside the VLAN is confined and reproduced to another VLAN. VLAN is frequently used to express a region of broadcast. Confining broadcast using VLAN frees bandwidth for user traffic which enhances functioning for the usual VLAN traffic.
2. VLAN creates cheap, simple, and flexible means to operate networks and is made using software. Thus, it may be configured simply and swiftly after evaluation to construct distinct physical LANs for many communication groups. A manager merely modifies the VLAN configurations without affecting re-cabling and nodes, in case regrouping of nodes is needed.
3. VLANs also offer better security by separating perceptive information of one VLAN from any other VLANs. Limitations can be enforced at the OSI layer 3 routing tool to avert routing of inter VLAN.
4. As a physical LAN switch may be shared by multiple VLANs, the use of the switch is augmented. It minimizes capital expenditure (CAPEX) in acquiring network devices for separate node groups.

The membership of a VLAN can be classified in various ways:
1. *Port-based*: Various port numbers are provided as per the services provided in the network. So, the port number of the same network is diverted as per the number so there is no conjunction in the network.
2. *Protocol-based*: In this type of VLAN, traffic is handled on the base of the protocol used in the network. Traffic following the same protocol will be diverted in the same network.

3. *MAC-layer clustering*: In VLAN at layer 2, Vswitches pass traffic to the MAC address of the connecting device. A large table of MAC address is stored in the memory for incoming packets; if the virtual port number on the virtual switch is not known, even then traffic will be handled easily.
4. *Network-layer clustering*: VLAN helps to create multiple layer 3 networks on a single physical network, for handling various virtual networks.
5. *Multicast grouping*: VLAN helps to reduce traffic in the network by forming various broadcast domains that divide the whole network into smaller networks; individual networks can then easily manage traffic.
6. *Policy grouping (basically for data and network security control)*: Traffic in VLAN is managed as per the various policies of network security, for example, fetching the data packet of a particular IP address that comes from a malicious hacker.

VLAN trunking permits traffic from multiple VLANs to navigate a solo network association. This skill is for solo association among any two network tools such as switches, storage systems, routers, and VMs along with multiple VLAN traffic navigating the similar route. The solo association via which multiple VLAN traffic may navigate is known as a trunk link.

VLAN trunking permits one port on a networked tool to be used for remitting or getting multiple instances of VLAN traffic over a trunk connection. The port, competent of moving multiple VLAN traffic, is known as a trunk port. To facilitate trunking, the remitting or networked tool should at least have a single trunk port configured on them. A trunk port on a networked tool is present in all the VLANs classified on the networked tool and moves traffic for all those VLANs. The method used to accomplish VLAN trunking is known as VLAN tagging.

7.6 TRAFFIC MANAGEMENT AND ITS TECHNIQUES

Resource management of various resource instances between various users in a cloud computing environment as per user requirement is called traffic management. Cloud computing is generally based on adaptive traffic management and control techniques.

In VDC, similar to a CDC, network traffic should be controlled to optimize both accessibility and functioning of networked resources. Load balancing is the main aim of controlling network traffic. It is a skill to allocate workload across multiple virtual or physical machines and equivalent network connections to avoid overconsumption or underconsumption of these resources and to optimize functioning. It is offered by dedicated hardware or software. In VDC, network managers have a suitable policy for allocation of network traffic across network connections and VMs. Network traffic governing skills may also be used to set up a policy to failover network traffic across network connections. In the case of a network malfunction, the traffic from failed connections will fail over to another accessible connection on the basis of a predefined policy. Whenever needed, network managers have a suppleness to modify a policy. When multiple VM traffic share bandwidth, network traffic governing skills certified assured service levels for the traffic created by every VM. Traffic governing skills permit a manager to set precedence for distributing bandwidth for various kinds of network traffic such as management, IP storage, VM, and VM immigration.

Load balancing is one of the key matters in cloud computing. It is a method which uniformly allocates dynamic regional workload across all the nodes in the entire cloud to prevent a condition where several nodes are too loaded, whereas others are doing little work or are idle. It assists in attaining a high user satisfaction and resource consumption ratio, improving the whole functioning and resource efficiency of the system. It also guarantees that each computing resource is allocated honestly and proficiently. It further averts blockage of the system that might happen due to unbalancing of the load. When one or more constituents of any service crash, load balancing assists in persistence of the service by executing fair-over, that is, in provisioning and de-provisioning of occurrences of the application without any failure. Resource utilization can be reserved to the least with appropriate balancing of load, which not only helps in making business greener but minimizes the cost. Scalability, one of the very essential characteristics of cloud computing, is also facilitated by load balancing.

In clouds, load balancing is a procedure which allocates the extra dynamic regional workload consistently across all the nodes. It is used to attain high user satisfaction and resource consumption ratio, making certain that every node is getting better functioning of the system. Appropriate load balancing may assist in consuming the accessible resources optimally, thus reducing resource utilization. It also assists in facilitating scalability, executing fail-over, and minimizing the response period preventing blockage and over-provisioning, and many more.

The network governing skills are as follows:
1. Technique 1: Balancing client workload—hardware
2. Technique 2: Balancing client workload—software
3. Technique 3: Storm control
4. Technique 4: NIC teaming
5. Technique 5: Limit and share
6. Technique 6: Traffic shaping

These will be discussed in detail in the following sections.

7.6.1 Technique 1: Balancing Client Workload—Hardware

The consumer load balancing service is normally offered by committed hardware and software such as a router and a switch. Hardware-based load balancing uses a tool, like a physical router or switch, to divide client traffic across multiple servers. The load balancing tool resides on the Internet and the server cluster. This facilitates all consumers to traverse the load balancing tool. Consumers use the IP address as it abstracts the authentic IP addresses of all servers in a group. The authentic IP addresses of the server are recognized to the load balancing tool that chooses where to send the request. Decision-making is normally managed by a load balancing policy like least connections policy, weighted round-robin, and round-robin policy. Round-robin rotates consumer links diagonally among servers.

Weighted round-robin permits a manager to describe a functioning weight to every server. Servers with superior weight value get a greater fraction of links throughout the process of round-robin. The least links uphold a similar number of links to all servers. Servers, which are competent of processing links quicker, get more links over time. As in Fig. 7.4 there are many processes in queue to run like p1, p2, p3, etc. Every process will get equal time interval; if process p1 runs and completes its allocated time interval, then the turn of the next comes automatically.

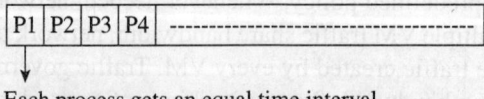

Each process gets an equal time interval

Fig. 7.4 Round-Robin distribution

7.6.2 Technique 2: Balancing Client Workload—Software

Software-based consumer load balancing is executed by software operating on a virtual or physical machine. DNS server load balancing is a normal illustration. In a DNS server, multiple IP addresses may be configured for a given name. In this manner, a cluster of servers may be mapped to a domain name to a separate server IP address in a round robin style. This facilitates consumers accessing similar domain names to distinguish IP addresses and thus remit requests to distinct servers.

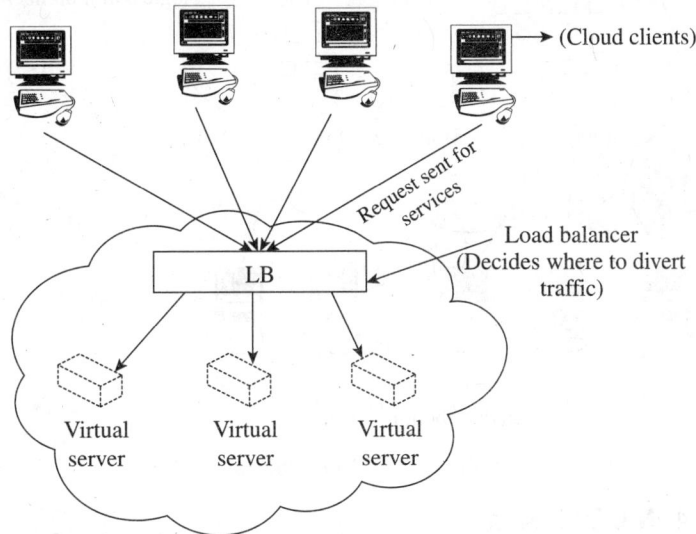

Fig. 7.5 Balancing client workload

The client sends a request for services to the network which comes to the load balancer and diverts traffic to the particular virtual server for handling and managing services in the cloud network as shown in Fig. 7.5. The load balancing is attained by using a unique driver on every server in a group that balances consumer's workload across clustered servers. The cluster offers an IP address (virtual IP address) to consumers, making the cluster seem as one server. This facilitates every incoming IP packet to arrive at every server in the cluster. The load balancing drive software separates the incoming packets and maps every request to a specific server. The other server in the cluster forces the request.

7.6.3 Technique 3: Storm Control

A storm arises as a result of the overflow of frames on a LAN or VLAN segment, developing unnecessary traffic and resulting in violated functioning of networks. A storm might arise with any cause such as denial-of-service attack from the user side, fault in executing protocol, or any sort of error in the network configuration. Storm control is a skill to avert a usual network traffic on a VLAN or LAN from being disturbed by a storm and hence improving network functioning. In case storm control is facilitated on a supported LAN switch, it supervises all inbound frames to a switch port and ascertains whether the frame is broadcast, multicast, or unicast. Then, it analyses the entire number of frames of a particular kind delivered at a switch port over a one-second time period. Then, the switch evaluates the amount with a pre-configured storm control limit. The switch port delays the traffic when the limit is attained and separates out succeeding frames over the next time period. The port will be out of the jamming condition if the traffic flows below the limit. Storm control limit can also be set as a fraction of the port bandwidth. Cloud strom can cause uneven distribution of storage etc., as shown in Fig. 7.6.

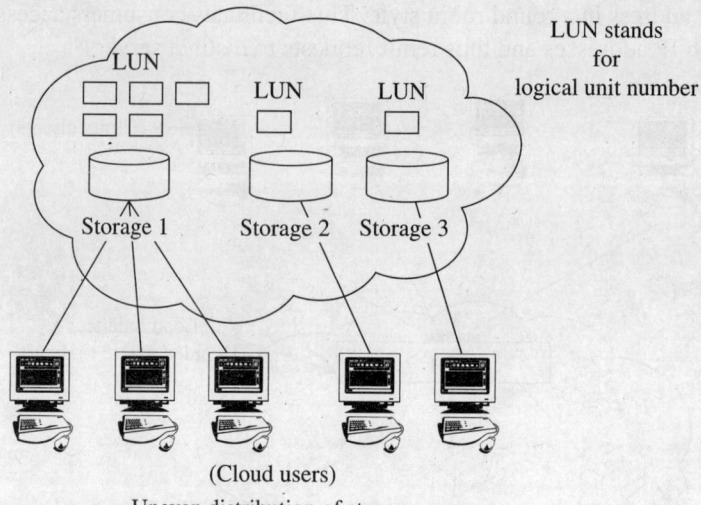

(Cloud users)
Uneven distribution of storage

Fig. 7.6 Storm control

7.6.4 Technique 4: NIC Teaming

NIC teaming is a skill which rationally groups physical NICs linked to a virtual switch. The skill balances traffic load across all or several physical NICs and offers failover in the case of an NIC failure or a network connection outage. NICs within a team may be configured as active and standby. Active NICs are used to forward frames, while standby NICs stay inactive. Load balancing permits allocation of all outbound network traffic across active physical NICs, providing superior throughput than a solo NIC might offer. A standby NIC will not be used for dispatching traffic unless a failure happens on one of the active NICs. In the event of NIC or connection failure, traffic from the failed connection will failover to another physical NIC. Failover and load balancing across NIC team members are managed as per the protocol of a virtual switch.

Another skill for load balancing is mapping between the source and target IP addresses of outbound physical and traffic NICs. A particular physical NIC forwards the frames with particular IP addresses. On a virtual switch, NIC teaming policies can also be allied to a port group.

7.6.5 Technique 5: Limit and Share

Share and limit are limitations which are used to manage various kinds of outbound network traffic such as management, IP storage, VM, and VM immigration, when these traffic kinds contend for the NIC or physical NIC team. They share and limit the enhanced levels of service for vital applications. They avoid input–output vital applications workload from being slowed down by less vital applications. 'Limit', just like its name, sets a limit on the highest bandwidth for traffic between NIC teams. The price is normally stipulated in Mbps.

'Shares' stipulate the relative priority for allocating bandwidth to different kinds of traffic when different types of traffic contend for a particular physical NIC. Share certifies that each outbound traffic kind gets its share of physical NIC based on its priority. Shares are specified as numbers.

7.6.6 Technique 6: Traffic Shaping

Traffic determination manages network bandwidth so that business-crucial applications have the needed bandwidth to certify the quality of service. Three limitations used for traffic determination in order to choke and mould the network traffic flow are standard bandwidth, peak bandwidth, and burst size. A standard bandwidth is configured to set the permitted data move rate (bits per second) across the allocated virtual switch or a port cluster over time. As this is a standard amount over time, the workload at a virtual switch may extend beyond the standard bandwidth for a lesser time period. The value proposed for the peak bandwidth decides the highest data shift rate (bit per second) sanctions across a virtual switch, assigned virtual switch, or a port cluster without dropping or rowing frames.

The cost of peak bandwidth is always superior to standard bandwidth. When the traffic rate at a virtual switch or allocated virtual switch port exceeds the standard bandwidth, it is known as burst. Burst is an irregular occasion and usually subsists for a lesser time period. The burst size classifies the highest sum of data (bytes) permitted to move in a burst, provided it does not surpass the peak bandwidth. Burst size is a computation of bandwidth multiplied by time period through which the burst survives. Hence, more superior the accessible bandwidth, lesser the time the burst may reside for a significant burst size. In case burst surpasses the configured size of the burst, the remaining frames will be wrinkled for later transmission. The frames will be plunged in case the line is packed.

7.6.7 Proposed Load Balancing in Cloud Computing

Load balancing that is presently prevalent in clouds is as follows:

Decentralized content alert load balancing It is a new content alert load balancing policy termed as workload and client aware policy (WCAP). It uses a unique and special property (USP) to identify the unique and special property of the request and computing nodes. USP assists the scheduler to determine the preeminent appropriate node to process the requests. It also assists in minimizing the ineffective time of the computing nodes, thus enhancing the consumption.

Server-based load balancing for Internet allocated services A new server-based load balancing policy for the web server is allocated all over the globe. It assists in minimizing the service response time by use of a procedure which restricts the redirection of requests to the nearest isolated servers without congesting them. A middleware is depicted to execute this procedure. In order to assist the web server for persisting overloads, it also uses a heuristic.

Join–Idle–Queue Join–Idle–Queue load balancing algorithm for dynamically scalable web services offers a huge level load balancing along with allocated dispatchers. Through eliminating load balancing work from the crucial way of request processing, it effectively succeeds to minimize load on systems as there is no overhead at the place of job arrival and the real response time too is not augmented.

A lock-free multiprocessing for load balancing (LB) It is a lock-free multiprocessing load balancing which prevents the use of shared memory in comparison to other multiprocessing load balancing that uses shared memory and maintains a user session lock. It may be simply completed by altering the Linux kernel. This assists in enhancing the whole functioning of the load balancer in a multi-core situation by operating multiple load balancing processors in a single load balancer.

Scheduling scheme on load balancing of virtual machine resources A scheduling scheme on load balancing of VM resources uses historical information and the present condition of the system to attain the finest load balancing and minimizes dynamic immigration with the use of an inherited algorithm. It assists in settling the matter of load-imbalance and high expense of immigration, hence attaining improved resource utilization.

Central load balancing policy for virtual machines (CLBVM) A central load policy for virtual machines balances the load uniformly in an allocated virtual machine or cloud computing conditions. This policy enhances the whole functioning of the system but does not believe in systems and the type of runtime errors it can handle.

Load balancing scheme for virtual storage (LBVS) It is a load balancing virtual storage scheme which offers a huge range of data storage mode and storage as a service. It uses a style for storage virtualization, that is, three-levels and load balancing is attained with the use of two load balancing modules. It assists in enhancing the ability of simultaneous access by using duplicate balancing, further minimizing the response time. It is attractive in catastrophe retrieval too.

Task scheduling algorithm based on load balancing A two-level task scheduling procedure based on load balancing is needed to meet the many needs of users and to acquire high resource consumption. It attains load balancing by first mapping jobs to virtual machines and then virtual machines to host resources in a way that enhances the response period of a job, appropriate consumption of resources, and the cloud computing environment's entire functioning.

Honeybee foraging behaviour A devolved honeybee-based load balancing skill is a nature-enthused algorithm based on self-association. By means of regional server activities, it upholds the overall load balancing. Global system functioning is enhanced with augmented system collection but as system volume is improved, throughput is reduced. Wherever different service kinds are needed, it is highly profitable.

Biased random sampling It is an allocated and scalable load balancing methodology which uses random sampling of the system realm to attain self-association, hence balancing the load across all nodes of the system. The functioning of the system is enhanced along with a high population of resources, hence resulting in an augmented throughput by efficiently consuming the augmented system resources.

Active clustering Active clustering load balancing is a self-aggregation algorithm that optimizes task assignments by linking services using the regional re-wiring concept. The functioning of the system is improved with high resources, thus augmenting the throughput by enhancing the functionalities of the system.

Load balancing procedure based on ant colony and complex network theory (ACCLB) The load balancing procedure based on ant colony and complex network theory in cloud computing uses scale-free and small-world features of a complex network to attain better load balancing. This skill overcomes heterogeneity, is adaptive to dynamic conditions, is outstanding in error tolerance, and has fine scalability, thus assisting in enhancing the functioning of the system.

Two-phase load balancing algorithm A two-phase scheduling algorithm which merges Load Balance Min-Min (LBMM) and Opportunistic Load Balancing (OLB) scheduling algorithm consumes higher implementing competence and upholds the load balancing of the system. LBMM scheduling algorithms reduces the implemented time of every job on the node, hence reducing the total time of completion. OLB scheduling algorithm maintains each node in working condition to attain the aim of the load balance. This mutual approach thus assists in an effective consumption of resources and improves the ability of work.

Event-driven Algorithms that react as per the event are event driven and can be analysed in various games. This algorithm analyses its constituents in comparison to the resources and the overall condition of the game session only after receiving aptitude proceedings as input, hence creating the game session load balancing activities. It is capable of scaling up and down a game session on multiple resources on the basis of the unpredictable user load.

Carton A procedure for cloud control known as Carton has been proposed by R. Stanojevic, which amalgamates the use of Distributed Rate Limiting (DRL) and Load Balancing (LB). DRL is used in order to be certain that the resources are allocated in a manner to maintain a rational resources distribution and LB is used to uniformly allocate the tasks to distinct servers so that the allied expenses may be reduced. For vigorous workloads, the server capabilities are adapted by DRL so that the functioning level at all servers is uniform. This algorithm is easy and simple to execute along with very low conversion and computation overhead.

Compare and balance A load balancing version is intended and executed in order to minimize the immigration time of virtual machines by shared storage, to load balance amid servers on the basis of their IO usages or processor and many more, and to maintain the zero-downtime of virtual machines in the process. An allocated load balancing is compared and the balance algorithm is also anticipated, which is based on sampling. Stability is accomplished very swiftly. This algorithm ratifies that the immigration of VMs is stable from high-rate physical hosts to low-rate host if every physical host has enough memory but this is a feeble hypothesis.

Overheads associated It decides the sum of overheads while executing a load-balancing algorithm at the same time. It is compiled of overhead, owing to jobs movement, inter-process, and inter-processor conversion. This could be reduced so that a load balancing skill may work effectively.

Throughput It is used to estimate the number of jobs to ensure complete implementation. It must be high to enhance the system's functioning.

VectorDot A new load balancing algorithm termed VectorDot has been proposed. It controls the hierarchical complexity of the data center and multidimensionality of resource loads across network switches, storage in nimble data centers, and servers which have storage virtualization skills and incorporated server. VectorDot uses dot products to differentiate nodes based on the articles needed and assists in switches, storage nodes, and servers.

7.7 VIRTUAL MACHINE MIGRATION SERVICES

VM migration is one of the vital strategies in the field of physical machine virtualization that permits applications to be clearly moved with their implementation settings across physical machines. Virtual machine migration is required for server consolidation (power saving), resource scheduling, and load balancing. For successful migration, interruption and migration time should be minimized.

Live virtual machine migration is a method which moves the whole operating system and its related application from one physical machine to another. The virtual machines are moved live with no interruption in the application working on it. The advantages of virtual machine migration comprise maintenance of physical server energy, load balancing amid the physical servers, and malfunction tolerance in situations of unexpected breakdown. The various virtual machine migration methods are given here:

Fault Tolerant Migration

Fault tolerance permits virtual machines to continue work if any component of the system crashes. This method migrates the virtual machine from one physical server to another physical server on the basis of the prediction of the breakdown. This method is used to enhance the accessibility of the physical server and avert degradation of applications.

Load Balancing Migration

The load balancing migration method intends to deliver load across the physical servers to enhance the scalability of physical servers in cloud setting. Load balancing helps in reducing the resource utilization, augmenting scalability, accomplishment of fail-over, over provisioning of resources, avoiding blockages, etc.

Energy Efficient Migration

The power utilization of a data center is mostly based on the consumption of servers and their cooling mechanism. The servers characteristically require up to 70 per cent of power utilization even at low consumption level. So, there is a want for migration methods which preserve the energy of servers by best resource consumption. Some of these are listed here:

Stop and copy-based migration It is a non-live migration method. The virtual machine totally stops working on the source machine and all the memory pages are copied to the target machine. After copying all the memory pages, VM happens on target. Downtime and migration time is similar for stop and copy-based migration since VM does not begin on goal host until the entire pages are transmitted to the goal. The disadvantage of this technique is that VM's services are totally unavailable until it has started on the target, causing augmented downtime.

Live migration Live migration of virtual machine permits the VM to migrate without any disruption while implementing its application. VM migration is a significant way for running applications and resources in big virtualized systems. It facilitates handling of resources to be dynamically reasonable in the complete virtualized system across physical host limitations and it permits applications to be dynamically shuffled to develop consistency and performance.

Precopy and post-copy migration are commonly used techniques for live migration in cloud computing, but both have different iteration steps.

Post-copy-based migration The VM, in post-copy, stops working on the source and only its implementation state (CPU, register, memory pages vital to begin VM on goal) is passed on to the aim machine and the VM starts working on the goal. Even then, all the memory pages are not transferred and continue to subsist on the source. When the VM requires a memory page, it creates a page fault and that consequent page is transmitted from the source to the target machine. When each of the memory pages is shifted to the target machine, the VM begins on the target host. In this technique, the page fault is one of the overheads as shown in Fig. 7.7. The steps included in the post-copy technique are as follows:
1. The virtual machine is on the source machine.
2. The execution state of the virtual machine is transferred before memory is transferred and if the page generates page fault then the requested page is transferred.
3. The virtual machine is activated on the target machine, later.

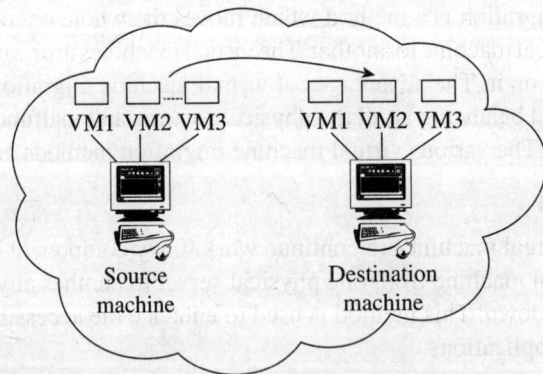

Fig. 7.7 Post-copy migration

Pre-copy-based migration Pre-copy technique is usually employed for live migration. In the beginning, it shifts each of the memory pages to the target machine. Then, iteratively, copies of pages are altered in the last round as shown in Fig. 7.8. The procedure is continual until the writable working set (WWS) happens to be small. When WWS turns small, it executes stop and copy functions and shifts dirty pages and the CPU state. WWS includes the pages altered in every round. The steps included in pre-copy migration are as follows:
1. Send all the memory pages to the target machine
2. Transfer the modified pages
3. Virtual machines activate the target machine

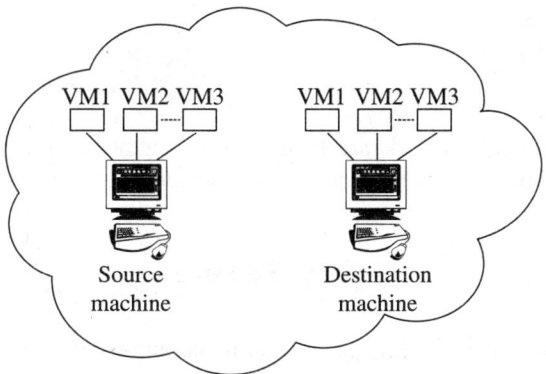

Fig. 7.8 Pre-copy migration

The functioning of any live VM migration approach can be estimated by the following metrics:
1. Preparation time: This is the time between starting migration procedure and shifting the VMs processor status to the aim node, throughout which the VM continues to perform.
2. Down time: This is the time when the VMs' implementation is blocked. It comprises the transport of processor status.
3. Pages transferred: This is the complete sum of memory pages shifted, comprising copies across all the time stages.
4. Resume time: This is the time between resuming the implementation of VMs and the end of migration; all necessities on the sources are eliminated.
5. Total migration time: This is the total time occupied by the migration procedure, from the beginning till the end. Total time is extremely significant as it influences the discharge of resources on both source and target nodes.
6. Application degradation: During the migration of virtual machines from one host to another, the application functioning, which is working on that VM, is violated.

Points to Remember

1. The network management techniques are as follows:
   (a) Technique 1: Balancing client workload—Hardware
   (b) Technique 2: Balancing client workload—Software
   (c) Technique 3: Storm control
   (d) Technique 4: NIC teaming
   (e) Technique 5: Limit and share
   (f) Technique 6: Traffic shaping
2. The benefits of network virtualization are as follows:
   (a) Hardware cost
   (b) Energy costs
   (c) Recoverability
   (d) Disaster recovery
3. VLAN allows you to have separate LANs among ports on the same switch.
4. VLAN trunking allows traffic from multiple VLANs to traverse a single network connection.
5. VLAN membership can be defined in several ways:
   (a) Port-based
   (b) Protocol-based

(c) MAC-layer grouping
(d) Network-layer grouping
(e) Multicast grouping
(f) Policy grouping

6. The various VM migration methods are fault tolerant migration, load balancing migration, energy efficient migration, stop and copy-based migration, and live migration.

Key Terms

Converged network adapter (CNA)   It is a computer input/output device which joins the performance of a host bus adapter (HBA) with a network interface controller (NIC).

Host bus adapter (HBA)   A host controller, host adapter, or host bus adapter connects a host system to other network and storage devices.

VLAN   A virtual local area network (VLAN) is a rational group of network devices, workstations, and servers which seem to be on a similar LAN in spite of geographically being situated at far distances.

VLAN tagging   The mechanism used to achieve VLAN trunking is called VLAN tagging.

VLAN trunking protocol (VTP)   It is a Cisco proprietary protocol which promulgates the definition of VLANs on the entire local area network.

Multiple-choice Questions

1. _____ allows physical servers to connect to the physical network.
   (a) NIC
   (b) HBA
   (c) CAN
   (d) All the above

2. _____ port allows virtual NIC to connect to the virtual switch.
   (a) VM port
   (b) Uplink port
   (c) Virtual port
   (d) None of these

3. VLAN provides _____ ways to manage a network.
   (a) Easy
   (b) Flexible
   (c) Less expensive
   (d) All the above

4. _____ allows traffic from multiple VLANs to traverse a single network connection.
   (a) Multicast grouping
   (b) Port based
   (c) VLAN trunking
   (d) None of these

5. Physical network provides connectivity _____.
   (a) Between physical servers and clients
   (b) Between physical servers and storage systems
   (c) Among physical servers
   (d) All the above

6. Hypervisor has _____.
   (a) Built-in functionalities
   (b) Network virtualization functionalities
   (c) Both (a) and (b)
   (d) None of these

7. The benefits of network virtualization are _____.
   (a) Energy cost
   (b) Software cost
   (c) Security
   (d) None of these

8. _____ is/are network components.
   (a) Virtual NIC
   (b) Virtual HBA
   (c) Virtual Switch
   (d) All the above

9. Storm control is done in _____ technique of traffic management.
   (a) Technique 2
   (b) Technique 3
   (c) Technique 5
   (d) Technique 6

10. In a DNS server _____ IP address can be configured for a given domain name.
    (a) Multiple
    (b) Single
    (c) Virtual
    (d) None of these

Review Questions

1. What is network virtualization?
2. Which network components are used in virtualization?
3. What are the various advantages and disadvantages of network virtualization?
4. What is a virtual switch? Explain in detail.
5. How is virtual LAN different from LAN?
6. What are the different tools used for network virtualization?
7. What are the features of the different components used in network virtualization?
8. What is load balancing? Explain with examples.
9. What is the need of network virtualization?
10. Explain traffic management technique and traffic shaping in detail.
11. Explain the various VM migration methods.

References

1. *Cloud Security A Comprehensive Guide to Secure Cloud Computing*, Ronald L. Krutz and Russell Dean Vines, ISBN: 978-0-470-58987-8, Wiley Publication, 2010
2. *Cloud Computing for Dummies*, Judith Hurwitz, Robin Bloor, Marcia Kaufman, and Dr. Fern Halper, ISBN-10: 0470484705,Wiley Publication, 1st edition, November 16, 2009
3. *Cloud Computing Technologies and Strategies*, Brian J.S. Chee and Curtis Franklin, Jr, ISBN 9781439806128, CRC Press, April 7, 2010
4. *Cloud Computing: A Practical Approach*, Anthony T. Velte, Toby J. Velte, Ph.D., RobertElsenpeter, ISBN-10: 0071626948, McGraw-Hill, 1st edition, November 1, 2009
5. *Grid and Cloud Computing*, Katarina StanoevskaSlabeva, Thomas Wozniak, and Santi Ristol, ISBN-10: 3642051928, Springer, 2010 edition, November 19, 2009
6. *Implementing and Developing Cloud Applications*, David E.Y. Sarna, ISBN-10: 1439830827, Publisher: Auerbach Publications, November 26, 2010

Answers to Multiple-choice Questions

1. (d)
2. (a)
3. (d)
4. (c)
5. (d)
6. (c)
7. (a)
8. (d)
9. (b)
10. (a)

CHAPTER 8

Virtualization Technology (At Desktop and Application)

> **Learning Outcomes**
>
> After completing this chapter, students will be able to:
> - comprehend desktop virtualization
> - describe techniques used for desktop virtualization
> - illustrate remote desktop services
> - explain hardware virtual machine
> - understand infrastructure of desktop virtualization
> - describe components of desktop virtualization
> - describe machine imaging
> - describe VM migration services management

8.1 INTRODUCTION

Desktop virtualization is actually a type of illusion provided to the user using different techniques. It involves encapsulating and delivering either access to an entire information system environment or the environment itself to a remote client device. The client with different operating systems and devices may use entirely different hardware architecture from that used by the projected desktop environment.

For IT organizations, desktop administration is expensive, manual, and time-consuming. As compared to desktop virtualization, server virtualization makes datacenters more quick and effective by advanced levels of accessibility, quicker application delivery, and enhanced utilization. In the rest of the chapter, we will understand desktop virtualization, its advantages and disadvantages, the technique used for virtualization, remote desktop services, tools used for providing these services, virtual desktop infrastructure, application virtualization, etc.

8.2 UNDERSTANDING DESKTOP VIRTUALIZATION

Desktop virtualization is a type of software technology used to separate the desktop and its connected application software from the physical device used by the client. In case of loss of any device or hardware, components will be restored after login from some other device. Remote desktop virtualization works in a manner similar to client–server model in which applications can be executed on any remote desktop with different operating systems and with the help of the protocol of remote display, a user can interact with the application as shown in Fig. 8.1.

Storage can play a significant role in the overall performance of virtual desktop infrastructure (VDI). The operating system, applications, and user data are all tied to a specific piece of hardware in a traditional operating system. Loss of a desktop's setting for virtualized applications or devices could

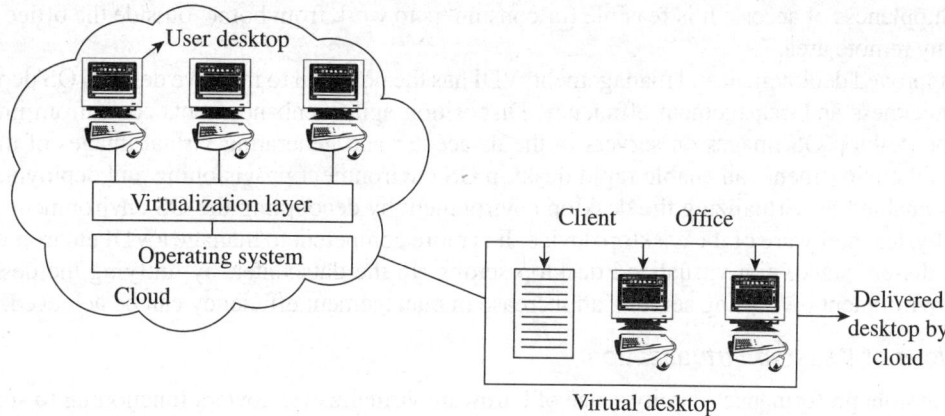

Fig. 8.1 Desktop virtualization

cause businesses to suffer because it affects the operating system, applications, user data and settings if data is not kept safe for future reference.

In a virtualized desktop, virtualization breaks the connection between hardware and the elements facilitate the IT staff to alter, update, and organize these elements independently for greater business quickness and improved response time. End users also get the benefits of virtualization because they get the same desktop, but with the added ability to access the computing environment from different kinds of devices and access from anywhere.

It is the capability of the virtualization to isolate or separate the operating system (OS), user configuration layers, and applications. The desktop virtualization permits you to update and administer one layer without disturbing the other layers. It also proposes the improved level of flexibility with smooth organization. The advantages of desktop virtualization include the following:

Advantages of Desktop Virtualization

1. Simpler provisioning of new desktops
2. Installation of new applications at cheap rates
3. Desktop image-management capabilities
4. Increased data security
5. Longer time given for customer desktop infrastructure
6. Protected reserved access to a business' desktop settings
7. Facilitation of thin clients: Desktop virtualization facilitates utilization of thin clients as endpoint machines. A chance has been generated through this to considerably cut down the price of endpoint hardware by swapping old PCs with a thin-client machine.
8. Improved security: Safety advantages for the desktop setting are also given by VDI. The advantages emanate from storing and managing the desktop OS setting on centralized servers placed in the datacenter, rather than on endpoint machines or disseminated desktops. If the desktop or laptop is lost or stolen, the user's desktop environment is still protected. Centralization of the desktop environment on servers in the datacenter, good management practices, and software can make implementation of security software updates more efficient.
9. Better business continuity and disaster recovery: Desktop business continuity and disaster recovery can be improved by implementing VDI. Business stability developments are facilitated by centralizing data in the datacenter and the desktop OS and applications, where supervisors can effortlessly execute recovery and backup operations.
10. Abridged PC repairs: It is much easier to maintain virtual desktops than the traditional PCs.

11. Suppleness of access: It is feasible for consumers to work from home, outside the office, or from any remote area.
12. Improved deployment and management: VDI has the potential to improve desktop OS deployment quickness and management efficiency. Disposition agility enhancements come from integrating the desktop OS images on servers in the datacenter and generating virtual images of the OS. A VDI environment can enable rapid desktop OS environment provisioning and deployment. This is enabled by virtualizing the desktop environment by decoupling the OS environment from the physical hardware of the desktop device. It is more competent to manage a VDI environment than a disseminated, non-virtualized desktop setting. In the datacenter, by unifying the desktop OS environment on hosting servers, an increase in management efficiency can be achieved.

Limitations of Desktop Virtualization

1. Possible performance scarcity—use of hardware virtualization lowers functioning to some level
2. Reliance on network connection: A VDI solution depends on the network connection to operate. If the endpoint tool of the consumer cannot attach to the hosting server, the consumer will not be capable of accessing applications, desktop, and data. In addition to reliability of connection, the network should have suitable bandwidth and low latency to provide a good user experience.
3. Challenges in introducing and retaining drivers for peripherals
4. Difficult to operate complicated applications
5. Augmented interruption in case of failure of network that may be prevented by using clustered file technique
6. Data of user not permanently deleted from the network
7. Expensive and complicated installation and supervision of VDI
8. Businesses executing VDI projects or desktop virtualization are aware of the needs of information technology. Reference architectures, guidelines, and other devices are offered by businesses to help in deciding the prices for installing virtual desktop infrastructure. The requirements for infrastructure alter extensively on the basis of whether the approach is client-hosted or server-hosted.
9. Highest percentage of physical memory is required by virtual desktops, though this fluctuates on the basis of the operating system, workload, applications, and other aspects.
10. VDI execution servers never need customer-hosted virtualization due to the execution of virtual machines on end-point machines.
11. As per network requirements, various virtual images are safely kept in the internal storage as well as in the network storage for future reference, and that is not an easy task.
12. Accumulative network investments are not usually needed for customer-hosted VDI as the network load is similar to the network consumption for normal PC running operations.
13. It may be tricky to comprehend the performance effect which a VDI installation will have on storage systems. The main focus of utilization guidelines concerning storage is how to estimate storage capacity necessities.
14. Unsuitable for high-end graphic applications: Typically, a VDI solution is not suitable for users who use high-end graphic applications. This is mainly due to the inability of the remote desktop delivery protocols in a VDI solution to provide the required performance levels for this type of application.
15. Additional infrastructure required: A VDI resolution needs extra storage, servers, and networking infrastructure. The sum of extra infrastructure needed depends on the functioning, scale, and service stage necessities of a corporation.

The dependence between the application and the underlying platform which comprises hardware and the operating system is being broken by application virtualization. Desktop virtualization is no more than the revised version of the modern enterprise desktop. Nowadays, due to the increasing popularity of virtualization, the appearance of the modern enterprise desktop is getting modified with the help of virtualization technology. Each product of virtualization is completely unique, be it the desktop, application virtualization, or server consolidation.

Virtualized desktops propose a higher level of suppleness and mobility which is unfeasible with a standard desktop, along with global access to a modified machine, without carrying any laptop. There is no uncertainty about the fact that the server hosted desktop virtualization may propose various benefits such as reduced support cost, reduced hardware cost, simplifying life cycle supervision, among others.

8.3 DRIVERS USED IN VIRTUALIZATION

The most common driver of desktop virtualization deployment is the need to improve client security. Driver is somehow related to security which is also important in business management and to manage the top challenges that IT professionals face when trying to promote desktop virtualization to the upper management.

While the main drivers behind desktop virtualization deployments are all about IT, once the technology is implemented, IT professionals see its benefits extending throughout the entire organization. They focus on business strategy and the way the end users work as per the business deal.

Forty-two percent believe that desktop virtualization increases user productivity by enabling workplace flexibility and decreasing downtime. It is believed by professionals that desktop virtualization will give better result if employees of an organization use the right tools without considering the hardware and infrastructure used by the clients.

Desktop virtualization has many important features, some of which are discussed in further sections.

8.3.1 Features of Desktop Virtualization Drivers

Reduction in cost of desktops   It eliminates the need to have desktop or laptops for individual employees.

Reduction in management cost of desktop   It is easy to manage desktops and their applications centrally or remotely which reduces the management cost.

Easy setting of desktops   Setting of desktops becomes very easy through a centralized management console. The cost of move-add-change is also reduced with desktop virtualization.

Reduced cost to refresh desktops   It is easy for any organization to move from any operating system to another without any expense. It is also easy to extend desktop life cycle and management.

8.4 TECHNIQUES USED FOR DESKTOP VIRTUALIZATION

The objective of desktop virtualization technology is to centralize the desktop's operating system (OS) at the data center to make security and management of desktops easy. Desktops hosted at the data center run as virtual machines, whereas end users remotely access these desktops from a variety of endpoint devices. Data centers manage how an application can be executed fluently and how it can be stored for future reference. The two desktop virtualization techniques basically used for providing services to users are as follows:
- Remote desktop services (RDS)
- Virtual desktop infrastructure (VDI)

Remote desktop services (RDS) are traditionally known as terminal services. In RDS, a terminal service runs on top of a Windows installation and provides individual sessions to client systems. These sessions can provide a thorough desktop experience while remotely accessing via a terminal services client. The workstation receives the visual feedback of the session while resource consumption takes place on the server.

Application delivery is more lively and rapid because applications are installed once on the server and can be accessed by the user without having to install the application locally. The security of the user environment is improved because the user's applications and data are stored, secured, executed, and accessed centrally instead of being located on the user's local desktop device.

A customized configuration and environment of servers is easy to handle with available tools, due to which a centralized operating system and applications make the user environment manageable and user friendly, when compared to distributed desktops managed at different locations.

Adding a new user environment is completed without having to install an OS or applications on the local endpoint device. Software updates, patches, and upgrades are also completed on servers instead of on the user's endpoint device. RDS is a mature technology, easy to implement, and scales well, as compared to a VDI solution. An RDS solution can support more users per server than a VDI solution. A typical RDS solution can support 250 or more users per server, compared to a typical VDI solution supporting 30–45 users per server. RDS is also less expensive to implement in terms of initial acquisition cost and supporting infrastructure. The application developed for desktop operating systems may not necessarily be compatible with server operating systems.

VDI and RDS are designed for providing services to users as per their requirement. However, the differences between RDS and VDI are shown in Table 8.1.

Table 8.1 RDS versus VDI

RDS	VDI
Separate virtual machines are not provided to the user	Separate virtual machines are provided to the users
Multiple operating systems' instances need not be managed	Multiple operating systems' instances need to be managed
Various users share the same virtual machines and operating systems	Same resources need not be shared
Full administration is not provided to the users because many instances of the same resources are shared by many users	User gets full administration over resources
Less resource utilization of CPU, memory elements, etc.	More resource utilization

8.4.1 Remote Desktop Services

Remote desktop services (RDS) are an important feature of Microsoft Windows Server which permits users to remotely access Windows applications and graphical desktops. The various technologies which are a part of remote desktop services are as follows:
1. Remote application, launched with Windows Server 2008, permits the user to access personal applications on a shared server. Applications served by the remote application appear like local software applications despite being implemented in the server. This is occasionally termed as 'application publishing' or 'seamless windows'.
2. Remote desktop virtualization host, launched with Windows Server2008 R2, permits users to dynamically link up to a virtual desktop allocated from a pool or an individual virtual desktop.
3. In remote desktop services, desktops or applications may be accessed from a range of customer's tools, operating systems along with Java clients, and HTML 5 browsers. Users observe and interact with remote desktop services' resources by way of remote display protocols. Microsoft offers the remote desktop protocol (RDP) with Windows; and third-party businesses may also develop their own protocols.

Along with the accessibility of high-speed Internet access, one can instantly host applications software remotely which will facilitate global trade access to shared applications effectively without the necessity of any significant computer knowledge or IT expert.

Advantages of RDS

1. Data recovery in disaster: There is no worry of misplacing any data due to disaster or theft, as all the files and credentials are stored in secure data centers. All correspondence with the remote desktop is encrypted to make certain that all correspondences are secured and safe from being hacked.
2. Working anywhere: This system allows users to travel with the computer system or laptop and work faultlessly from anywhere and anytime.
3. Cost effective: This remote desktop system will save the expense of software because it normally comes with the remote IT system package.

Disadvantages of RDS

1. Requirement of powerful RDS: Since various computers are managed by a centralized RDS, the capability of RDS must be powerful and sufficient in order to bear the functional load of multiple computer systems.
2. Requirement of RDS monitoring: The remote desktop service is the foremost source of risk of downtime. The whole system will collapse in case the remote desktop service crashes, unless an RDS monitoring system is in place.
3. Requirement of reliable network: The complete functioning of the system is affected by the integrity of the network. The complete system will crash in case the network of remote desktop service is disrupted.
4. Requirement of right adjustment in network: The network must be familiar and make certain that there should not be any blockage during the establishment of the remote desktop services.
5. Knowledgeable administrator: The administrator must be an expert, have essential knowledge, and be in touch during working hours.

8.4.2 Infrastructure for Desktop Virtualization

Virtual desktop infrastructure (VDI) refers to the hosting of a desktop OS running in a VM on a server in the virtual data center (VDC). A user has full access to the resources of the virtualized desktop. The server-hosted desktop virtualization solution approach is sometimes called virtual desktop environment (VDE). VDI allows a user to access a remote desktop environment from an endpoint device via a remote desktop delivery protocol. The hosted remote OS and associated applications are shown on the user's endpoint device display and controlled via the endpoint device's keyboard and mouse. For the user, the experience is very similar to using the remote desktop services (RDS) solution, except that the desktop OS is running in a VM hosted on a server, instead of on a remote user session on a single server OS.

The VDI architecture consists of several components that work together to provide an end-to-end solution. The main components are endpoint devices, a connection broker, and VM hosting servers.

Advantages of VDI

1. Low price in buying desktop computers
2. Centralized client operating system management
3. Swift client implementation
4. Reduction in the costs of desktop
5. Reduction in the cost of electricity
6. Enhanced security of data
7. Protected remote access
8. Lesser applications compatibility troubles

Disadvantages of VDI

1. Printing normally involves third-party appends
2. Scanning is natively unsupported
3. Bi-directional audio is natively unsupported
4. Exhibit protocols are unsuitable for graphic design
5. Needs low-latency association between the virtual infrastructure and customer
6. Needs enterprise class server hardware and storage areas network for VMs permanently delivered to particular users
7. Needs trained IT staff

8.5 COMPONENTS FOR DESKTOP VIRTUALIZATION

The VDI architecture consists of several components that work together to provide an end-to-end solution. The main components are:
- Endpoint devices
- A connection broker
- VM hosting

The number of VMs that a single server can support depends on several factors including hardware, software, configurations, and user workloads of the desktop VMs. The desktop VMs may be running any desktop OS supported by the hypervisor. In VDI, each VM may be dedicated to a specific user (persistent desktop) or allocated in a pool (non-persistent desktop). A VM pool shares VMs for concurrent use by many users.

VM pools have the potential to save VM disk storage requirements. When provisioning a VM, a template or image can be used as a basis for VM creation, settings, and disk. In the case of demand, advanced provisioning technology permits a VM to be provisioned to use a single image, rather than assigning an entire disk image. For each consumer VM, merely a single image is utilized to provision the VM.

The option has the potential to save a significant amount of VM disk storage. The savings result in provisioning a VM from a single image, thereby not requiring a full VM disk image for every VM. To set up and organize the connection between the desktop VM and the endpoint machine which is working on the VM-hosting server, a connection broker is liable. The connection broker provides manageability, security, reliability, and scalability benefits. A connection broker is generally needed as part of the VDI solution for a larger or more complex environment.

The user would be configured to directly connect to the same VM by a computer name or IP address. It is important to determine whether the connection broker is compatible and supports the hypervisor that is used by the VM hosting server. VM hosting servers are responsible for hosting desktop VMs that are remotely delivered to the endpoint devices. Type 1 hypervisors are most suitable for this type of solution due to their performance and scalability benefits. Additionally, they support a greater number or density of VMs than Type 2 hypervisors.

A VDI solution may potentially introduce a significant number of new servers and added storage into the datacenter. To execute desktop virtualization, a major necessity is consumer state virtualization. The consumer state comprises the data of consumers in addition to OS configuration settings and applications. Usually, PCs of consumers have the authoritative copy of settings and data of consumers. The three main challenges with managing the user state are as follows:

1. The first challenge is to back up user data and settings that are scattered from PC to PC and restore the user's productivity after a laptop is lost or stolen.

2. The second challenge is to migrate the user state when the OS is refreshed.
3. The final challenge is to make data available to the user, regardless of the PC used.

With user state virtualization, organizations store user's data and settings in a central location. The result is that users are free to travel, and their data and settings follow them. User state virtualization can also reduce the liability to update systems as per requirements. The central copy of the data is on the network. Therefore, it is effortlessly reinstated in case of a stolen or misplaced PC and the locations of the user may be re-applied mechanically.

8.6 APPLICATION VIRTUALIZATION

Fundamentally, application virtualization software combines OS resources and isolates them within a virtualized container along with the application that accesses them. This technology offers skills to install applications without altering or making any variation to the file system, underlying OS, or registry of the computing platform in which they are installed as shown in Fig. 8.2.

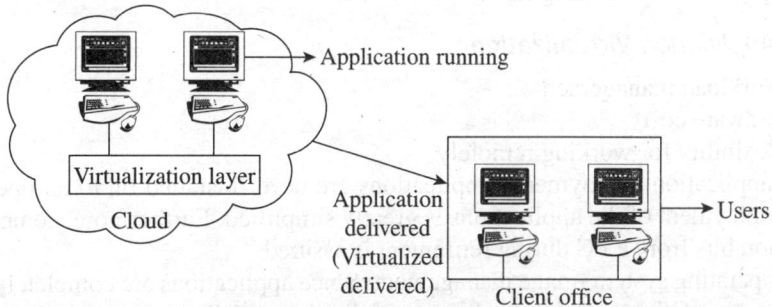

Fig. 8.2 Application virtualization

Virtualized applications are secured from hidden fraud which might be caused due to installation amendments. One such illustration is where Microsoft Access databases have been engaged by an organization by means of a discrete version of Microsoft Access than the standard of corporation. As two versions of Microsoft Access cannot be deployed on the same computing platform at the same time, they must be virtualized to overcome this matter and must be used concurrently. The following points are to be considered because there are various settings where discrepancy may occur if numerous applications or versions of the same applications are deployed on the same computing platform.
1. Applications should be served in an inaccessible environment.
2. Operating system resources and the applications should be comprehended in a virtualized container.
3. Reliability of applications and operating systems should be guaranteed.
4. Divergences among various applications or discrete versions of the same application should be avoided.

Virtualization is the separation of the logical unit from the physical unit. Correspondingly, application virtualization includes separating the physical customer tool from the administration of the application itself. Application encapsulation packages the application in a self-contained executable package that does not rely on a software installation or an underlying OS for any dependencies. From the system on a USB key or through local storage, this package is available. Since these applications contain the ability to run just as standalone executables, they would not need any means to be mounted in the customer machine locally where they operate.

Application streaming involves transporting application-specific data or resources to the client device when the application is executed. Only a minimum amount of data is delivered to a client before the application is launched. Hence, the first time, application launches very quickly and the load on the network is also reduced. Additional features of the application are delivered on demand or in the background without user intervention.

Application packages are stored on a (centralized) server. Application streaming is suitable in a well-networked environment. Streaming involves the use of a locally installed agent on the client machine. This mediator has the functionality to arrange and sustain the virtual environment for every application. The mediator pays attention to administration jobs and is a chief element in the streaming performance. Technology categories that fall under application virtualization include the following:

- Streaming of application: Before startup, rather than delivering the whole application, portions of the application's code, settings, and data are delivered according to their requirement.
- VDI or desktop virtualization: The application is introduced in blade PC or VM which also comprises the operating system (OS). This makes management of infrastructure and formation of virtual desktops easy to grant access of virtual desktops. VDI may normally fill up the gaps wherever applications' streaming fails.

Advantages of Application Virtualization

1. Improved workload management
2. Reduced hardware cost
3. Increased flexibility for working remotely
4. Simplified application deployment: Applications are never installed on to an operating System; hence the deployment of the applications is greatly simplified. Furthermore, complete removal of all application bits from a PC during retirement is assured.
5. Simplified operating system image management: Since applications are completely different from the OS, managing OS images is simpler, especially during OS patches and upgrades. It helps to create a more dynamic desktop environment, in which the desktop is an aggregation of separately-managed components.
6. Elimination of resource conflicts: Since each application has its own virtual OS resources, resource and application conflict issues are eliminated.

Limitations of Application Virtualization

1. All software cannot be virtualized. For example, applications that require a device driver or 16-bit applications that require shared memory space cannot be virtualized.
2. Some types of software cannot be virtualized, such as anti-virus packages and applications that require heavy OS integration.

8.6.1 Tools Used for Application Virtualization

Various tools are used for application virtualization and some of them are listed below.

Microsoft Application Virtualization (App-V)

It is just a part of the vendor's complete virtualization solution. Microsoft virtualization includes server virtualization through Hyper-V, desktop virtualization through Virtual PC and Microsoft Enterprise Desktop Virtualization (MED-V), presentation virtualization through terminal services, and profile virtualization (roaming profiles, folder redirection, and so on) through various technologies embedded in its operational systems.

Within App-V, Microsoft provides a complete virtual application management solution. From management servers that provide streaming and downloading of virtualized applications to data stores that house content, Microsoft provides thorough virtualization architecture.

VMWare ThinApp

VMWare's ThinApp application virtualization is unique as it does not require a client. As the ThinApp virtualized applications are also MSI packages, they can be deployed using the reporting and inventory capabilities of existing corporate software deployment tools.

Tools of ThinApp packages created by one version work with the same user device and applications packaged by a new version. Application virtualization allows administrators to work with different users of different apps, which can be carried from one desktop to another through different media like USB drives. VMware centralizes ThinApp administration and also automates various virtualization tools for Windows applications.

The advantages of ThinApp include the following:
1. Fewer arguments between applications.
2. Supports identical application with different versions: It has the ability to run efficiently, different versions of the same application under a similar Windows environment.
3. Keeps applications on virtual desktops: It keeps applications on virtual desktop to support an environment for executing the programs, relatively storing the whole applications in the local area, for example, C: Program Files.
4. Supports another memory: Application virtualization not only supports virtual desktops but also executes if we keep that application in some memory device and execute that from anywhere.
5. Support encapsulation: Installation of thin clients is not required to install every client at the destination where it is running.

Flexera Software Supporting Application Virtualization

Application virtualization has been supported by Flexera Software in two main fields—consulting and product tendering. Flexera Software Consulting Services supports the Flexera Software model. Experienced Flexera Software mentors may direct a corporation to perceive the advantages of every technology for the particular objectives, permitting an apparent assessment of suitable technology for an exclusive budget and situation.

Most importantly, Flexera Software Consulting Services helps organizations move from developing an application virtualization plan to implementing a working solution.

8.7 HARDWARE VIRTUAL MACHINE (HVM)

Dedicated software called hypervisor is used to make machines virtual to share resources. Hypervisors make multiple virtual hardware, which are isolated from each other and make virtual machines run various operating systems such as Unix, Linux, or Windows operating system on the same physical machine. Virtualization reduces the need of physical machines and reduces maintenance cost of hardware, energy consumption, and cooling consumptions. Maintenance of virtual machines is very easy. Disaster recovery, backups, or various administration tasks are also easy to do with virtual machines.

A hypervisor is an operating system that performs in a systematic mode. The hypervisor lies at the lowest levels of the hardware. Since in cloud computing you want to support numerous distinct operating environments, the hypervisor turns out to be a perfect transport means as shown in Fig. 8.3.

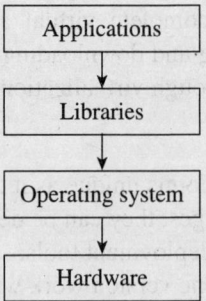

Fig. 8.3 Operating system and application linking

A virtual machine is also known as a guest and the virtualization tool helps to handle multiple virtual machines on a single physical machine. Software or hardware virtualization technique is used to make a physical machine a virtual machine. Depending on the application, there are two types of virtual machines:
1. System virtual machines allow sharing of physical resources among various virtual machines.
2. Process virtual machines allow programming that is platform-independent.

The virtual machine supervisor is known as a hypervisor. The work of the hypervisor is to manage the processor, memory, and other resources of firmware. The hypervisor performs like a traffic officer, permitting numerous operating systems to work on a similar tool without needing binary alterations or source codes. Every operating system seems to have the mainframe, memory, and other resources of firmware for itself, but in actuality, the hypervisor manages the mainframe and its resources, allotting what is required to every operating system consecutively.

Hardware virtualization is a developing technology which can turn out to be foremost, particularly for server platforms. Virtual hardware behaviour comprises EFI and BIOS, accessible virtual PCI slots, the highest number of CPUs, the greatest memory design, and other features typical to hardware. When you generate a virtual machine, you may acknowledge avoiding hardware edition, which characterizes the host on which you generate the virtual machine, or a previous edition. You may employ a previous hardware edition in the following conditions:
1. To regulate testing and installment in a virtual environment
2. If you do not require the facilities of the newer edition
3. To maintain compatibility with previous hosts

Virtual machines, along with hardware editions earlier than edition 8, may work on ESXi 5.0 hosts but do not encompass all the facilities accessible in hardware edition 8. The hardware edition of a virtual machine emulates the virtual hardware behaviour supported by a virtual machine. Such behaviour characterizes the physical hardware accessible on the ESXi host on which you generate the virtual machine. For instance, you could not employ 1011GB of memory or 32 virtual processors in virtual machines with hardware editions earlier than edition 8.

The vSphere Web Client or the vSphere Client permits you to advance virtual machines simply to the newest hardware edition. In case virtual machines do not encompass to remain companionable with previous ESXi/ESX hosts, you may advance them on ESXi 5.0 hosts. In such matters, they are advanced to edition 8.

To sustain virtual machine compatibility with ESXi/ESX 3.5 hosts, it should be made compatible with the latest hardware or machine that is used for application. You may generate, amend, and operate diverse virtual machine editions on a host in case the host supports that edition. Occasionally, virtual machine measures on a host are restricted or the virtual machine has no access to the host.

A virtual machine may encompass a previous hardware edition than that of the host on which it works in the subsequent instances:
1. You use a virtual machine generated on an ESXi/ESX 4.x or a previous host to an ESXi 5.0 host.
2. You generate a virtual machine on an ESXi 5.0 host by employing a prevailing virtual disk which was generated on an ESXi/ESX 4.x or previous host.
3. You append a virtual disk generated on an ESXi/ESX 4.x or a previous host to a virtual machine generated on ESXi 5.0 hosts.

A VM is described as a physical machine by software which has its individual array of virtual hardware on which an application and operating system may be overloaded. Along with virtualization, every virtual machine is offered with reliable virtual hardware despite the fundamental physical hardware which the host server operates. The VMware system manager better knows the internal mechanism of a virtual machine that must assist in everyday infrastructure administration jobs.

While you generate a VM, avoid array of virtual hardware allotted to it. As an administrator of cloud computing environment, many virtual hardware can be added or removed and most virtual hardware may merely be appended or eliminated even as the VM is powered off, with the exclusion of hard disks.

8.8 UNDERSTANDING MACHINE IMAGING

A virtual machine image is like a template that is used for creating a new case. We can choose any image from the available catalogue for making images or saving images from running available instances. After image creation, the software is configured as per the setting given or default settings. Images for operating systems or for databases, application servers, or other applications are available for users. Images typically reduce data related to runtime operations, such as data swapping and configuration files with IP addresses or host names.

8.9 PORTING APPLICATION

Porting is a method of making software adaptive to every situation for which it was not initially written or planned to perform. It is also compatible with different hardware configurations. Writing software from scratch is not an easy task, but it is more beneficial if software is adaptive as per hardware infrastructure and in every situation it comes up with good and accurate results. Software designers frequently argue their product is portable, suggesting that it will take only small attempts for it to perform on a platform of a consumer. The three favoured platforms are those from UNIX, Apple, and Microsoft, making it simpler to build software that is transferable. Yet, in the well-established system market, porting remains a significant issue. To simplify portability, modern editors have converted to a machine-free intermediate code.

Customer requirements and platforms are generally different from each other, but for availing services of the cloud environment, customers have to interact with the cloud services provided by the cloud providers. IT professionals already comprehend that a cloud service could give an option and possibly, a very profitable delivery channel to sell anything the business wants to. It might be a service, software, or a new product line. Porting your subscription to a cloud situation facilitates you to expand all of the guaranteed profits of the cloud such as ease-of-use, elasticity, scalability, and countless resources to consumers and potential consumers who symbolize new sources of income. However, the track from initiated product to cloud-based service is only a drag-and-drop scheme.

As IT decision-makers investigate and intend to shift apps to the cloud, there are a few terms of concern they must be familiar with, going in. For instance, EnterpriseDB, a supplier of enterprise-class services and goods based on Post-greSQL, presents such a blueprint and proposes several directions on guiding the stages along the track and avoiding potential drawbacks.

8.10 VIRTUAL MACHINE PROVISIONING

Virtual provisioning is intended to reduce storage management by permitting storage managers to meet the demand for capacity on-query. Virtual provisioning provides a host, file, or application system an illusion that it has extra storage than is physically offered. Physical storage is allotted particularly when the data is written, instead of when the application is originally aligned.

Virtual provisioning may lessen power and cooling charges by reducing on the quantity of redundant storage tools in the group. Consequently, virtual provisioning happened to be a part of the green data center and green computing schemes. The concern for virtual provisioning is that it needs managers to vigilantly supervise the handling of virtually provisioned resources to guarantee that no virtual disks become filled, which results in storage faults for mission-serious applications.

8.11 VIRTUAL MACHINE MIGRATION SERVICES MANAGEMENT

Virtualization means taking particulars of physical hardware and giving virtualized resources for prominent applications. A vital trait of a virtual machine is that the software working within it is bounded to the resources and concepts offered by the VM. The software layer which offers virtualization is known as a virtual machine monitor (VMM) or hypervisor. It virtualizes each resource of a physical machine, thus determining and sustaining the accomplishment of numerous virtual machines. Virtualization may offer noteworthy advantages in cloud computing by allowing virtual machine migration to equalize loads diagonally across the data centers. Migration is mostly made for dynamic resource administration. Its chief aims are discussed below:

Load balancing   Resources are equally distributed among the requested clients so there should be balanced access of all the resources. This prevents a number of machines from getting congested in the presence of lightly loaded machines with sufficient auxiliary capability. Live migration may be used to equalize the arrangement. The total system load may be balanced by moving VMs from overloaded PMs to under-loaded PMs.

Server consolidation   Consolidation of server will result in lesser power utilization and hence lessening the entire operational charges for data center management. On the basis of load conditions, under-used machines having resources beneath a limit and overloaded machines having resources over a certain limit are recognized, and migrations are provoked to compactly pack VMs to increase resource handling on all PMs and relieve resources of PMs, if feasible.

Coldspot and hotspot mitigation   The discovery of coldspots and hotspots is based on limits that are decided by the data center possessor or based on the service level agreements stated by the consumers. Generally, a higher resource handling value near the threshold is decided as the upper limit and an extremely low resource handling value is decided as the lower limit. PMs having threshold values beyond the upper limit are decided to have produced hotspots, and those handling values less than the lower limit are supposed to have created coldspots. The former means over-consumption and the latter means under-consumption.

Points to Remember

1. The advantages of desktop virtualization include cheaper price of installing new applications, easier furnishing of new desktops, desktop promotion abilities, amplified data safety, better revive cycle for consumer desktop framework, and safe remote access to a venture desktop setting.
2. Desktop virtualization is not altered and contains a new feature of the modern enterprise desktop.
3. Remote desktop services (RDS) is customarily called terminal services. It is a blanket term for characteristics of Microsoft Windows server which permits consumers to distantly access Windows applications and graphical desktops.
4. The advantages of remote desktop are as follows:
   (a) Data recovery in tragedy
   (b) Operation from anyplace
   (c) Economical
5. The disadvantages of remote desktops are that it needs strong RDS, needs RDS scrutinizing, needs dependable network, needs proper alteration in network, and needs a well-informed supervisor.
6. The advantages of virtual desktop infrastructure (VDI) are cheap rate in buying desktop computers, centralized consumer OS management, speedy customer disposition, diminution in desktop support expenses, enhanced data safety, safe remote access, and less application compatibility problems.
7. The benefits of application virtualization are:
   (a) Enhanced workload administration
   (b) Abridged hardware charge
   (c) Amplified suppleness for remote working
8. A simplified application deployment/retirement involves easy operating system image management and abolition of resource arguments.
9. Some of the tools for application virtualization include Microsoft Application Virtualization, VMWare ThinApp, and Flexera Software Supporting Application Virtualization.
10. Porting makes software adaptive to every situation for which it was not initially written or planned to perform.
11. Virtual provisioning reduces storage management by allowing storage managers to meet the demand for capacity on query.
12. Virtual machine migration is mostly done for dynamic resource administration. Its chief aims are load balancing, server consolidation, and coldspot and hotspot mitigation.

Key Terms

Application encapsulation Application encapsulation packages the application in a self-contained executable package that does not rely on software installation or an underlying OS for any dependencies.

Application streaming Application streaming involves transporting application-specific data/resources to the client device when the application is executed.

Application virtualization Application virtualization is the technique of separating the application configuration layer from the operating system. It helps us to run applications on clients desktops, servers, and laptops without actually being installed on them, and it can be administered from a central location.

Browsers A software application used to locate, retrieve, and display content on the World Wide Web, including web pages, images, videos, and other files.

Datacenter A data center is a centralized repository for the storage, management, and diffusion of data and information.

Hypervisors A hypervisor, also known as a virtual machine manager, has a provision to make a single hardware host that can be shared by multiple operating systems.

Remote desktop A remote desktop is a different program found on most operating systems that allows a user to access an operating computer system's desktop. We can access it through the Internet or another network.

Virtual desktop environment The server-hosted desktop virtualization solution approach is sometimes called virtual desktop environment (VDE).

Virtual machines A virtual machine (VM) is actually a software program or operating system that makes physical machines' behaviour like a separate computer, and is also capable of performing tasks that look like a separate computer.

Multiple-choice Questions

1. Advantages of desktop virtualization are/is _____.
   (a) Increased data security
   (b) Simpler provisioning of new desktops
   (c) Desktop image-management capabilities
   (d) All the above

2. The benefits of virtual desktop infrastructure (VDI) include _____.
   (a) Reduction in desktop support costs
   (b) Reduction in electricity costs
   (c) Improved data security
   (d) All the above

3. What is not true about remote desktop?
   (a) Recovery of data during disaster
   (b) Work from anywhere
   (c) Increased speed
   (d) Cost effective

4. Transporting application-specific data/resources to the client device when the application is executed is called _____.
   (a) Application encapsulation
   (b) Application streaming
   (c) Remote desktop
   (d) None of these

5. A program that allows multiple operating systems to share a single hardware host is called _____.
   (a) Virtual machine
   (b) Hypervisor
   (c) Remote desktop
   (d) None of these

6. Software that cannot be virtualized is _____.
   (a) Antivirus software
   (b) Software that required shared memory space
   (c) Application that require heavy OS integration
   (d) All the above

7. The server-hosted desktop virtualization solution approach is sometimes called _____.
   (a) Virtual desktop infrastructure (VDI)
   (b) Virtual desktop environment (VDE)
   (c) Both (a) and (b)
   (d) None of these

8. Virtualized desktops offer a greater level of _____ that is impossible with a standard desktop.
   (a) Flexibility
   (b) Mobility
   (c) Both (a) and (b)
   (d) None of these

9. Advantage of application virtualization includes:
   (a) Improved workload management
   (b) Reduced hardware cost
   (c) Increased flexibility for working remotely
   (d) All the above

10. The disadvantages of remote desktop are
    (a) Powerful remote desktop services (RDS) required
    (b) RDS monitoring required
    (c) Reliable network required
    (d) All the above

Review Questions

1. What is virtualization and how is it different from desktop virtualization?
2. What are the various advantage and disadvantage of desktop virtualization?
3. Explain the various techniques of desktop virtualization?.
4. What are the various components of desktop virtualization?
5. What do you understand by application virtualization?
6. What are the benefits of virtual desktop infrastructure?
7. What do you understand by remote desktop?
8. What are the limitations of application virtualization?
9. What are the various tools in application virtualization?
10. What is the technology that comes under application virtualization?
11. Explain the applications of hardware virtual machine (HVM)?
12. Why is virtual machine migration imaging very important for sensitive transaction area like banks?
13. How virtual machine provisioning important at the time of disaster?

References

1. *Cloud Security A Comprehensive Guide to Secure Cloud Computing,* Ronald L. Krutz and Russell Dean Vines, ISBN: 978-0-470-58987-8, Wiley Publication, 2010
2. *Cloud computing for Dummies,* Judith Hurwitz, Robin Bloor, Marcia Kaufman, and Dr. Fern Halper, ISBN-10: 0470484705,Wiley Publication, 1st edition, November 16, 2009
3. *Cloud Computing Technologies and Strategies,* Brian J.S. Chee and Curtis Franklin, Jr ISBN 9781439806128, CRC Press, April 7, 2010
4. *Cloud Computing: A Practical Approach,* Anthony T. Velte ,Toby J. Velte, Ph.D.,Robert Elsenpeter, ISBN-10: 0071626948, McGraw-Hill, 1st edition, November 1, 2009
5. *Grid and Cloud Computing,* Katarina StanoevskaSlabeva, Thomas Wozniak, and Santi Ristol, ISBN-10: 3642051928, Springer, 2010 edition, November 19, 2009
6. *Implementing and Developing Cloud Applications,* David E.Y.Sarna, ISBN-10: 1439830827, Auerbach Publications, November 26, 2010
7. *Market-oriented cloud Computing: Vision, Hype, and Reality for Delivering IT Services as Computing Utilities. In High Performance Computing and Communications,* R. Buyya, C.S. Yeo, and S. Venugopal, 2008. HPCC'08. 10th IEEE International Conference on pp. 5–13 IEEE, 2008
8. Advantage and Disadvantage of Remote Desktop:-http://ezinearticles.com/?Remote-Desktop-Service---Advantages,-Disadvantages-and-Its-Monitoring&id=6437670
9. Benefits of desktop virtualization: http://medtechmedia.com/RCPDF/VMware_BetterPatientCare_Virtually%20There.pdf
10. Remote desktop application: - https://technet.microsoft.com/en-us/magazine/hh315808.aspx, last accessed in May 2018
11. Virtual machines:-https://www.vmware.com/support/vsphere5/doc/vsp_esxi50_u1_rel_notes.html, last accessed in May 2018

Answers to Multiple-choice Questions

1. (d)	3. (c)	5. (b)	7. (b)	9. (d)
2. (d)	4. (b)	6. (d)	8. (c)	10. (d)

CHAPTER 9

Cloud Infrastructure Management and Migration

> **Learning Outcomes**
>
> After completing this chapter, students will be able to:
>
> - comprehend various service creation tools
> - describe the web application programming interface
> - describe the unified management software
> - understand cloud service management
> - describe the way to access cloud
> - understand cloud migration
> - describe banking on cloud

9.1 INTRODUCTION

Nowadays, in order to manage the environment of cloud computing, almost all new and already established dealers have certain kinds of tools. These tools can scrutinize, administer, customize, and negotiate to work easily and efficiently among users.

A dynamic provisioning system might not be needed unless your cloud implementation is mission critical or quite static. In such a case, customary tools for resource deletions, variations, or additions integrated with the product might be sufficient.

In the rest of the chapter, we will discuss the tools for administrating the cloud, cloud management products, unified management software, the various cloud providers and traditional IT service providers, and the qualities of different web browsers.

9.2 ADMINISTRATING CLOUDS

Various suppliers possess products structured for cloud computing management, such as OpenQRM, Managed Methods, VMware, and Cloud Kick, together with established names such as CA, BMC, IBM, Tivoli, and HP. In order to give alerts on likely problems, each product uses specific methods, in addition to tracking performance tendencies.

Although their different characteristics set them apart from one another, they are all concentrated towards a single idea, which is to supply information regarding cloud computing systems. Equivalent main features are provided by the main cloud substructure managing products which are as follows:

1. Almost all of these assist in designing and furnishing new items and in eliminating useless items.
2. Almost all offer a common set of reports on status such as response time, used quota, uptime, etc.
3. Almost all of these assist distinct clouds forms (often stated as hybrid clouds).

When it comes to meeting these three standards, it has been observed that only a few suppliers present comprehensive means in handling metrics and managing provisioning in hybrid environments. They are Zeus, Morph, RightScale Kaavo, and Scalr. Cloud suppliers offer certain options to meet the first and second standard, like CloudWatch by Web Services of Amazon.

The well-established and branded companies which are famous for their conventional data center monitoring appliances fail to compete in the cloud market. Their products are the restate of current appliances which provide nothing else than alerting and reporting tools.

HP company Open View, also known as Operating Manager, can administer cloud-based servers, but in the same way as administered by some other server. At present, the company BMC also has nothing new to offer other than its customary tools (although it functions on cloud management tools).

It offers:
1. Ways to monitor and manage the cloud
2. Cloud supervising and cloud service administration for suppliers
3. New information on cloud management
4. Licensing and pricing for tools of cloud management

Nowadays, the best infrastructure provisioning and management alternatives accessible are as follows:

RightScale

At present, RightScale is one of the main suppliers. Similar to other suppliers in the emerging market, they also propose free editions with confine on capacity and features, intended to familiarize you with the product. The product of RightScale is classified into three components which are as follows:
1. Cloud management environment:
   (a) Multi-cloud engine
   (b) Cloud-ready server template and best practice deployment library
   (c) Adjustable automation engine
2. Cooperative cloud tips from RightScale:
   (a) Initiation of server in the cloud by means of Server Templates
   (b) Organization of servers with RightScale deployments
   (c) Scalable batch processing by way of RightGrid automation

The main interface which the users will have along with the software is RightScale's management environment. It is intended to turn a user during the introductory process of migrating the cloud by the means of library and templates. Then the environments are managed with the help of the management environment tool, specifically continuing manufactures and guaranteing the availability of resource. The supporting companies are Amazon, Rackspace Eucalyptus, GoGrid, and Multi-Cloud Engine. The next best infrastructure provisioning and management alternatives accessible is called Kaavo.

Kaavo

A range similar to RightScale has been given by Kaavo. The product is used:
1. To handle demand variations through automatically adding up or eliminating resources
2. For single-click of complicated multi-tier appliances in the cloud
3. For ciphering preserved data in the cloud
4. To manage run-time environment and automation of workflows without human interference
5. For run-time organization of relevant infrastructure within the cloud

The essential product of Kaavo is known as IMOD. Provisioning, changes, and configuration to the environment of the cloud has been controlled by IMOD and also in the hybrid model across various suppliers. Similar to other main CIM players, IMOD of Kaavo holds the top position among the masses by handling applications' layers and infrastructure.

The multi-cloud single system tool is one of the significant characteristics in IMOD. For example, a database backend can be created by users in Rackspace whilst setting their presentation servers on Amazon. Supporting Eucalyptus in the private space and Rackspace and Amazon in the public space is a strong selling point while it should be taken into account that Eucalyptus can be supported by most aspects of cloud management, and also supports Amazon.

Well-programmed and monitoring tools have been proposed by both RightScale and Kaavo to make certain that internal metrics such as SLAs and information are accessible clearly. The demands of these SLAs could be met with the help of dynamic allotment. Kaavo and RightScale both propose the skill to maintain templates and to alleviate the implementation of multi-tier systems.

Zeus

The durable and trustworthy Web server made Zeus famous. Although it did not have a good market share, it had a long list of top-tier clients. Along with Apache and to a smaller-level, controlling the market, Zeus acquired its proficiency in server space's application and developed the Application Delivery Controller specimen of the Zeus Traffic Controller. To test the availability, conventional load balancing tools were used by it which created or terminated supplementary insistence in the cloud, hence supplying tool provisioning. Presently, this has been assisted by Zeus on the platform of RackSpace and slighter level to Amazon.

Scalr

Scalr is a new project introduced on Scalr.net and Google Code which, on the Amazon platform, builds vibrant clusters similar to that of RightScale and Kaavo. Just like Rightscale, it also assists in upsizing and downsizing, depending upon the custom building of images, traffic demands, and snapshots for every server or server type. As Scalr is a new launch, it does not assist the varied number of applications, platforms, databases, and operating systems unlike leading competitors who stick to conventional designing.

Morph

The functionality in its own private space has been proposed by Morph, thus refilling the provisioning space and management as an application. It is intended at the business enterprise looking to install a private cloud. The Morph CloudServer, which is a top-tier product, is embedded on the IBM BladeCenter and also assists numerous virtual machines.

The Eucalyptus cloud computing platform and Ubuntu Linux operating system is its core. Targeted at the administer service provider market, the formation of private clouds and the active provisioning in these clouds has been allowed by Morph. As a result of its open-source roots and involvement in open-cloud associations, Morph provides customized and stylish platforms by providing guidance at each and every step.

CloudWatch

Amazon CloudWatch is a service that provides customers' facilities to monitor applications, systems, and also provides you with easy solutions by giving you the facility to collect metrics, logs, and events in a real-time system about a resource.

In CloudWatch for EC2, a central management console, the same one as used by the Amazon Web Services, manages all load balancing, monitoring, and dynamic provisioning known as auto-scaling. *Automatic scaling* is generally used in cloud computing, where the total amount of resources in a server is measured in terms of the number of active servers, and scaling is done on the basis of load at a particular instant of time. Installing of supplementary software and other websites to retrieve appliances is not needed in it. As this product is not meant for those business enterprises which require hybrid support, Amazon users must be aware that it is efficient and heavy just like other business markets.

Due to an excess of devices in the market, it is essential for the data manager to originate the evaluation earlier and to watch the progress of the market. This modification to the basis of the infrastructure of IT is both fast and enormous. It is the need of the hour to have a review of products and a regular amendment of plans, along with a market watch scrutiny of companies. It is well known that RightScale has been leading the market but other businesses are also in the race and making competition tough with precise observations of the market.

9.3 CLOUD MANAGEMENT PRODUCTS

The framework of cloud infrastructure is made up of the following components (refer to Fig. 9.1):
1. Physical infrastructure
2. Virtual infrastructure
3. Applications and platform software
4. Cloud infrastructure management and service creation tools

Application and platform software	Service creation tools
Virtual infrastructure	
Physical infrastructure	

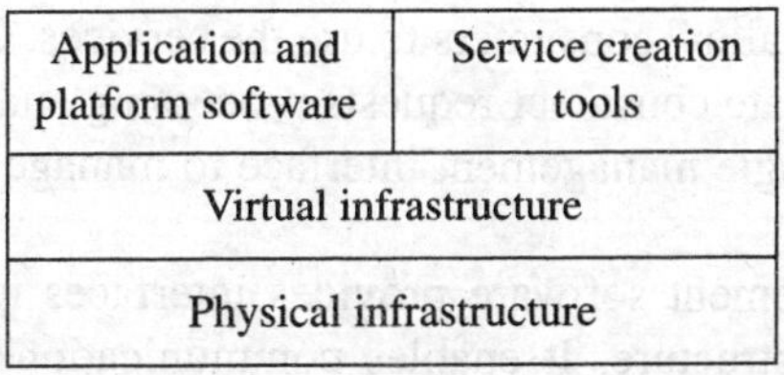

Fig. 9.1 Framework of cloud infrastructure

Physical Infrastructure

Physical infrastructure includes physical IT resources which comprise physical network components such as switches, routers, physical adaptors, physical servers, and storage systems. Physical servers are linked with one another, to the storage systems, and to the clients through physical networks such as IP SAN, FC SAN, and IP network.

Cloud service providers may use physical IT resources from one or more data centers to provide services. Even if physical IT resources can be kept at multiple data centers that are far from each other, connectivity must be established among them. The connectivity facilitates data centers at different locations to work as a single unit and resources can also be shared as per user requirement.

This enables both migration of cloud services across data centers and provisioning of cloud services using resources from multiple data centers.

Virtual Infrastructure

Virtual infrastructure consists of the following resources:
- Resource pools such as CPU pools, memory pools, network bandwidth pools, and storage pools
- Identity pools such as VLAN ID pools, VSAN ID pools, and MAC address pools
- Virtual IT resources consist of the following:
  (a) VMs, virtual volumes, and virtual networks
  (b) VM network components such as virtual switches and virtual NICs

Virtual IT resources gain capacities such as CPU cycles, memory, and network bandwidth and storage space from the resource pools. Virtual networks are defined using network identifiers such as VLAN IDs and VSAN IDs from the respective identity pools. MAC addresses are assigned to virtual NICs from the MAC address pool.

Applications and Platform Software

Applications and platform software layers include a suite of software such as the following:
- Business applications
- Operating systems and database
- Software required to build environments for running applications
- Migration tools

Applications and platform software are hosted on VMs to create Software as a Service (SaaS) and Platform as a Service (PaaS). For SaaS, applications and platform software are provided by cloud service providers. For PaaS, only the platform software is provided by the cloud service providers. Consumers export their applications to the cloud. In Infrastructure as a Service (IaaS), consumers upload both applications and platform software to the cloud. Cloud service providers supply migration tools to consumers, enabling deployment of their applications and platform software to the cloud.

Cloud Infrastructure Management and Service Creation Tools

Cloud infrastructure management and service creation tools are responsible for managing physical and virtual infrastructure. They enable consumers to request for cloud services. They provide cloud services based on consumer requests and allow consumers to use the services. Cloud infrastructure management and service creation tools automate consumer requests processing and creation of cloud services. They also provide administrators a single management interface to manage resources distributed in multiple virtualized data centers (VDCs).

Virtual infrastructure management software provides interfaces to construct virtual infrastructure from underlying physical infrastructure. It enables communication with tools, such as hypervisors and physical switch operating systems, and also configuration of pools and virtual resources with the assistance of these tools. In a VDC, compute, storage, and network are used. By using distinct virtual infrastructure management software, resources are organized separately.

Physical servers and networks are handled separately using compute management software and networks appropriately. Apart from this, unified management software is also another facility that combines various infrastructure of virtual cloud into a single unit.

9.4 UNIFIED MANAGEMENT SOFTWARE

Unified management software interrelates with all individual virtual infrastructure management software and gathers data on the accessible virtual and physical infrastructure patterns, connectivity, and consumption. Unified management software accumulates this information and offers a combined outlook of IT resources scattered in VDCs. This facilitates a manager to watch accessibility functioning and capability of virtual and physical resources centrally.

A single management interface is offered by unified management software to generate virtual pools and resources. It is used to facilitate a manager to insert independence and aptitude to the available pools. This eliminates the administration of storage, compute, and network resources unconnectedly using local management software.

The vital purpose of unified management software is to generate cloud services. It executes a string of procedures to generate cloud services. Unified management software facilitates a manager to rate pools. Resource rating is a method to classify pools based on abilities such as aptitude and function. Multiple rating levels can be identified for every kind (e.g., network, compute, and storage) of pool. Three rating values are used to indicate the three distinct rating levels.

Resource package is a method of amalgamating a rated compute pool with a rated storage pool and a rated network pool. A memory pool as well as a CPU pool are involved in the compute pool. The amalgamation facilitates a cluster of physical servers from which the compute pool is generated, to use the network and storage pools for shifting and saving data correspondingly. The incorporated pools are provided a bundle name and are considered the only unit. A bundle can be associated with platform software or an application to allow PaaS and SaaS.

IaaS is an exception, where only network, storage, and compute resources are vital. The correlation permits a particular platform software and application to use particular bundle resources.

A cloud service supplier characteristically sustains multiple resource bundles with distinct permutation of rating values for network, storage, and compute pools. Every bundle is used to generate a cloud service that succeeds in the abilities of the pools in the bundle.

Unified management software assists in classifying cloud services. It permits a manager to roll all the services together with their service traits. The service traits are as follows:
1. Network bandwidth, CPU, storage ability, and memory which are to be assigned to services from distinct bundles
2. Name and explanation of platform and software applications
3. VDC position (bundle position) from where resources are to be assigned
4. Backup strategy, such as the position of the backup data and the number of backup copies of a service case. For instance, a backup strategy might be to generate two copies of VM files and to sustain the copies in a similar VDC or shift to another VDC.

Unified management software facilitates generating a variety of cloud services along with varied service traits. Services based on abilities of the bundle resources are connected. Service traits are related with VMs and are used to offer a service. On the basis of the kind of service (i.e., IaaS, PaaS, or SaaS), VMs may or may not host applications and platform software.

Unified management comprises the following:
1. Automation of IT sequence with incorporation into accessible IT systems' management tactics
2. Self-service portal and service catalog for IT resources along with on-demand provisioning
3. On-demand provisioning offered along with self-service portal and service catalog for IT resources
4. Resource management for efficient operation of hardware infrastructure groups
5. Automatic workload for carrying effectual batch and event-driven project business measures
6. Life cycle management from request to retirement
7. Strategy-based administration destined for improved handling and governance
8. Virtual and physical assets administration
9. Automatic network provisioning
10. Automation and setting up for huge data and business enterprise aptitude workloads
11. Resource allocation comprises generating service cases and assigning resources from bundles to service cases when customers ask for services. At the occasion of generating service cases, VMs are built and incorporated with virtual volumes (virtual disks) and VLANs. Platform software and application can be deployed on the VMs. The service cases get storage, network, and compute capacity from suitable bundles. The allotment of aptitude and software deployment pursues traits described for the service.

A web-based user interface has been provided to customers by user access management software. Customers can use the interface to demand for cloud services. User access management software interrelates with unified management software and dispatches every service requirement. The unified management software supplies these services that are made accessible to the customers through user access management software.

The manager is facilitated by the user access management software to generate and print service catalog. A service catalog is a planned manuscript with information concerning every cloud service accessible to customers. It comprises information regarding service expenses, demand procedures, and traits. User access management software authenticates customers before dispatching their requirements to unified management software. It sustains a database for every customer account. User access management software observes usage or allotment of resources associated with a cloud service case. A chargeback report is created according to the allotment or usage. For supplying transparency, the report is traceable to customers as well.

9.5 PROCESSES IN CLOUD SERVICE MANAGEMENT

Cloud service administration comprises a set of organizational procedures that connect the distribution of cloud services to customers. Generating and distributing services involve giving customers what they desire.

Cloud service management procedures perform in the environment to make certain all the service tasks are carried out as committed. Businesses, despite having top service conception devices, are many a time, unsuccessful in carrying out services to the desired quality and do not meet business needs. This is because of inadequate service management procedures.

Sometimes, services offered by cloud suppliers are not delivered by them as the supplier has a scarcity of resources, or a customer is incapable of using a service for a considerable session because of an uncertain fault in the infrastructure of the supplier. Cloud service suppliers should make use of appropriate service management procedures to supply cloud services. Therefore, there is a need to recognize the actions and purposes in every service management procedure.

Processes included in cloud service management (refer to Fig. 9.2):
- Service benefit and configuration administration
- Capacity administration
- Performance administration
- Incident administration
- Problem administration
- Availability administration
- Service catalog administration
- Financial administration
- Compliance administration

These procedures are discussed in detail in the following sections.

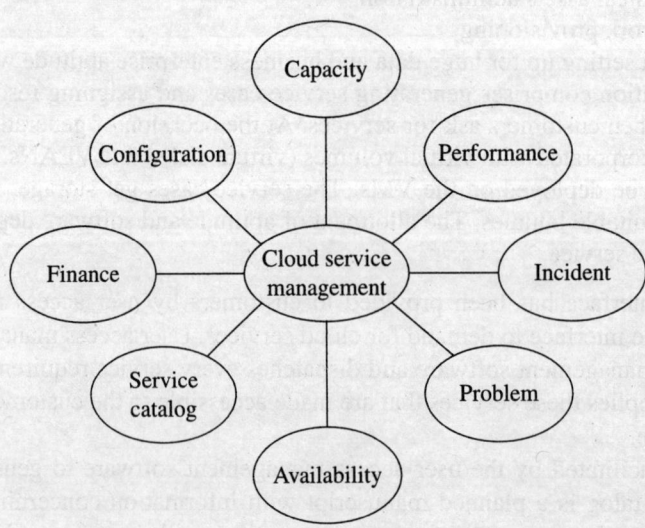

Fig. 9.2 Process administration involved in cloud service management

9.5.1 Service Benefit and Configuration Administration

Service asset and pattern administration sustains information regarding cloud infrastructure resources such as storage display, spare elements, and physical servers. The information comprises manufacturer name, customer IDs (CIs), license status, inventory status, serial number, account of amendment, edition, and position.

It retains information on used and accessible abilities of CIs and any matter associated with the CIs. It also sustains information on the interrelationships among CIs such as a VM to a service, a service to its customer, a VDC to its site, a physical server to a control transfer data to the server, and a physical server to a VM hosted on the server. This guarantees that design objects are analysed as incorporated elements. Accordingly, it assists in recognizing the root reason of the crisis and measuring the influence of every alteration in the association.

Service asset and design management sustains all the information regarding configuration objects in one or more databases which are known as configuration management database (CMDB). This database is used by every cloud service management procedure to transact with troubles or to comprise alterations into cloud infrastructure and services. Service asset and design management modernizes CMDB when novel design objects are installed or when traits of design objects vary. It occasionally examines the authenticity of information on design objects to make sure that the information it sustains is an accurate description of the configuration items used to provide cloud services.

9.5.2 Capacity Administration

Cloud administration deals with the management of various cloud computing products and services provided by cloud computing. Capacity administration guarantees that a cloud infrastructure is capable of meeting the mandatory requirements for cloud services in a price efficient way. The consumption of IT infrastructure resources is supervised by capacity management. It recognizes over-consumed and under-consumed resources.

Capacity administration is accountable for setting up future IT infrastructure necessities for cloud services. It collects information on the past and present consumption of resources and setup tendency on aptitude utilization. Based on the tendency, it predicts development in customer requirement for aptitude in the future.

9.5.3 Performance Administration

Performance administration involves monitoring, measuring, analysing, and improving the performance of cloud infrastructure and services. Performance management monitors and measures performance, such as response time and data transfer rate, of the cloud infrastructure resources and services. It analyses the performance statistics and identifies resources and services that are performing below the expected level.

Performance administration guarantees that the entire infrastructure resources accountable for supplying cloud services are met or exceed the mandatory functioning level. It executes alterations in resource design to enhance functioning of resources.

Overconsumption of resources is a major cause for lack of performance. Performance administration decides the necessary aptitude of cloud infrastructure services and resources to meet the predictable performance level. It performs collectively with capacity administration and executes alterations associated with resource performance.

9.5.4 Incident Administration

An unintended incident can affect cloud services or lessen the service quality, like an infected functioning. An event might lead to breakdown of service. Incident administration ensures cloud services along with the necessary traits to customers when events initiate lack of service or any trouble.

Incident administration arranges events on the basis of their strictness and reinstates cloud services inside a decided time frame. It attempts to recover cloud services as soon as possible by amending the malfunction or fault which instigated the event. Incident administration records the event history along with particulars of the event indications, cloud infrastructure resources which create the cloud service, severity of the incident, time to determine the incident, depiction of the fault, and the event determination data. The event history is used as an input for problem administration.

If incident administration is incapable of deciding and amending the reason behind an event, the fault-rectification activity is transmitted to problem administration, and incident administration supplies a temporary treatment. Incident administration might comprise numerous support clusters to support fault tolerance.

9.5.5 Problem Administration

Problem administration prevents events from recurring and reduces the unfavourable influence of events which may not be avoided. It lists troubles on the basis of their influence to the company and takes remedial measures. It recognizes the basic reason of a trouble and prompts the most suitable solution for the trouble. If an entire solution is not accessible, problem administration offers techniques to eradicate or lessen the influence of a trouble. It preemptively investigates the event history and recognizes service breakdown likely to occur. It recognizes and resolves faults before any trouble takes place.

Problem administration also records the trouble history with particulars on the indications, the cloud infrastructure resources which create the cloud service, the time to solve the problem, the severity of the trouble, fault depiction, and the resolved data. The trouble history offers a chance to study and control future problems.

9.5.6 Availability Administration

Availability administration makes certain that the accessibility necessities of a cloud service are continuously met. It summarizes and executes the process and technical characteristics necessary to accomplish the declared accessibility of a service.

Availability administration assists when server outcomes in the services failover to a further accessible server in the group. It guarantees that the corporation continuity procedures, cloud infrastructure, and devices are suitable to meet the necessary accessibility level. It constantly evaluates and scrutinizes the declared accessibility and the attained accessibility of cloud services and recognizes the areas where the accessibility ought to be enhanced.

Availability administration facilitates in recognizing regions for accessibility enhancement. The problem and incident management offers a major contribution to availability administration by figuring out the reasons of any failure and by keeping track of time needed to recommence services.

Enhanced customer service and price efficiency for the cloud service supplier are guaranteed by availability administration. It lessens the period for customers to connect with the service desk. This enhances customer satisfaction and helps improve the reputation of the cloud service supplier.

9.5.7 Service Catalog Administration

Service catalog administration comprises generating and sustaining a service catalog. It guarantees that the information in the service catalog is the latest and correct. It brings in usefulness and is clear while recounting service offerings in the service catalog. It guarantees that the service depiction is precious and definite to customers.

Corporation technologies and drivers are forever changing, and accordingly, cloud services are required to undergo modifications. Service catalog administration constantly evaluates service offerings in a service catalog and improves the catalog to comprise new services and alterations in the service offerings.

In service catalog administration, an important activity is to symbolize cloud services in a way that evidently discloses the worth of the services. Characteristically, every service offering in a service catalog is presented using a record.

9.5.8 Financial Management

Financial administration comprises estimating the price of supplying a service. The price comprises ongoing operational expenditures (OPEX) such as cooling, power, and facility cost, capital expenditure (CAPEX) such as attaining and installation prices of cloud infrastructure, and management expenditure like labour charge.

Financial administration manages investments and decides the IT budget for cloud infrastructure and function for a fixed time period. It decides the cost that the customer is likely to pay for a service and guarantees profitability. It facilitates the cloud service supplier to regain the price of supplying cloud services from customers.

It also scrutinizes and reports on consumption and distribution of resources by customers. This guarantees that the customers pay for what they use in reality. It characteristically carries out a series of activities to implement chargeback for supplying cloud services.

9.5.9 Compliance Administration

Compliance administration makes certain that the cloud infrastructure resources, cloud services, and service creation procedures fulfil the strategies and authorized demands. It guarantees that the compliance needs are satisfied at the same time as provisioning cloud services and configuring cloud infrastructure. Compliance administration mainly comprises the following:
1. Strategies and rules
2. External legal demands

Sticking to *strategies and rules* applies to both cloud service suppliers and customers. Strategies and rules might be on designing the finest practices, safety rules like physical infrastructure upholding timeline, roles and responsibilities of manager, and information backup agenda, and alteration of procedures like cloud infrastructure services and resources.

External legal demands are data secrecy laws forced by distinct nations. These laws can identify geographical sites in order to save consumer data and prohibit alteration or removal of data throughout its maintenance period. Several nations do not permit fiscal data to traverse country boundaries. In such instances, compliance administration ought to guarantee that the cloud infrastructure which offers the desired service is situated inside the border of these nations and data access is controlled by the populace of those nations.

Compliance administration occasionally considers compliance examination in infrastructure services and resources. If it finds out any difference from the compliance requisite, it initiates remedial measures.

9.6 CLOUD PROVIDERS AND TRADITIONAL IT SERVICE PROVIDERS

Traditional IT providers control the software, hardware, storage, and networks for their customers. The IT service provider handles the whole setting whilst the consumer pays the licensing bill for the software. The infrastructure is handled by the service provider according to its own convenience. The consumer signs a long-term agreement with the traditional service provider which jointly approves service terms. In order to fulfil the requirements of one consumer, an environment is characteristically modified by these IT providers. To raise the demand for cloud-based services, lower capital costs and better flexibility are required.

Nowadays, various new development projects are tracked on the cloud, signifying an augmented confidence business enterprise, ready cloud services for commercial use including test and development, critical applications, and data analysis or batch processing.

Cloud providers always offer clouds apps with advanced features as given here:
- Data can be stored locally, even on offline mode.
- Web browsers along with custom-built appliance installed on the Internet connect devices such as mobiles phones and desktops.
- Access to a broadscale of services such as application development platforms, on-demand computing cycles, and storage is available.

The difference between traditional service providers and cloud service provider (as shown in Table 9.1) can also be discussed on the basis of the following parameters.

Table 9.1 Difference between traditional IT services and cloud services

	Traditional IT services	Cloud services
Data	If there is a requirement for higher bandwidth or storage, you should upgrade your package. These packages are generally deployed on a monthly or yearly subscription.	According to your requirement, cloud services permit you to alter the bandwidth and storage. When you are not using bandwidth, you need not pay for it.
Performance	When any issues occur, you need to be worried	A backup facility is provided by cloud services that gets activated during issues in the main server. The data is retrieved as well as saved within a secure period.
Security	Less secure	More secure

Data Limits and Availability

Along with selecting your host provider, you also select a package service. If there is a requirement of more bandwidth or storage by you, you should upgrade your package. Charges of these packages generally depend on a monthly or yearly subscription.

According to your requirement, cloud service permits you to alter the bandwidth and storage. When you are not using bandwidth, you need not pay for it.

Performance

When you are a particular web host, it means you trust the technical team of the host in order to make the whole performance perfect. When you use cloud services, you not only get website hosting, but a lot more. When any problem is encountered, you need not be worried about backup or running all the components. A facility for backup is provided by cloud services that get activated during problems in the main server. The data is retrieved as well as saved within a secure period.

Security

While using cloud provider services, most businesses are worried about the safety of their secret data. Cloud providers, in order to ensure the security of your data, will work with you as they are aware of the importance of security. When your whole business working depends on websites, selecting a good cloud provider ensures that your site runs properly.

9.7 HOW TO ACCESS THE CLOUD

With the help of cloud, it becomes feasible for you to access your data at any time from any place. Cloud providers have software and hardware essential for running your enterprise appliances. Even small corporations have to invest capital for purchasing new memory space. A company can buy additional space or lessen their subscription according to the growth of their business or their requirement of less storage space.

For accessing the cloud, an Internet connection is required. If you wish to see the particular document which you have stored in the cloud, you have to first set up an internet connection through any mobile, broadband, or wired/wireless connection. The advantage of this is that you can access the same document anywhere and anytime with the help of tools that can access the Internet. These tools can be a phone, desktop, tablet, or laptop. Every provider offers a certain function so that users can manage their clouds according to their form. While selecting a provider, you should compare your requirements to the available cloud services. The requirements of your cloud will fluctuate according to your plan to use the space and the means allied with the cloud.

You can buy additional storage space at any time from your cloud provider according to technological requirements, thus your cloud provider will offer services on a pay-as-you-use method. For accessing cloud services and tools, some other tools are required. These include a platform that supports a cloud environment, web application, web browsers, etc.

9.7.1 Platforms

A platform refers to the way in which a cloud computing environment is supplied to you. The framework of a web application involves maintaining the expansion of dynamic web applications, web services, and websites. The purpose of a framework is lessening the expenses in web development which occurs with regular activities.

Early in the web's life, hypertext was mostly hand-coded Hypertext Markup Language (HTML) which was published on web servers. HTML provides users with a facility to change the web page as per the requirement. Apart from this, static pages can also be made dynamic using the Common Gateway Interface (CGI). This allows external applications to interface with web servers.

9.7.2 Web Applications

The decision of choosing a web application on the cloud depends on the type of providers available and the services they offer. Google offers a variety of applications geared towards productivity. Force.com allows you and others to create your own apps and then make them available for others to use.

Started as a free service in August 2006, Google Apps is a set of applications which comprises the following:
- Start page for designing a customizable home page on a particular domain
- Gmail webmail services
- Google Talk instantaneous messaging and Voice Over IP
- Google Calendar, shared calendaring

Nowadays, Google services are used by hundreds of academia and more than 100,000 small companies. A premium service known as Google apps premier edition is being provided by Google. This offers unique features which are as follows:
1. Ten gigabytes storage per user—Around 100 times more storage space than that of the standard commercial mailbox, purging the necessity of deleting emails repeatedly.

2. APIs for business incorporation—APIs for single sign-on, mail gateways, and data migration permit businesses to further modify the service for unique situations.
3. Almost 99.9 per cent uptime service level agreements for high accessibility of Gmail as well as Google crediting and monitoring consumers in case of failures of service levels.
4. 24/7 support for serious problems comprising comprehensive business hours' telephonic support for managers.
5. Optional advertising—By default, advertising can be turned off, but if needed, companies can decide to take in significant target-based ads of Google.
6. Low fee—Due to affordable and low annual fee per customer account per year, it is easy to provide these applications to everybody in the business.
7. Along with Google talk, Gmail, start page and Google Calendar, all versions of Google apps also involve other customized tools if required by the user.
8. Google docs and spreadsheets—It helps the groups to work together on documents and spreadsheets without emailing documents back and forth. Several workers can steadily work on a document at the same time. All alterations are recorded for editing and managerial controls, permitting businesses to define limitations on sharing of documents.
9. Gmail for mobile devices on BlackBerry—Gmail, meant for mobile services, offers the same experience like conversation view, search, and synchronization of the desktop edition on BlackBerry handheld tools for Google apps' users. Gmail for mobile tools joins the list of other mobile alternatives for Google apps and BlackBerry users who already comprise a multiple range of calendar tools along with Google Talk.
10. Application level control—Permits managers to adjust services to business strategies like distribution of documents or calendars outside of the business. In order to offer additional alternatives and assessment to clients of Google Apps Premier Edition, Google Enterprise Professional associates like Postini and Avaya are coming up with a number of solutions based on Google apps together with advanced security, email gateway, synchronization of Google calendar, and assimilation of third-party with Google Talk also providing migration, implementation, and support services.

9.7.3 Web Application Programming Interface

While assembling your apps, you are expected to use web application programming interfaces (APIs). There are a range of APIs in the market and the one used by you would be based on your skills and the company selected by you for cloud services. Different APIs are used by different cloud servers.

An API is a suite of programming instructions and values to access a web-based program. Software companies issue their APIs to the public so that other software developers may invent products which are controlled by its services.

A personal API has been launched by Amazon for its site developers so that data maintained at the Amazon website can be effortlessly accessed by them. By means of API of Amazon, a third-party website can directly associate with products available on the Amazon site. APIs permit one program to clear with the other one. Via APIs, programs can clear one another without interference from the user. It also permits you to purchase anything at Amazon and insert your credit card data. Amazon uses an API to transmit your credit card information to distant applications, which verify the working of APIs.

API identifies the approach in which two things will communicate. The calls back and forth are controlled by web services with the support of APIs. Web services refer to having a set of standards along with XML, the programming language which permits applications to communicate through the Internet. XML is the language of common-purpose markup. It illustrates prepared data in such a way that it can be readable to both computers and humans.

APIs can be used by your programmer by programming existing or new applications to create the correct XML messages for utilization of distant applications. Businesses that launch their own API generally act as part of a bigger software development kit (SDK) which involves the API, documentation, and programming devices. Web services and API are invisible to your users as they access the cloud. XML is not the only standard that makes APIs work. Other standards include the following:

1. Simple object access protocol (SOAP)—It encodes XML messages so that they can be received and understood by any operating system over any type of network protocol.
2. Universal description, discovery, and integration (UDDI)—It is an XML-based service of the directory that permits businesses to enroll themselves, correlate with each other, and collaborate using web services.
3. Web services description language (WSDL)—It is the SOAP of UDDI. WSDL is the XML-based language that businesses use to describe their services in the UDDI creators.

Google Gadgets

To search the emails, files, web history, and chats, desktop search application, Google Gadgets, is used. It works like Google, in the sense that this new application makes it feasible for users to find information on their computers quickly and effortlessly.

The Google Gadgets API is composed of three languages:

1. XML—This language is generally used for writing gadget specifications. A gadget is just an XML file that can be easily found.
2. HTML—HTML is the markup language used to develop static pages on the web. XML is used to define rules both in human readable language and machine readable form used with markup language and with other tags available in it that can be used to define text based format. XML is easily understood by internet, intranet, and other applications.
3. JavaScript—It is the scripting language you can use to add dynamic behaviour to your gadgets.

The Google data APIs provide you with a facility to read and write data with simple standard protocol. They cover a wide range of business services that can be used for linking your applications within and outside of the cloud infrastructure.

Some of the Google data APIs are given below:

- Google apps APIs
- Google base data API
- Blogger data API
- Google book search data API
- Google Calendar data API
- Google Code Search data API
- Google Contacts data API
- Google Documents List data API
- Google Finance Portfolio data API
- Google Health data API
- Google Notebook data API
- Picasa Web Albums data API
- Google Spreadsheets data API
- Webmaster Tools data API
- YouTube data API

9.7.4 Web Browsers

To connect to the cloud, you need an interface, which is a web browser. Browsers tend to mostly be the same, but with some subtle functional differences. Internet Explorer enjoys the highest market share of browser usage. Mozilla's Firefox accounts for 20.78 per cent and Apple's Safari 7.13 per cent, while Google Chrome has less than 1 per cent of the market share. The remaining 2 per cent of the market includes products such as Camino, Opera, etc.

Internet Explorer

Internet Explorer 8 supports and brings a new look with enhanced capabilities to support everyday tasks such as searching, browsing websites, and printing. The big change in IE 8 is its rendering modes. The progressive evolution of the web has necessitated that browsers such as Internet Explorer include multiple content-rendering modes both supporting strict interpretation of certain web standards and also supporting behaviours designed to maintain compatibility with existing websites.

Internet Explorer 8 has been designed with the following representing modes:
1. The first one reflects the execution of the current web standards of Microsoft.
2. The second one reflects the execution of web standards of Microsoft at the time of launching of Internet Explorer 7 in 2006.
3. The third one is based on rendering techniques of the web during the initial period. The latest rendering mode is forward looking and specially designed by web designers, whereas the rest are there to facilitate similarity with the innumerable sites which are presently augmented for the earlier versions of Internet Explorer.

Though Internet Explorer 8 comprises significant end-user innovations, it was further intended with IT managers and developers in mind. Microsoft engineered Internet Explorer 8 for compatibility with prevailing websites by fulfilling some of the vital standards for the development of websites. Internet Explorer 8 also featured better portability for business enterprises through the improved support of Active Directory Group Policy through which IT managers could easily install and centrally administer the browser on all the desktops within their network.

Mozilla Firefox

Firefox 3 was launched by Mozilla in June 2008 which was the main update to its open-source, the famous free browser. Firefox is the conclusion of three years of labour of thousands of security experts, developers, and testers from all around the world and also localization and support communities. Firefox 3, accessible in almost 50 languages, is two to three times faster than its precursor and provides an additional 15,000 enhancements with an innovative smart location bar, malware fortification, and wide work to upgrade the performance and speed of the browser.

Firefox 3 has been developed on the best of the Gecko 1.9 platform, resulting in a more subjective, easier-to-use, and safer product. Less memory is used by Firefox during its operation in comparison to its earlier issues. The redesigned page interpretation and layout depicts that users can see web pages two to three times faster than that of Firefox 2.

Firefox has increased the security bar. The latest phishing protection and malware helps in protection from worms, spyware, viruses, and Trojans to keep users secure on the web. Firefox allows users to confirm authenticity of the site. The open-source process of Mozilla has affected the skills of thousands of security experts around the world.

Users of Firefox modify their browser along with more than 5,000 add-ons. Add-ons of Firefox permit users to administer jobs such as uploading digital pictures, listening to music, online marts, and watching the weather forecast—everything is through accessibility from the browser. The browser helps users to locate and install add-ons with the new Add-ons Managers.

Safari

Safari 3.1 is declared by Apple as the fastest web browser of the world for Window PCs and Mac; it loads web pages 1.7 times faster than Firefox 2 and 1.9 times quicker when compared to Internet Explorer. JavaScript is operated by Safari six times faster than other browsers. It is the foremost browser that supports the latest ground-breaking web standards required to serve the future generation of favourably interactive experiences of Web 2.0. Safari 3.1 is reachable as free download. It features a natural browsing experience along with easily managed tabs, an amalgamated ability to 'find' which displays the number of matches in a page, drag and drop bookmarks, and a built-in reader to quickly scan the latest information and news.

Safari 3.1 is the first browser to support CSS animations and the first to support new audio and video tags in HTML 5. It also supports CSS web fonts by providing designers with unlimited fonts to design new websites.

Safari 3.1 for Mac OS X needs Mac OS X Tiger or Mac OS X Leopard version 10.4.11 and atleast 256 MB of memory. It is structured to operate on any Intel-based Mac or Mac with PowerPC G3, G4 or G5 processor, and built-in Fire Wire.

Safari 3.1 for Windows needs Windows Vista or Windows XP with atleast 256 MB memory along with a system of at least 500MHz Intel Pentium processor.

Chrome

Chrome is a venture of Google into the market of open-source browsers. During the beginning of the Internet, web pages were normally nothing more than text. However, nowadays, the web has developed into an influential platform which facilitates users to collaborate with colleagues and friends via web applications including email, listening to music, watching videos, managing finance, editing documents, etc. Google Chrome was created for the web of today and tomorrow's applications.

Chrome Cloud

For cloud computing, chrome is a great device. It expands the cloud into the computer of your company. This is mostly due to the power of the V8 JavaScript engine and built-in Google Gear. Google Gears are too open-source and permit potent web applications by addition of new features to the web browser. The main API elements of Gear are as follows:

1. A worker pool module which offers parallel implementation of code of JavaScript
2. A desktop module which allows web applications to interrelate with the desktop more logically
3. A database module which can save information locally
4. A geolocation module which allows web applications to discover the geological position of the users
5. A local server module which serves and accumulates application resources such as images, HTML, JavaScript, and many more

Chrome will allow desktop and web applications to merge, uploading everything onto the cloud so that users do not have to think about them. Chrome is an application that supports both online and offline web applications. There are a number of ways of connecting with the cloud and on that basis you have customized environments and tools.

9.8 MIGRATING TO CLOUDS

A corporation's aim of migrating to the cloud must be a clear perceptive of what the cloud may and may not do it. Preparing a roadmap for installation may then be pursued. A well-formed cloud policy needs thorough deliberation of every cloud service kind, installation module and access alternative considered against specific application characteristics of the company. It is also vital to bear in mind that several applications can never be appropriate for a cloud situation. At the highest limit, several applications might not fit in anywhere.

Noticeable cloud applicants are applications which may perform on extremely modified uniform infrastructure. The progress to the cloud is an evolutionary method. A full-grown immigration policy will be expected in various objects, but among these, three are the most vital—organizational customs, IT governance, and virtualization.

Virtualization is an introductory skill for cloud computing. The more virtualized the infrastructure, the more advanced the resource consumption inside the shared pool. Various companies have worked on improving their IT services as per the demands of the user, realizing that doing so may augment elasticity and enhance operational proficiencies. The necessity to accept powerful IT service administration and superiority turns out to be even more vital beneath the cloud model, where services are provisioned dynamically and not attached to particular portions of the infrastructure. Corporations, which have not accepted IT service administration, will wish to do so as a preliminary step towards the cloud.

Some of the advantages and disadvantages of clouds are as follows:

Advantages

1. Scalable—Nearly all cloud-computing services are payable as per a monthly charge. Therefore, if your business expands, you may order additional server space.
2. Nearly zero provisioning cost—Along with the cloud, you need not establish a server and waste the man-hours it takes to get one, up and working.
3. Money can be saved for other means—It lessens the expenses involved in setting up a novel infrastructure.
4. Fewer IT infrastructure staff to administer—Along with cloud computing, you need not employ a technical group to administer and scrutinize the cloud.

Disadvantages

1. Scarcity of control—Servers might not be directly administrated by you, but even now you are accountable for your data. Before deciding on a cloud service, you must inquire about the backup system, safety, and upholding policies. Decide what happens to your data if the company modifies hands or moves out of business, and understand that your company even possesses the information and may get it from the cloud whenever you need it.
2. Integrating systems—It is impossible for everybody to shift a corporation totally to the cloud due to the systems it has constructed already.
3. Speed—Along with the data transfer speed, cloud-based services sometimes do not communicate among themselves during low-speed connectivity.
4. Cost—As there is no up-front assets' investment associated with cloud services, the technology is yet to have long-standing expenses' investments. The expenses linked with downtime, renewing of native computers to access the system, and unavoidable unpredicted faults are all drawbacks for drifting to the cloud.

9.8.1 Challenges in Migration to and from the Cloud

Successful cloud migrations need adequate resources and time. Migration timeline is even lengthier for businesses with a plenty of data. The process in this case might continue for six months or more. In order to prevent such lengthy timeline and other malicious surprises such as concealed costs, it is better to take a record of all your data and interview important content owners or stakeholders. Third-party devices might help businesses to comprehend how much data they have and also watch out for rest of important factors which might greatly influence migration costs and time—like customizations made to information architecture and legacy systems.

Although Microsoft leads the market supreme, businesses explore multiple dealers in order to accomplish their productivity and collaboration requirements. The three main dealers—Google, Microsoft, and Amazon,—control the cloud market, whereas most businesses use multiple dealers' apps instead of asking employees to follow one set of devices.

With the lack of third-party support, controlling cloud apps might be a budget buster. The biggest amount allied with controlling cloud-based productivity and collaboration apps is the job of IT department.

Through outsourcing cloud management, IT departments can concentrate on larger initiatives such as innovation or and safety training for staff.

Safety remains the biggest obstacle to cloud adoption. Although various businesses have made the jump to the cloud, almost one quarter is still uncertain to migrate—mainly because of concerns over safety. In a survey, almost 53 per cent of respondents mentioned safety as their prime obstacle for adopting and effectively controlling their cloud apps.

9.9 BANKING ON CLOUD ECONOMICS

It is tough for many corporations to forecast exactly the real expenses of operating any known application in the data center. A specific server can be used to support some distinct applications. How do you exactly estimate how much of your private resources are devoted to only one application? There might be a specific month when employees are renewing a single application, while in another month, they might have to troubleshoot other applications. Some departments are dynamic users, whereas some others may hardly have any effect on it. Even though technically you can scrutinize for personal use, doing so would need more operating cost than the value of it.

The cloud computing module is a modern conception of computation which offers a number of advantages for its adopters, for example, that of the same physical infrastructure being easily shared by many users with virtualized infrastructure. Such an online computing module has been broadly used in the western world and assumed to have some trade and financial effects.

For predicting the effects of the cloud computing acceptance, various models are built. Several strategy executions comprise the support of the cloud computing adoption in banks and universities for comprehending the advantage of efficient usage and scalability of computing resources.

 Points to Remember

1. Virtualization is a key feature that supports cloud computing. A cloud with a more virtualized infrastructure has higher resource utilization.
2. MAC addresses are assigned to virtual NICs from the MAC address pool.
3. Virtual infrastructure management software provides interfaces to construct virtual infrastructure from the underlying physical infrastructure.
4. Firefox 3 is two to three times faster than its predecessor.
5. The cloud infrastructure framework consists of the following components:
   (a) Physical infrastructure
   (b) Virtual infrastructure
   (c) Applications and platform software
   (d) Cloud infrastructure management and service creation tools
6. Processes in cloud service management include service benefit and configuration administration, capacity administration, performance administration, incident administration, problem administration, availability administration, service catalog administration, financial administration, and compliance administration.
7. For accessing cloud services and tools, a platform that supports a cloud environment, web application, web browsers, etc. is required.
8. Successful cloud migrations need adequate resources and time.
9. Safety remains the biggest obstacle to cloud adoption.

Key Terms

Asynchronous JavaScript and XML (AJAX) It is a group of web development techniques used for creating interactive web applications.

HTML It is the markup language used to format the pages on the web. It is generally responsible for the static portions of your web pages.

JavaScript It is the scripting language you can use to add dynamic behaviour to your gadgets.

Simple object access protocol (SOAP) SOAP encodes XML messages so that they can be received and understood by any operating system over any type of network protocol.

Universal description, discovery, and integration (UDDI) UDDI is an XML-based directory that allows businesses to list themselves, find each other, and collaborate using web services.

Web services description language (WSDL) WSDL is the SOAP of UDDI. WSDL is the XML-based language that businesses use to describe their services in the UDDI.

XHTML Extensible Hypertext Markup Language

XML This is the language you use to write gadget specifications. A gadget is just an XML file, placed somewhere on the web where Google can find it.

Multiple-choice Questions

1. Kaavo core product is called:
   (a) IMOD
   (b) CIM player
   (c) Rackspace
   (d) None of these

2. The components of a cloud infrastructure framework is/are:
   (a) Physical infrastructure
   (b) Virtual infrastructure
   (c) Cloud infrastructure with service creation tools
   (d) All the above

3. Which is/are included in resource pools?
   (a) CPU pools
   (b) Memory pools
   (c) Storage pools
   (d) All the above

4. Mac addresses are assigned to virtual NICs from the:
   (a) VLAN ID
   (b) MAC address pool
   (c) VSAN ID
   (d) None of these

5. Application and platform software are hosted on VMS to create:
   (a) SaaS
   (b) PaaS
   (c) Both (a) and (b)
   (d) None of these

6. A compute pool implies:
   (a) CPU pools
   (b) Memory pools
   (c) Both (a) and (b)
   (d) None of these

7. Compliance management includes:
   (a) Policies and regulations
   (b) External legal requirements
   (c) Security rules
   (d) All the above

8. The disadvantage of AJAX is/are:
   (a) Difficult to bookmark
   (b) That there is no standard body behind AJAX
   (c) That it does not history engine in a browser
   (d) All the above

9. Google Gadgets API consists of ___ language.
   (a) XML
   (b) HTML
   (c) JavaScript
   (d) All the above

10. One of the advantages of migrating to cloud is:
    (a) The lack of control
    (b) The integrating system
    (c) That it is scalable
    (d) None of these

Review Questions

1. What is the application of virtual infrastructure management software?
2. What is unified management software?
3. What is the process of cloud service management?
4. How are cloud providers different from traditional IT service providers?
5. What are the various requirements to access the cloud?
6. What are the advantages and disadvantages of migrating to the cloud?
7. What are the various features of a browser?
8. What are the advantages of Google Chrome over other browsers?
9. What are the different components included in the cloud infrastructure framework?
10. Write a short note on Google Gadgets.
11. Why is banking on cloud computing important before migrating to it?
12. What is the important feature due to which organizations want to migrate to the cloud?
13. How is Safari different from other browsers that are used for cloud computing?
14. What types of services are provided by the unified management software?

References

1. *Cloud Security A Comprehensive Guide to Secure Cloud Computing*, Ronald L. Krutz and Russell Dean Vines, ISBN: 978-0-470-58987-8, Wiley Publication, 2010
2. *Cloud Computing for Dummies*, Judith Hurwitz, Robin Bloor, Marcia Kaufman, and Dr Fern Halper, ISBN-10: 0470484705, Wiley Publication, 1st edition, November 16, 2009
3. *Cloud Computing Technologies and Strategies*, Brian J.S. Chee and Curtis Franklin, Jr, ISBN 9781439806128, CRC Press, April 7, 2010
4. *Cloud Computing: A Practical Approach*, Anthony T. Velte, Toby J. Velte, Ph.D., RobertElsenpeter, ISBN-10: 0071626948, McGraw-Hill, 1st edition, November 1, 2009
5. *Grid and Cloud Computing*, Katarina StanoevskaSlabeva, Thomas Wozniak, and Santi Ristol, ISBN 10: 3642051928, Springer, 2010 edition, November 19, 2009
6. *Implementing and Developing Cloud Applications*, David E.Y. Sarna, ISBN-10: 1439830827, Auerbach Publications, November 26, 2010

Answers to Multiple-choice Questions

1. (a)
2. (d)
3. (d)
4. (b)
5. (c)
6. (c)
7. (d)
8. (d)
9. (d)
10. (c)

CHAPTER 10

Security Issues of Cloud Computing

> **Learning Outcomes**
>
> After completing this chapter, students will be able to:
>
> - understand security objectives in cloud environment
> - explain the security services of cloud computing
> - explain the security techniques used in virtual machine (VM)
> - describe challenges of cloud security
> - comprehend physical security of cloud computing
> - describe design principles used in cloud security
> - understand cloud software testing and its need
> - describe cloud software requirements
> - discuss common threats and vulnerabilities in cloud computing
> - understand various legal matters in cloud computing

10.1 INTRODUCTION

Reliable cloud computing may be analysed as a computer safety design which is intended to defend cloud systems from malicious attacks and impositions, and make certain that computing resources will perform in a particular, conventional behaviour as planned. A reliable cloud computing system will defend data in operation with applications and hypervisors against illegal access to information and apply encryption to defend sensitive data.

Governments and corporations have listed the advantages of cloud computing as follows—upholding accessibility to services, data reliability, simplicity, privacy, liability and responsibility, generating faith and reliability via support, and guaranteeing values. Cloud computing has issues related to security, which is why cloud users are always not sure about the security of data that they maintain on the cloud. The safety issues concerned with cloud computing are high in the case of public clouds whose computational resources and infrastructure are handled by an external party which conveys services to the common public through a multi-occupant platform. Cloud users worry about the threats associated with maintaining data on the cloud; some of these are discussed in this chapter.

10.2 SECURITY CONCERNS OF CLOUD COMPUTING

From a safety point of view, there are eight threats that users encounter while transferring to and saving data in the cloud.

Handling of data by third party The supplier works on all aspects of handling data, from carrying out updates to uploading to safety controls. Although cloud suppliers might guarantee your data is secure, nobody is a 100 per cent confident about this.

Cyber attacks Every time you save data on the Internet, you are at risk of a cyber attack. This is one of the main challenges of using a cloud, as large amounts of data are saved by all kinds of users on similar cloud systems.

Insider threats Once a worker gets access to your cloud or provides others access to this, all the data, from consumer data to secret information and intellectual property, can be revealed.

Government intrusion Government supervision programs and contestants (who are competitors having the same goals and who can take advantage of your data) are not the only ones who might want to look into your data.

Legal liability Threats associated with the cloud are not restricted to safety. They also comprise its consequences, like court cases filed against or by you.

Lack of standardization A supplier might encompass the newest safety attributes, but owing to the common scarcity of cloud consistency, there are no definite rules amalgamating cloud suppliers.

Lack of support As all the cloud suppliers want a good reputation with their consumers, they market their products with attractive schemes, confusing the consumers in the process.

Constant risk Identity management and access control are fundamental functions required for secure cloud computing. The simplest form of identity management is logging onto a computer system with a user ID and password, but genuine identity management is needed for cloud computing, along with robust authorization, authentication, and access control.

While using cloud resources there is always an element of doubt in the minds of cloud users—is the data safe or not. Hackers always try to take advantage of what you are keeping in the safe zone.

Since price and user-friendliness are the two big advantages of cloud computing, the cloud supplier should build upon the following rules for providing better safety:
1. Where is the data? The cloud supplier must agree in writing, to provide the safety level needed for its consumers.
2. Who has access? Access management is the primary worry, as insider attacks are a big threat.
3. What are your rigid needs? You should make sure that your cloud supplier is capable of arranging the requirements and accessibility of data.
4. Do you have the right to inspect? The cloud supplier must agree in writing to the conditions of inspection.
5. What kind of training does the supplier propose for its workers? Recognizing how a supplier guides its workers is significant.
6. What sort of data categorization system does the supplier employ? The consumer should recognize the kind of encryption being employed.
7. What are the service level agreement (SLA) conditions? The SLA acts as an agreement of assured services between the consumer and the cloud supplier that identifies the level of services that will be offered.

8. What is the long-term feasibility of the supplier? Cloud providers should be a consistent service provider in the same field, otherwise he or she would not be able to provide feasible services to the users and would not stay for long in the same business.
9. What happens if there is a safety break? If safety is breached due to any reason, the support you will get from the cloud supplier must be clear.
10. What is the catastrophe recovery/corporation permanence strategy? The means by which data may be recovered in case of natural vulnerabilities and catastrophe has to be discussed.

The various cloud computing attacks are discussed in the following sections.

10.2.1 Threats to Infrastructure, Data, and Access Control

In cloud computing, various network intrusion matters arise. Some of them are argued as follows:

Denial of Service

When the web server or the network server is besieged with numerous service requests which damage the network, the service denial option will not be able to keep up with the influx of requests and the client's legitimate requests may not be authenticated by the server. For instance, hacking may not stop the functioning of the web server from providing services. In cloud computing, the hacker, by sending thousands of requests to the server, attacks the server so that it becomes incapable of responding to regular customers. Thus, the server will not be able to work appropriately. The solution to such an attack is to lessen the user's privileges connected to the server.

A denial-of-service attack (DoS attack) or distributed denial-of-service attack (DDoS attack) is an attempt to make a network or machine resource inaccessible to its anticipated consumers. Usually, it encompasses one or more person's actions for provisionally or indefinitely interrupting or deferring the host's services when connected to the Internet. For overcoming the target resources, the following means are used for a DoS attack:

1. Loading up the target's hard drive storage space via e-mail attachments or huge file transfers
2. Disconcerting the target host's subnet mask, creating a disturbance of the subnet routing of the target
3. To take network connections, utilizing all the resources of the goal which result in the rejection of added network connections

Man in the Middle Attack

This is an issue of network security which occurs due to the improper configuration of secure socket layer (SSL). For instance, during communication between the two parties if the SSL is not installed properly, all the information shared between the two parties could be hacked by the middle party. To avoid such an attack, installation of the SSL must be proper and checked before communication with legitimate parties.

Network Sniffing

Network sniffer is another form of hacking and is a serious matter of network security. In this, encrypted data is hacked via the network. For instance, hackers hack passwords that are improperly encrypted during communication. If the communication parties fail to use encryption techniques for data security, hackers, as a third party, easily trap the data during transmission. An alternative solution to ward off this attack is to use encryption techniques to secure the data.

Port Scanning

There are several issues concerned with port scanning. Hackers can use these ports since Port 80 (HTTP) is always open and is used for providing services to the users. Some other ports for example, 21(FTP), are open only when required. Hence, ports can be secured by encryption until the server software is properly configured. An alternative solution to prevent such an attack is by using a firewall to secure data from port attacks.

SQL Injection Attack

SQL injection attacks are those where special characters are used by hackers to return the data. For instance, in SQL, the query's scripting ends where the clause can be customized by adding further data in it.

Cross Site Scripting

In this kind of attack, the user enters the correct URL of a website, whereas on another site, a hacker redirects the user to his/her website and hacks its identification. The hacker gets access to confidential information of the user.

To properly understand the threats of cloud computing offers, it is essential to comprehend the techniques involved in security of communication to detect, correct, and protect errors so that reliability, accessibility, and secrecy of communications over networks can be maintained.

This involves the following:
1. Security of communication and network which is related to data, multimedia, voice, and duplicate programs in terms of wide area, remote access, and local area networks
2. Extranet/Internet/Intranet in terms of gateways, firewalls, router, and numerous protocols

To make cloud computing technology reliable among cloud users, there are many security objectives that should be achieved by every cloud provider, and some of these are discussed in the next section.

10.3 CLOUD INFORMATION SECURITY OBJECTIVES

The software should be capable of challenging most attacks and handling potential attacks. The following are the security objectives of cloud information:

Reliability The software should be able to implement all its features and work accurately under a variety of circumstances, including attacks.

Secrecy, veracity, and accessibility Secrecy, veracity, and accessibility are referred to as CIA (confidentiality, integrity, and availability). It is the foremost aim of cloud security. Secrecy refers to the divulging of intended or unintended, unofficial disclosure of information. Secrecy in cloud systems is necessary for asset privileges, traffic investigation, encryption, etc.

Intellectual property rights Intellectual property (IP) comprises innovations and plans, and literary and creative works. Rights to intellectual property are protected by copyright acts that defend conceptions of the mind and copyrights that are approved for novel innovations.

Encryption Encryption involves jumbling of messages so that they cannot be interpreted by an unofficial unit, even if they are interrupted. The number of attempts needed to decrypt the message is reflective of the power of the encryption input and the strength and excellence of the encryption algorithm.

Accessibility Accessibility guarantees consistent and appropriate access to cloud computing resources or cloud data by legitimate users. Accessibility assures proper functioning of systems when required. Additionally, this guarantees that the safety services of the cloud system are working properly.

Every corporation is expected to apply stringent security measures. The following sections discuss how cloud computing corporations should maintain the safety, secrecy, integrity, and accessibility of data.

10.3.1 Confidentiality

'Safety' is of primary concern for outsourcing information technology services and, especially, for shifting managerial applications, data, and other resources to a public cloud computing situation. Corporations must consider risk-based criteria in examining accessible secrecy and safety alternatives for determining the uploading of managerial tasks into a cloud setting.

The safety policies of cloud computing are as follows:
1. Workers (cloud users) must be provided guidance on associated technologies.
2. Background check of workers is essential.
3. Access limitations must be set for employees.
4. Code word amendments within a stipulated time are mandatory.
5. A code word for hardware or server offered by a dealer must not be used.
6. The physical position of the server is important—cloud suppliers must maintain storage tools in safe places with appropriate physical defences.
7. Firewalls should be deployed and its strategies, arrangements, and regulations amended on a customary basis.
8. Antivirus updates should be made regularly.
9. Data must be erased from servers and backup tools when the service is eliminated or the server is eradicated from the cloud.
10. System file updates and patch updates must be performed precisely.
11. System logs should be maintained.

10.3.2 Cloud Computing Environment and Accessibility

The liabilities of both the corporation and the cloud supplier are divided on the basis of the service module. Corporations utilizing cloud services should be aware of the liabilities over the computing situation and the suggestion for secrecy and safety. Promises equipped by the cloud supplier to support secrecy and safety claims should be documented for future correspondence.

Knowing the processes, strategies, and technological rules utilized by a cloud supplier is a requirement to assess the secrecy and safety threats involved. It is also vital to understand the technologies employed to provide services and the importance of secrecy and safety of the system. Particulars regarding the system design of a cloud may be examined and employed to create a whole image of the safety given by the secrecy and safety rules, which develop the capability of the corporation to assess and act on threats precisely, utilizing suitable processes and techniques for constant scrutiny of the safety condition of the system.

10.3.3 Organizational Security and Privacy Requirements

The public cloud supplier's default usually does not replicate a precise corporation's safety and secrecy requirements. From a threat perceptive, the appropriateness of cloud services depends on the corporation functions and the penalty from the rational risks faced by it. Corporations must ensure that every public cloud computing environment is arranged, installed, and administered in order to assess their secrecy, safety, and other needs.

Selection of workers, data possession and exit privileges, break warnings, segregation of occupant applications, data encryption and isolation, trailing and reporting service efficiency, and agreement with rules and regulations are vital details that a company should always convey to the cloud user.

With the increasing number of cloud suppliers and an array of services to opt from, corporations should implement care while choosing and allocating tasks to the cloud.

10.3.4 Client-side Computing Environment Requirement

Cloud computing includes both a server and a consumer side. With stress characteristically placed on the former, the latter may be simply ignored. Services from diverse cloud suppliers, with cloud-based applications built by the corporation, should impose more precise commands on the consumer regarding safety and secrecy.

Web browsers are a chief component of consumer-side access to cloud computing services. Consumers might also involve small applications which operate on desktop and mobile tools for accessing services. The numerous accessible plug-ins for web browsers are disabled for safety reasons. Many browsers do not offer updates for keeping data and systems safe from unauthorized users.

10.3.5 Cloud Security Services

Powerful administration procedures are essential for functioning and sustaining a safe cloud computing system. Secrecy and safety procedures involve scrutiny of the information system resources of corporations and assessing the execution of strategies, values, measures, controls, and rules which are employed to set up and protect the accessibility of resources of the information system. The corporation must assemble and study accessible data about the condition of the system and as frequently as is necessary for controlling secrecy and safety threats, for every layer of the corporation.

Controlling and assessing threat in cloud computing systems can be tackled, as major parts of the computing situations are under the power of the cloud supplier. The corporation should guarantee that secrecy and safety rules are executed accurately, function as planned, and meet managerial needs.

Cloud computing is based on the safety of numerous personal elements. Moreover, besides elements for common computing, there are other elements such as those for resource metering, self-service, data replication, quota management, workload administration, and service-level scrutiny. Many of the abridge interfaces and service concepts provided by cloud computing address the basic fundamental difficulty which influences safety. Corporations must guarantee, to the highest degree, feasible security and that secrecy and safety are sustained on all cloud computing procedures.

10.3.6 Integrity

Integrity, from the perspective of computer systems, refers to techniques for ensuring that the data is genuine, correct, and protected from illegal user alteration.

Digital signatures, hashing methods, and message verification codes are used for protecting data integrity. Integrity troubles are in large scale because of the multi-tenancy feature of clouds, although cloud computing presents great prospectives for efficient working and reduction in expenses. As clouds are mostly used for data storage, data integrity is the chief matter of the consumer side as after transferring data to the server, consumer will have no control over the data.

10.4 CLOUD SECURITY DESIGN PRINCIPLES

Earlier, computer software was written without taking safety into consideration. However, due to the growing complexity and regularity of malicious attacks against information systems, up-to-date software is of paramount importance. Along with cloud computing systems looking for meeting diverse purposes such as rate, dependability, functioning, safety, and sustainability, trade-offs need to be made.

The following are some of the tools used in cloud security:

Qualys Qualys is used to secure devices and web apps, without the requirement of any extra hardware or software. The company also analyses and ensures that your system is free from threats. You can also solve the problem of malware using Qualys. It is used to scan all web apps for vulnerabilities and safe data while using SaaS, IaaS, and PaaS.

White Hat security White Hat security refers to carefully listening to protect your website from the very beginning, that is, from the coding process. It facilitates the Sentinel product suite as a service to protect your websites using various products. It provides you with information pertaining to current threats to avoid coding vulnerabilities into the website. Sentinel helps you to assess web apps for vulnerabilities and gives you information about various loopholes in the application.

Okta Okta offers an identity management tool to acertain who is where and why. You can collect information about employees working at the backend and frontend. It also supports and manages logins for all applications including Google Apps, Salesforce, etc.

Proofpoint Proofpoint is specially designed to find loopholes in emails. It supports various email pops with the weakest links.

Zscaler Zscaler has an efficient and advanced tool for security and monitors all the traffic in a network of a particular cloud.

DocTrackr DocTrackr is a security tool that supports file sharing services. While transferring data from one system to another, data changes at many levels or it could be used for malicious work. DocTrackr works to prevent these.

Vaultive Vaultive supports tools for networks to protect and encrypt data.

Technologically capable hackers may discover a technique to force an entry into a computer system, provided they have sufficient resources and time. The aim is to comprise a system that is adequately safe.

The following are the major security design principles that must be kept in mind:

Least Privilege

The belief of minimum opportunity refers to the fact that a personal, procedural, or other kind of unit must be provided with the least resources and opportunities for the least amount of time to fulfill an assignment. Privileges such as read, write, and access are not necessary to be provided to all types of users. For example, the clerical staff in a bank do not have to access managerial-level data for taking decisions at various stages.

Separation of Duties

Separation of responsibilities gives users a sense of duty and modules are always divided into subparts for active participation of all users and for completion of the task on time. For instance, signatures of more than one person would be needed for approval to proceed further for completion of a task.

Defence in Depth

Defence in depth is the application of various layers of safety in which a succeeding layer will offer safety in case a preceding layer is broken due to some reason.

Defence in Multiple Places

At different levels, there are various authentication levels so that everyone trying to access the data have to give necessary authentication so that only the right person is able to access that data, keeping the data safe from the internal and external world.

Layered Defences

A plurality of information security and finding methods is used so that accessing vital information does not become easy for everyone.

Security Robustness

According to the importance of the information system, an estimate of the potency of information is to be ascertained and the expected threats measured.

Deploy KMI/PKI

Various security measures are used for keeping data safe from the external world, for example, the use of public key infrastructures (PKI) and robust key management infrastructures (KMI). PKI and KMI deal with cryptography that maintain a record of the various symmetric and asymmetric keys used for different types of plain text and cipher text during cryptography.

Deploy Intrusion Detection Systems

Apart from the firewall system, an intrusion detection system must also be implemented, so that an alarm is raised if there is any problem in the network.

Fail-safe

Fail-safe means that if a cloud system crashes, it must crash to a situation where the safety of the system and its data are not negotiated. In a state where the renewal of a system is not done mechanically, the crashed system must allow access to the system manager and not to other users, until safety powers are reinstated.

Economy of Mechanism

The mechanisms used should support a comprehensive and simple plan for implementation of security measures, so that unintentional access can be filtered out and stopped to safeguard the data.

Complete Mediation

In complete mediation, each request regarding accessing information should pass through an applicable and effective agreement process. For controlling and safeguarding data from external access, an uninterrupted supply of services, with smooth and flexible components, along with various checks are provided to users.

The entire process of intrusion requires the following:
1. Recognition of the unit making the access demand
2. Confirmation that the demand has not been altered since its commencement
3. Application of suitable approval processes
4. Reconsideration of previously authorized needs by a similar unit

Leveraging Existing Components

The safety levels of cloud implementation should be utilized to their maximum capacity. Appraising the situation and status of the existing safety means and guaranteeing that they are working to their best will significantly progress the safety bearing of an information system.

Authentication and support facilities are needed to ensure genuine access to data. Confirmation is a procedure to make sure that documentations of an asset or user are authentic so that no illegal access to information is permitted. Multi-factor authentication is a unique technique for substantiation that believes in collectively incorporating many features for authenticating a user.

Endorsement is a procedure to provide accurate access privileges to a user on resources. Endorsement describes the restrictions of the access privileges of a user on a resource, for instance, read-write access or read-only access on a file. Moreover, reviewing is a procedure to evaluate the efficiency of safety enforcement means.

10.5 CLOUD SECURITY SERVICES

Cloud computing necessitates that the following properties be fulfilled to make cloud services secure.

Authentication

Validation is the examination of proof of identity of a user. It creates the identity of the user and makes sure that users are who they claim to be. For instance, a user gives an identity (user ID) to a computer sign-in screen and then offers a code word. The computer system validates the user by confirming that the code word matches the person giving the ID.

Authorization

Authorization refers to the privileges and rights approved to a person who is allowed access to information assets and computer resources. Once an identity of a user is established, the process of approval decides the degree of system rights held by a user.

Auditing

For supporting operational assurance, corporations employ two fundamental means— scrutiny and system audits. These means may be utilized by the cloud supplier, the cloud consumer, or both, according to the asset design and installment.

An IT evaluator audits the following functions:

System and transaction controls   It deals with the different controls, checks, and constraints used for carrying out transactions.

Systems' development standards   It deals with the type of standards (used during system development) to be provided to the users.

Backup controls   It gives details about the backup facilities for taking a backup of various transactions for future references.

Data library procedures   It gives details about the libraries that are needed for running a particular application.

Data center security   It provides details about the security that a cloud provider uses for providing adequate security to the cloud data center.

Contingency plans   It provides details about the emergency plan that a cloud provider uses in the case of an emergency, with the services provided by them at the time of disaster.

Additionally, IT evaluators can suggest improvements to controls and they frequently contribute to an extension procedure of systems to assist a corporation to avoid expensive reengineering after execution of the system log. An audit trace is a compilation of events that are documented, and is further engaged to assist in the tracking of data, from original transactions to associated reports and proceedings, or backward, from reports and proceedings to their respective sources.

Audit traces might be restricted to a particular time or they might include every action on a system. Audit logs should record the following:
1. The transaction's date and time
2. Who processed the transaction
3. At which terminal the transaction was processed
4. The security events relating to the transaction

Besides these, an evaluator must inspect audit logs for the following as well:
1. Modifications done
2. Modification repeatitions
3. Computer operating practices
4. If every instruction is reliably commenced by the user
5. Recognition and substantiation efforts
6. Resources and files accessed

Accountability

Accountability is the capability to decide the procedures that a person inside a cloud system can handle and to recognize that specific person. Audit traces and logs maintain an account of liability and may be employed to perform investigation studies to examine sequential incidents and the procedures or persons associated with such incidents. Accountability is related to the view of no denial, in which a person may not effectively reject the working of an activity.

10.6 SECURE CLOUD SOFTWARE TESTING

Cloud testing utilizes the cloud infrastructure for software testing. For guaranteeing high levels of services and for avoiding unexpected situations, testing is required. There are various types of testing, such as compatibility, stress, load and performance, browser, latency, and functional, as shown in Fig. 10.1.

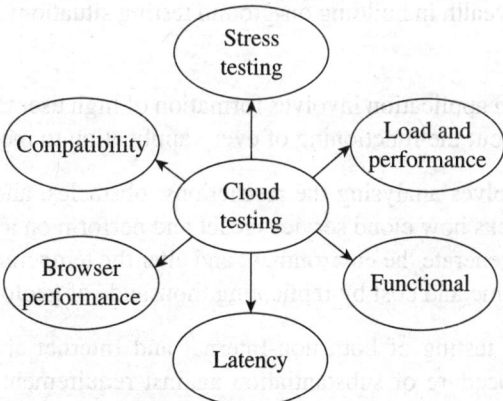

Fig. 10.1 Types of testing

Unlimited effective storage, speedy accessibility of the infrastructure through accessibility, scalability, and flexibility of disseminated testing reduce the execution time of testing of large applications and are useful in proper working of the applications.

10.6.1 Need for Cloud Testing

Cloud computing offers efficient and flexible resources via which scalable computing power and varied services, application services, and business procedures to individuals and corporations are distributed as services to users anytime and wherever they need it.

A conventional strategy to examine software requires high charge to replicate user action from diverse geographic sites. Firewalls involve expenses on software, hardware, and their preservation. Depending on the applications, especially where there are an unexpected numbers of users, cloud testing can become more efficient.

Cloud-based software testing involves the various types of testing that make the cloud provider confident that the services are working properly based on application and infrastructure. It has four main purposes:

1. To guarantee the importance of cloud-based applications installed in a cloud, with their operational services, business procedures, and system working with scalability based on an array of application-based system necessities in a cloud.
2. To legalize Software as a Service (SaaS) in a cloud system, with software scalability, functioning, measurement, and safety based on some financial scales and pre-defined SLAs.
3. To verify the offered mechanical cloud-based operational services, for instance, auto-provisioned operations.
4. To examine inter-operation ability and cloud compatibility among SaaS applications in a cloud infrastructure.

10.6.2 Types of Testing

Testing of various cloud services at the cloud provider-end and client-end is necessary to make sure that all the services of a cloud provider are working properly. The following are the types of testing that are important for cloud computing:

Stress test   Stress test is employed to decide the capability of applications. It is vital for every application to perform efficiently even under extreme strain to maintain reliability. Stress testing guarantees this by producing peak stacks employing simulators. However, the rate of producing such scenarios is huge. Rather than spending wealth in building on-ground testing situations, cloud testing proposes scalable and reasonable options.

Load test   Load testing of an application involves formation of high user traffic and assessing its reply. There is also a need to carry out the functioning of every application to meet certain norms.

Performance test   This involves analysing the restrictions, obstacles, and limiting elements of functioning testing. This test checks how cloud services react and perform on a specific workload. By using cloud testing, it is simple to generate the environment and alter the temperament of traffic on-command. This efficiently lessens the time and cost by replicating thousands of geologically overwhelmed users.

Functional test   Functional testing of both non-Internet and Internet applications may be achieved using cloud testing. The procedure of substantiation against requirement or system needs is accomplished on the cloud rather than on-location.

Compatibility test   Using cloud, diverse operating systems may be generated on order, making compatibility testing easy.

Browser performance test   Authentication of support of applications for numerous browsers and functioning may be achieved without effort. Numerous devices facilitate automatic website testing from the cloud.

Latency test Cloud testing is used to assess the latency among the activity and the analogous reply for any application after installing it on the cloud.

These days, cloud computing has altered the technique of computation and rendering services to consumers, for instance, it alters the means of supplying and running computing resources, such as databases, CPUs, and storage systems. Cloud computing not only conveys novel business chances, but also initiates several 'chief effects' on software testing. A chief effect is called Testing as a Service (TaaS) on clouds. TaaS cloud infrastructure is deemed as a novel business and service module, wherein a supplier assumes software testing actions of a given application system in a cloud infrastructure for consumers as a service based on order.

10.6.3 Importance of Cloud Testing

Compared to recent forms of software testing, cloud-based testing has exclusive benefits:
1. It reduces costs by controlling the computing resources that clouds require. Virtualized resources are efficiently employed and cloud infrastructure shared to eliminate the need for specific computer resources and certified software in a test laboratory.
2. It takes the benefit of on-command test services (by a third-party) to accomplish large-scale and effectual synchronized online corroboration for Internet-based software on clouds.
3. It easily influences scalable cloud system infrastructure for testing and evaluating system scalability and functioning.

10.6.4 Forms of Cloud-based Software Testing

There are four diverse types of cloud-based software testing as listed here. All of them have diverse purposes.

Testing SaaS on clouds It guarantees the importance of a SaaS in a cloud, based on its operational and non-operational service necessities.

Testing of clouds It authenticates the importance of a cloud from an outer vision based on the cloud's particular abilities and service characteristics. SaaS, cloud dealers, and end users are moving towards this kind of testing.

Testing inside clouds It confirms the importance of a cloud from an internal outlook based on the internal infrastructures of a cloud and specific cloud abilities. Cloud dealers may operate this kind of testing as they have access to internal infrastructures and associations among SaaS(s) and mechanical abilities, supervision, safety, and administration.

Testing over clouds It examines cloud-based service applications over clouds, comprising hybrid, personal, and public clouds based on system-stage application service stipulation and necessities. This typically is operated by the cloud-based application system suppliers.

The following are the major Testing as a Service (TaaS) service capabilities:

TaaS process management It proposes test project administration and procedure control.

QoS necessities management It supports accounting and modelling of software testing and QoS necessities, comprising quality guarantee modeling.

Test environment service It offers, on order, test situation services to create the needed virtual cloud-based infrastructure and computing resources with the devices essential according to the necessities.

Test solution services It proposes different types of methodical testing and test group and administration services.

Test simulation services It creates on order test simulation with chosen characteristics and supports the essential data generation or test message.

On-order test service It offers on order test implementation services based on chosen plans and testware.

Trailing and scrutiny service It permits test engineers to trail and scrutinize different plans at different stages in or over clouds for the testing function.

TaaS pricing and billing It facilitates TaaS dealers to give consumers selectable testing services based on pre-defined costing modules and invoicing services.

10.6.5 Internet-based Software Testing vs Cloud Testing

The differences between Internet-based software testing and cloud-based software testing are shown in Table 10.1.

Table 10.1 Internet testing vs cloud testing

	Internet-based software testing	Cloud-based software testing
Testing objectives	Guarantees the importance of system operations and functioning based on certain stipulations	Guarantees the importance of operations and functioning of applications, clouds, and SaaS by controlling a cloud system
Testing as a service	Internal interior software testing as engineering assignments	Concurrent on-order testing service proposed by a third-party
Testing and execution time	Offline test implementation in a test lab; it also tests goods prior to distribution	On-order test implementation by third parties. Online test implementation in a public cloud and offline test implementation in a personal cloud
Test simulation	Replicated online user access and online traffic data	Online or virtual user access replication and traffic data replication
Function validation	Validating element operations, system operations, and service characteristics	Cloud service or SaaS operations across application operations
Security testing	• Operation-based safety aspects • User secrecy • Server/Consumer access safety • Procedure access safety • Message or data reliability	• Cloud/SaaS safety aspects, comprising scrutiny and measurement • User secrecy in different web consumers • Laterally application safety over clouds • SaaS/Cloud API and connectivity • Security testing with virtual/real-time tests in a vendor's cloud

10.6.6 Cloud Testing Environment

Based on the application, there are three types of cloud test environments:
1. A cloud-based business test, wherein application dealers install web-based applications in a cloud to legalize their importance in a cloud infrastructure
2. A public or private cloud test, wherein dealers install SaaS applications
3. A hybrid cloud test, wherein dealers install cloud-based applications on a hybrid cloud infrastructure to confirm their importance

Cloud/SaaS-oriented Testing

These testing actions are generally operated within a cloud by engineers of the cloud or SaaS dealers. The chief purpose is to guarantee the service proposed in a SaaS. These engineers should undergo amalgamation, entity testing, system function decline, and legalization testing, in addition to scalability and functioning assessment. As SaaS and clouds typically offer some service APIs and connectivity interfaces to their consumers, it is necessary for engineers to authorize these APIs and connectivity in a cloud situation. Additionally, SaaS-based or cloud-based safety services and working aspects should be tested. Besides these, function testing and scalability assessment in a cloud are extremely significant and vital to SaaS or cloud dealers, as this guarantees the importance of cloud suppleness for supporting cloud and SaaS services within a cloud.

Online-based Application Testing on Clouds

This testing is generally executed for confirming online application systems on a cloud by using a cloud-based comprehensive user and traffic access. This is a general usage of cloud technology for assisting existing online application dealers to accomplish online-based system operation testing and functioning assessments on a cloud by extracting the benefits of clouds so that scalable and different computing resources on a cloud may be employed without using any internal test. While applications are associated with inheritance systems, the connectivity importance among the inheritance systems and the under-test application installed on a cloud must be allowed.

Cloud-based Application Testing over Clouds

This testing refers to engineering actions that are completed to guarantee the importance of a cloud-based application crossing diverse clouds. While applications are expanded to be installed and implemented over diverse clouds, novel testing jobs are required to guarantee its reputation. Unlike the earlier two types, the principal testing purpose here is to guarantee back-to-back application over clouds. This proposes that system amalgamation, function legalization, scalability measurement, and functioning assessment be managed with diverse cloud technologies. It is not easy to understand the tasks involved in inspection system interoperability, compatibility, and connectivity among diverse clouds.

10.7 SECURE CLOUD SOFTWARE REQUIREMENTS

Secure cloud software requirements refer to consumer software needs and potentials; this stage is before the software plan stage. The necessities have been designated as accurate, clear, thorough, and indisputable. The necessities of the information system safety strategy corresponding to software reassurance must be evaluated to make certain their constancy and accuracy. The two kinds of safe software studies that must be carried out are as follows:

Internal It is important to ensure that the software are absolute, accurate, and steady with the associated design necessities. The study must tackle the following:

1. Security constraints
2. The software's non-functional properties
3. The software's positive functional requirements

External It is important to decide the following:

1. The software guarantee necessities tackle the authorized rigid and necessary strategy matters.
2. The non-operational safety necessities symbolize an appropriate putrefaction of the system's safety targets.
3. Software guarantee necessities never clash with the system's safety targets.
4. The software is flexible.

Cloud system software necessities' engineering depends upon the interface with the user, and the result of the procedure comprises both functional and non-functional software functioning attributes. Future software security necessities, beginning from a resource viewpoint, offer an effectual technique for tackling cloud software safety necessities. Some basic properties are as follows:

Specific The requirement must be clear, specific, and as comprehensive as possible.

Measurable The necessity must be computable to make sure that it has been met, via scrutiny, testing, or both. Necessities should be practical to meet as well.

Attainable The system should be capable of making known the necessity for specific conditions.

Realizable The necessity should be possible under the system and the business enterprise should grow steadily. There may be various units according to user necessity and the system must work at the same time to meet all the necessities.

Traceable The necessity must be traceable, both the forward and backward directions, all through the progress life cycle. Necessities must be inaccessible as well so as to make them simple to legalize or trail all through the progress life cycle.

Appropriate Necessities must be legalized, thus guaranteeing that they originate from a genuine need or command and that other necessities are not more suitable.

Reasonable Encountering the necessity is actually feasible in the software.

A further harmonizing technique for operating cloud software safety necessities engineering is a target-oriented pattern wherein a target is a software purpose. The kinds of targets which one aims for are operational targets, non-operational targets, code accuracy, and safety sturdiness.

One execution of target-oriented necessities engineering is the non-operational necessities that offer a base for deciding whether a target has been achieved or not. Non-operational necessities comprise features of a software system such as reliability, performance, cost, security, maintainability, and accuracy as shown in Table 10.2.

Table 10.2 Non-operational necessities

Reliability	Software must be consistent in case it works according to the needs of the user and restrains work appropriately where required.
Performance	Software functioning must be accurate and spontaneous.
Security	Software must be secure, keeping in mind that the users' secure data must not be disclosed to unauthorized users.
Accuracy	The software should give the correct outcome under different circumstances.
Cost	The software should be realistic so that all the users may utilize it regularly.
Maintainability	Alterations in software are also simply diverted by the software according to the needs of the user.

10.8 SECURE DEVELOPMENT PRACTICES

The information that an organization processes must be classified according to the organization's sensitivity to its loss or disclosure. The possessor of the information system is answerable to define the sensitivity level of the data as per a defined classification format.

The following classification terms are typically used in the private sector and are applicable to cloud data:

Public data Information that is similar to unspecified information, and information of businesses that cannot be categorized into sets, can be treated as public. Even if its unofficial disclosure might be anti policy, it is not supposed to adversely or critically affect employees, clients, and companies.

Sensitive data Information that requires a higher level of classification than normal data is called sensitive information. This information is protected from loss of confidentiality as well as from loss of integrity due to unauthorized alteration. Confidential data must be protected with many wrappers. Loss of data is harmful to the company and it destroys its reputation. This categorization is for data that needs special security so that it is reliable, by securing it from illegal deletion or modification.

Private data This categorization is concerned with personal data which is for use within the company. Its unofficial revelation might have an adverse and serious effect on the company and its employees.

Confidential data This categorization is concerned with the most secret data of the company, which is often handled the company. Its unofficial revelation might have a serious and adverse effect on clients, business partners, stock holders, and/or the company itself. This information is exempt from disclosure under the provisions of the Freedom of Information Act or other applicable federal laws or regulations.

Cloud software functions generally define what the software has to accomplish to perform a task securely. Secure cloud software requirements can be achieved by the following practices:

Handling Data

A lot of data is sensitive and needs special treatment. As the Internet is dynamic, personal and sensitive information is placed on cloud servers. There was no need to treat this confidential information carefully five years back, whereas other data, like code words, have always needed careful attention. Instances for the treatment of significant or perceptive data are as follows:

Code words must in no way be conveyed clearly. They must always be encrypted. Code words must in no way be seen on the screen of the user when they are entered into the computer. Although asterisks (*) are seen, care should be taken to make sure that it is all asterisks.

If feasible, code words must always be encrypted with one-way jumble. This will ensure that nobody is able to take out the code word from the server. The single technique to crack the code word would be via brute-force cracking. With one-way muddling, genuine code words are not evaluated to substantiate the user. If the code words cannot be decrypted, users would not be given their code words when they do not remember them. Credit card and other fiscal information must in no way be transmitted openly.

Cloud servers must lessen the transmission of sensible data like credit card information. This applies to reports that might be utilized for in-house use, for example, development, status, and troubleshooting reports.

Code Practices

Absolutely essential information must be mentioned in the cloud server policy. An attacker will spend many hours investigating but the information may not be recovered easily. Remarks, names, and other private information must be avoided.

Software packages of the third-party, such as FTP servers and web servers, frequently offer signs which state the edition of the software which is in operation. Hence, there are checks to ensure that an invader does not get access to too much information.

Language Options

The language used in the program has certain defects as well. One of the most often exposed weaknesses in cloud server applications is a liable outcome of the utilization of C and C++. C language is not capable of discovering and preventing inappropriate memory allotment and the onus is on the programmer to execute secure programming methods. Good coding procedures will be confirmed for margin restrictions to make sure that operations are properly carried out. This needs an immense amount of control from the programmer. When it comes to performance, even the most knowledgeable developers may ignore these tests periodically. The Java Virtual Machine (JVM) is liable for slowing down of buffer. The inherent safety mechanism of Java is one of the causes of its popularity. Malicious language must not be probable in Java.

Physical Security of Systems

Physical access to the cloud servers must be constrained. Any cloud server is susceptible to an attacker with limitless time and physical access to the server. In addition, physical troubles might cause the server to include down time (for additional details, refer to Section 10.16). This is likely to be an accessibility malfunction which you may consider as one of the main security standards of the CIA.

To ensure server accessibility, the following items should be offered:
1. An uninterruptible power supply (UPS)
2. Fire security to lessen the tools and personnel loss
3. Sufficient airing and cooling
4. Sufficient workplace and lighting for supporting and advancement of the system
5. Confined physical access to the server (unauthorized people should not have close access to the server)

Informal connections may also lead to outages. Any access to the server place must be noted for later evaluation. The supply must be controlled and scrutinized. The physical safeties planned must expand to the network cables and additional tools (like routers) which are vital to the functioning of cloud servers. To sustain individuality of active users, outer links should integrate the following controls to defend IT resources.

1. At least, every outer link should integrate a firewall and employ safe gateways to permit in-house users to unite to outer networks. In case the user accesses is derived from an external confined network, the user should be recognized and authenticated at the entry way. The in-house domain name systems (DNSs) must be concealed.
2. Utilize outer substantiation databases.
3. Dial-up modems must not be connected to computers which are associated with the in-house network.
4. Endorse outer links before use. Outer links must be sporadically evaluated by an autonomous association.

Any software shares three safety requirements, which are as follows:
1. It should be reliable under predictable working circumstances and remain reliable even under unapproachable working circumstances.
2. It should be reliable in its personal deeds and in its incapability to be negotiated by an attacker via utilization of susceptibility or insertion of malicious policy. It should be robust.
3. Cloud software planning associated to operational safety and protected assets are discovered in the perspective of the cloud software requirements. Protected necessities for safety-related cloud software functions normally classify what the software has to achieve to work on a job steadily.

10.9 VULNERABILITY ASSESSMENT TOOLS FOR CLOUDS

Cloud computing gives the image of numerous virtual machines on one physical infrastructure. There are cases where safety is more complicated to sustain when unique traits of a cloud are united with more conventional safety matters. The cloud is merely an environment wherein the user is provided particular rights. Precise attacks are conferred as well, including session riding attacks, virtual machine breakouts, etc. It is impossible to completely defend some features of the cloud. Gathering a vulnerability evaluation to the cloud infrastructure is both essential and feasible. For vulnerability evaluation, some of the well known available tools in the market include WebSAINT, ImmuniWeb, BeyondSaaS, Dell Secure Works, etc.

10.10 CLOUD ARCHITECTURAL CONSIDERATION

A wide range of features influence the execution and functioning of cloud safety designs. There are common matters concerning rigid wants, safety administration, devotion to paradigm, safety consciousness, and information categorization. Then, there are more particular architecturally associated fields, comprising reliable hardware and software, offering a safe implementation setting, creating safe communications and hardware strengthening via micro architectures discussed in the following subsections.

Micro Architecture

Computer architecture refers to the association of the primary components to work efficiently. The chief hardware elements of a digital computer are memory, central processing unit (CPU), and input/output tools. A fundamental CPU of a common digital computer consists of an arithmetic logic unit (ALU), one or more accumulators, control logic, a program counter, an instruction register, multiple general-purpose registers, and some on-chip local memory.

The ALU carries out logical and arithmetic operations on the binary words of the computer. The components of the CPU which are used to support execution on the difficult design are referred to as micro architecture. A micro architecture plan can integrate the following:

Pipelining It augments the functioning of a computer by overlying the steps of diverse directions. For instance, if the order cycle is separated into three branches—obtain, decipher, and implement—directions may be overlapped to augment the implementation pace of the directions.

Superscalar processor It is a processor which facilitates the synchronized implementation of diverse instructions in both similar and diverse pipeline phases efficiently.

Very-long instruction word (VLIW) processor It is a processor wherein a solo order looks over a single synchronized operation. For instance, the order could identify and simultaneously implement two operations in a single order.

Multi-programming It implements two or more programs concurrently on one processor (CPU) by broken implementation among the programs.

Multi-tasking It implements two or more subprograms or jobs at the same time on one processor (CPU) by broken implementation among the jobs.

Multi-processing It implements two or more programs at during a similar occasion on diverse processors. In symmetric multi-processing, the processors share similar memory, operating system, and data, whereas in equivalent multi-processing, many processors are utilized.

Multi-threading It means that jobs should be synchronized to share resources and operate within a procedure. In a multi-processing system, strings work in equivalence.

Simultaneous multi-threading (SMT) It refers to multiple strings operating on one core. SMT is particularly expensive in improving the speed of encryption computations which are broadly utilized in protecting the transactions of a cloud. Micro architecture may be intended as hardware accelerators for operations such as arithmetic, encryption, and safe web transactions to support cloud computing.

10.11 SECURE EXECUTION ENVIRONMENT AND COMMUNICATIONS

In a cloud environment, applications are operated on diverse servers in a distributed manner. Additionally, cloud computing is employed to run and accumulate enormous sums of data in database applications which are co-situated with information pertaining to previous users. Therefore, it is enormously significant for the cloud dealer to offer a safe implementation situation and safe interactions for consumer storage and applications.

In a cloud environment, applications work on diverse servers in a disseminated manner and these applications interrelate with the external world and other applications might enclose perceptive information whose unfortunate access would be destructive to a consumer. Additionally, cloud computing is gradually being utilized to handle and accumulate enormous sums of data in database applications which are also misplaced with information of other users. Therefore, it is enormously vital for the cloud dealer to offer a safe implementation situation and safe communications for consumer applications and storage.

Arranging computing platforms for safe implementation is a versatile job and in various cases it is not worked on appropriately, owing to parameters which are occupied. This gives opportunities for malware to utilize weakness, such as downloading codes fixed in the data and having the code implemented at a high dispensation stage.

In addition to administering safe communications among the computing resources in-house, in a corporation, transfer of applications to the cloud needs a reassessment of the communications safety. Such communications apply to both data in action and data at break.

10.12 IDENTITY MANAGEMENT AND ACCESS CONTROL

Identity administration and access control are the primary operations needed for safe cloud computing. The easiest type of identity administration is logging on to a computer system by means of a user ID and password. Though factual identity administration is needed for cloud computing, stringent access control, support, and confirmation are also needed. It must decide what resources are certified to be accessed by a procedure or user by employing technology like smart or biometrics cards, and decide at what time a resource has been accessed by unoffical units.

10.13 VM SECURITY RECOMMENDATIONS

In addition to the safety measures discussed, it is strongly suggested that each virtual machine also has the following safety checks:
1. Deploy anti virus software—As virus security software proposes safety different from spyware, it is advised to utilize Windows Defender on your Windows virtual machines for extra protection. Defender is used along with Windows. To discover it, click the Start button and type 'Defender' in the search box.

2. Select strong passwords—Weak passwords may be deduced, hence providing somebody else access to your system and your files. Generate passwords which are no less than eight characters in length, including numbers, lower- and upper-case symbols, and letters.
3. Maintain operating systems efficiently—It is vital to maintain your host and virtual operating systems.
4. Sustain replicas for every machine (host and virtual) for security concerns—If any guest is more vulnerable than other guests or your host, it might get access to a reunion of the rest of your system.
5. Regulate host access—Access to the host should be regulated.

10.13.1 VM Security Techniques

As with any cloud computing environment (a virtualized environment), users worry about the safety of the data they store on the cloud. The subsequent safety execution methods are needed for a majority of computer systems and are superior practices for virtualized systems. Such regions comprise physical safety, patching, and isolated administration methods. Setting the host operating system vulnerability in the operating system of the host computer may run into the virtual machine operating system.

Thus, the finest practice methods should be executed to sustain the safety of the fundamental technology. Several of these methods comprise the following:

1. Employ strong passwords like extended, difficult-to-deduce passwords with symbols, numbers, and letters. Modify these frequently.
2. Stop unnecessary programs or services, particularly networked services.
3. Complete substantiation for access control is a must.
4. The host must be personally firewalled.
5. Repeatedly patch and renewal the host.

Some of the safety measures are explained in detail.

Restraining physical access to the host For making data safe, it should have restricted access and self-control at numerous levels. Various access permissions are given to the employees as per the duties of the employees in the company.

Employing encrypted communications Encryption technologies like encrypted virtual private networks (VPNs), safe HTTP (HTTPS), secure shell (SSH), transport layer security (TLS), and many more must be utilized to offer safe communications among the guest domain and the host domain, or from hosts to administration systems. Encryption will assist in preventing these uses as man-in-the-middle (MITM), session hijacking, and spoofed attack.

Immobilizing background tasks Most conventional server operating systems contain various low-precedence procedures which are planned to operate after prime business hours.

Updating and patching Time-to-time updating of the security tools for providing defence to the cloud computing is essential on the virtual machine.

Retaining backup From a security point of view, regular backup of data needs to be maintained for future access.

10.14 CHALLENGES TO CLOUD SECURITY

Computer software was not always written with security in mind, but because of the increasing frequency and sophistication of malicious attacks against information systems, software design methodologies, these days, include security as a primary objective. Cloud computing systems are designed to meet various objectives such as performance, price, security, reliability, and maintainability. To win the reliability of consumers, security is the main issue and concern.

Internal Clouds Intrinsically Insecure

As businesses operate on private clouds, incidents of security breach tend to be frequent. Recognition abilities have to be cloud-specific and operational abilities like patch management should be incisive.

Lack of Risk Awareness and Security Visibility

Businesses need to bear the challenging aspects of cost, control, and visibility while using public cloud services. This is an important aspect from a security point of view because clients maintain very sensitive data on the cloud.

Confidential Information Requiring Safer Storage

One of the toughest jobs in cloud computing is to store confidential information securely. Several approaches are implemented for the security of data and for making it easily accessible to the consumers. The security aspects deal with encoding the data but the crucial questions are how and where to encode.

Insecure Applications

For years, security of applications has been a matter of concern. Whenever possible, it is better to redraft an application for the deployment of a cloud. This lets the application's parts to make amendments independently and tend to be more powerful and distributed.

More Vigorous Authorization and Authentication

Many profitable solutions are available for authentication and authorization of clouds. Each business has its specific means to administer authorization and authentication.

It is to be ascertained if an existing authentication method might work properly and in a reliable and safe manner for users working in a cloud environment. To prevent attacks, a higher authority always maintains checks and constraints to validate the authorization and authentication of every user.

10.14.1 Computer Security Incident Response Team

Computer security incident response teams (CSIRTs) shape the keystone of synchronized event reactions and computer safety information sharing for governments and big corporations all around the world. This module has worked for treating malicious movement on the conventional Internet. Though the initiation of cloud computing has formed a novel array of confronts for safety experts in protecting the platforms which distribute the cloud, it is not sure if conventional CSIRTs are presently able to offer similar support for cloud computing platforms and their suppliers. The attention to possessions, which is a characteristic of cloud computing, means that the cost of 'maintain' events within the cloud will be very different from 'conventional' events. As a result, the cloud safety alliance has instigated the cloud CISRT originality.

Even though cloud computing is clearly constructed upon conventional Internet services, infrastructure, and protocols, such elements are taken mutually in new techniques. The definitional traits of cloud computing, such as multi-occupancy, suppleness, resource sharing, and on-order provisioning, contain data which makes it difficult to understand conventional CSIRT operations. Besides, the corporation modules of cloud computing encapsulate many levels of consumers and suppliers within one virtual infrastructure.

10.15 RISK ISSUES

The aim of the risk evaluation process is to detect the probable sources of risk while working in a cloud environment. This crucial procedure is needed before shuffling operations to the cloud, particularly when the decision is associated with public clouds.

The several steps that are involved in this procedure are as follows:

Identifying sensitive and critical assets Careful evaluation of every asset, such as applications processes and data, should be needed to evaluate how sensitive and critical an asset is for the business. Sensitive assets are those which have high business value for the company. Therefore, these assets should be operated in full safety mode or else the company could lose its reputation in the business market. Critical assets are essential for running the company. The name of the company in the market should not be harmed and there should be no loss of confidential information.

Identification of potential risks While working in a cloud environment, it is very essential to identify and analyse all the potential risks. It is the responsibility of the cloud provider to ensure the security of data at any cost or else there could be threat to the reputation of the company.

Classification of risks into severity levels When complete classification of the risks involved with working in the cloud has been done, these risks are required to be classified into several severity levels such as no risk, low risk, high risk, moderately high risk, and very high risk.

Association of potential risks with critical assets According to the risk appraisal for the asset, a customer judges the expressed terms and conditions of the prescribed agreement with a cloud service provider (CSP). CSP needs to determine all the advantages and disadvantages before signing any agreement in detail with the client so that they can also be aware of the numerous risk factors.

10.16 PHYSICAL SECURITY OF SYSTEMS

Cloud customers have no control over their personal data. Cloud customers essentially lose control over physical security when they move to the cloud, since genuine servers can be placed wherever the providers choose to place them. As physical cloud infrastructure supports various cloud customers collectively, its safety is essential to both its customers and the CSPs. CSP seeks to provide better services to clients but procedures, policies, and processes are significant elements for successful physical security which can protect the device and information assembled in the hosting center.

Server security issues consist of identifying details of server applications such as the following:
1. Determining whether the server will be used for general purposes or a specific application
2. Analysing the network services offered on the server
3. Analysing users and groups of users to whom access rights are given on the server (this comprises deciding their particular access privileges as well)

On the basis of these facts, appropriate measures for protection have to be determined consisting of the following:
1. To reveal user authorization and authentication mechanisms
2. If the server has unused hardware components such as drives, USB ports, or NICs, they must be disabled or detached. The same must be done in virtual machines. Virtual machines aim to move towards green computing.
3. Physical security protection means including safety of the server that will be housed in the premises

Usual security measures which need to be set for protecting the physical cloud infrastructure involve the following:
1. Letting a port in a disabled or an unconfigured condition so that unidentified components or tools cannot link to the infrastructure
2. 24×7×365 on-site premise security where the cloud's physical infrastructure is housed
3. Biometric authentication-based access for the premises
4. Closed circuit TV cameras to track movement throughout the service

Besides the aforementioned measures, cloud environments also need additional measures for the guest operating system (OS) and application levels. Hence, prevention measures taken for further security are as follows:

Prohibiting applications from cloning executable files One of the ways used by hackers is to make exposed applications into clone executable files of their preference. Hence, a vital act for strengthening the application is to prohibit it from initiating other executables, other than the trusted one. Cloning the executable files stops the functioning of several applications.

Prohibiting applications from modifying or designing executable files Another method which hackers use is converting the exposed application into designing or modifying executable files of their preference to pop up in the malicious program attacking the system. This malicious program can finally be implemented and activated. Hence, it is essential that applications are not permitted to design or modify any executable file during their working.

Prohibit applications from amendments at sensitive areas It is necessary to prevent applications from undergoing changes at sensitive fields of the guest OS as a registry key in the Windows operating system. Modification in OS may cause loss of data and stop various applications.

10.17 INPUT VALIDATION AND CONTENT INJECTION

User input that cannot be trusted must be verified and validated at all the ends. User inputs are checked at various levels to prevent loss of data and to maintain integrity. Content injection occurs when the cloud server takes input from the user and applies the content of that input into commands or SQL statements. Essentially, the user's input is injected into a command that is executed by the server. Content injection can occur when the server does not maintain clear distinction and separation between the data input and the commands executed.

10.18 DATABASE INTEGRITY ISSUES

Database integrity requires the following three goals:
1. Prevention of the alteration of data by unoffical users
2. Prevention of the unintended or unoffical alteration of data by authorized users
3. Preservation of both internal and external consistency:
   (a) Internal consistency: Ensure that internal data is consistent
   (b) External consistency: Ensure that the data stored in the database is reliable. External reliability means that the item number recorded in the database for every section is equivalent to the item number which actually subsists in that section.

10.19 REGULATORY ISSUES

Cloud computing consists of applications, platforms, and infrastructure segments. Each segment performs different operations and offers different products for businesses and individuals around the world.

The business application includes Software as a Service (SaaS), utility computing, web services, platform as a service (PaaS), managed service providers (MSPs), service commerce, and Internet integration. We cannot be sure that data at cloud services is secure. There are various security concerns for cloud computing as it includes several technologies along with databases, virtualization, networks, transaction management, concurrency control, resource scheduling, load balancing, memory management, and operating systems.

Hence, security concerns for several of these systems and technologies are relevant to cloud computing. For instance, the network which intersects the systems in cloud need to be protected and mapping of the virtual machines to the physical machines needs to be carried out steadily. Data safety includes encrypting the data and guaranteeing that proper policies are imposed for sharing of data. The security matters in cloud computing are as follows:

(a) Servers and applications' access
(b) Transmission of data
(c) Virtual machine security
(d) Network safety
(e) Data safety
(f) Data confidentiality
(g) Data reliability
(h) Data setting
(i) Data accessibility
(j) Data segregation
(k) Security policy and conformity
(l) Patch management

In reputed data centers, access to servers is restricted and controlled to manage on-premise connections that are outside the cloud data centers. In a cloud environment, the physical location of information is not known. In cloud computing, administrative access should be managed on the Internet, taking into account risk and exposure. Numerous security policies and access privileges are provided to the administrator and higher authorities of the company.

It is extremely vital to confine administrative access to information and watch this access to uphold changes in system control. Issue of data access is mostly associated with security policies offered to the user during data accessing. Several companies possess their own security policies on account of which every employee may have access to a specific set of data. The security policies in some companies do not give employees access to some types of information.

10.20 LEGAL MATTERS IN CLOUD COMPUTING

For businesses, cloud computing is fast acquiring popularity as an substitute to traditional software licensing. Although the innovation has taken efficiency and convenience levels to new heights, it also brings a gale of legal implications.

Consumers must bear in mind the legal risks during negotiation of an agreement for these services. In cloud computing, the consumer's data is hosted on a remote server that might be controlled by the provider or a third party, situated in Hong Kong or overseas, and that might be exclusive to one consumer or shared amid many.

Consumers should have the power to access their data whenever required. It is especially vital that the consumer can do so when either:

- The contract is terminated or
- The service provider becomes indebted or else closes down business

As the requirement to get a copy of the data upon end of the contract appears apparent, the contract's premature termination is generally accompanied by conflicts. Hence, it is essential that the contract does not permit the service provider to conceal access to data until a conflict over fees or any other matter is solved. The problem is that breakdown often happens without alert and the consumers' rights to access remote applications and data then may be at the tenderness of a liquidator or administrator.

Consumers may secure themselves to some degree by obtaining regular copies of their data, so that they will have an up-to-date copy in the case of a sudden breakdown. Moreover, even having the data may be of limited use in case the application is inaccessible. Consumers may succeed to negotiate an 'escrow' arrangement where an application's copy is held by an independent third party and given to the consumer if the service provider is in debt. It is also vital to concede the format that the service provider uses to provide the data. The provider should supply the data in an open format that permits the consumer to shift to another provider or bring the compatible function in-house.

Certainly, reliability is crucial to the success of any cloud computing provider and most business-oriented providers will provide robust service levels for reassuring consumers. In case of unavailability of the remote server, the consumer's business might have to be put on hold, hence it needs to be made sure that the service levels given by the provider are acceptable for their requirements.

In addition, consumers need to make sure that they get a refund in case the service levels are not met by the service provider. If service levels breakdown frequently, the consumer must have the right to abolish the contract. Safety and disaster recovery measures are vital elements of traditional IT infrastructure and hence consumers must be sure that their cloud computing provider has appropriate adjustment in place.

The contract must contain necessities to assure that the data of consumer will be kept safe by the service provider. This is especially vital in case the data involves personal information of employees or consumers or important commercial details. Some types of data such as legally privileged information and patentable inventions might lose their legal protection in case revealed to a third party. Consumers should ask for legal advice in case they plan to store this kind of data on the cloud.

The contract must specify when the service provider is allowed to access the data of consumer and when it is permitted to open it to third parties. The contract must state what the service provider is needed to do in the case it is legally needed to disclose information to governmental authorities. The contract must deal with the question of which party affords the risk in case of safety breaks. In case of the service provider bearing the risk, the consumer must need the provider to have proper insurance for covering the potential damages. Now, cyber security policies are accessible from various insurers.

A data center may face the interruption or damage from terrorist attacks, earthquakes, fires, floods, computer viruses, telecommunication failures, power loss, computer denial of service attacks, and other efforts to damage systems. The provider must have redundant servers and remote back-ups of data for ensuring the continuity of service in such cases. In case services are disturbed or data is lost, the service provider must afford the expenses and costs incurred by the consumer. The consumer should also need the provider to have proper insurance to cover such cases. More issues emerge in case the service provider or the remote server is situated outside Hong Kong.

Various nations have privacy laws that confine the personal information transfer outside their borders. If personal information from one jurisdiction is processed or stored on a server in other location, the consumer will be required to abide with the legal regulations in the nation from where the data is transferred. These differ from nation to nation. If the service provider is situated outside Hong Kong, the consumer must intend to have the contract governed by the law of Hong Kong and ensure that the parties submit to the jurisdiction of the Hong Kong's courts. In case of any disagreement by the service provider, the customer should at least make sure that the contract has a proper optional dispute resolution mechanism such as mediation or arbitration, for minimizing the risk of being drawn into expensive litigation in a foreign nation.

10.21 INFORMATION PRIVACY AND LAWS

Cloud data privacy matters are among the significant concerns of organizations moving to the cloud. In most countries as well as organizations, data privacy policies are relevant when personally identifiable information (PII) is composed and stored. When this data is uploaded onto the cloud, it offers a unique challenge as cloud computing resources are circulated and it becomes difficult to find out the location of data and accessing of data at any particular time.

The laws pertaining to cloud data's privacy differ with countries. For instance, Germany has the strictest laws, whereas the European Union protects personal data more safely than the United States.

10.22 COMMON THREATS AND VULNERABILITIES

A threat is an incident that can cause harm to a system and create loss of reliability, secrecy, or accessibility. Threats may be malicious like the intended alteration of confidential data, or accidental like an error in a transaction computation or accidental deletion of a file.

A system's vulnerability is a weakness that is open to risks. Reducing the susceptible features of the system can reduce such threats. The common threats to both cloud and traditional infrastructure include the following:

Eavesdropping Eavesdropping is a primary cause of failure of confidentiality. This type of network attack consists of unauthorized interception of network traffic. Some network broadcast techniques such as satellite, mobile, wireless, and PDA are exposed to attacks. Snooping may take one of these two forms:

Passive eavesdropping Secretly monitoring or listening to transmissions that are unauthorized by either the sender or receiver

Active eavesdropping Tampering with a transmission to create a covert signaling channel, or actively probing the network for infrastructure information

Eavesdropping and probing are often the preliminary steps to session hijacking and other network intrusions.

Fraud Falsified transactions, data manipulation, and altering of data integrity for gain

Theft Theft of information or trade secrets for profit or unauthorized disclosure, and physical theft of hardware or software

Sabotage Denial-of-service (DoS) attacks, data integrity harm, etc.

External attack Gain infrastructure information, locate an unsecured modem line, and the insertion of a malicious code or virus

Several attacks are intended at disrupting service, but some are focused on illegally obtaining sensitive information, while others try to mislead or cheat.

10.23 LOGON ABUSE

Logon mistreatment refers to users accessing services of a superior security level that is actually not permitted to them. In distinct network imposition, this sort of abuse principally focuses on those users who might be genuine users of a diverse system or users having a lower security categorization.

It is also possible for intruders to pretend to be another user (e.g., an attacker socially engineering passwords from an Internet service provider (ISP)).

10.24 INAPPROPRIATE SYSTEM USES

The non-official or personal use of a network by non-certified users, like surfing the Internet for banned sites, is inappropriate. The utilization of network services for reasons other than business may be deemed as abuse of the system.

While most employers do not enforce extremely strict web surfing rules, occasional harassment proceedings may result from employees accessing pornography sites and employees operating private web businesses using the company's infrastructure.

10.25 NETWORK INTRUSION

It is a substantial challenge to secure the virtual network as virtual switches may hardly be noticeable to system administrators, who mostly implement safety at the network level. Since the virtual network traffic might by no means leave the server, it is not possible for the security administrator to observe VM-to-VM traffic or intercept it, and therefore, be able to understand what that traffic is being routed towards. Therefore, logging of the VM-to-VM network movement in a single server and confirmation of virtual machine access for rigid reasons is a little difficult. It is also difficult to rectify or watch the misuse of virtual network resources and bandwidth consumption in VM-to-VM.

Therefore, for managing and observing VM-to-VM traffic, a firewall service is needed. Virtual firewall (VF) offers a firewall service that completely works on the hypervisor. The regular packet of supervising and filtering of the VM-to-VM traffic is supplied by the VF. The procedure of discovering actions that can negotiate the reliability, accessibility, or secrecy of a resource is known as intrusion detection (ID).

The following are the three key types of technologies which are currently in use for ID:

Server-based IDS The activity log encompassing system calls, application logs, file systems modifications, etc., is studied. It works well for supervised systems and might analyse applications running on the computer.

Network-based IDS The network traffic and communicating nodes are studied. It might manage the network traffic for identifying DOS attacks, vulnerabilities, port scans, etc. This type of IDS inhabits the network and, therefore, is relatively inaccessible from malicious applications. Therefore, it is moderately less vulnerable to attacks. However, it poorly studies managed systems and looks at malevolent application activities running on these systems. Lest the network traffic is encrypted, there is no effective means for the network-based IDS to decrypt the traffic for analysis.

Integrated IDS It uses a server-based network and techniques amalgamation. It studies network traffic along with system activity logs. Firewalls manage the access between networks for preventing problems, contrary to which IDS finds many opportunities to get into a network. The only applicable means to make sure that these possibilities must be clogged after an assault is to restore the working system from the initial medium, smear the scraps, and restore every information and application. Piggybacking in the network area means that hackers gain illicit access to a system via authentic connection of the consumer in a condition such as when a user logs off improperly or leaves a session open, allowing an illicit user to resume the session.

10.26 SESSION HIJACKING ATTACKS

Session hacking is the act of controlling the individual session or making a corroboration session ID. It requires a hacker service to be constrained, brute-controlled, or having repeal-engineered

IDs to seize control of the web application session of a certified consumer even if that session is not yet sustained.

Session hijacking, known as transmission control protocol (TCP) session hijacking, is a method of managing the web consumer session by obtaining the session ID of the permissible consumer. The moment the session ID of a consumer has been accessed, the hacker may execute all that the consumer is expected to execute on the network.

Usually, the session ID is reserved in a cookie or URL. Corroboration processes are approved at set-up, for mass communications. Between sessions, hijackers take advantage of the situation. The nuisance might or might not be perceptible on the basis of the user's technical knowledge and the type of assault. Unless a website terminates to react in a possible or customary way to the input of the consumer or discontinue responding totally for the anonymous reason, the probable reason for this is session hijacking.

A system's illicit access might be accomplished through session hijacking. In such an attack, the attacker hijacks a session between a consistent consumer and a network server. Later, it also reinstates the computer IP address to that of the server and the consistent consumer continues the conversation thinking that it is chatting with another consistent consumer.

10.27 FRAGMENTATION ATTACKS

IP fragmentation attacks generally use different IP datagram divisions as TCP filtering devices are excessively proficient to conceal TCP packets. The following are the two examples of this type of attack:
1. A little portion is passed on by the hacker that crashes several TCP header fields into a second portion. If the filtering devices of the target do not execute the least section size, this illegal packet might be conveyed via the target network.
2. Subsequent packets overwrite the target address information of the real packet and later the target filtering device approves the second packet. This might happen if the target filtering device does not execute the smallest portion to counteract along with non-zero counteracts.

10.28 CLOUD ACCESS CONTROL ISSUES

Several safety matters of cloud computing are as follows:

XML Signature Element Wrapping

For web services, XML signature element wrapping is the most popular assail. It is used for guarding the element name, feature, and value from illegal parties but is unable to protect the place in the recognition. The intruder directly trails to damage the system. The invader aims at the constituent by working the SOAP messages and placing something he/she likes. This assail, sometimes, uses a third-party certified digital certificate. We can use certificate agencies and a combination of XML signature with Web Services Security (WSS) to a specific constituent.

Browser Security

Browser security is the second matter. When a consumer sends a request to the server through a web browser, the web browser requires utilization of the secure socket layer (SSL) to encrypt the credentials to legalize the consumer. SSL's point-to-point support indicates if a third party is present. Later, the host might decrypt the data.

Hackers conceal themselves and use a new individuality. In case intruders mount packages on an intermediary host, the intruders may get the consumer's documents and use them for authorization in the cloud system.

Therefore, dealers must use WSS perception on web browsers as WSS performs at the message-level, using XML encryption for constant encryption of SOAP messages that do not have to be decrypted at negotiator hosts.

Cloud Malware Injection Attack

Another issue is that of cloud malware injection attacks which attempt to harm a virtual machine, malevolent service, or application. Malevolent software or codes are used to access the cloud setting. Once the malevolent software is introduced into the cloud environment, the intruder considers the malevolent software to be an authentic request. It is not easy to determine what the authentic data are. If an affluent consumer enquires about a malevolent service, only then are malicious users detected.

Hackers upload the virus program into the cloud arrangement. Once the cloud arrangements are activated for an authentic service, the entry of the virus is accomplished and the cloud setting is affected. The consumer requests the malevolent program to check on the cloud. In case of a virus infected cloud, it is disseminated to all the consumers. A virus infects the consumer's device. Therefore, authenticity of the received messages must constantly be checked. The original image or request file should be stored by using jumble functions and it must be equated with the jumble value of all impending service requests. Authentic jumble values are produced by the hacker for dealing with cloud systems.

Flooding Attacks

The fourth issue is flooding attack. Since cloud systems constantly expand in size whenever the requests from customers increase, new service requests are initialized by the cloud systems to retain the requirements of a customer.

Flooding attack refers to disbanding a huge sum of trash requests for certain services. As soon as the intruder chucks an enormous amount of requests by proposing more resources, the cloud system will try to execute, flanking to the requests and ultimately the system consumes all the resources and becomes incompetent to distribute services to customary requests from consumers. Then, the invader assails the services. We may prevent the assail by an intrusion detection system that might sift through the malevolent requests.

Data Protection

The most essential factor in cloud computing is data protection. It must be hard for the cloud's consumers to competently guarantee the behavior of the cloud supplier and be sure that information is administered in a certified way.

Incomplete Data Deletion

In cloud computing, incomplete data deletion is a hazard, since imitations are produced at numerous places in a server. Deletion of correct data is unfeasible as copies of data are saved as an imitation but are unavailable.

Thus, virtualized private networks must be used to make the data safe and use inquiries which will eliminate the whole data from the main servers together with its imitations.

Lock-in

In case a consumer wishes to move from one cloud supplier to another, or back to a home IT setting, the charge of access control in the cloud should be equivalent with the value of the confined information.

Appropriate access controls facilitate complete accessibility. Accessibility guarantees that certified consumers of the system have continuous and timely access to the information in the system. Consistency and utility are the aims of additional access control. Access control must offer security from unanticipated, unintentional, or illicit change of data. With this security, the external and internal consistency of the data might be conserved. Data privacy must be evenly maintained and data accessibility given on a timely basis. These features cover the consistency, accessibility, components, and privacy of the safety of a data system. Accountability features enable the activities of a system to be customized to suit individuals.

Points to Remember

1. Confidentiality refers to the prevention of intentional or unintentional unauthorized disclosure of information.
2. Passwords should never be transmitted in the open.
3. Testing in the cloud leverages cloud computing environments and seeks to simulate real-world user traffic as a means of load or stress testing of websites.
4. Software requirements engineering is the process of determining customer software expectations and needs, and is conducted before the software design phase.
5. Security is prominent only two times in the development life cycle, that is, during requirements definition and testing.
6. Cloud testing is utilized to measure the latency between the action and the corresponding response for any application after deploying it on clouds.
7. Load testing of an application involves creation of heavy user traffic and measuring its response.
8. The aim of the risk evaluation process is to detect the probable sources of risk while working in a cloud environment.
9. The principle of least privilege maintains the minimum privileges and resources for the minimum period of time required for completing a task.
10. Audit logs should record the following:
    (a) The transaction's date and time
    (b) Who processed the transaction
    (c) At which terminal the transaction was processed
    (d) Various security events relating to the transaction

Key Terms

Accountability It refers to a system's capability to determine the actions and behaviour of a single individual within a system and to identify that particular individual.

Authentication It is the testing or reconciliation of evidence of a user's identity. It establishes the user's identity and ensures that the users are who they say they are.

Authorization It refers to the rights and permissions granted to an individual or process that enables access to a computer resource.

Availability It ensures that authorized users are reliable and ensure authorized user for accessing compute, storage, and network resources available on cloud computing. Availability also ensures data availability to cloud users even in the case of failure of data.

Confidentiality It provides the required secrecy of information and ensures that only endorsed users have access to data. In addition, it restricts illicit users from accessing information.

Confidentiality, integrity, and availability   Confidentiality, integrity, and availability are sometimes known as the CIA triad of information system security.

Defence in multiple places   Information protection mechanisms placed in a number of locations to protect against internal and external threats.

Denial-of-service attack (DoS attack) or distributed denial-of-service attack (DDoS attack)   It is an effort to make a machine resource or network resources not accessible to its intended users.

Deploy intrusion detection systems   A system that supports intrusion detection mechanisms for detecting intrusions, evaluating information, examining results, and take action as per the requirements.

Deploy KMI/PKI   Use of robust key management infrastructures (KMI) and public key infrastructures (PKI).

Eavesdropping   Eavesdropping is the primary cause for the failure of confidentiality.

Encryption   Encryption involves scrambling messages so that they cannot be read by an unauthorized entity, even if they are captured.

Fail-safe   Fail-safe means that if a cloud system fails, it should fail to a state in which the security of the system and its data are not compromised.

Fraud   Falsified transactions, data manipulation, and other altering of data integrity for gain is called fraud.

Identification   It is the means by which users claim their identities to a system.

Integrity   It ensures that illegal changes to information are not allowed. The objective of this is to detect and protect against unauthorized variation or deletion of information.

On-demand test service   It provides on-demand test execution services based on selected schedules and test wares.

QoS requirements management   It supports book keeping and modelling of software testing and QoS requirements, including quality assurance modelling.

RAID   It refers to the redundant array of independent disks.

Sabotage   Sabotage includes denial-of-service (DoS) attacks, data integrity harm, etc.

Security robustness   Robustness ensures working of information security and its flexibility during any situation, and evaluates the performance of the security system on various parameters and how the system reacts to various security issues.

Session hijacking   It is the act of taking control of a person's session following the acquiring of or producing an authentication session ID.

Software requirements engineering   It is the process of determining customer software expectations and needs, and it is conducted before the software design phase.

SQL injection attacks   These are attacks where a hacker uses special characters to return the data.

TaaS pricing and billing   It enables TaaS vendors to offer customers selectable testing service contracts based on pre-defined pricing models and billing services.

TaaS process management   It offers test project management and process control.

Test environment service   It provides on-demand test environment services to establish the required virtual cloud-based computing resources and infrastructures as well as the tools necessary as per the requirements.

Test simulation services   It establishes on-demand test simulation environments with selected features and supports the necessary test message or data generation.

Test solution services It offers diverse systematic testing solutions and testware generation and management services.

Theft Theft includes the theft of information or trade secrets for profit or unauthorized disclosure, and physical theft of hardware or software.

Multiple-choice Questions

1. Which two security functions should be delivered by firewalls in a cloud network infrastructure installation?
   (a) Prevention of distributed denial of service
   (b) Single user access for management operations
   (c) Unified threat management such as antivirus and web filtering
   (d) Both (a) and (c)
   (e) Blocking host name look-up of any system that is external to the cloud

2. Which one of the following is the most important security consideration when selecting a new computer facility?
   (a) Local law enforcement response times
   (b) Proximity to competitors' facilities
   (c) Aircraft flights paths
   (d) Utility infrastructure

3. The typical function of secure socket layer (SSL) in securing wireless application protocol (WAP) is to protect transmissions:
   (a) Between the WAP gateway and the wireless device
   (b) Between the web server and WAP gateway
   (c) From the web server to the wireless device
   (d) Between the wireless device and base station

4. How can confidentiality of information be achieved?
   (a) By ensuring enough resources to make information available for all users
   (b) By preventing unauthorized changes
   (c) By regularly backing up information
   (d) By restricting access to information

5. What is location information used for in the cloud?
   (a) To determine the geographical location of the user of an application
   (b) To determine the identity of a user of an application
   (c) To determine whether a user of an application is online
   (d) To determine who has accessed a document stored in the cloud

6. Software is _____ if it works as per user requirements and constraints work properly at different conditions.
   (a) Accurate
   (b) Reliable
   (c) Secure
   (d) None of these

7. Scrambling messages so that they cannot be read by an unauthorized entity, even if they are intercepted, is _____.
   (a) Confidentiality
   (b) Reliability
   (c) Encryption
   (d) All the above

8. Audit logs should record the following for security purpose _____.
   (a) The transaction's date and time
   (b) At which terminal the transaction was processed
   (c) Encryption
   (d) All the above

9. Software requirements engineering is the process of determining_____.
   (a) Customer software expectations and needs
   (b) Software design phase
   (c) Software requirements
   (d) All the above

10. Which of these is/are true regarding the security policy for cloud computing?

(a) Antivirus updates must be done without fail.
(b) Patch updates and system files updates have to be conducted accurately.
(c) System logs must be maintained
(d) All the above

11. Design principles of security include:
(a) Least privilege
(b) Separation of duties
(c) Defence in depth
(d) All the above

12. Testing or reconciliation of evidence of a user's identify is:
(a) Identification
(b) Authentication
(c) Authorization
(d) Privacy

13. The most sensitive business information that is strictly intended for use within the organization:
(a) Public data
(b) Sensitive data
(c) Private data
(d) Confidential data

14. Passwords used in handling data should:
(a) Not be clear while sending
(b) Be encrypted
(c) Not be part of a query string
(d) All the above

15. One of the drawbacks of 'C' language is that it:
(a) Cannot prevent buffer overflow
(b) Not based on OOPs
(c) Improper memory allocation
(d) None of these

16. It ensures that the data stored in a database is consistent with the real world.
(a) Internal consistency
(b) External consistency
(c) Integrity rule
(d) None of these

17. Sabotage includes:
(a) Denial of service attack
(b) Data integrity harm
(c) Both (a) and (b)
(d) None of these

18. TCP session hacking is also known as:
(a) Session hacking
(b) Denial of service attack
(c) Fragmentation attacks
(d) All the above

19. Fraud refers to:
(a) Falsified transactions
(b) Data manipulation
(c) Altering of data integrity for gain
(d) All the above

20. _____ means that the number of items recorded in the database for each department is equal to the number of items that physically exists in that department.
(a) External consistency
(b) Internal consistency
(c) Integrity
(d) All the above

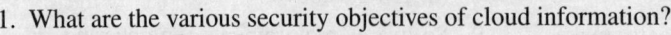

Review Questions

1. What are the various security objectives of cloud information?
2. Why it is necessary to secure data in a cloud environment?
3. What needs about security must be kept in mind when finding a cloud provider for an organization?
4. What are different design principles of cloud security?
5. What do you mean by least privileges?
6. Explain the various cloud security services.
7. What do you mean by cloud software testing?
8. What are the different types of testing?
9. What do you mean by goal oriented software security requirements?
10. What are the requirements of secure cloud software?
11. What is the computer security incident response team (CSIRT)?

12. What are the different security techniques for a virtual machine (VM)?
13. Why is security of cloud necessary?
14. How can we provide security in a cloud environment?
15. What are the challenges when it comes to keeping the cloud secure from malicious users?
16. What the various design principles of security for cloud computing?
17. What do you understand by physical security of data?
18. What are the various security issues of cloud computing?
19. Explain a denial-of-service attack.
20. With the help of an example, explain what SQL injection attacks are.
21. What are the benefits of defence in multiple places?
22. What do you understand by integrity in cloud security?
23. Explain what are session hijacking attacks.
24. What do you understand by logon abuse?
25. Discuss the different security tools available for applications, to make cloud application efficient and secure.

References

1. *Cloud Security A Comprehensive Guide to Secure Cloud Computing*, Ronald L. Krutz and Russell Dean Vines, ISBN: 978-0-470-58987-8, Wiley Publication, 2010
2. *Cloud computing for Dummies*, Judith Hurwitz, Robin Bloor, Marcia Kaufman, and Dr. Fern Halper, ISBN-10: 0470484705, Wiley Publication, 1st edition, November 16, 2009
3. *Cloud Computing Technologies and Strategies*, Brian J.S. Chee and Curtis Franklin, Jr, ISBN 9781439806128, CRC Press, April 7, 2010
4. *Cloud Computing: A Practical Approach*, Anthony T. Velte, Toby J. Velte, Ph.D., RobertElsenpeter, ISBN-10: 0071626948, McGraw-Hill, 1st edition, November 1, 2009
5. *Grid and Cloud Computing,* Katarina StanoevskaSlabeva, Thomas Wozniak, and Santi Ristol, ISBN-10: 3642051928, Springer, 2010 edition, November 19, 2009
6. *Implementing and Developing Cloud Applications*, David E.Y.Sarna, ISBN-10: 1439830827, Auerbach Publications, November 26, 2010
7. *Forms of Cloud-based Software Testing*, http://seij.dce.edu/Paper%201.pdf
8. Internet-based software testing, http://www.ijera.com/papers/Vol2_issue4/EC24817824.pdf, last accessed in May 2018
9. Cloud testing: A review http://www.academia.edu/7404462/Cloud_Testing_A_Review_Article, last accessed in May 2018
10. Cloud Computing Top Threats: https://cloudsecurityalliance.org/media/news/ca-warns-providers-of-the-notorious-nine-cloud-computing-top-threats-in-2013/

Answers to Multiple-choice Questions

1. (d)	5. (a)	9. (a)	13. (d)	17. (c)
2. (d)	6. (b)	10. (d)	14. (d)	18. (a)
3. (b)	7. (c)	11. (d)	15. (a)	19. (d)
4. (d)	8. (d)	12. (b)	16. (b)	20. (a)

CHAPTER 11

Computing Platforms

Learning Outcomes

After completing this chapter, students will be able to:

- comprehend online analytical processing (OLAP)
- explain performance monitoring tools
- list quality of service (QoS) issues in cloud computing
- describe sky computing
- understand various cloud computing platforms like Xen cloud platform
- discuss service-level agreement
- describe various computing platforms
- describe third-party technology
- explain MapReduce in cloud computing
- comprehend Hadoop

11.1 INTRODUCTION

For availing the services offered by cloud providers, cloud users need various platforms to work efficiently with different applications. The various services that are provided to cloud users include SaaS, PaaS, and IaaS. All these services have different platforms and customized tools as per user requirements.

The cloud management software is a part of the software which is responsible for the entire process of identifying the physical machine, receiving the IP address sent from the network, and producing the virtual machine. The first element is the physical machine, which is an amalgamation of the operating system and hardware. Cloud management software must be flexible enough to work on distinct operating systems and the hardware of sellers. The second element is a network that comprises dynamic host control protocol (DHCP) and domain name system (DNS). The network elements must be planned to deal with both the virtual machine and the host demands. The third element is the hypervisor which offers a structure to work on virtual machines (VMs). The fourth element is image storage; this is where the VM images are saved. The fifth element is the front end that permits users to request for the VM and permits a cloud manager to modify configurations. The sixth element is the cloud management software, for example, Nimbus, OpenNebula, Eucalyptus, etc.

In the rest of the chapter, we shall discuss the various management products, service oriented architecture (SOA) and cloud computing, online analytical processing, software vendors, cloud performance monitoring tools, quality of services in cloud computing, Intercloud, sky computing, various cloud computing platforms, third party technology, etc., in detail.

11.2 EXPLORING CLOUD MANAGEMENT PRODUCTS

For better performance over a cloud network, operations over it should be properly managed and monitored. Cloud has the attractive feature of virtualization that adds to the complexity of virtual infrastructure management. Cloud management products and software must have the ability to handle errors, security, performance, and responsibility. Cloud management is necessary and includes both types of management at the cloud level as well as on-premise management of resources.

The cloud environment consists of physical resources, networking devices, hypervisor, storage system, management software, and an interface to work smoothly. The cloud management software obtains a demand from the consumer, receives the consequent virtual machine's image file to administer it, and forwards a demand to the hypervisor to generate a virtual machine. It then requests for network parameters of the machine and assigns an IP to the virtual machine. The basic network management features (refer to Fig. 11.1) are as follows:

1. Resource management of various resources available for cloud computing
2. Security implementation at various levels in cloud computing for users to avail the services and various tools offered by the provider
3. A proper monitoring system, that is, time-to-time management of various systems in cloud computing
4. Policy management, that is, management as per the policy defined by the cloud provider for various applications, data migration, data deletion, etc.
5. Resource maintenance, that is, the resources utilized by a cloud user change from time to time; resource management and maintenance also change accordingly

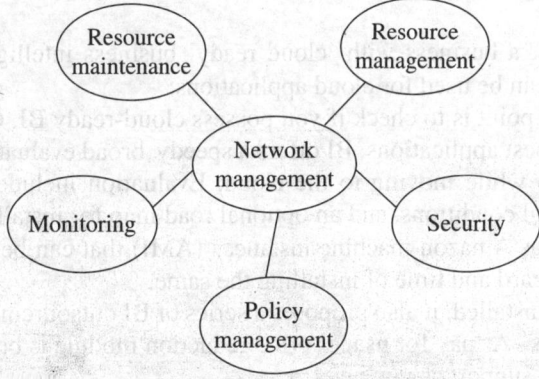

Fig. 11.1 Network management features

11.3 SOA AND CLOUD COMPUTING

SOA is a service-oriented architecture which manages software systems and consists of various interacting services. It is a computing package to support various software systems according to the business domain. Service providers and consumers play an important role in SOA. It is responsible for managing the services offered by them so that consumers can demand services as per the need. The service agreement is negotiated and signed by both the provider and consumers before availing any services. The agreement consists of the nature of the service, how to use various services, charges for the services, etc. Both the provider and consumer can belong to different organizations or parties. Technical complexity is not disclosed to consumers. Web services technology supports implementation of SOA. It also supports inter-operation facilities on various platforms and programming environments. Generally, SOA supports various standards such as HTTP and XML. Web services are basically designed on various languages as per the choice of the developer. Users can find out detailed documents, libraries, and tools as per the requirement of the application which can be easily downloaded and appended to the application.

Cloud service suppliers require architecting declaration using a service-oriented approach to distribute services with the expected stages of scalability and flexibility. SOA is a software design for constructing business applications. The projected approach manages existing assets and also produces new dealings which are supple, convenient, and constrained.

SOA is actually giving businesses a new approach for designing a more efficient IT infrastructure and system that is helpful as it swiftly reacts to threats.

The chief features of SOA are depicted in more detail as follows:
1. SOA is a black-box constituent design. The black box permits you to recycle the prevailing applications of the corporation. Users do not need to know each aspect of what is within every constituent, reducing any kind of complexity.
2. Elements of SOA are arranged to connection via corporation procedures to distribute a distinct stage of service. SOA generates an easy agreement of constituents which, mutually, carry a versatile business service. Parallelly, SOA should offer suitable service stages. The constituents also guarantee a reliable service stage. Service stage is attached to the best practices of complete trade, usually mentioned to business process management (BPM). BPM concentrates on the efficiency of business procedures, whereas SOA permits IT to assist in these business procedures.

11.4 ONLINE ANALYTICAL PROCESSING

Online analytical processing (OLAP) is a method used for answering multi-dimensional queries in a computing environment.

OLAP is used to market a business with 'cloud ready' business intelligence (BI). The following points explain how OLAP can be used for cloud applications:
1. Preparation: The first point is to check if you possess cloud-ready BI. Cloud specialists will help you to decide on the best applications. BI offers a speedy, broad evaluation of all the chief aspects you should look into while moving to the cloud. Evaluation includes price-reduction studies, modified technological conditions, and an optional road map for installing the cloud.
2. Installment: OLAP has Amazon machine instances (AMI) that can be customized, considerably lessening both the hazard and time of installing the same.
3. Support: After being installed, it also proposes a series of BI outsourcing services to deal with and support user decisions. A 'pay for usage' price-reduction module is beneficial. The elastic cloud model offers as much support as you need.

11.5 BUSINESS INTELLIGENCE

Every business has to come up with some guidelines for taking decisions in the company. Cloud computing plays an important role in this. It has appropriate strategies so that decisions can be taken in favour of the business. Cloud computing can be used as a tool for the collection, analysis, presentation, and dissemination of business information and data. BI also supports online analytical processing, data mining, process mining, complex data processing, and predictive and prescriptive analysis.

Many financial and functional features are supported by cloud BI. Some of the functional features are:

Execution and installment speed Each service is instantly accessible without any lengthy phases, be it application installment, infrastructure, etc., resulting in time reduction.

Elasticity It can manage the computing power depending on varying necessities.

Concentration on core power BI apps are controlled by experts and the focus is on their core abilities.

Lowered overall charge of possession Capital expenses are converted into functional expenses, so that payment can be made as per use.

On-demand accessibility Services support distant and mobile users, all of which may be controlled by a cloud platform, be it database storehouses, data administration, etc., by using diverse browsers.

There are many reasons for the slow acceptance of cloud BI. These are given here:

Data safety Safety usually comprises accessibility, authenticity, and privacy of the data that is vital for consuming the cloud. Since businesses require high levels of safety, suppliers worry about the acceptance of their products.

On-premise incorporation Speedy progress to the cloud is not practical for everybody.

Lack of power Service-level agreements should be discussed between the cloud provider and cloud user at the beginning. It is complicated to get service level agreements (SLAs) from cloud suppliers. Data management, data possession, consistency, and safety of services are some of the chief concerns.

Dealer maturity Dealers come up with many proposals regarding their services; this confuses consumers.

Performance Performance with huge data is for a while not very satisfying.

Pricing modules There is lack of a uniform pricing module, making it difficult for consumers to make a decision. Consumers have to predict the return on investment (RoI), in particular, what revenue or price reduction does a specific contract offer.

If an organization decides to move to the cloud, the benefits for businesses can be categorized as follows:

Financial benefits It includes the direct impact of a new deal or technology on the organization's budget and economic growth.

Non-financial benefits It includes the impact on operational changes. It also includes improvement in performance and results, for example, level of improvement in customer satisfaction, better information, and reduced cycle time.

Financial RoI has three metrics for an organization:

Payback period The required time period for the benefits to pay back the cost of the project to be invested

Net present value (NPV) The value of future benefits estimated as per today's money value

Internal rate of return (IRR) The benefits are recalculated as per the interest rate.

The non-financial RoI benefits are as follows:
1. *Customer satisfaction index (CSI)*: Apart from financial benefits, there are some intangible benefits like customer satisfaction; if a customer is satisfied, the business graph will definitely grow in an unpredictable manner.
2. *Independent agencies' rating*: Independent decision and rating can be done with the help of available data, which can be used for future predictions as well.
3. *Better time utilization*: At-the-glance view of data is not only helpful in predicting the trends in the future, but is also the best way to utilize the time for evaluating complex data.
4. *Quality of data for various applications*: Data should always be flexible and support each and every type of application. Data processed by every application can be used for various decision support systems.

5. *Public relation*: Better application support by the service provider guarantees better relations with the client.
6. *Risk avoidance*: The available data is used in decision-making and reduces risks to the client's business.
7. *Change in decision-making process*: Prediction with the help of data is always useful to change decisions for the future, on the basis of present data and evaluation.

Calculation of Three Financial RoI Metrics

To calculate the metrics, we first need to list down the cost and return of the organization. Cost and returns are estimated for x years, where x is the life of BI implementation in number of years. Generally, the life span of BI implementation is 3 to 5 years.

Financial RoI metrics = Cost and returns for x years

where x = number of years

The BI implementation cost has two components:
1. *Capital expense*: Generally it includes one-time investment cost like one-time hardware cost, software licence procurement, etc.
2. *Operational expense*: It refers to expense after a certain period of time (e.g., support services cost, annual maintenance contract, etc.)

11.6 INDEPENDENT SOFTWARE VENDOR

Self-governing software dealers or independent software vendors (ISVs) offer software which support and operate on diverse hardware and operating systems. Platforms such as Microsoft, IBM, Hewlett-Packard, and Apple are offered to consumers. They also support ISVs, together with different business offers. Usually, many applications that function on a platform have additional appraisals. Platform makers such as Microsoft and IBM make applications even though they do not have the resources, and in several cases, the link required for building them.

Several ISVs concentrate on a precise operating system such as AS/400. IBM also has ISV applications. There are additional ISVs for a specific application area, such as engineering and building software, mainly for high-end UNIX-based workspace platforms.

Some of the software vendors are explained here:

Apica

Apica offers high-tech cloud-based SaaS functioning devices which experiment, advance, investigate, and supervise all the features of a web infrastructure for recognizing feasible and existing matters. Broad decisions of Apica are intended to guarantee successful migration to the cloud.

Chef

Chef is an open-source arrangement, administration, and amalgamation structure which assists designers and system managers to construct and uphold completely automatic server infrastructure based on the best execution and proficiency.

CloudOpt

CloudOpt proposes centralized services which unite a completely integrated supervising and helpdesk system along with unmatched system engineers to offer consumers with extraordinary values. It processes completely controlled infrastructure resolutions at negligible expenses.

CloudPassage

CloudPassage is a security SaaS business, offering the private server security of commerce and is purpose-made for lithe cloud systems. The corporation deals with the technological challenge of dealing with high volumes of data for cloud hosting, so a consistent physical location for network administration is important.

CodeFutures

CodeFutures is the foremost supplier supporting database functioning devices which drastically enhanced consistency and scalability. It offers a highly scalable method for enhancing the throughput and wide-range functioning of high-contract, database-centric corporation applications.

11.7 CLOUD PERFORMANCE MONITORING TOOLS

As a consequence of the popularity of cloud computing applications and the shift from networked application services to the cloud, there is no need to manage resources at the user end. There are basically five cloud monitoring tools.

Zenoss cloud monitoring   This is prepared by Zenoss to monitor hybrid, private, and public clouds with an amalgamated visibility and offers synchronized alertness of the whole infrastructure. Zenoss guarantees significance via a model-driven cloud functions' administration system that maintains a broad record of the network, hardware, and software tools used.

RevealCloud   It is a server functioning and scrutinizing device offered by CopperEgg. It offers wide visibility, transversely, to both public and personal cloud environments. It uses a cross-association exploratory that assists functional groups in rapidly locating and isolating the main reasons for problems on the cloud. It is intended to be utilized on the server side. The following features are offered by RevealCloud:

(a) It offers alarms and visibility that alert managers time to time when problems are discovered.
(b) It offers instantaneous results, scrutinizing server functioning every five seconds.
(c) It offers process, OS, and system scrutiny as well.

RevealUptime   It is another product from CopperEgg that best matches RevealCloud for offering associated data among end users. This permits managers to better understand what their users are feeling in relation to the servers and the cloud.

Gomez APM   Gomez application performance management (APM) of Compuware offers a different attitude to cloud analysis of applications. The device offers thorough information on the root cause of troubles and what effect it has on the whole system and corporation. This permits IT groups to work on the issues immediately and prioritize the serious ones. The major characteristic of this APM is its error area isolation.

Rackspace Cloud Monitoring   It is an API-driven supervising system that permits managers to generate or use APIs depending on their needs and can work with every tool including mobiles. This permits managers to be over their Rackspace-hosted infrastructure that comprises ports, protocols, and websites. It is imperative to choose a managing tool that works best for the cloud infrastructure and the provider.

11.8 QUALITY OF SERVICE ISSUES IN CLOUDS

Service quality is the capability of supplying diverse services to consumers (data flows or applications) and guarantee a certain standard. Quality of Service (QoS) rules are many and are reliant on the application.

The general service arrangement is as follows:
1. Delay: Time taken for a flow of packages to move from the source to the target
2. Loss: The possibility that a data flow is lost
3. Bandwidth: Maximum speed at which the source might convey data

Service situation in the cloud depends on SLAs that signify an agreement made between the service supplier and the consumer with non-functional provisions of the service, specifically QoS. SLA takes into account service charge, liability, and penalty in case of agreement infringements.

SLAs are necessary to administer the procedure of resources in cloud computing. In the process of conciliation, a combined assessment is made among the service supplier, service user, and parties, from the perspective of cloud computing. Service quality is the skill to propose different priorities to applications, users, or an assurance of a specific performance level.

11.9 INTERCLOUD

The Intercloud is a unified universal 'cloud of clouds' and an expansion of the Internet 'network of networks' on which it is established. In 2007, the expression was first used from the perspective of cloud computing. In early 2009, it became popular and has been used to explain the data center of the future as well.

The Intercloud circumstances are based on the chief concept that every individual cloud does not contain countless physical resources or ubiquitous geographical marks. If a cloud oversupplies the storage and computational resources of its infrastructure, or is appealed to employ resources in characteristics where it has no marks, it would not be capable of satisfying these appeals for service allotments transmitted from its consumers. The Intercloud circumstances would tackle these conditions where every cloud would employ storage, computational, or any type of resource of the infrastructure of additional clouds. This is a correct interpretation of how the Internet works, in that a service supplier, to which an endpoint is connected, will send or access traffic starting from the source/target of its service region using Internet navigation practices with other service suppliers with whom it has an agreed switch.

11.10 SKY COMPUTING

In the existing cloud computing environment, everyone wants to be isolated into protected, proprietary systems. With an intention to achieve this objective, numerous attempts of the research society are dealing with matters like general programming form, open customary interfaces, sufficient service phase arrangements, or portability of applications. In this environment, we argue regarding the want for an open-source cloud application programming interface and a platform intended for growing multi-cloud-oriented applications. A platform which permits the installment of element-based applications in a cloud environment considering diverse cloud suppliers is Sky computing (refer to Fig. 11.2). Sky suppliers consist of the following:
1. Collective utilization of multiple clouds
2. Platforms, apps, resources, and diagonally autonomous clouds are employed
3. Services except those of every personal cloud
4. Smoothness of various clouds
5. Customers of cloud suppliers
6. Superior computing and information systems laboratory

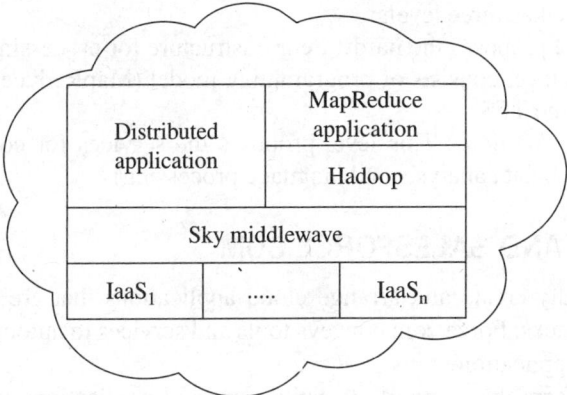

Fig. 11.2 Example of Sky computing architecture

11.11 XEN CLOUD PLATFORMS

The Xen cloud platform (or XCP) is an open-source virtualization platform which offers distinct cloud computing and virtualization. XCP comprises the Xen hypervisor, the Xen API device load, and amalgamations for networking, storage, etc. Added functionalities accessible in XCP include the following:
1. Virtual machine lifecycle—live photographs, migration
2. Resources offered—flexible networking and storage
3. Announcement, advancement, etc.
4. Updation facilities
5. Coordinated functioning, supervising, and warning
6. Support and patterns for Linux and Windows guests
7. Open vSwitch support suite
8. Storage XenMotion live Immigration (VDI immigration, cross-pool immigration)

Let us look at the XCP feature matrix for the entire list of characteristics.

XCP merges server workloads, allows reductions in administration, cooling, and power expenses, and hence contributes to environmentally maintainable computing, an augmented facility to adjust to varying IT situations, an optimized utilization of prevailing hardware, and an enhanced stage of IT consistency. The Xen Cloud Platform is certified beneath the GNU general public licence (GPL2). XCP appears in two alternatives:

- The XCP can be downloaded from Xen.org. This edition of XCP deploys on your host from an ISO, offering an out-of-the-box server virtualization and cloud computing platform after launch.
- XCP tool stack packets (or XCP-XAPI packets) permit you to put up an XCP-like environment from packets which are distributed through the packet administrator of the operating system of your host. XCP-XAPI packets are single and accessible from supported Linux allotments (presently Ubuntu and Debian). XCP-XAPI packets offer more flexibility in customizing with versatile functionalities.

11.12 TPLATFORM

Tplatform is a cloud platform which offers an expansion platform for web mining applications started on Google cloud technologies and performs as a PaaS. Their infrastructure is supported by these three skills—a scalable file system known as Tianwang File System (TFS) that is similar to the Google file system (GFS), the Big Table data storage, and the MapReduce programming module.

The Tplatform structure has three levels:
1. *PC group*: This level proposes the hardware infrastructure for processing of data.
2. *Infrastructure*: This level consists of programming model (MapReduce), distributed data storage means (BigTable), and TFS.
3. *Data processing applications*: This level proposes the services for consumers to develop their application (e.g., web data analysis and language processing).

11.13 FORCE.COM AND SALESFORCE.COM

Force.com offers to rapidly create and arrange cloud applications that are secure and scalable with customized application stacks. Force.com conveys tools and services to automate businesses and is also compatible with mobile application.

Force.com is the platform that supports to build powerful applications without writing any code. Applications can be built using dragging and dropping components of App Builder. Force.com also has powerful cloud databases with enhanced features that support application work. You can also connect your application with external data sources and effortlessly use it in any application.

Apex is a platform with force.com that supports object-oriented programming language with code writing and customized applications. Apex code also supports powerful business applications to create triggers and run as per the event generated before or after the event.

Force.com also has robust security controls to check authorization and authentication at every level. You can create new profiles, edit profiles, and change various permissions as per user need. We can also change control over data using various constraints available with the tools.

Salesforce provides services for encrypting sensitive information. It also supports applications for monitoring user data and history of user access. It offers you a rich suite of features such as profile of user, real-time status update, etc. Applications are easily available to work with a group or an individual.

11.14 APACHE VIRTUAL COMPUTING LAB

VCL is a free and open-source cloud computing platform with the prime objective of distributing devoted, customized compute environment to users.

NCSU offers an isolated access service which permits you to keep a computer with a preferred array of applications for yourself, and distantly access it on the Internet. This service is stimulated by the Apache Software Foundation's Virtual Computing Lab (VCL) software.

Development of VCL began in 2004 as a joint project of the Office of Information Technology (OIT) and the College of Engineering (COE) to proficiently use hardware reserves and to offer distant access to a variety of superior compute necessities by NCSU researchers, students, and faculty.

In November 2008, NCSU contributed the VCL source code to the Apache Software Foundation (ASF) as part of constant attempts to develop the VCL and to promote open source growth. NCSU persists to be deeply concerned in the growth of VCL via the open-source populace at ASF.

With constant assistance from the OIT, College of Engineering, corporate, and academic partners, the ASF VCL software offers a service which effectively supports a broad series of users with varied computing requirements athwart the UNC system.

The Apache Software Foundation offers assistance for the Apache of open-source software business enterprise. The VCL code base was given by NCSU and approved into the Apache Software Foundation in November 2008. The Apache VCL is a rising organization and welcomes everyone who wishes to contribute, to connect.

The compute situations in VCL may vary from plain (to describe a virtual machine's operating efficiency) software to a group of authoritative physical servers operating multifaceted high performance computing (HPC) replication.

VCL supports many kinds of compute resources comprising physical bare-metal appliances, virtual machines hosted on numerous diverse hypervisors, and conventional computing lab computers which you would usually discover on a university campus. The interface of the user comprises a self-service web portal. By using the portal, users choose from a record of modified situations and create conditions.

Secretly, the forecast elements assembled into the web portal decide which compute resources to allocate for the conditions. The demanded situation is then dynamically provisioned, protected, and organized to permit isolated access by the user. The user, afterwards, distantly unites to the isolated compute situation by using a desktop or any of the other supported protocols.

11.15 ENOMALY ELASTIC COMPUTING PLATFORM

Enomaly's service provider is a principal platform which distributes a total 'cloud in a box' platform for transporters and hosting suppliers who desire to propose an IaaS service to their consumers. Enomaly elastic computing platform (ECP) service provider offers a significant and easy consumer self-service interface, a consumer-facing API, powerful multi-occupant safety, theme engine, a rigid allocation system, and flexibility, and controls dynamic and provisioning engines. The services provided by the Enomaly Elastic computing platform are given here:

Customer dashboard First of all, customers have to log in. The control panel demonstrates virtual machine power and control functions, VM depository functions, and records system faults. Service suppliers may append their personal content.

Advanced disk management Advanced disk management of ECP offers the facility to simply connect a variety of storage capacities. Sparse disk support (thin provisioning) of ECP offers a facility to a hosting corporation for storing data that has advanced disk management.

Further, quick VM replication offers a rapid and simple means to copy VMs for backup or speedy parallel scaling of applications.

11.16 MAPREDUCE

MapReduce is a programming module for dispersion of huge data arrays with a parallel, distributed algorithm on a group. It supports runtime environments for managing large volumes of data. Generally, database management is based on relational data models, and for large database handling, this type of model does not work efficiently as data is in an unstructured form. Keeping data in rows is not feasible when we are handling huge amounts of data, hence at that time data is organized in file form. The concept of distributed workflows is used for handling large data.

A MapReduce program consists of a Map () process and Reduce () process which operates a precise function. The 'MapReduce System' (also known as 'framework' or 'infrastructure') coordinates with distributed dispersed servers, operating different assignments at the same time, organizing communication and data shifts among numerous fractions of the system, and offering for idleness and error tolerance. Figure 11.3 demonstrates MapRduce. MapReduce libraries have been printed in various programming

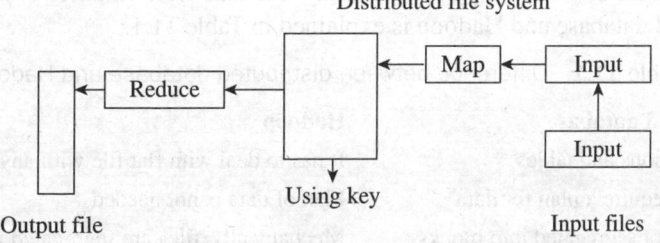

Fig. 11.3 MapReduce platform

languages, with diverse stages of optimization. A famous open-source execution is Apache Hadoop. Google initially invented the structure for its Web page indexing. Its new structure restores the previous indexing algorithm.

The computation logic used in MapReduce has two functions, map() and reduce():
1. An operation called 'Map' permits various points of the distributed group to allocate their work.
2. An operation known as 'Reduce' is intended to lessen the concluding form of the results of groups into a single production.

Figure 11.1 shows the MapReduce platforms. In a distributed file system, input is taken in the form of a file and after applying Map () over it using some key, the file is reduced to make a single entity which is the actual output after all the processing. It reduces work on a group of service and is extremely scalable. It has many types of execution that are offered by multiple programming languages, example C, C++, etc.

11.17 HADOOP

Hadoop is an open-source structure that is designed for processing large data sets. It is an application programming model developed by Google which implements MapReduce for providing basic operations for data processing. Map and Reduce work on the data which is given as input by the user and provides processed output as shown in Fig. 11.4. Hadoop offers run time environment to the user. Yahoo sponsors Apache Hadoop. Yahoo also administers the largest Hadoop in the world and tries to make Hadoop a complete package for data processing.

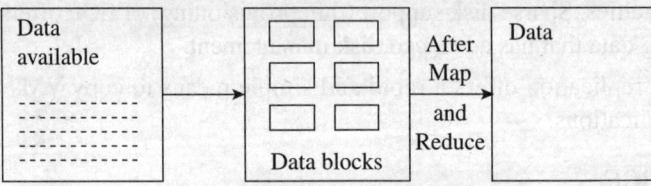

Fig. 11.4 Hadoop

Hadoop is a Java programming-based free structure which is employed in a distributed computing environment for dispensation of big data arrays. It is, in fact, the Apache Software Foundation sponsor scheme. It supports applications to operate on systems along with thousand joints of terabytes. Speedy data transport is possible among nodes which assist the system for ceaseless functions. It lessens the threat of catastrophic system collapse and uncertainty among users.

In Google's MapReduce, a specific application is divided into numerous parts. The operating system favoured by it is Linux and Windows. Hadoop is, in fact, offers a Java interface which supports resourceful, scalable, and reliable distributed computing.

Hadoop file system (HDFS) controls data duplication on this file system to figure out any hardware breakdown or data failure owing to any reason. Since Hadoop is printed in Java, apart from this, it supports other languages as well. Response time may fluctuate from minutes to hours. The differences between a distributed database and Hadoop is explained in Table 11.1.

Table 11.1 Difference between distributed database and Hadoop

Distributed database	Hadoop
It has relations and tables	It has to deal with flat file with any set-up
It should require a plan for data	Plan of data is not needed
Files are not segregated into blocks	Mechanically, files are segregated into blocks

11.18 CLOUD MASHUP

It is a technology or computing resource on the Internet assembled from various sources that can be used by an application developer to develop a new service. We can use data, presentations, or tools (can be assembled from more than one source) for developing a new service according to the requirements.

Mashups are generally available free of cost and have free access. Mashups are interactive and easy to use. It also provides us with a richer interactive tool. Application developers need not develop much code for any mashup application.

Web 2.0 is the frequently used mashup in cloud computing. Too many features are not supported by Web 1.0. So, Web 2.0 was brought in to reduce all those anomalies. Google tools also support users to use the functionalities in various applications. Web 2.0 is a web technology in which users have control over the interaction or presentation as cloud computing is an inexpensive way of computing with storage- and software-like facility. Web 2.0 is also supported by Wikipedia, Google application, etc.

A mashup is a computing platform for an application which merges and utilizes data or functionalities from more than one source to generate a novel service. Merging numerous applications into one will assist in giving data in a more valuable and serviceable form. Such applications are typically hosted on the cloud.

The Google Maps API is famous as it facilitates designers to construct web applications whose output information is a further clear representation.

Platform Mashups

The novel kind of mashup, which we recognize nowadays, merges cloud computing services and amalgamates them into one application or service. A fine illustration of cloud computing service composition is Amazon's GrepTheWeb. Nevertheless, the current declaration of Appirio's ReferMyFriends App demonstrates that cross-cloud mashups are feasible too. Other illustrations for cross-cloud mashups are Facebook and EC2 back-end, and Force.com and AppEngine back-end. There are various attractive mashup options.

11.19 OPENNEBULA

OpenNebula is a cloud computing tool for running various distributed data center infrastructures. The OpenNebula tool controls a virtual infrastructure of the data center to construct hybrid, public, and private executions of infrastructure as a service. OpenNebula is a free and open-source software, put through the necessities of the Apache Licence edition 2.

OpenNebula coordinates network, storage, virtualization, security, and scrutinizing technologies to install multi-layer services as virtual machines on distributed infrastructures, merging both isolated resources and data center cloud resources as per the allotment strategies.

The tool includes characteristics for administration, amalgamation, scalability, accounting, and safety. It also declares consistency, portability, and interoperability, offering managers and cloud users the option of a number of cloud interfaces (vCloud, OGF Open Cloud Computing Interface, Amazon EC2 Query) and hypervisors (VMware, KVM, and Xen), and may put up manifold software and hardware amalgamations in a data center.

OpenNebula was a guiding corporation at the Google Summer of Code 2010. It is subsidized by C12G. OpenNebula is utilized by telecom operators, hosting suppliers, IT services suppliers, supercomputing centers, international research plans, and research labs. A number of other cloud resolutions employ OpenNebula as the kernel service or cloud engine.

11.20 NIMBUS

In the outsourcing of computational resources, a revolution has been generated by Infrastructure clouds as they facilitate users to provision resources customized to their needs, comprising the accurate software load and implementation opportunities on a pay-as-you-go basis. Users require techniques to permit the on-order resources to share an arrangement and safety environment, and guarantee consistency and scalability in the situation.

Nimbus Platform offers an amalgamated array of devices. The main objective behind this is to allow users to shift to the cloud smoothly and rapidly, mechanizing and assisting much of the procedure. Some of the contemporary Nimbus Platform tools are explained here:

Cloudinit.d   Cloudinit.d is a tool for deploying, scrutinizing, and managing cloud applications. In case the application is only cloud or multi-cloud, easy or intricate, VM-based, bare metal, or any amalgamation of the above, cloudinit.d is intended to build the synchronization and administration of that application simple.

Phantom   Phantom is a service which offers auto-scaling and high accessibility for compilations of resources installed over multiple IaaS cloud suppliers, permitting users to extend consistent and scalable applications.

11.21 GOOGLE APP ENGINE

Google App Engine is a PaaS presentation which allows you to construct and operate applications on the infrastructure of Google. App Engine applications are simple to construct, sustain, and scale since data storage and traffic require alteration. Along with App Engine, there are no other servers for you to sustain. You just upload your application and it is set to go. The features supported by the Google app engine are as follows:

Support trendy languages   You can easily build your application using Java, Ruby, Python, PHP, etc.

Elasticity   Customized form of features is available for applications that are also elastic in nature.

Complete control   Users do not have to focus on infrastructure management and so they can fully manage an environment with the help of codes available.

Google App Engine assists apps written in a variety of programming languages:
1. Java: By using App Engine's Java runtime setting, you may construct your application using customary Java techniques.
2. Python: App Engine includes standard Python libraries and a fast Python interpreter.
3. PHP: App Engine utilizes Google's cloud platform services under the cover when you entitle standard PHP tasks.
4. Go: App Engine includes a Go runtime situation.

Google App Engine makes it simple to construct and arrange an application which works consistently even under excessive load and with great sums of data. It comprises the following characteristics:
1. Mechanized scaling and load balancing
2. Planned jobs for activating events at particular times or normal intervals
3. Integration with other APIs and Google cloud services

Applications work in a safe, sandboxed situation, permitting App Engine to allocate demands diagonally across many servers, and scaling servers to sustain traffic needs. Your application works within its individual safe, consistent situation which is free of the operating system, hardware, or physical position of the server.

Selecting an App Engine Environment

You may manage your applications in App Engine by standard or supple environment. You may also opt to concurrently employ both environments for your application and benefit from it.

Arranging your applications by means of a microservice design aligns the best with App Engine, particularly if you choose to employ both environments. There are various issues to judge when deciding which environment is best suited to your application and its services. Utilize the following segments to understand and learn which environment best meets your requirements of application.

Operating the App Engine supple environment means that your application requests work within Docker containers on Google Compute Engine virtual machines (VMs).

Usually, applications which obtain reliable traffic face regular traffic variations, or those that rally the parameters for scaling up and down steadily are more cost effectual in the supple environment:

1. The VM examples employed in the environment are resumed on a weekly basis. During resumes, management services of Google apply many essential operating systems and safety updates.
2. You constantly have root access to Compute Engine VM cases. By evasion, secure shell access (SSH) to the VM cases in the supple environment is immobilized. If you opt, you may facilitate root access to your app's VM cases.
3. The geographical area of the VM cases employed in the supple environment is decided by the site which you state for the App Engine application of your cloud platform plan. The management services of Google guarantee that the VM cases are co-sited for best performance.

11.22 MICROSOFT HYPER-V

Microsoft Hyper-V is a server virtualization platform established by the Microsoft Corporation that offers virtualization services via hypervisor-based simulations.

Microsoft Hyper-V is a server hypervisor which permits association of a single physical server into several virtual servers, each one sharing the hardware resources of the host server and driven by Hyper-V. Hyper-V, which works both independently and along with others, was developed to enhance server consumption and lessen capital expenses for importing an internal physical server.

Hyper-V is the main buildup to Microsoft's cloud computing and virtualization product subscriptions and presents a total non-stop performance. Hyper-V offers the basic performance to produce a virtualization layer above the physical layer of the server machine of the host and allows guest operating systems to be mounted and handled via an integrated administration support.

Hyper-V divides a fraction of a physical machine into child segments and assigns them to distinct guest working systems, with Windows Server 2008 performing as the main parent/host. It also allots suitable software and hardware resources for the entire guest working system it is hosting as they do not have straight access to the crude compute hardware resources and depend on Hyper-V.

Virtualization augments the ability of IT administration and the accessibility of IT resources and applications. QNAP Turbo NAS (QNAP are specialized hardware used for file sharing, storage management, and virtualization policy and support various cloud services) offers a high-functioning, consistent, and reasonable storage platform for virtualization applications such as vSphere, VMware, Citrix XenServer, and Microsoft Hyper-V.

Additionally, QNAP offers the virtualization platform that is accessible on the QTS App center and facilitates virtualized desktop functions on Turbo NAS for running multiple virtual machines. The virtualization platform converts a Turbo NAS into a 2-in-a-box NAS which could work both as a seamless NAS and as a virtualization system.

Hyper-V works on the principle of isolation of virtual machine supported by a hypervisor. The logical partition is divided into parent and child partitions. Parent has direct access to the hardware device, whereas the child does not have access to physical processors. Hyper-V works on user and kernel mode with the hypervisor and hardware, as shown in Fig. 11.5.

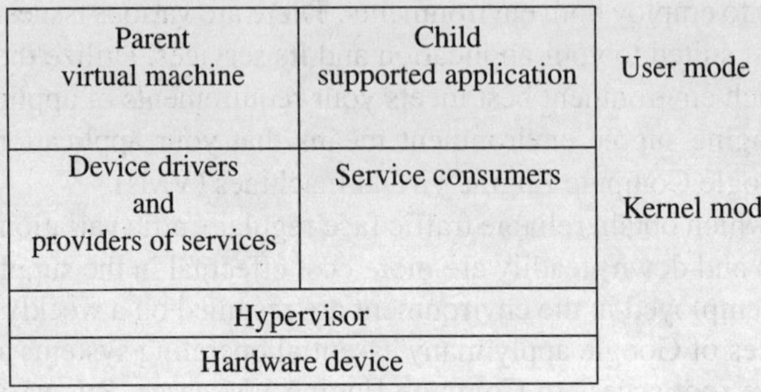

Parent virtual machine	Child supported application	User mode
Device drivers and providers of services	Service consumers	Kernel mode
Hypervisor		
Hardware device		

Fig. 11.5 Hyper-V

11.23 MICROSOFT AZURE

Microsoft Azure is a cloud computing service formed by Microsoft to build, deploy, and manage services and applications via data centers of the Microsoft network running worldwide. It offers SaaS, PaaS, and IaaS and supports various diverse programming devices, languages, and structures, comprising Microsoft-specific and third-party systems and software. More than 600 Azure services are listed in Microsoft, of which some are covered here:

1. Famous software packages, virtual machines, and IaaS permits customers to initiate all-purpose Linux virtual machines and Microsoft Windows, with preconfigured machine images.
2. Environment letting developers App services, PaaS, effortlessly advertises and handles websites.
3. Websites' high-density hosting permits developers to make sites using PHP, ASP.NET, Python, or Node .js, and may be installed using Mercurial, Git, FTP, Team Foundation Server, or uploaded via the portal of a customer. This characteristic was declared in the sample form in June 2012 at the event of Meet Microsoft Azure. Consumers may generate websites in ASP.NET, PHP, Python, Node.js, or pick from some open-source applications from a gallery for installation. This encompasses one feature of the PaaS presenting the Microsoft Azure Platform. In April 2015, it was renamed web Apps.
4. Web Jobs are applications which may be installed on a web App for executing background processing. This may be quoted on an agenda, on order, or may run continuously. The table, queue, and blob services may be used for communicating between Web Jobs and Web Apps and to supply state.
5. Mobile engagement accumulates synchronized analytics which emphasize the behaviour of customers. It offers push notifications to mobile tools as well.
6. Hockey App may be employed to build, issue, and beta-test mobile apps.
7. Storage services offer SDK and REST APIs for accessing and storing data on the cloud.
8. Table service allows programs to store prepared text in paneled sets of units which are accessed by a divider key and main key. It is a NoSQL non-relational database.
9. Blob service permits programs to accumulate binary data and unstructured text as blobs which may be accessed by an HTTP(S) path. It offers safety means for managing access to data as well.
10. Queue service allows programs to correspond asynchronously through messages by means of queues.
11. File service lets access and storing of data on the cloud by means of the SMB protocol or the REST APIs.

12. Azure search offers text explores and a division of OData's structured filters by means of SDK or REST APIs.
13. DocumentDB is a NoSQL database service which executes a division of the SQL SELECT proclamation on JSON documents.
14. Redis Cache is a controlled execution of Redis.
15. StorSimple controls storage jobs between cloud storage and on-premises devices. SQL database, previously recognized as SQL azure database, works to generate, scale, and expand applications into the cloud by means of Microsoft SQL server technology. It also incorporates with Hadoop and Microsoft system center, and active directory.
16. SQL data warehouse is a data warehousing service intended to control data intensive and computational enquiries on datasets above 1 tera byte (TB).

The Microsoft Azure Service Bus permits applications working on Azure sites or off site tools to correspond with Azure. This assists in making consistent and scalable applications in a service-oriented architecture (SOA). Four diverse kinds of communication means supported by the Azure service bus are as follows:

1. *Event hubs* offer telemetry and event access to the cloud at a substantial level, with high reliability and low latency. For instance, an event hub may be used for tracking data from cell phones like a GPS location synchronized in actual time.
2. *Queues* permit one-way communication. Messages would be sent to the service bus queue by the sender application and read by the receiver from the queue. Although there may be numerous readers for the queue, just one would process a particular message.
3. *Topics* offer one-way communication by means of a subscriber plan. It is similar to a queue, though every subscriber will obtain the message's copy sent to a topic. Additionally, the subscriber may sort down messages on the basis of particular criteria described by the subscriber.
4. *Relays* offer bi-way communication. Unlike topics and queues, a relay does not accumulate in-flight messages into its personal memory. Rather, it simply passes them on to the target application.

Media Services

Microsoft Azure has been explained as a 'cloud layer' over numerous Windows Server systems that utilize Windows Server 2008 and a modified edition of Hyper-V, well-known as the Microsoft Azure Hypervisor for providing services' virtualization. Reliability and scaling are managed by the Microsoft Azure Fabric Controller.

Azure offers an API built on XML, HTTP, and REST which permit a developer to interrelate with the services offered by Microsoft Azure. In addition, Microsoft offers a customer-side controlled class library which summarizes the works of interrelating with the services. It also amalgamates with Git, Eclipse, and Microsoft Visual Studio.

Besides interacting with services through API, customers may handle Azure services by means of the web-based Azure portal that attained general availability in December 2015. The portal lets customers browse active resources, amend settings, commence new resources, and analyse basic monitoring data from active virtual services and machines.

11.24 AJAX

Asynchronous JavaScript and XML (AJAX) is a unit of web development techniques used for generating interactive web applications. By means of AJAX, data can be recovered from the server asynchronously by web applications. As done in the settings, there would be no interference with the behaviour and the display of the current page.

AJAX is an expression which symbolizes a broad range of web technologies which can help web applications to communicate with the server without disturbing the current status of that page. AJAX refers to the following technologies:
1. The document object model for the active display of and interfacing with data.
2. For presentation, cascading style sheets (CSS) and extensible hypertext markup language (XHTML) are used.
3. The XML HTTP requests object in order to communicate asynchronously.
4. For control and interchanging the data, extensible style sheet language transformations (XSLT) and XML are used.
5. JavaScript in order to bring all these technologies collectively.

Merits

1. Many times, pages on a website have similar information. In case those pages were implicit, similar matter would be found on each page. AJAX permits a web application to repossess new information and alter how the matter is shown. This is very competent, diminishes the quantity of bandwidth used, and lessens load times.
2. Using a contemporary request permits the web browser of the user to be more collaborative and speedily react to inputs of consumers. The consumer might even make out the application to be quicker.
3. Associations to the server are concentrated, as style sheets and scripts simply require to be downloaded one at a time.

Demerits

1. Animatedly produced web pages do not turn up in the history engine of a browser; hence clicking on the Back button would not restore the last seen page.
2. An animatedly produced web page is complicated to bookmark.
3. In case JavaScript is disabled or if a browser does not support AJAX, the functionality of AJAX cannot be utilized.
4. After AJAX, there is no standards body; hence there is no broadly assumed best practice for testing AJAX applications.
5. Presently, printed SLA is stipulated by the provider so that the user is also pleased by the services, and the services might be reasonable, planned, and estimated with the service of other providers too.

11.25 EMC

EMC cloud service suppliers propose EMC powered public, private, and hybrid cloud platforms with better service-level agreements (SLAs), enhanced consumer service, and verified platforms. Configurations vary from on-premises, and EMC support services and applications as per customer requirements.

VMware and EMC have the mutual goal of bringing pioneering services and solutions, allowing service and businesses' suppliers to construct a software-defined data center (SDDC), change their operations, and convey ITaaS. Fundamental to this alteration is cloud computing and virtualization, conveying utmost IT agility and competence. VMware and the powerful answers, which simplify administration, enhance data strengthening and augment functioning while offering safety of the IT environment.

VMware and EMC share a mutual spirit to convey an SDDC design which pools, summarizes, automates, and handles every IT resource in a computerized and software-defined way. The instrumentation of data center services is computerized with VMware vCloud suite athwart the entire software-defined constituents—network, compute, and storage.

EMC ViPR, the foremost software-defined storage product, is an expansible software platform which summarizes storage with all its exclusive abilities, from physical groups to a sole group of virtual storage. Storage managers later produced virtual storage groups which they could handle at the virtual layer as per computerized strategies. Data services, such as file, object, and block data services, work over the platform and control the exclusive traits of the virtual storage groups and pools. EMC software-defined storage offers particular VMware integrations with interfaces into the VMware vStorage APIs (VADP, VASA, VAAI) athwart the EMC storage range (Avamar, XtremIO, Isilon, data domain, VNX series, VMAX Family). EMC ViPR will merge with vRealize Operations and VMware vRealize Automation to computerize provisioning and develop functioning, capability and configuration administration through the servers, applications, storage environments, and networks.

11.26 NETAPP

NetApp is an American data management and computer storage company having its headquarters in Sunnyvale, California. NetApp storage provides software and hardware platforms offered by NetApp for distinct organizations in different industries. Both software and hardware work mutually to drive ability and lower price at all levels of storage tools. NetApp storage intends to minimize the expanded space, which is needed for IT storage like failover protection, backups, and snapshot copies. The outcome is more utilizable storage per gigabyte.

NetApp storage consists of diverse storage application platforms like the distinct fabric-attached storage (FAS) hybrid storage groups. This further comprises the storage working system that uses an integrated storage design, which at the infrastructure layer helps control prices and augments ability; this is extremely significant for virtualized environments and cloud computing.

Make your business powerful with a reliable array of organization data services through your hybrid cloud setting. The data fabric permitted by NetApp offers the data control you require, while allowing the alternative in cloud suppliers you desire. Maintaining the verified storage competence, scalability, and accessibility of the world's number 1 celebrated storage operating system, NetApp is clustered to Data ONTAP.

11.27 CLOUD SERVICE SUPPLIERS AND THREATS

Business executives and IT professionals often inquire about the inequality among cloud models and traditional outsourcing from a safety point of view.

Common cloud controls are well-known controls connected with traditional IT services which are relevant to cloud-based services too, and whose evaluation systems are developed.

Delta cloud controls are higher-threat control regions which have specific significance to cloud settings and whose cloud review systems are less developed.

A business enterprise or organization assessing a cloud platform may have a record of 100 controls to scrutinize, from IT management procedures, information safety strategies and threat management, to antivirus, recovery, and capability management. Each of these regions offers a particular level of threat. As resources are forever limited, spending an equal quantity of time investigating each of the 100 controls without considering their significance or threat is possible to leave the higher threat control regions (e.g., visualization) inadequately inspected and the company uncovered.

Subsequently, shift on to the higher threat and newer delta cloud controls that have specific consequence to the cloud. Your group might not be as skilled in assessing these controls and your current review programs might not defend them adequately. The delta cloud controls division of this guide offers an outline of 12 cloud computing delta control regions. These regions comprise various approvals for examining and assessing these cloud controls and traditional outsourcing models, mutually from a people and process viewpoint. For the majority, this experience and knowledge may be shifted to cloud models. The consumer has to identify business necessities, comprising functional and non-functional necessities.

11.28 SERVICE LEVEL AGREEMENT

Service level agreement (SLA) is an agreement between the customer and service provider who offers a variety of services distributed by the supplier in computable conditions. Before providing services to the cloud users, the service provider has an agreement with the user as per the requirement and service provided to the user. As per Fig. 11.6, we have various cloud users and each has a different requirement which is monitored continuously by SLA monitoring agent. QoS measurement and SLA manager continuously measure the services given in the SLA of users. If it is fine, then cloud services are granted to the users. SLA managers also instruct resource management time-to-time for providing quality services to the users.

The fundamental metrics which SLAs might identify are as follows:
1. The extent of time that services will be available
2. Overall number of users served concurrently
3. Accurate functioning standards to occasionally evaluate functioning
4. Plan declaration for network variations which might possibly influence users
5. Response time for a range of troubles
6. Access
7. Usage information that will be offered

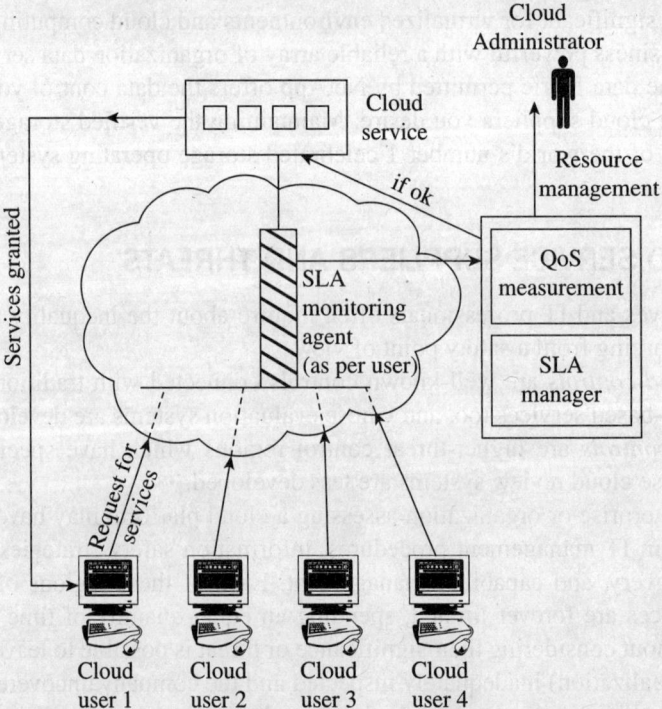

Fig. 11.6 Service level agreement management

Requirements of SLA

1. *Safety*: A customer should know his/her safety provisions and what combination prototypes are essential to assemble those necessities.

2. *Data encryption*: Data should be encrypted for making data secure during any transaction. The details of the encryption algorithms and access direct strategies must be particular.
3. *Privacy*: Fundamental privacy fear is tackled by necessities like encryption of data, removal, and maintenance. An SLA must clearly state how the cloud supplier segregates applications and data in a multi-occupant situation.
4. *Data maintenance and removal*: How does your supplier confirm they obey the rules, maintenance rules, and removal strategies used?
5. *Hardware removal, destruction*: When should hardware be removed and destroyed?
6. *Regulatory agreement*: If rules are made compulsory as a consequence of the data being handled, the cloud supplier should be capable of attesting the agreement.
7. *Lucidity*: For decisive applications and data, suppliers ought to be practical in informing customers when the conditions of the SLA are broken. This comprises infrastructure matters such as function and troubles, and safety events.
8. *Guarantee*: The supplier is supposed to be liable for determining necessary guarantee.
9. *Performance descriptions*: What is meant by uptime for a customer? How will the server perform at peak load and off load?. These questions are answered in this parameter.
10. *Scrutinizing*: You may desire to identify an impartial third-party association to analyse the functioning of the supplier.
11. *Audit ability*: Since the consumer is accountable for each break which leads to failure of data or accessibility, it is vital that the customer be capable of checking the processes and systems of the supplier. The SLA must make it apparent when and how such reviews occur. They may be expensive and troublesome to the supplier.
12. *Metrics*: The metrics of an SLA should be unemotionally and openly distinct.
13. *Offering a machine-intelligible SLA*: This may permit for an automatic, vibrant variety of a cloud agent. In other words, if your SLA needs the agent to employ the cheapest probable supplier for a number of assignments but the most safe supplier for others, such a mechanization makes it a potential.
14. *Human interface*: Self-service is one of the fundamental features of cloud computing, but your SLA must take into consideration that human interface can also be required by the cloud consumer.

When various users are requesting for cloud services, there is an SLA monitoring system which works according to the constraint and agreement as per the user requirement and services of users. SLA management also works to keep a record of the various services, quality of services, and resource management as per the report given by the SLA manager, as shown in Fig. 11.6.

11.29 THIRD-PARTY TECHNOLOGY

Before the Internet came along, you would buy software, typically with a licence, and deploy and operate it on your computers similar to purchasing a music CD and playing it in your residence. Beneath the cloud model, the software is operated online by a third-party supplier, and you access it via your Internet browser. You do not deploy something on your personal computer and do not really possess any software; instead of purchasing a product, you are leasing a service. Third-party concept is also very valuable in providing security to the cloud data center.

Technologically inclined people are thrilled about cloud computing. There is hardly anything that one needs to be concerned about. While you lease a car, the protection, upkeep, and crash assistance are all taken care of by the leasing company. Similar is the case with cloud services as when you employ these, there is no worry regarding deploying it, preserving it, downloading updates, or maintaining it safely. This needs to be taken care of by the service provider.

With clouds, you have the ability to push the operational IT work to other people. This actually reduces the risk to the cloud service provider. Efficiently outsourcing the skill not only reduces the threat and unanticipated expenditure, but also makes the work smooth and swift. If you can spend lesser time on maintenance, you could use the extra time creating technology to perform important functions that assemble the needs of your corporation.

Nevertheless, the utmost advantage of the cloud is economics. Let us go back to the lease-a-car theory. While you purchase a car, there is enormous direct expenditure. You never get that money back if the car is not used by you daily, or even if you sell it. After five years, you will have an old car that no one else would want to purchase, and if it starts giving trouble, it will cost more and more to repair. However, your leasing car is forever an existing model that can be used as per the requirement.

This is the situation with cloud services too. There is no straightforward charge. You will disburse a less, expected, flat-rate monthly payment per user for the software which is used by you and which indicates that you may scale up or down as your corporation requires order.

You can expand or contract the number of resources you are controlling. Thus, spending on technology which used to be a major capital expense for even small businesses now becomes an operational expense. Cloud providers provide the ability to change, adapt to the promising needs of the business.

Unlike deployed software, you will forever have access to the newest edition as well. While a novel edition of a service is launched, it is immediately made accessible to each subscriber, providing you access to devices that will keep your corporation at the highest level of competitiveness.

Operating software online also has several built-in advantages:

Work from wherever you want Software that was deployed on a computer only worked on that computer. Business owners, these days, work from their homes, office, and even airport lounges. With the cloud, you will not only have access to your software at all times, but you can also sign in and continue from where you left off.

Collaborate with customers, dealers, and contemporaries You may share access to your cloud workplaces. It denotes that you could work on documents, presentations, suggestions, etc., along with other populace and increase the limits of your place of work to clients as well.

Limit threat of catastrophe and expedite catastrophe recuperation One of the chief economies of cloud computing is that a fine cloud supplier will contain superior safety and flexibility than you may ever expect to afford. They will save your data securely and steadily. In case your workplace is broken into (or, more probably, you abandon your laptop on a train), your data is secure and instantly available online from another appliance.

The disadvantages are as follows:
1. Third-party technology involvement in cloud computing sometimes leads to a risk of security issues between the cloud user and the cloud service provider.
2. For various technical issues, sometimes, a third party will not work very efficiently as per expectation.

Points to Remember

1. Six elements of the cloud environment are physical machine, network, hypervisor, image storage, and cloud management software.
2. Service oriented architecture (SOA) manages software systems and consists of various interacting services.
3. Online analytical processing (OLAP) is a method that is used for answering multi-dimensional queries in a computing environment.
4. The financial and functioning features supported by cloud business intelligence (BI) comprise execution and installment speed, elasticity, concentration on core power, lower overall charge of possession, and on-demand accessibility.

5. The reasons for slow acceptance to cloud business intelligence are data safety, on-premise incorporation, lack of power, dealer maturity, performance, and pricing modules.
6. Some of the independent software vendors are Apica, Chef, CloudOpt, Cloud-Passage, and Code-Futures.
7. There are basically five cloud monitoring tools—Zenoss, RevealCloud, RevealUptime, Gomez APM, and Rackspace.
8. Service situation in the cloud depends on SLAs that signify an agreement made between the service supplier and the consumer with non-functional provisions of the service, specifically 'quality of service' (QoS).
9. The Intercloud is a unified universal 'cloud of clouds' and an expansion of the Internet 'network of networks' on which it is established.
10. A platform which permits the installment of element-based applications in a cloud environment considering diverse cloud suppliers is Sky computing.
11. The Xen cloud platform (or XCP) is a chief open-source virtualization platform which offers distinct cloud computing and virtualization.
12. Tplatform is a cloud platform which offers an expansion platform for web mining applications started on Google cloud technologies and performs as a Platform as a Service (PaaS).
13. Force.com offers to rapidly create and arrange cloud applications that are secure and scalable with customized application stacks.
14. Virtual computing lab is a free and open-source cloud computing platform along with the prime objective of distributing devoted, customized compute environment to users.
15. MapReduce is a programming module for dispersion of huge data arrays with a parallel, distributed algorithm on a group.
16. Hadoop:
    (a) Deals with flat file with any set-up
    (b) Does not require Plan of data
    (c) Mechanically, in Hadoop, files are segregated into blocks.
17. Cloud Mashup is a technology or computing resource on the Internet assembled from various sources that can be used by an application developer to develop a new service.
18. OpenNebula is a cloud computing tool for running various distributed data center infrastructures.
19. Nimbus Platform offers an amalgamated array of devices to allow users to shift to the cloud smoothly and rapidly, mechanizing and assisting much of the procedure.
20. Google App Engine is a Platform as a Service (PaaS) presentation which allows you to construct and operate applications on the infrastructure of Google.
21. Microsoft Hyper-V is a server virtualization platform established by the Microsoft Corporation that offers virtualization services via hypervisor-based simulations.
22. Microsoft Azure is a cloud computing service formed by Microsoft to build, deploy, and manage services and applications via data centers of the Microsoft network running worldwide.
23. The Apache Software Foundation (ASF) VCL software established at NCSU offers a service which effectively supports a broad series of users with varied computing wants athwart the UNC system.
24. Asynchronous JavaScript and XML (AJAX) is a unit of web development techniques used for generating interactive web applications.

Key Terms

Capital expense (Capex) Generally, it includes a one-time investment cost like one-time hardware cost, software licence procurement, etc.

Internal rate of return (IRR) The benefits recalculated as per interest rate

Net present value (NPV)   The value of future benefits estimated as per today's money value

Online analytical processing (OLAP)   It is computer processing that supports users for extracting data as per the requirement and view data from different perspectives.

Operational expense (Opex)   It requires an expense after a certain period of time, for example, support services cost, annual maintenance contract, etc.

Payback period   The required time period for the benefits to pay back the cost of the project to be invested

Service oriented architecture (SOA)   It is a software design and software architecture design pattern based on distinct pieces of software providing application functionality as services to other applications.

Multiple-choice Questions

1. The important feature of cloud business intelligence is/are:
   (a) Execution and installment pace
   (b) Elasticity
   (c) Concentration on core power
   (d) All the above

2. The reason for the sluggish acceptance speed to cloud is/are:
   (a) Data safety
   (b) On-premise incorporation
   (c) Lack of power
   (d) All the above

3. The required time period for the benefits to pay back the cost of the project to be invested is:
   (a) Net present value (NPV)
   (b) Internal rate of return (IRR)
   (c) Payback period
   (d) None of these

4. The value of future benefits estimated as per today's money value is:
   (a) Net present value (NPV)
   (b) Internal rate of return (IRR)
   (c) Payback period
   (d) None of these

5. The benefits recalculated as per interest rate is/are:
   (a) Net present value (NPV)
   (b) Internal rate of return (IRR)
   (c) Payback period
   (d) None of these

6. Fundamental metrics of service level agreement is/are:
   (a) Reaction time for a range of troubles
   (b) Access accessibility
   (c) Usage information which will be offered
   (d) All the above

7. Requirements of SLA is/are:
   (a) Safety
   (b) Data encryption and privacy
   (c) Data maintenance and removal
   (d) All the above

8. Operating software online has which intrinsic advantages?
   (a) Work from anywhere
   (b) Collaborate with customers, dealers, and contemporaries
   (c) Limit the threat of catastrophe and accelerate catastrophe recovery
   (d) All the above

9. A cloud computing device kit for running assorted disseminated data center infrastructures is:
   (a) OpenNebula
   (b) Map Reduce
   (c) Amazon
   (d) None of these

10. Hadoop's features include:
    (a) It can deal with flat file with any set-up.
    (b) Plan of data not needed.
    (c) Mechanically, files are segregate into blocks.
    (d) All the above

11. Sky computing means:
    (a) Collective utilization of multiple clouds
    (b) Smoothness of various clouds
    (c) Both (a) and (b)
    (d) None of these

Review Questions

1. Explain the various monitoring tools of cloud performance.
2. What do you understand by service level agreement?
3. Describe the various cloud quality of services' issues in cloud computing.
4. Why is business intelligence important in a cloud environment?
5. What is the importance of intercloud?
6. What are the advantages of sky computing?
7. What is MapReduce?
8. What is the role of a third party in cloud computing?
9. What are the various vital metrics of SLA?
10. What are the various services provided by Enomaly's service provider?
11. Discuss the importance of service level agreement.
12. Explain the financial and non-financial benefits of business intelligence.

References

1. *Cloud Security A Comprehensive Guide to Secure Cloud Computing*, Ronald L. Krutz and Russell Dean Vines, ISBN: 978-0-470-58987-8, Wiley Publication, 2010
2. *Cloud Computing for Dummies*, Judith Hurwitz, Robin Bloor, Marcia Kaufman, and Dr. Fern Halper, ISBN-10: 0470484705, Wiley Publication, 1 edition, November 16, 2009
3. *Cloud Computing Technologies and Strategies*, Brian J.S. Chee and Curtis Franklin, Jr, ISBN 9781439806128, CRC Press, April 7, 2010
4. *Cloud Computing: A Practical Approach*, Anthony T. Velte, Toby J. Velte, Ph.D., RobertElsenpeter, ISBN-10: 0071626948, Publisher: McGraw-Hill, 1 edition, November 1, 2009
5. *Grid and Cloud Computing,* Katarina StanoevskaSlabeva, Thomas Wozniak, and Santi Ristol, ISBN-10: 3642051928, Springer, 2010 edition, November 19, 2009
6. *Implementing and Developing Cloud Applications*, David E.Y.Sarna, ISBN-10: 1439830827, Publisher: Auerbach Publications, November 26, 2010
7. *Market-oriented Cloud Computing: Vision, Hype, and Reality for Delivering IT Services as Computing Utilities*, In High Performance Computing and Communications, R. Buyya, C.S. Yeo, and S. Venugopal, 2008, HPCC'08, 10th IEEE International Conference on pp. 4–13 IEEE, 2008
8. *Mastering Cloud Computing*, Rajkumar Buyya, Christian Vecchhiola, S. ThamaraiSelvi, Tata McGraw Hill Education Private Limited, 2008
9. *Cloud Computing and Virtualization*, V. Rajeswara Rao, V. ShubbaRamaiah, BS Publication, ISBN-10: 9383635045, Publisher: BS Publications/BSP Books, 2014

Answers to Multiple-choice Questions

1. (d)
2. (d)
3. (c)
4. (a)
5. (b)
6. (d)
7. (d)
8. (d)
9. (a)
10. (d)
11. (c)

12 CHAPTER

Advanced Technologies in Cloud Computing

Learning Outcomes

After completing this chapter, students will be able to:

- comprehend cloud computing trends and cloud development tools
- describe media clouds, security clouds, and application-specific clouds
- use cloud descriptor language
- compare various cloud-aware applications
- discuss the need of green computing
- explain third-party technology
- understand the concept of Bigtable and IOT
- describe T-Systems and CometCloud

12.1 INTRODUCTION

Many advanced technologies, application services, etc., are regularly introduced in cloud computing for providing better services to users. The cloud data center consists of many IT and non-IT equipment for smooth functioning of the services provided to users. There are many open challenges in the context of energy-efficient management of data center and carbon emission to the data center of cloud computing. Cloud computing reduces the investment on hardware and software by providing various tools to the users. It is also supportive to reduce energy consumption up to a certain extent. All the technical problems and issues are handled by the cloud providers so cloud users are free to focus on the core business issues. The cloud is focused on auto updating of various services and applications. Cloud computing also offers premium security services for protecting the cloud environment from unauthorized access, alteration, and malicious users.

Many advanced, distinct features are available to cloud users, but how we use it in a secure way to make application of cloud more accessible is important. This is going to be discussed in this chapter along with the various advanced technologies available in the market.

12.2 CLOUD COMPUTING TRENDS

Cloud computing is a paradigm shift in the world of technology. As a technology trend, it has changed the meaning of technology in recent years. It is a progressive technology and the several trends recognized by analysts and professionals are given here.

High Commercial Importance

Due to the many advantages of cloud computing, companies have come forward to make cloud an essential business requirement. Organizations have to know how to use this technology to optimize their investments.

Cloud computing helps to streamline software, business processes, and services accessed by the organization.

Hybrid Cloud Computing

Hybrid cloud computing refers to the merging of public and private cloud computing. Companies are using cloud computing (both public and private) to enhance their internal applications and framework. It is predicted that these services will augment the business and financial status of the company. The requirement for optimal cloud experiences is foremost for the companies which are accepting this technology. The trend is expected to grow as cloud computing expands across different industries and markets. While keeping in mind the various advantages of cloud computing, many organizations have migrated into it.

Dedicated Cloud Applications for Mobile

Today, cloud computing applications are available with a simple platform and with interface accessible on mobiles. To make cloud computing familiar among businessmen and employees, many applications are accessible on the mobile to make optimal use of the applications of the cloud.

Cloud Computing Information Security

As security is one of the most common issues of cloud computing, in the near future, new encryption techniques and security protocols with enhanced features will be developed. Figure 12.1 shows cloud service securities provided to various cloud clients. With the help of the virtualization tool, the same physical resources are allotted to more than one client. Apart from the different applications and facilities provided by the cloud provider, it is also one of the duties of the provider to take care of the information of the client associated with the cloud.

We can take the example of two companies, as shown in Fig. 12.1, who can take cloud services from the same cloud provider. Clients who are using these services on behalf of the companies are not aware of the security measures and tools used by the cloud provider to provide services to the cloud users. Various security levels and authentication tools are used by the cloud providers to make cloud services and applications secure while interacting with cloud clients who are accessing the cloud services subscribed to by the company.

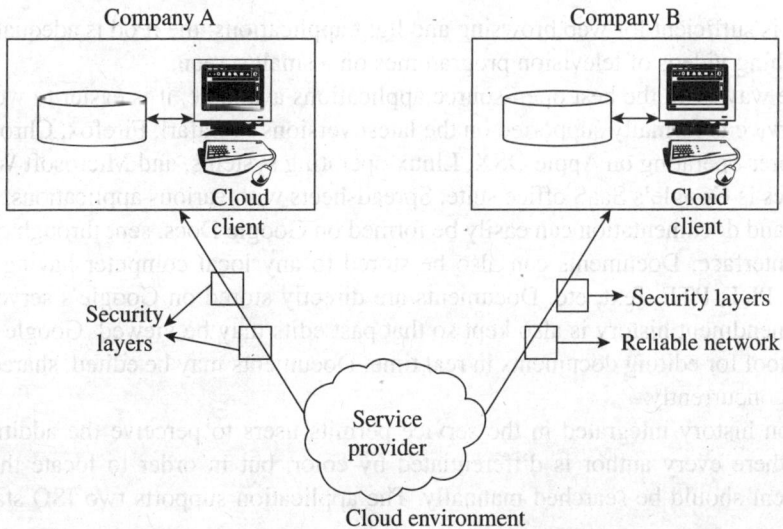

Fig. 12.1 Cloud service securities

12.3 UNDERSTANDING CLOUD TOOLS

For accessing facilities provided by cloud providers, many tools are available in the market. Vendors such as Atlassian, PivotalLabs, and others give the opportunity to work as PaaS. A company that provides tools for cloud development is CollabNet, which has focused products and services.

CollabNet offers clients various opportunities to join and makes an announcement every time with new style about how to access tools and better features. Various services are offered to clients to assist in the operation of applications, to a huge number of infrastructure approaches.

Hybrid cloud IT is adopted by CollabNet for various application development and deployment life cycles. The steps include the following:
1. Centralized control with transparent tools and processes is enhanced on the cloud.
2. Encourage reusability by creating a robust coding community.
3. Give preference to development processes by standardizing tools, workflows, and processes automation.
4. In a secure, accepting and optimal way, there is a hybrid approach using public and on-premise private cloud resources.

At present, there is a great deal of argument on which mobile applications are superior. For managing and monitoring cloud computing, various tools are available, some of which are as follows:
1. AppDynamics—It is used for monitoring various applications in the cloud computing environment.
2. Nimsoft—It allows cloud clients as well as the service provider of the cloud to monitor the application.
3. ManageEngine—It is a tool used for cloud monitoring.
4. NetEnrich—It is also used as a cloud monitoring tool.
5. NetRelic—It is mostly used for server as well as application monitoring.
6. Rackspace—It is a tool used for monitoring third-party cloud services.
7. SplunkStorm—It is mostly used to analyse performance parameters in a cloud application.
8. Aternity—It is used for platform monitoring (e.g., virtual machines, physical machines, etc.).
9. Compuware Gomez—This is a type of SaaS platform used for performance management of application.

12.4 CLOUD WITH DIVERSELOOK

The notebook is sufficient for web browsing and light applications; the iPod is adequate for listening to music or watching videos of television programmes on a small screen.

In the same way, with the best open-source applications available, it is easier to work, as in Google Docs. This service is formally supported on the latest versions of Safari, Firefox, Chrome browsers and Internet Explorer operating on Apple OSX, Linux operating systems, and Microsoft Windows.

Google Docs is Google's SaaS office suite. Spreadsheets with various applications, presentations for the company, and documentation can easily be formed on Google Docs, sent through email or imported via the web interface. Documents can also be stored to any local computer having formats such as ODF, HTML, PDF, RTF, Text, etc. Documents are directly stored on Google's server to prevent loss of data and amendment history is also kept so that past edits may be viewed. Google Docs serves as a collaborative tool for editing documents in real time. Documents may be edited, shared, and opened by various users concurrently.

The revision history integrated in the service permits users to perceive the additions made in the documents, where every author is differentiated by color, but in order to locate these changes, the whole document should be searched manually. The application supports two ISO standard document formats—OpenDocument (for both opening and exporting) and Office Open XML (for opening only). Google docs not only support many formats but can also be used for document sharing purpose. Sharing feature with good accessibility makes it popular among company and businesses.

Google Docs has enjoyed a swift rise in popularity among students for education and indifferent educational institutions. Google Cloud Connect is a plug-in for Windows Microsoft Office 2003, 2007, and 2010 which can instinctively save and synchronize from Excel spreadsheets, Microsoft Word documents, or PowerPoint Presentations to Google Docs in Microsoft Office or Google Docs format. A copy of Google docs is instinctively updated every time the Microsoft Office document is stored. The Microsoft Office document is synchronized when online, while it can be edited offline. Google Cloud Sync retains earlier Microsoft Office document versions and allows multiple users to collaborate by working on the same document at the same time.

You can also use it as Visual Basic for Applications (VBA) in Microsoft Office and as Google Spreadsheets. Google sites also incorporate Google Apps Script to write code within documents. The scripts can be activated either by user action or by a trigger in response to an event. GoogleDocs suite now includes Google Forms and Google Drawings. Google Forms is actually a tool for gathering information through different modes.

Google Drawing permits users to collaborate forming, distributing, and editing drawing or images. You can access Gmail account from any place, explore it all at the same place, and in no way require moving to a new account. Google Calendaris used to organize schedules, all in one place.

With Google Docs offline, a local version of the document list and editors is also available, along with the documents. Features of Google App Engine:
1. Google App Engine supports Python.
2. PiCloud is a cloud computing platform that integrates into Python. It allows developers to control the computing power of Amazon Web Services (AWS).
3. When using the Python library, known as cloud, PiCloud will integrate effortlessly into your existing code base. You would require registering a PiCloud account for using this package.
4. Without a PiCloud account, the cloud library can also be used as a simulator. The simulator uses the multiprocessing library and the simulated service can then run jobs locally across all CPU cores.

12.5 MEDIA CLOUDS

Media cloud is an open platform which permits scholars to answer quantitative queries regarding the matter of online media. With the help of media cloud, journalism critics and scholars may look at what types of stories are covered by which media sources, what type of language is used by the media channels in combination with different stories and how stories circulate from one media channel to other media clouds.

The vertical market cloud is focused on the notion of influencing the vast amount of isolated reporting ability which has been provided by the worldwide Internet. Media cloud is a system which allows you to perceive the course of media. The Internet is basically varying the approaches of forming and distributing news; however, there are some inclusive styles to understand the temperament of these changes. Media cloud automatically builds a collection of news stories and blog posts from the web, applies language processing, and gives you ways to analyse and visualize the data. Media cloud is a huge data set of news assembled from newspapers, other reputable news associations, and blogs along with a set of facilities and devices to evaluate those data.

12.6 SECURITY CLOUDS

Securing the cloud is one of the issues that is an obstacle for cloud vendors, to save data from unauthorized and malicious users. We have back-end security processing from Check Point Corporation, where scanning of email was controlled at the Check Point data center, which permitted sophisticated safety features to be proposed on comparatively economical firewalls intentionally designed for home use. Figure 12.2 shows distinct security parameters by different cloud providers. Various services and applications are supported by distinct cloud providers and on the basis of user requirement a single company can take advantage of various services. Different security tools are used by cloud providers as per the terms and conditions of the company. Some cloud providers use digital signature for securing data, whereas some use digital signature and encryption to provide security and authentication.

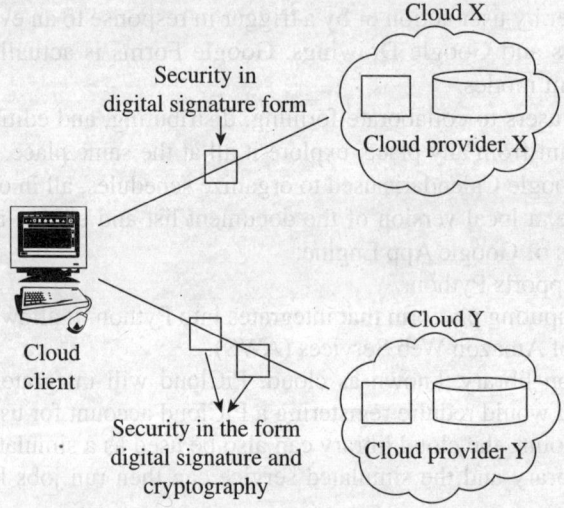

Fig. 12.2 Distinct security parameters by different cloud providers

Many cloud service providers are focused not only on characterizing attacks swiftly, but also being constricted to supply safety reviewing of Internet feeds prior to the attacks reaching a company, and closing attacks before they have a possibility to shoot up and do actual harm. We have different techniques of securing data and one among them is using antivirus, which has the caliber to find the virus that is characterizing the same virus under different names.

Security is one of the obstacles for many organizations to migrate in the cloud environment. This is why cloud providers always try to make cloud network secure by providing various security measures and policies to the users. As shown in Fig. 12.3, security management in cloud computing management and security policies are always an interface for users to enter the cloud network. It is not possible for every one to enter into the cloud network without knowing the key for decrypting the encrypted data.

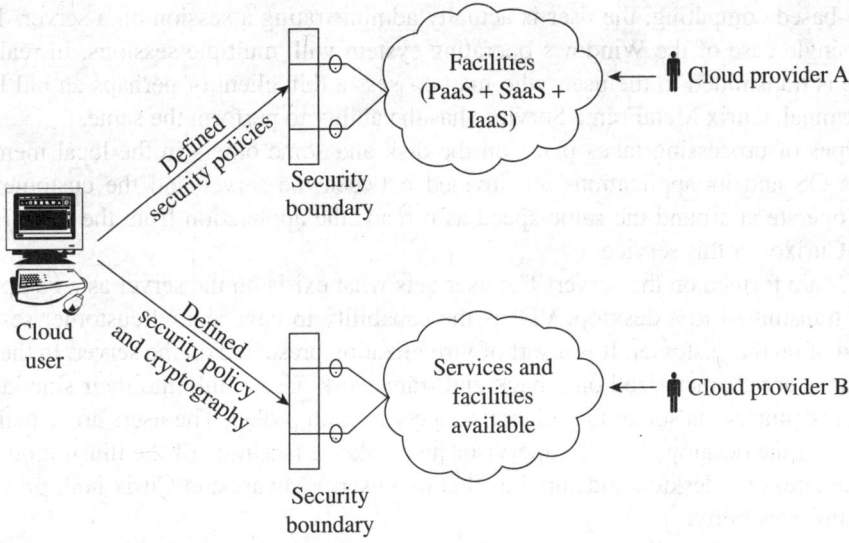

Fig. 12.3 Security management in cloud computing

12.7 APP-SPECIFIC CLOUDS

Some applications are specially designed to support cloud platform, or are hosted on a cloud infrastructure, whilst other applications are different. Rationally, each application may either partially or fully exist on the cloud.

Various application-specific cloud software are available and their features help you to make decisions as to whether to run your specific application in the cloud or not.

12.7.1 Virtualized Desktop

Cloud application also supports a virtualized desktop for accessing various applications. It is well known that a PC is managed from the data center, not from the desktop. Therefore, virtual desktop infrastructure (VDI) is an environment where one desktop resource is shared by many users and non of them are aware of which resource they are sharing in the environment.

Virtualized desktop refers to files, applications, data, etc., that are separated from the real desktop and saved on a server in a data center. It is well known that in an organization, the annual support charge per PC is somewhere around three to five times the price of the PC itself. After the time period of around four years, PCs become outdated; this can be updated by vitalizing the desktop as it helps to control and centralize support with regular updating. Regulating infrastructure, which requires supervision through virtualization, makes it easier to optimize.

Client desktop virtualization can be done through:
- Session-based computing
- The operating system
- VDI
- PC blade

Customer virtualization includes imitating a complete PC in software on a data center server and illustrating the user interface on a graphic terminal. Computers have become effective to perform this and it is not easy for users to discover the difference between desktop and customer virtualization.

In session-based computing, the user is actually administrating a session on a server. The server is managing a single case of the Windows operating system with multiple sessions. In reality, only the screen image is transmitted to the user, who may possess a thin client or perhaps an old PC such as a Microsoft terminal. Citrix MetaFrame Services has the ability to perform the same.

Certain types of processing takes place on the disk and some others in the local memory. Hence, the Windows OS and its applications are divided between the server and the customer. Streaming applications operate at around the same speed as it reads the application from the disk. Both Hewlett Packard and Citrixoffer this service.

Virtual PCs are formed on the server. The user gets what exists on the server as a complete PC. The graphics are transmitted to a desktop. VDI is the capability to have shared customer sessions on the server instead of on the customer. It is a sort of virtualization presented on the server. In the VDI model, virtual machines are characterized on a back-end framework. Users link into their simulated desktops from several consumers via something known as a connection broker. The users are actually accessing the illustration of the desktop. The IT supervisor just makes a facsimile of the illustration (server copy used as a template) of a desktop and supplies that to a user. VMware and Citrix both provide software that delivers this capability.

The PC blade is actually a distinct type of server computer which has a single computer board slotted into the blade cabinet having a built-in power supply. The numbers of PC blades are not included in the server blade.

Virtualization includes a shift in view from physical to logical, considering IT resources as logical resources instead of discrete physical resources. With the use of virtualization in your settings, you can proficiently merge resources such as networks, processors, and storage into a virtual environment that offer the following advantages:
1. Merger to reduce the cost of hardware
2. Workloads optimization
3. Responsiveness and flexibility of IT

Virtualization means formation of flexible alternatives for real resources, alternates which have similar operations and external interfaces like their accessories but which differ in features such as performance, cost, and size. These are also referred to as virtual resources.

Virtualization offers many virtual resources to users without any need to worry about the actual physical location of the resources by virtualizing physical resources into shared pools of resources. After virtualization, a single physical resource looks similar to many virtual available resources. Moreover, virtual resources may have features and functions which are unavailable in their basic physical resources.

System virtualization generates various virtual systems in a single physical system. Virtual systems have independent operating environments to use virtual resources. Hypervisors are firmware components or software which can virtualize system resources.

If you are operating heterogeneous techniques in your service network, you should choose the hypervisor which has support for your presently running operating systems. Although all hypervisors are not equally formed, all of them provide nearly the same features. On the basis of hypervisor selection, features of hardware virtualization can be predicted. Coordinating this information to needs of a business will be at the basis of the decision made by you.

12.8 GROUPWARE CLOUDS

Today, different software with exciting facilities are accessible to make it easy for use. CompuServe is one case wherein all sorts of applications are accessible, along with some collection, similar to the applications of groupware.

Google Docs and Google University ought to be one of the more contemporary applications of desktops in the clouds. Along with complete worksheets, word processing, and presentation devices, offerings of Google provide shared workspaces without the need of apps being deployed on the desktop other than a web browser which supports Java.

DirectAccess is intended to lessen redundant traffic on the community network by simply transferring traffic proposed for the community network via the DirectAccess server, or the supervisor can be selected to propel the entire traffic via the community network.

Direct access might validate the user and support corroboration like a smart card. IT supervisors may check which intranet resources particular users could access by using DirectAccess. PC-over-IP (PCoIP) supports graphics-related applications. Compacted frames or bitmaps are transferred to the remote customer.

Further, while communicating compacted bitmaps or structures, we may amend it considerably. With usually less bandwidth and higher latency on a WAN connection, fewer images are produced rapidly.

With 'Padalog desktop', you can now move your paper-based planner onto the cloud and access it from the office. Either your desk or a from-out-of-data registered to 'Padalog desktop' can be quickly and safely checked, directly from your smartphone or tablet device. In addition, if your device is lost or stolen, an administrator can easily lock the account or remotely delete the data for safety.

The following are the advantages of DirectAccess:

Working outdoors, the office is simpler than ever It augment the efficiency of mobile workers by linking them flawlessly and more steadily to their community network whenever they have Internet access. Direct access permits the network of the community to share files, intranet websites, and professional applications with an Internet connection.

Direct isolated machines more efficiently IT supervisors can handle mobile computers by revising Group Policy settings and circulating software updates whenever the mobile computer has internet connectivity, even when the user is not logged on. It is flexible to give IT the chance to service isolated machines on a normal basis and guarantee that mobile users remain up to date with policies of the company.

Augment safety and access control Direct access uses IPv6-over IPsec to encrypt data spread over the Internet to maintain the safety of data because it moves to various networks. Figure 12.4 shows resource replication for security purpose. Various virtual instances are available for cloud users and after a time interval, replication of virtual servers are kept in a physical storage device for future references.

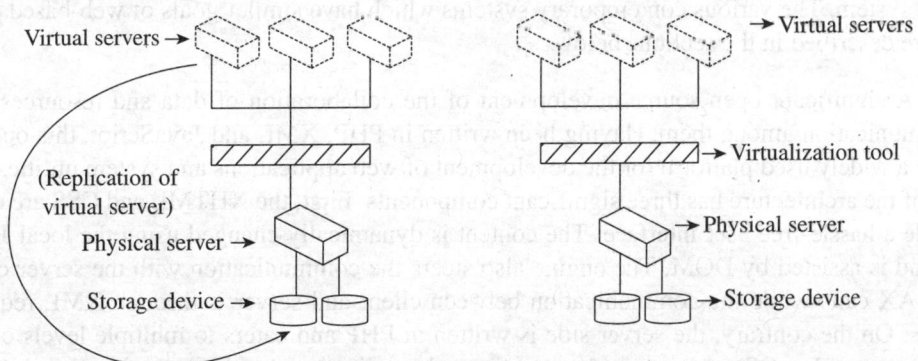

Fig. 12.4 Resource replication

With the help of virtualization tools, physical resources like servers can become virtual for providing services to various users. As actual storage devices are attached to the physical servers, after some interval of time, replication of the virtual server is saved in the physical storage device. In case of any type of damage, actual data is kept intact at the physical location.

12.9 MOBILE CLOUD COMPUTING

Mobile cloud computing (MCC) is the integration of mobile network computing, wireless networks, and cloud computing used to develop rich applications for mobile users. The architecture of mobile cloud computing is shown in Fig. 12.5. MCC not only brings the benefits to mobile users but also for network operators and cloud providers. MCC is helpful to build and deploy mobile applications very fast by using cloud services. MCC provides mobile users with processing services and data storage in clouds.

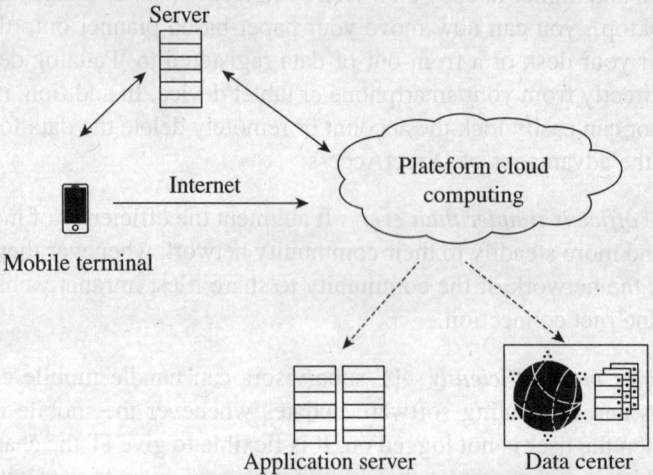

Fig. 12.5 Mobile cloud computing architecture

With the rapid development of new forms of cloud and mobile computing, it is necessary that operating systems must evolve so that all devices in a given network can appear to be accessed by the same operating system framework and common set of applications are maintained. As a result, the internet or the cloud could potentially be supported and managed by a huge virtual operating system like the proposed system. The various contemporary systems which have similar goals of web-based operating system are described in the sections below.

EyeOS A significant open source development of the collaboration of data and resources by users and communication among them. Having been written in PHP, XML and JavaScript, this open source project is a widely used platform for the development of web applications and system utilities. The client side of the architecture has three significant components. First, the XHTML and CSS are employed to provide a hassle-free user interface. The content is dynamically changed using the local JavaScript engine and is assisted by DOM. The engine also steers the communication with the server conducted using AJAX calls while the communication between client and server is through XML requests and responses. On the contrary, the server side is written in PHP and caters to multiple levels of abstractions. The aim of EyeOS was to provide an entire web application development framework but it falls short under certain constraints. Though the user interface provides a sufficiently good response, there are some issues that curb the usability. Communication between server and client has to be initiated by the client and thus it accumulates in latency and server load. This entire setup is not suitable for computation of intensive applications on the client or server side. Though it is accessible on mobile devices, network latency and bandwidth constraints are of major concern and do not support the usage of all kinds of applications that are deployed on such a platform.

HP Palm OS HP WebOS is Palm's proprietary mobile operating system designed and developed to run on the Linux kernel. The first version was run on the Palm Pre that was released on Sprint. It has been designed to run on a diversified hardware, supporting a range of screen sizes and resolutions. It works best on a touch panel device. Being built around a web browser, it requires a CPU, a meagre amount of memory, and an internet connection to interact with the user interface. It is a unique combination of Palm and open source components, which provide user space services. This is referred to as core OS. Neither the application developers nor the end users have access to the core. The core uses Linux 2.6 as a base along with standard driver architecture with a boot loader. It aids an ext3 file system and internal and FAT32 file systems. The core also covers a wide range of services, ranging from operating system services, middleware, and wireless and media subsystems. The application runtime environment is operated by the user interface system manager which can be manipulated by the user as well. The framework also provides access to widgets and palm services. It shows the presence of a feature called synergy that helps to integrate information pages similar to the other available Webkit-based browsers. A web-based approach is used to sync data from other third-party applications. Some significant downside in this development is that the library of applications is smaller when compared to those of Apple and Android. In addition, it is comparatively difficult for developers to code and build applications on this platform.

Open Mobster It is a critical open source platform that is used for integrating mobile applications with the cloud. Some of the noteworthy features include data synchronization, real time push notifications, and remote procedure call. Data synchronization is available using a simple API which functions smoothly in both online and offline modes but do not require any special sync related programming efforts on the developer side. Real time push notifications use socket approaches for text messages and email alerts. This is also done using a simple API. Remote procedure call is invoked using the simple RPC mechanism without going into low level programming. There is presence of a management console that is used to administer the cloud server [10]. There is a software stack that is installed on a mobile device and has specific services. Network services help in establishing a reliable network connection with the cloud server. Database service manager manages and stores all the local data related to the applications that are installed on the mobile device.

Advantages of MCC

Flexibility It allows to access data from cloud from anywhere through mobile network.

Real time application Since all the data and applications are managed externally through cloud, they can be updated and accessed at real time with very little effort and also enable simultaneous access across multiple devices thus encouraging collaborative working.

Multiple platform support Since data and applications are stored in the cloud, with mobile cloud computing, it is not mandatory to stick to a certain platform, thus enabling multiple platform support.

Low cost option Depending on your volume of usage, MCC is mostly free of upfront cost or has minimal upfront cost. Like any other pay-for-use service, it comes without the hefty fees charged for licensing and upgrades.

Disadvantages of MCC

Data security   It is the major concern when it comes to cloud computing. Even though there are options available to encrypt as well as password protect the data, it can still lead to major damages if there is a security breach and not undertaken properly.

Performance issues and connectivity   Since MCC is internet driven, your location and access to the internet will affect your functioning. For example, in an area with only 2G network, expect slow access.

Mobile Cloud Computing (MCC) Applications

1. Cloud based m-learning—It is the combination of e-learning and mobility. In comparison with the traditional m-learning, cloud-based m-learning solves the problems of low transmission rate and limited storage of educational resources.
2. Mobile e-governance—In recent days, many government organizations have started providing the services through mobile for easy reachability purpose.
3. Mobile banking—Many commercial transactions are performed through online mobile banking applications.
4. Guidance with the help of mobile—Mobile technologies are providing assistance in many cases, such as guiding pedestrians while crossing the road, especially those who are blind or visually impaired and, offering text transcription for hearing impaired people.
5. Cloud-based mobile rural healthcare—Rural people and the people suffering with chronic diseases could use mobile healthcare technologies to continuously monitor their health.
6. Gaming with mobile—With the help of large computing resources available in cloud, it is very easy to offload the games in the server.
7. Mobile e-commerce—M-commerce allows users to do online shopping, online transactions through mobile and mobile advertisements, etc.

Examples of MCC Applications

In case of face recognition, the law enforcement agencies are using facial recognition software as a crime-fighting tool. MCC can be effectively used for real-time face recognition by moving the processing and the storage of data out from mobile devices to the cloud.

Similarly, mobile cloud learning in the context of higher education enables students to engage themselves in continuous learning and assessment system. Mobile cloud computing can be used in many flipped class rooms, online quizzes, continuous performance monitoring, etc.

12.10 CLOUD COMPUTING ENVIRONMENT OPEN-STACK

There are various sets of software tools available for building and managing cloud computing platforms such as public and private clouds. Tools support users to deploy virtual machines and instances to handle different tasks for managing a cloud environment. For example, a mobile application that requires communicating with the remote server can communicate with users across different instances, and all of them can communicate with one another. Anyone who is authenticated can access the source code, make changes or modifications, and freely share those changes.

For controlling a huge collection of compute, storage, and various networking resources in the cloud data center, a cloud operating system is used—this is called an open stack. Users directly interact with the dashboard to support the administrator and provide control for handling resources easily through an interface.

Docker is a novel open platform that comes in a cloud computing environment to support developers, and administrators for handling and running distributed applications, and support operations of applications inside the software container. This provides an additional layer of abstraction and virtualization at the operating system level. Docker supports the resource isolation feature of Linux kernel. This tool packages the application and its dependents in a container and helps to run on the server. It is used to support easy portability, isolation of application, and enhance elastic feature as well.

12.11 SELECTION OF CLOUD APPLICATION

Cloud computing, which permits users to access their applications hosted on servers over the Internet, carries responsibilities and new benefits for developers. For developers who host the program in a public PaaS, several suppliers render APIs that permit the application to request for more resources than required by the application. Services of the cloud should mechanically extent whenever required, and as per the requirement of the application service quality should also change.

Now-a-days particularly, developers ought to look out for applications, and the sessions of users should be considered in the application code. For a simple application, the user might want to save some sort of state and feature. This is one of the requirements of databases or objects, even now, to store the information state of the user. It is the basis why most web applications never store data on front-end servers. It is the section which generally wants scale. Moreover, dealing with databases is not the same always. In a cloud environment, the notion of relational database is nearly dead. In fact, nearly all PaaS carry the concept of 'storage engine', where the deflation model is encouraged. As tables are distributed athwart various machines for scalability, many old notions are not worthy in this. Alternatively, functioning may augment due to the result of the ability to fetch database information on various servers at the same time.

Creating an application hosted in the cloud varies from the first day of an on-premise installation. Various layers can be extracted, and assorted resources accessible on the Internet can be utilized. For instance, you can save information on Amazon's S3, consume application logic which operates in a totally discrete area, and host your presentation stratum on Facebook. Apart from the features of the cloud-aware application, there are some tools, varying from notebooks, tablets, desktop computers, smartphones' home automation, car entertainment systems, and many more, which progress towards specialism. The facilities accessible in these tools differ as well, for instance, battery, audio, camera, screen size, keyboard, Internet connectivity bandwidth, etc.

To move towards the cloud and make applications cloud alert, you merely require to learn your business and consider what can and needs to be transferred on to the cloud, beginning with small groups and individuals and later shifting to mid-sized associations. By determining what is to be transferred to the cloud, you should actually be able to figure out what you wish out of the cloud. In case you are using the cloud for PaaS or SaaS, you ought to examine which applications are most suitable for protection on the cloud. You can send all kinds of data to the cloud. You can manage applications online and store particular files as well. Microsoft's Document Connection device appears with Microsoft's unified communications asset along with its Office set of applications.

12.12 CLOUD DESCRIPTOR LANGUAGE

Cloud descriptor language uses the feature of XML like schema exchange. Cloud descriptor language sometimes uses scripting language for its application.

Scripting Languages

Scripting means writing codes, scripts, or programs to support the software environment which computerizes the implementation of the jobs that can alternatively be implemented in person, manually. Environments which can be computerized via scripting comprise web pages inside a web browser, the shells of operating systems (OS), software applications, etc.

As scripting is not a language, many languages do not support the implementation of scripting. C++ implementations are rarely used, because it requires more time to write a program as compared to other scripting languages like Python. Normally, a scripting language is distinguished by the following properties:

1. Ease of writing—Scripting languages are very fast and have simple syntax, and easy semantics and error handling.
2. Operating system services—Scripting is generally intended on desktops, restraining the portability wants of the pre-built libraries.
3. Interpretation of source code—Non-scripting languages anticipated for big programs are frequently precompiled in at least some logic for better performance.
4. Comparatively loose structure—Java as a scripting language is not simple to use because of the regulations regarding classes. In many enterprises, development is not done with traditional accumulated programming languages. However, along with scripting languages, scripts are exclusive programs that operate on the server and show a web page after they are operated. Scripts are very valuable and used by vibrant web page scheming which has content that alters with time.

There are various languages that support script writing for websites, for example, PHP, Perl, ASP, and JSP. As a script allows for complete automation of the process, new entries are displayed as soon as users sign the guest book. All the script entries are stored on the server, so it can be displayed immediately.

Perl

Perl has mainly been used to write CGI scripts. High-traffic websites like Amazon.com use Perl comprehensively. Often, Perl is used as a bond language, connecting those interfaces and systems together, which were not particularly intended to inter operate, altering or dealing huge amount of data for tasks like designing reports. Perl code may be made transportable across UNIX and Windows. Perl is usually used for simplifying packaging and upholding of software. With the use of Perl, graphical user interfaces (GUIs) might be built. For instance, Perl is normally used to facilitate user interface with Perl scripts. These interfaces can be synchronous or asynchronous.

Python

The Python programming language has obtained fame as one of the constituents of the LAMP (Linux, Apache, MySQL and Python/Perl/PHP) board. Python has been observed as a new tool which is liked by the programmer, and vital languages such as Python and Ruby have appeared as substitutes to languages such as C# and Java. Software with many attractive features are available for the user, such as App Engine, Google, the Zope application server, web framework, etc. Python is a commanding progressive programming language which is employed in an ample range of application domains. Python rarely assesses Perl, Ruby, Java, Scheme, or Tcl. The peculiar features of Python are as follows:

1. Simple, legible syntax
2. Procedural code can be easily uttered
3. Code can be developed in modules
4. Supports error handling if there is any exception

5. Supports dynamic data types
6. Broad standard libraries
7. Code or modules support other languages too

12.13 GREEN COMPUTING

The centralized maintenance of software packages, data backups, and balancing the volume of user demands across multiple servers or multiple data center sites are the various benefits of the cloud. In contrast, a public cloud is hosted on the Internet and designed to be used by any user with an Internet connection to provide a similar range of capabilities and services. Cloud computing may propose energy savings in terms of computing and storage services, principally if the end user drifts to the use of a computer or a workstation of lower capacity and lower energy utilization. Due to increase in data centers, cloud computing leads to increases in network traffic and the associated network energy consumption. The matter of energy utilization in information technology tools has increased considerably in recent years and there is mounting appreciation of the want to direct energy utilization athwart the whole information and communications technology (ICT) sector. It was estimated that data centers accounted for roughly 1.2 per cent of the total United States electricity utilization in 2005. The broadcast and switching networks in the Internet account for a further 0.4 per cent of total electricity utilization in broadband-enabled countries.

'Green computing' is used to signify the effective use of resources in computing. This word usually associates to the use of computing resources in concurrence with augmenting financial feasibility, shrinking environmental effect, and guaranteeing social responsibilities. Green computing is greatly associated with other similar activities such as encouraging the use of recyclable resources.

Electronic products environmental assessment tool (EPEAT) is one of the by-products of green computing. EPEAT goods act to enhance the life and effectiveness of computing goods. Furthermore, these goods are intended to reduce maintenance activities, lessen energy expenses all through the life of the good, and permit the recycling or reuse of several resources.

Energy Star acts as a sort of voluntary mark granted to computing goods which succeed in reducing consumption of energy. Energy Star is directed to goods such as television sets; the computer checks temperature control instruments such as refrigerators, air conditioners, and analogous goods.

Cloud computing is an engineering challenge to manage the power consumption of large data centers and associated cooling. The organization of power utilization in data centers has directed to a number of significant enhancements in the efficacy of energy. Cloud computing infrastructure is lodged in data centers and has extensively benefitted from these developments.

As given in Fig. 12.5, we can see that various services are provided by the cloud provider to the users, and due to this, heavy load in the data center emission of CO_2 is also more. However, we can apply strategies to make computing green; then cloud computing becomes green computing. Methods such as virtualization or sleep scheduling of computing resources in cloud computing data centers enhance the energy proficiency of cloud computing. Even as it is significant to comprehend how to reduce energy utilization in data centers which host cloud computing services that is also liable for global warming up to some amount, it is also vital to think about the energy needed to transfer data to and from the end user and the energy utilized by the end-user interface. Government directives, though well-intentioned, are just a part of an inclusive green computing attitude. Working habits of corporations and computer users may be customized so as to lower the unfavorable effect on the universal environment. Some of the steps that may be taken are as follows:

1. Power-down the CPU and all tangential through comprehensive periods of inoperativeness
2. Attempt to perform computer-related jobs during adjacent, concentrated spans of time, keeping hardware off, the rest of the time

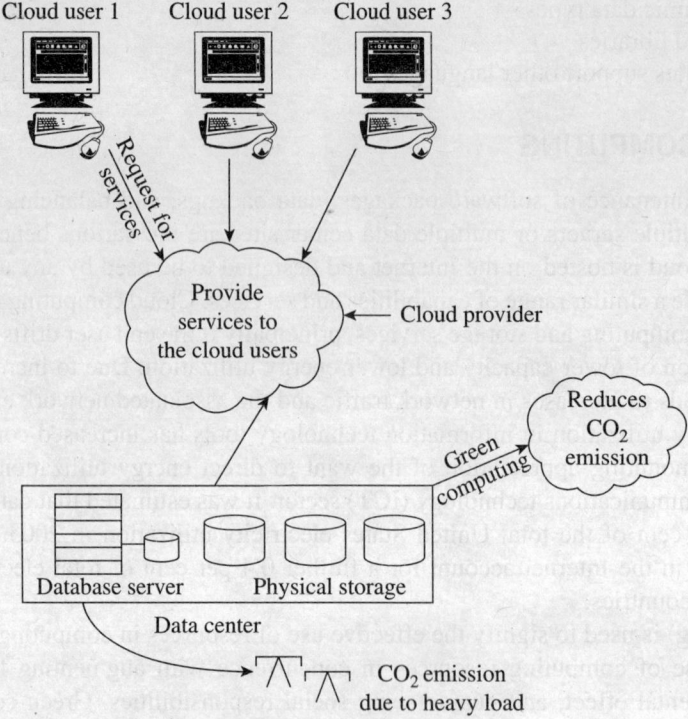

Fig. 12.5 Green computing

3. Power-up and power-down energy-intensive tangential like laser printers as per demand.
4. Instead of cathode ray tube (CRT) monitors, try to use liquid crystal display (LCD).
5. Whenever conceivable, use notebook computers in place of desktop computers.
6. Use the power-management characteristics to switch off hard drives and exhibits after a few minutes of inoperativeness.
7. Reduce the use of paper and recycle waste paper appropriately.
8. Dispose e-waste as per local, state, and national policies.
9. Utilize substitute energy funds for data centers, servers, and computing workstations.
10. One of the foremost outcomes of green computing was the Sleep mode act of computer monitors that keeps an electronic tool of the consumer on standby mode when a predetermined phase of time passes, during which the activity of the user is undetected.

12.14 WORKLOAD PATTERN FOR CLOUDS

As many companies are migrating towards cloud technology because of its many advantages, data is only going to increase which is saved by the cloud users. This is why cloud data stores have been responsible for big data management. A difficult challenge for organizations is moving large amounts of data on cloud environment and its management is also not so easy. Aspera is now a solution for big data clouds problem. Cloud computing becomes a practical, conventional solution for data processing, storage, and distribution. This computing lets users easily scale out infrastructure and pay as per the usage.

Big data is a term for data sets and has challenges such as analysis, capture, search, sharing, storage, transfer, visualization, and security of information. Certain advanced technologies are still required to extract value from the data set.

Various researchers have advised that commercial DBMS is not appropriate for handling enormously large-scale data. One database server has the limit of cost and scalability, which are the two vital aims of big data processing. For adapting numerous large data processing models, D. Kossmann offered four distinct architectures on the basis of classic multi-tier database application architecture that are paneling, imitation, disseminated control, and caching architecture. It is apparent that the optional suppliers have distinct business models and aim for distinct types of applications. Google appears to be more concerned with small applications along with light workloads, whereas Azure is presently the most reasonable service for average to big services. Most current cloud service suppliers are using hybrid architecture which is competent to fulfil their real service needs. Big data architecture comes from three important features—disseminated file system, and semi-structured and non-structural data storage.

Until now, researchers were unable to amalgamate the vital characteristics of large data. Some believe that large data is the data which we are unable to process utilizing pre-existing skill, technique, and hypothesis. The world is now turning into a 'defencelessness' era whilst immeasurable data is being created by society, business, and science. Large data is always a new challenge for data administration and even for the entire IT industry.

Large data storage and administration-related technologies of data administration systems are unable to meet the requirements of large data. In addition, the rising pace of storage ability is much lesser than that of data; hence a revolution of information framework is required. We want to achieve hierarchical storage architecture. Earlier, computer algorithms were unable to efficiently handle storage of data which is directly obtained from the real world, because of the heterogeneity of large data. So, the method to rearrange data is an important concern in large data management. Virtual server skill can aggravate the difficulty, increasing the vista of overcommitted resources, particularly if communication is deprived amid the storage administrators, application, and server. We as well require resolving the blockage troubles of the high-associated I/O and the only-named node in the current master-slave system model.

In large data computation and investigation, while processing an inquiry within large data, speed is an important requirement. As the process might take time (since it cannot navigate all the associated data in the entire database in a little time), index will be the best option. Presently, indices in large data are only looking at simple kind of data, whilst large data is becoming more intricate. The amalgamation of a suitable index for large data and advanced preprocessing skill will be an enviable resolution when we meet such problems. Application parallelization and divide-and-conquer are the usual computational models for impending large data troubles. However, receiving added computational resources is not as easy as just upgrading to a bigger and more prevailing machine on the soar. The conservative serial algorithm is incompetent for the large data. If there is sufficient data parallelism in the application, consumers can take the benefit of the reduced cost model to use hundreds of computers for a short time. As a concern of big data security, using online data application of cloud, a large number of companies can significantly lessen their IT cost. Privacy and safety influence the large data storage and processing, as there is enormous utilization of third-party infrastructures and services which are utilized to host significant data or to execute important operations. The scale of applications and data rise exponentially, and bring a large amount of dynamic data scrutinizing and safety fortification. Unlike conventional safety techniques, safety in large data is mostly in the form of how to process data mining, without revealing the perceptive information of consumers. Current technologies of privacy fortification are mostly based on static data sets, whereas data is forever animatedly changed, including data prototype, variants of attributes, and accumulation of new data. Hence it is a challenge to execute effectual privacy fortification in this multifaceted condition. Additionally, regulatory and legal matters also need to be taken care of.

12.15 THIRD-PARTY TECHNOLOGY

Before the advent of the Internet, you would buy software, typically with a licence, and deploy and operate it on your computers, similar to purchasing a music CD and playing it in your residence. Beneath the cloud model, the software is operated online by a third-party supplier and you access it via your Internet browser. You, by no means, deploy something on your personal computer and do not really possess any software, as instead of purchasing a product, you are leasing a service. Third-party concepts are also valuable in providing security to cloud data center.

The tech generation is thrilled about cloud computing. There is hardly any technology for you to be concerned about. While you lease a car, the protection, upkeep, and crash assistance are all taken care of by the leasing company.

Nevertheless, the utmost advantage of the cloud is economic. Let us go back to the lease-a-car theory. While you purchase a car, there is an enormous direct expenditure. You never receive that money back if the car is not used by you daily, or even if you sell it. After five years, you will encompass an old car that no one else desires to purchase, and if it goes off beam, it will charge more and more to repair. However, your leasing car is forever an existing model, and you just disburse to use what you require, when you want it.

This is the situation with cloud services as well. There is no straightforward charge. You will disburse a less-expected, flat-rate monthly payment per user for the software used by you and which indicates that you may scale up or down as per your corporation's requirements.

You can expand or contract the number of resources you are controlling. Thus, spending on technology which used to be a major capital expense for even small businesses now becomes an operational expense. The cloud provider gives us the ability to change, adapting to the promising needs of the business.

Unlike deployed software, you will forever have access to the newest editions as well. While a novel edition of a service is launched, it is immediately made accessible to each subscriber, providing you access to devices that will remain in your corporation at the highest levels of competitiveness.

Operating software online also conveys several built-in advantages:

Work from wherever you want Software that was deployed on a computer only worked on that computer. Businessmen nowadays work from residences and the office and airport lounges and along with the cloud, you will not only have access to your software at all times, but also be able to sign in and continue from where you left off.

Collaborate with customers, dealers, and contemporaries You may share access to your cloud workplaces. It denotes that you could work on documents, presentations, suggestions, etc., along with other populace, and increase the limits of your place of work to clients as well.

Limit threat of catastrophe and expedite catastrophe recuperation One of the chief economies of cloud computing is that a fine cloud supplier will contain superior safety and flexibility than you may ever expect to afford. They will save your data securely and steadily. In case your workplace is broken into (or, more probably, abandon your laptop on a train), your data is still secure and instantly available online from an additional appliance.

Examples of Third Parties

Dropbox, a SaaS vendor, uses the services of a third-party IaaS vendor, like Amazon Web Services. For availing services, they have to agree on some service conditions and agreements. Security threats and lack of control are always involved if the internal data of a cloud is handled by third parties or external sources.

As given in Fig. 12.6, company A offers various exciting services to the users but for the physical storage of data, company A involves third-party company B. Users are unaware of the services of company B because they know that they are taking services from company A.

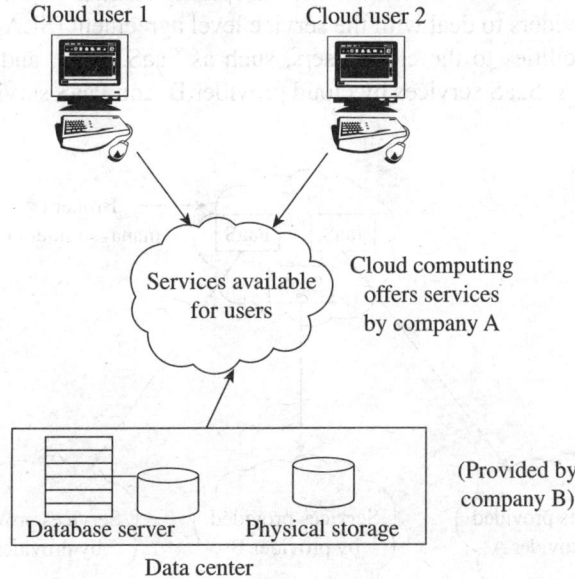

Fig. 12.6 Third party technology

12.16 INTERCLOUD

The Intercloud is a unified universal 'cloud of clouds' and an expansion of the Internet 'network of networks' on which it is established. In 2007, the expression was first used in the perspective of cloud computing. In early 2009, it became popular and has since then been used to explain the data center of the future as well.

The Intercloud circumstances are based on the chief concept that every individual cloud does not contain countless physical resources or ubiquitous geographic marks. If a cloud oversupplies the storage and computational resources of its infrastructure, or is requested to employ resources in characteristics where it has no marks, it would still be capable of satisfying these appeals for service allotments transmitted from its consumers. The Intercloud circumstances would tackle these conditions where every cloud would employ the storage, computational, or any type of resource of the infrastructure of additional clouds. This is the correct communication regarding how the Internet performs, in which a service supplier, to which an end point is connected, will send or access traffic starting to source/target the beginning exterior of its service region using Internet navigation practices with other service suppliers with whom it has an agreed switch.

Cloud technology is now playing a key role in handling the rapid increase of data. It is not possible for a single cloud to handle everything as per user demands. For providing better service, various clouds' providers have to communicate with each other to share their resources. This is actually what we call Intercloud computing. Resource management with regard to agreement and services are still one of the challenges of Intercloud computing.

An intermediate party that can communicate between two or more parties for sharing resources among them is known as 'cloud broker' or simply 'broker'. Broker also introduces the cloud users to the cloud service provider (CSP) and vice versa.

A cloud broker offers an interface to cloud users with multiple cloud facilities. This interface can be managed and can share the resources of multiple clouds. The broker introduces users to various cloud providers and services that are better for them according to their requirements. The broker also assists various service providers to deal with the service level agreement (SLA). As shown in Fig. 12.7, the broker offers three facilities to the cloud users, such as SaaS, PaaS, and IaaS. IaaS services are offered by cloud provider A, SaaS services by cloud provider B, and PaaS services are offered by cloud provider C.

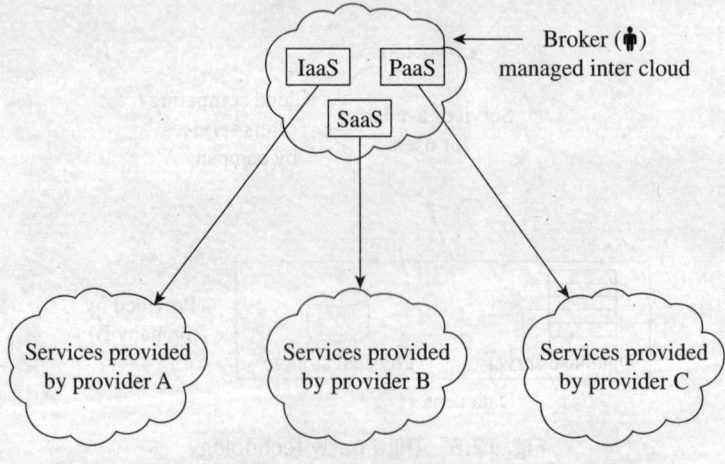

Fig. 12.7 Intercloud

12.17 AZURE CLOUD SERVICES

Powerful applications with advanced features having application-oriented customization techniques are available in Azure cloud services. The following are the steps that show how services can be set up as per our requirements.

The steps to start Azure cloud services are as follows:
1. Azure SDK for Visual Studio 2013 helps to set up a development environment and Visual Studio Express will be installed with SDK.
2. First of all download and unzip the folder (Solution file).
3. Start Visual Studio.
4. The File menu helps you to choose an open project and after navigating open the solution file.
5. For building solutions, press CTRL+SHIFT+B. You can also manually install the solution file by going to the Manage NuGet Packages of the Solution dialog box and then click the Restore button given on the top right.
6. In Solution Explorer, select ContosoAdsCloudService from the start-up project.
7. You can run the application by Pressing CTRL+F5.

8. Visual Studios have tools if you are running cloud service projects locally. Storage emulator uses an SQL Server Express LocalDB database in Azure cloud storage.
9. Click on Create an Ad.
10. You can enter data and also select the .jpg image to upload.
11. After clicking, the app goes to the Index page.
12. You can thumbnail after refreshing.
13. Organize the application to Azure.

After this, you can run the application in the cloud environment:
1. First create Azure cloud service as discussed next.
2. Then create the Azure SQL database followed by Azure storage account.
3. Configure the solution with Azure SQL database as per your requirements.
4. Configure Azure storage account as discussed.
5. Arrange the project with Azure cloud service.

The steps to create Azure cloud services are as follows:
1. Open the Azure classic portal in the browser.
2. Click New -> Compute -> Cloud Service -> Quick Create.
3. Enter a unique URL prefix in the URL input box.
4. Choose the area to organize the application.
5. Select the region closest to your customers and this specifies the data center for your cloud service hosting.
6. Now click Create Cloud Service.

The steps to create an Azure storage account are as follows:
1. Click New > Data Services > Storage > Quick Create in the Azure classic portal.
2. Enter a unique URL prefix in the given URL box to your storage account.
3. From the Region drop-down, you can choose for the cloud service.
4. From the Replication drop-down, select locally redundant.
5. Then, click Create Storage Account.

12.18 BIGTABLE

Expansion of Internet facilities and digital communications has led to a widespread requirement of storage systems with efficient accessibility of stored data items. Conventional database systems make use of relational databases which is comprised of several tables made up of rows and columns. These rows and columns are named. These systems generally follow ACID properties—that is atomicity, consistency, isolation, and durability. However, generally with large scale dataset, these properties are difficult to maintain along with maintaining good availability and tolerance on network partitioning. Hence for huge and extremely distributed environments, databases posing ACID properties become difficult to manage and here arises the need for alternate databases which can deal with high availability and performance.

Bigtable is one of such alternate databases which have been specially designed for huge storage of data. It is a storage system for distributed environment made in the form of large table. The size of this large table can range up to petabytes of data. This data can be present across several thousand machines. Bigtable is capable of handling millions of queries made by millions of users at an instant and millions and trillions of images and information pieces.

The credit of developing Bigtable goes to Google. Google formulated the Bigtable in 2005 and this was made used in several of its services. According to the Google's White Paper, the definition of Bigtable is as follows:

"Bigtable is a distributed storage system for managing structured data that is designed to scale to a very large size—petabytes of data across thousands of commodity servers. Bigtable is a sparse, distributed, persistent multidimensional sorted map. The map is indexed by a row key, column key, and a timestamp; each value in the map is an uninterrupted array of bytes."

Structure of Bigtable

Bigtable can be visualized as a map which is accessible through indexing. This indexing is done by three values—(a) row key, (b) column key, and (c) timestamp. Every value is in itself an array of bytes.

Bigtable is a huge structure comprising of rows and columns. The access to these is done by a (key, value) pair. The key corresponds to the rows and the value refers to the set of columns.

The structure of Bigtable poses some striking features as—distributed, sparse, multidimensional, time-based, sorted, and persistent.

1. Persistent—This property establishes that all data keeps getting stored on disk persistently.
2. Sparse—This property tells that the table structure could use varied number of columns for various rows, in which some may remain empty as well.
3. Distributed—The meaning of being distributed in terms of Bigtable structure is that data storage in the table can be done across various machines. These can be tens of thousands in numbers.
4. Sorted—Bigtable is structured as a map, which is an associative array. Associative arrays are generally not sorted, since the values can be accessed by hashing, etc. However, Bigtable shows a difference here and keeps its records in sorted form through its key values. The keys can be sorted in a manner such that data records, which are related to each other, are stored together.
5. Multi-dimensional—Indexing of the table in Bigtable structure is done by its rows. Every row, on the other hand, is comprised of column families which can be one or more than one in number. A column family may contain one or more than one named columns. These are normally defined during the creation of table. A column family usually stores data of the same type. All the columns are generally compressed within a column family in a Bigtable. The combination of rows, column families, and columns in a bigtable gives a three-level naming hierarchy for accessing data.
6. Time-based—Time is an important parameter for Bigtable structure. There can be kept various versions of data in a column family. For an application to access a certain data from the column family, it needs to specify its timestamp. If the application fails to do so, it will get access to the latest version of the requested data.

Tablets

A tablet refers to the subdivision of a table into subtables consisting of a collection of rows. A subset or a certain number of rows from among the many rows of the Bigtable can be taken and kept together in form of a subtable, which is known as a tablet. This can also be termed as a unit of distribution for Bigtable used for load balancing.

Timestamps

Every data record in the cells of the Bigtable can have multiple versions of its content. To identify these versions separately, a timestamp is used. These timestamps are made up of 64 bits and these can be real time or assigned by a client. While accessing the data, if no timestamp is mentioned, then the latest existing version of the data is made available, otherwise the most recent version earlier than the specified timestamp is made available.

Columns

The content stored by a column may be a single short value which can be just a bunch of bytes or may also be large. Bigtable construct does not associate any type with the column. A Bigtable can possess columns within a column family. The columns can also be created dynamically. The number of columns in a Bigtable can be huge ranging to hundreds of thousands or millions, but a column family for a row can consist of only a fraction of them. The number of column families in a table is usually small (ranging to atmost hundreds), while the number of columns can be unlimited.

Construction of Bigtable

A Bigtable consists of:
1. Client library
2. A master server
3. Several tablet servers

A client library is linked with user's code. A master's server is used for coordinating different activities. Tablet servers have the provision of getting dynamically added or removed.

The responsibilities of a master server include:
(a) The work of assigning tablets to various tablet servers is done by the master server. Thus, master server helps in balancing the load of the tablet server.
(b) Garbage collection for files in GFS
(c) Creation of Column family and table, i.e., management of schema changes

The responsibilities of a tablet server include:
(a) Management of a set of tablets. These tablets can be 10-1,000 tablets per server.
(b) Handling read/write requests made to the tablets.
(c) Splitting and managing the tablets if the size of the table gets huge.

In order to perform reads or writes over the data, the clients need to directly communicate with the tablet servers. Google File System (GFS) is used by the Bigtable implementation for storage of both logs and data files.

Aspects such as monitoring of health, scheduling of jobs, and failure management are handled by a software referred to as the cluster management system.

12.18.1 Chubby

Bigtable provides another important and highly available service known as Chubby. It is a distributed lock service. Chubby provides management of leasing of resources and also storage of configuration information. The working of Chubby involves usage of five active replicas. From these, one is chosen as a master to serve requests. In this, to make the service to work, a majority of replicas should be in the running state. To keep the replicas in a consistent state, Paxos is used. Every file or directory in a Chubby can work as a lock. The namespaces to these files and directories are provided by the Chubby.

Responsibilities of a Chubby in a Bigtable Construct include:
1. Ensuring presence of only one active master
2. Storing access control lists
3. Discovering tablet servers
4. Storing the bootstrap location of Bigtable data

12.18.2 Development of Bigtable

The development of Bigtable starts with a single tablet. As this table grows, it splits into further multiple tablets, each of whose size can be around 100 to 200 MB. A Bigtable grows in a three-level hierarchical form. The three-level hierarchy (Fig. 12.8) includes matter in such form:
1. First Level-Root Tablet—It stores the locations of various metadata tablets.
2. Second Level-Metadata Tablet—It stores the locations of various user data tablets.
3. Third Level-User Tablet—It stores the user data or information.

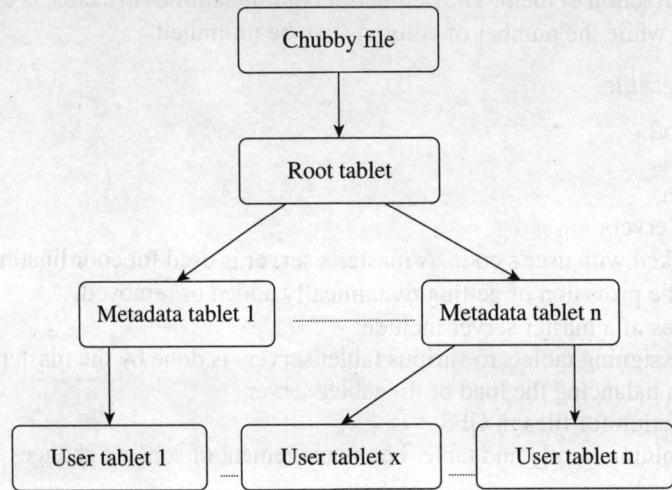

Fig. 12.8 Bigtable's three-level hierarchical view

The storage in a Bigtable is done at three levels. The Root Tablet is the top-level which stores the table IDs of several Metadata tablets in a unique Metadata Table. Each row of the Metadata tablet stores a user Tablet's Table Id and end row information.

Management of tablet servers is done by Chubby. A tablet at a time can be assigned to only one tablet server. On initiation of a tablet server, a uniquely named file is created. This uniquely named file is in Chubby servers' directory and the tablet server acquires an exclusive lock on it when it is created.

The master tablet server is responsible for monitoring the Chubby servers' directory to discover new tablet servers. The functions of master, upon its creation, are as follows:
   (a) Acquires a unique master lock in Chubby—This is done to disallow multiple masters from initiation.
   (b) Looks for active tablet servers, by scanning the Chubby's server directory.
   (c) Identifies which tablet is assigned to every tablet server by communicating with them.
   (d) Acquires the knowledge of the full set of tablets by scanning the Metadata Table.
   (e) Creates a set of unassigned tablet servers.

Bigtable can be replicated across various data centers to ensure availability through multiple Bigtable clusters.

12.19 CLOUD USAGE FOR BIG DATA ANALYTICS AND INTERNET OF THINGS

It is discussed in the sections below.

Big Data

Big data has endured much earlier and the Internet of Things (IoT) commences into the scenario in order to perform analytics. Information is stated as 'Big Data' when it reveals the four V's—volume, variety, velocity, and veracity. This equates to a huge quantity of data which may be structured and unstructured both, where velocity denotes to the data processing speed and veracity ascertains its uncertainty.

The Internet of Things

The idea of Internet of Things (IoT) plans to take a vast range of things and convert them into smart objects—everything from watches to refrigerators, cars, and train tracks. Products, which usually would not be coupled to the Internet and are capable to get and process data, are supplied with sensors and computer chips to gather data. However, unlike chips used in smartphones, mobile devices and PCs, these chips are mainly used to gather data which signifies product performance and consumer usage patterns.

The IoT is basically the means which collects and sends data. Information from IoT tools exists in large data and is computed against it. IoT will shortly touch each phase of our lives—manufacturing, transportation (i.e., traffic lights, cars, and smart train tracks), smart homes (i.e., thermostats and voice activated appliances), as well as customer goods such as wearables, smartphones, etc.

This troublesome technology needs new infrastructures, including software and hardware applications, along with an operating system. Ventures will be required to deal with the flow of data which begins flowing in and evaluate it in real-time since it develops by the minute. In this case Big data comes in; Big data analytics devices are suitable for dealing masses of data transferred from IoT tools, generating a continuous flow of information. However, just to distinguish the two, the IoT carries the information from which Big data analytics can take the information for creating the insights needed of it. Since the IoT carries data on a different scale, the analytics solution should integrate its requirements of speedy incorporation and processing followed by a correct and quick eradication.

IoT companies associate the growing number of data sets that help them to obtain real-time responses and accustom to changing tendencies, solving the challenge of size without agreeing on the performance. The internet has spread across various technological platforms and billions of people in the world. With this spread getting wider, new technologies and devices have evolved. Examples include smart phones that have reached every person in the world, smart watches, and smart homes equipped with sensing technologies for smart energy, water management, etc. The internet lies as the backbone for all of these devices and technologies.

The interconnection of devices and cloud leads to new business cases and smart solutions leading the way to Internet of Things (IoT). A thing in IoT can be a device such as heat sensor or a cloud service that detects the heating level or the person requesting the service. So, IoT can be viewed as a triangle of devices, cloud and the end users as shown in the Fig. 12.9.

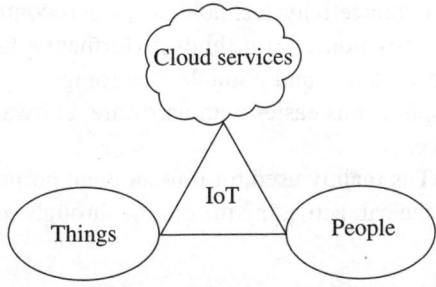

Fig. 12.9 IoT Triangle

IoT can be generically thought of as connecting things to the internet and using that connection to provide some kind of useful remote monitoring or control of these things. It is about harmonizing the way humans interact with devices and the environment using some common public services.

IoT in its culmination can be defined as the one that creates an intelligent, invisible network environment that can be sensed, controlled, and programmed. IoT-enabled products employ embedded technology that allows them to communicate, directly or indirectly, with each other or the Internet (refer to Fig. 12.10 which shows monitoring one's healthcare via cloud).

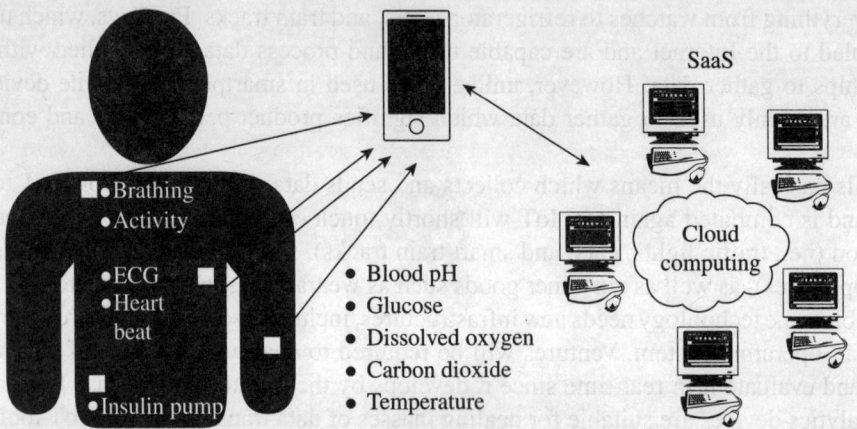

Fig. 12.10 IOT Enabled Healthcare monitoring with cloud

IOT is considered as a process of accessing any information by everyone from anywhere. This is described as follows:
1. Everyone—With the advent of technological advancements, anyone can connect their devices or products or sensors to the IoT; and even threshold conditions can be applied.
2. Everything—Any object or device can be connected to the cloud to extend the capabilities of devices and provide security to the entire IoT ecosystem.
3. Everywhere—Because of internet and intranet access, the developed framework can be accessed from anywhere and everywhere. Based on the wireless sensor networks and network topologies' advancements, accessing an IoT framework is not a big issue.

Applications of IOT

Applications of IOT are vast. For example, Texas Instruments (TI), a global semiconductor design and manufacturing company, offers cloud-ready system solutions with the industry's broadest IoT-ready portfolio of wired and wireless connectivity technologies, microcontrollers, processors, sensors, and analog signal chain and power solutions. From high-performance home, industrial and automotive applications to battery-powered wearable and portable electronics or energy-harvested wireless sensor nodes, TI makes developing applications easier with hardware, software, tools and support to get anything connected as an IoT device.

In automotive appliances, IoT is mainly used for infotainment purposes such as connecting between the phones and the speakers of the car, activating the engine through voice control, etc.

Using global networking technologies with IoT, one can track the location and find the place for parking the vehicle. For example, it can be Bluetooth headset or GPS tracker. These devices facilitate the user to help enhance their health and wellness and gather information around the user.

In home automation systems, IoT applications include monitoring and controlling the devices inside a home in an intelligent way. They include lighting and temperature control among the connected appliances for effective use of energy. In some another level, smart building management systems include smart cities equipped with smart city lights, residential e-meters, surveillance cameras for traffic control, pipeline leak detection, etc. Healthcare IoT applications include remote monitoring of patients, for example, heart rate, blood pressure level, etc.

Architecture of IOT

We need to get a wider view of the IoT playground. To do that, the key players must first be identified. We classify the *IoT players* into three clusters—Things, Gateway, and Network and Cloud (refer Fig. 12.11).

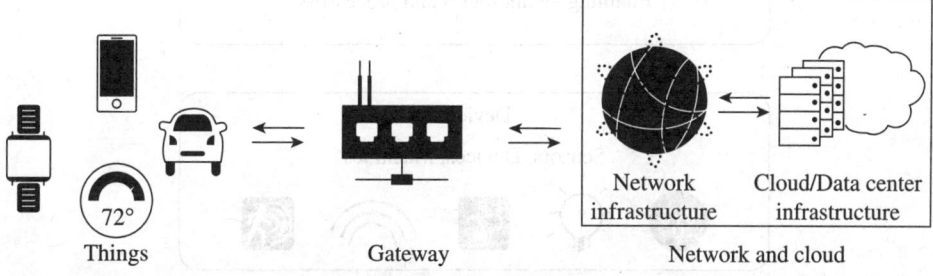

Fig. 12.11 The IOT Players

1. Thing—A thing can be a human being with attached sensor, an animal with a RFID chip, the vehicle with sensors to alert the driver for some condition or any other object containing the IP address.
2. Gateway—It is the mediator or bridge between the thing and cloud. Here, the thing speaks to the gateway and then gateway communicates with the cloud and vice versa.
3. Network and Cloud—This one contains various services helpful to the user for performing specific action according to user requirements.

The different devices and environments needed in IoT can be layered as shown in the Fig. 12.12. The sensors and devices needed in the IoT environment form the bottom layer. The different types of sensors can be temperature, pressure, moisture, etc. The data captured by the sensors needs to be processed using processors and enabling technologies. The technologies include RFID detection, motion sensing, etc. Some of the technologies that enable these devices are discussed further in the Wireless Sensor networks' section. Examples include Bluetooth, Wi-Fi, etc. The processed data can be stored using cloud infrastructures and thus, in turn, provide different IoT services. The different types of IoT services include home automation, healthcare services, energy management, and emergency services, among others.

Challenges of IOT

Developing the different layers of technology for the horizontal nature of the IoT requires developers and designers to deliver on the most basic challenges, including:

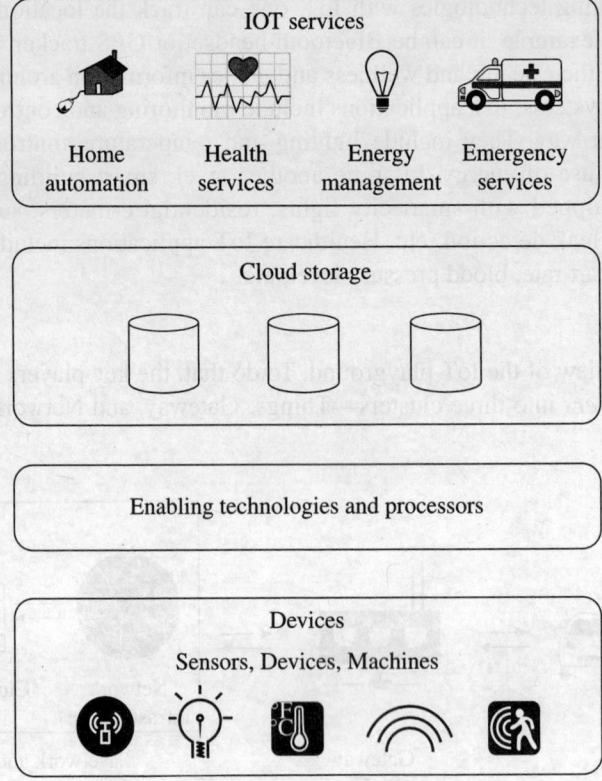

Fig. 12.12 Architecture of IoT

Power management Most of the objects in the IoT environment are required to be battery powered and use energy intelligently. Some devices need to be more energy efficient. The challenge is to make the management of power to these devices, objects, and equipment in an easy manner.

Connectivity In the global technological environment, wide variety of different wired and wireless standards are used to connect the devices or objects. However, there is not just one universal connectivity standard. The challenge is to design and develop the common connectivity standards to communicate one with the other.

Rapid evolution The IoT world is constantly changing and updating. New things are being added every day. The challenge faced by the industry is with the unknown use cases, devices, and applications. For this, there is a need to develop a flexible environment in all facets.

Complexity Every day, many devices and equipment are developed by industry. However, the problem occurs when the newly launched devices are not connected to the IoT environment. Good and flexible design and development is essential to get more things to be connected. Additionally, the design and development should be understandable by an average user who does not have much technical background.

There are several fundamental features that a 'thing' has to encompass to be a good IoT solution. Among these, the most important features are energy efficiency, security, data handling, and simplicity.

Energy efficiency As the number of devices grows, even small amounts of excessive power is a noticeable waste. When it comes to power, the challenge is to ensure that adding internet connectivity does not impose a change to the power supply. In other words, ideally it should fit within the existing power budget headroom. For example, the MSP430, being an ultra-low power MCU, ensures that the IoT application takes minimal power.

Security mechanism Providing security to the data and cloud networks is always a challenging issue. This challenge should be strengthened in IoT environment given the more number of entry points and a higher possibility of breach in those points. For every security solution for IoT environment or in any technological environment, there is an equivalent threat. There is a never ending fight towards better security.

Data handling Higher density of node happens with large number of deployment of end points. It requires higher capacity demand and accessible storage.

Simplicity The IoT design system should be simple and scalable so that if more devices are added to the system or removed from the system, the environment need not be modified.

12.19.1 Different Aspects of IoT Systems

Role of cloud computing With the integration of IoT and cloud computing domains, we can find numerous applications in various fields such as healthcare, agricultural, web forecasting, etc. Cloud computing platforms offer the number of service and deployment models used to bring flexibility and scalability to data. IoT applications use a variety of processing power and memory resources. So, the adaptability of cloud services is required to deal with new requirements, firmware, or system updates and offer new capabilities over time.

Role of Big Data Many more advanced IoT systems depend on the analysis of vast quantities of data. There is a need, for example, to extract patterns from historical data that can be used to drive decisions about future actions. IoT systems are thus often classic examples of 'Big Data' processing.

Real time Most of the IoT applications run in real world environment so that the data flows in continuous manner among different objects. There is a need to give on-time response to different events.

Distributed IoT systems can span whole buildings, cities, and even the globe. Wide distribution can also apply to data, which can be stored at the edge of the network or stored centrally. Distribution can also be applied to processing since some processing takes place centrally (in cloud services), but it can also take place at the edge of the network, either in the IoT gateways or even within (more capable types of) sensors and actuators. Today, there are officially more mobile devices than people in the world. Mobile devices and networks are one of the best known IoT devices and networks.

Heterogeneous systems IoT systems are often built using a very heterogeneous set up. This applies to sensors and actuators, and also to the types of networks involved and the variety of processing components. It is common for sensors to be low-power devices and it is often the case that these devices use specialized local networks to communicate. To enable internet scale access to devices of this kind, an IoT gateway is used.

Scalability Scale for IoT system applies in terms of the numbers of sensors and actuators connected to the system, the networks which connect them together, the amount of data associated with the system and its speed of movement, and also in terms of the amount of processing power required.

12.20 COMETCLOUD

A COMET Cloud (CCS) consists of a cloud service and data modem which is directly adaptable with an array of services. The CCS data modem is accessible with CDMA and GSM (International) connectivity. Averaged data is supposed to secure cloud site internationally an hour and domestically nearly 15–20 minutes. Modem location is available automatically from the involved GPS. With the CCS modem, the first year of data service is included.

With each COMET Cloud, a safety link is provided to a custom dashboard. The dashboard is from where the data is clearly seen, charted, and downloaded. By the use of Met One Instruments' updated COMET Software, downloaded data can be stored, displayed, analysed, and reported. Map overlays could be carried into the dashboard on which the sensor can be sited. The serial number of sensor is the ID number on the data report and map location. In the cloud, data are stored for up to two years. After the completion of two years, the oldest one is overwritten by new data. Data may be exported for analysis and reporting. By computer or any tablet or smart phone, COMET Cloud site can be accessed.

CometCloud offers:
1. Infrastructures services for dynamic coordination and federation in order to enable on-demand scale-down, scale-up, and scale-out
2. Programming support in order to enable programming models and services range for autonomic management and operation of the applications and infrastructure

CometCloud provides us the facility with scheduling like monitoring, analyser, managing data, etc. CometCloud works as an interface between cloud application and cloud user by providing support like research site, etc. as shown in Fig. 12.13.

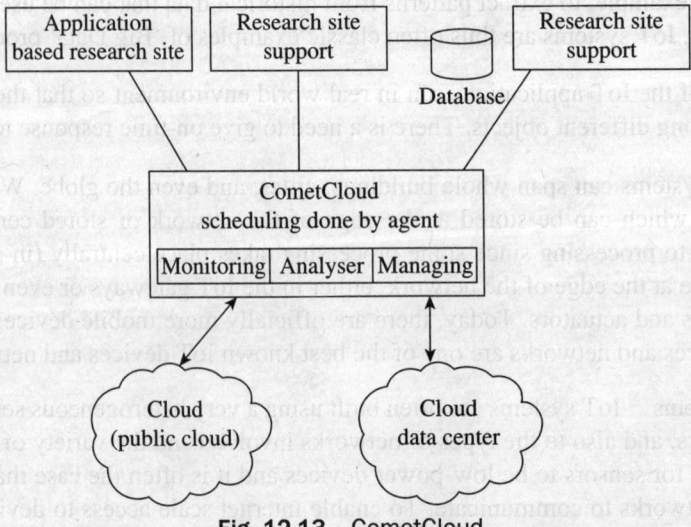

Fig. 12.13 CometCloud

12.21 T-SYSTEMS

Deutsche Telekom, one of the largest IT services companies in Germany, is the founder of T-Systems. Most of existing IT businesses and service of Deutsche Telekom were then incorporated and assimilated under the control of one single company, T-Systems. In 2008 Cognizant, global IT services provider and T-Systems entered into a global cooperation. In India, Cognizant took over operations of T-Systems. T-Systems is a market leader in Germany as well as working for the German government.

In order to support its global partners, T-Systems opened another branch in India known as T-Systems ICT India Pvt. Ltd. The company with its head office in Pune and another 'Point of Production' in Bangalore, is expanding in order to offer its ICT services to global customers of T-Systems International.

T-Systems, the IT service provider hand of German telco Deutsche Telekom, made announcement that the company plans to assimilate all of its cloud services onto a new unified, fully-redundant cloud infrastructure platform. The company informs its standardization efforts will help to improve the flexibility and automation of its services, and permits enterprises to execute more data privacy policies and robust data residency.

According to the company, it will standardize its cloud services, which includes its IaaS and collaboration and software services on its Dynamic Cloud Platform moving ahead, starting with its Munich datacenters, in conjunction with Cisco, fully redundant (based on "twin-core" principle) and linked with 10GbE between each datacenter, the platform was developed.

According to T-Systems, bringing all its heterogeneous offerings together on a single platform will increase the flexibility of services and get a higher level of automation to the back-end datacenter operations and network.

As shown in Fig. 12.14, virtual private network of an organization may have various types of department like heads quarter of the organization, manufacturing department etc. With the existing network, organizations can connect with other private cloud (supported by T-Systems), public cloud, etc.

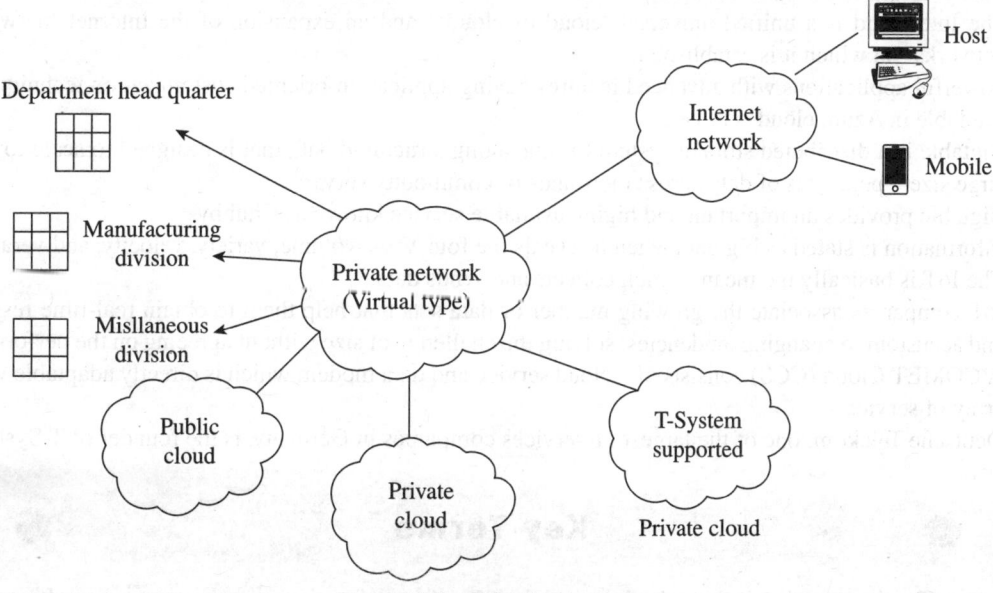

Fig. 12.14 T-System working

Points to Remember

1. Native applications are designed for particular devices and their supporting operating systems.
2. Perl is frequently used as an adhesive language, binding mutually systems and interfaces which were not specially intended to interoperate, changing or dispensing on huge amounts of data for jobs like generating reports.
3. Virtualization is generally employed to physical hardware resources by merging manifold physical resources into shared pools from where users obtain virtual resources.
4. Native apps are generally faster, whereas mobile cloud apps use mobile device browsers.
5. Google drawings support the creation, modification, and sharing of images or drawings among many users simultaneously.
6. Media cloud is an open platform, open source which permits scholars to answer quantitative queries regarding the matter of online media.
7. Securing the cloud is one of the issues that is an obstacle for cloud vendors, to save data from unauthorized and malicious users.
8. Virtual desktop infrastructure (VDI) is an environment where one desktop resource is shared by many users and non of them are aware of which resource they are sharing in the environment.
9. Mobile cloud computing (MCC) is the integration of mobile network computing, wireless networks, and cloud computing used to develop rich applications for mobile users.
10. Google App Engine supports Python.
11. For controlling a huge collection of compute, storage, and various networking resources in the cloud data center, a cloud operating system is used—this is called an open stack.
12. Cloud descriptor language uses the feature of XML like schema exchange. Cloud descriptor language sometimes use scripting language for its application.
13. Green computing is used to signify the effective use of resources in computing.
14. The Intercloud is a unified universal 'cloud of clouds' and an expansion of the Internet 'network of networks' on which it is established.
15. Powerful applications with advanced features having application-oriented customization techniques are available in Azure cloud services.
16. Bigtable is a distributed storage system for managing structured data that is designed to scale to a very large size—petabytes of data across thousands of commodity servers.
17. Bigtable provides an important and highly available service known as Chubby.
18. Information is stated as big data when it reveals the four V's—volume, variety, velocity, and veracity.
19. The IoT is basically the means which collects and sends data.
20. IoT companies associate the growing number of data sets that help them to obtain real-time responses and accustom to changing tendencies, solving the challenge of size without agreeing on the performance.
21. A COMET Cloud (CCS) consists of a cloud service and data modem which is directly adaptable with an array of services.
22. Deutsche Telekom, one of the largest IT services companies in Germany, is the founder of T-Systems.

Key Terms

Bigdata Cloud computing is an authoritative technology for performing complex computing. It eradicates the cost and need to sustain computing hardware, memory space, and software used for computing. Enormous growth in data or big data is produced through cloud computing, which is a challenge.

Green computing Efficient use of computing or resources to save energy is known as green computing.

Media cloud An open-source-type platform to permit researchers to answer questions or easily interact with the online media is known as media cloud.

Perl Perl is mostly used by the system administrator. It is an all-purpose program that supports writing short programs to be entered or run through the command line interface.

PiCloud It is a cloud-computing platform that integrates into Python. It allows developers to control the computing power of Amazon Web Services (AWS) without having to manage, maintain, or configure their own virtual servers.

Python Python is a powerful programming language that is easy to understand. It has proficient data structures with an effectual object-oriented programming approach. Python is a perfect language for scripting and various applications.

Scripts Scripts are special programs which run on the server and display a web page after they run. Scripts are very useful and used by dynamic web page designing that is content which changes with time.

Multiple-choice Questions

1. Device features are directly accessed by _____.
   (a) Mobile cloud applications
   (b) Native applications
   (c) Both (a) and (b)
   (d) None of these

2. Speed is faster in _____.
   (a) Mobile cloud applications
   (b) Native applications
   (c) Both (a) and (b)
   (d) None of these

3. Phython is a _____.
   (a) Scripting language used with Java
   (b) Server-side language
   (c) Web application framework
   (d) None of these

4. Google Docs has the _____ suite.
   (a) SaaS
   (b) PaaS
   (c) Iaas
   (d) None of these

5. Python has _____.
   (a) Strong introspection capabilities
   (b) Very high-level dynamic data types
   (c) Both (a) and (b)
   (d) None of these

6. In _____, the server runs a single instance operating system with multiple sessions.
   (a) Session-based computing
   (b) Operating system streaming
   (c) Virtual desktop infrastructure
   (d) All the above

7. The properties of a scripting language is/are _____.
   (a) Ease of use
   (b) Operating system facilities
   (c) Interpreted from source code
   (d) All the above

8. A native application is built for
   (a) A particular device
   (b) Its operating system
   (c) Both (a) and (b)
   (d) None of these

9. Google Docs serves as a collaborative tool for editing documents in real time so documents can be _____.
   (a) Shared by multiple users simultaneously
   (b) Opened by multiple users simultaneously
   (c) Edited by multiple users simultaneously
   (d) All the above

10. Popular languages in which you can write scripts for your website are:
    (a) PHP
    (b) Perl
    (c) ASP (Active Server Pages)
    (d) All the above

Review Questions

1. Explain the importance of green computing.
2. What is mobile computing?
3. What do you understand by media cloud?
4. How can you make your application cloud aware?
5. How can you make data secure on mobile computing?
6. How can you say that data is secure on cloud computing?
7. What are the different cloud descriptor languages?
8. What are the differences between mobile cloud applications and native applications?
9. What are the parameters to be considered in the near future to make the cloud more accessible?
10. What are the important features of Python language that support cloud computing?
11. What do you understand by app-specific clouds?
12. How can we remove carbon emission for survival of mankind?
13. Which tool is most useful to cloud users who are using community cloud? What is the essential requirement of the same?
14. How can we say that cloud has a high level of authentication and security checks for users?
15. Discuss the various parameters which explain that a cloud user is satisfied with the services provided by the cloud provider?
16. Discuss Big Data, IOT, and Bigtable.
17. Explain T-System and CometCloud.

References

1. *Cloud Security A Comprehensive Guide to Secure Cloud Computing*, Ronald L. Krutz and Russell Dean Vines, ISBN: 978-0-470-58987-8, Wiley Publication, 2010
2. *Cloud Computing for Dummies*, Judith Hurwitz, Robin Bloor, Marcia Kaufman, and Dr. Fern Halper, ISBN-10: 0470484705, Wiley Publication, 1st edition, November 16, 2009
3. *Cloud Computing Technologies and Strategies*, Brian J.S. Chee and Curtis Franklin, Jr, ISBN 9781439806128, CRC Press, April 7, 2010
4. *Cloud Computing: A Practical Approach*, Anthony T. Velte, Toby J. Velte, Ph.D., RobertElsenpeter, ISBN-10: 0071626948, McGraw-Hill, 1st edition, November 1, 2009
5. *Grid and Cloud Computing*, Katarina StanoevskaSlabeva, Thomas Wozniak, and Santi Ristol, ISBN-10: 3642051928, Springer, 2010 edition, November 19, 2009
6. *Implementing and Developing Cloud Applications*, David E.Y.Sarna, ISBN-10: 1439830827, Auerbach Publications, November 26, 2010
7. *Market-oriented Cloud computing: Vision, Hype, and Reality for Delivering IT Services as Computing Utilities*. In High Performance Computing and Communications, R. Buyya, C.S. Yeo, and S. Venugopal, 2008. HPCC'08. 10th IEEE International Conference on pp. 4–13 IEEE, 2008.
8. *Mastering Cloud Computing*, Rajkumar Buyya, Christian Vecchhiola, S. ThamaraiSelvi, Tata McGraw Hill Education Private Limited, 2008
9. *Cloud Computing and Virtualization*, V. Rajeswara Rao, V. ShubbaRamaiah, ISBN-10: 9383635045, BS Publications/BSP Books 2014
10. *Cloud Computing Concepts, Technology, and Architecture*, Thomas Erl, Zaigham Mahmood, Ricardo Puttini, ISBN-10: 0133387526, Pearson publication, 1st edition, May 10, 2013

11. Compilers, architecture, and synthesis for embedded systems (CASES), pp. 238–246, Nov 2001.
12. http://www.ibm.com/developerworks/cloud/library/cl-mapreduce
13. Steinke, B.: Reconfigurable object based multimedia display communication system for Smartphones. *Information and Telecommunication Technologies, 2008. APSITT. 7th Asia-Pacific Symposium on*, IEEE, 2008
14. Barth, A. and Jackson, C. and Reis, C.: Google Chrome Team. The security architecture of the chromium browser. *WWW2009*, April, 2009.
15. Lawton, G.: Moving the OS to the Web, *Computer Journal*, Vol. 41, No. 3, 2008, p.16–19

Answers to Multiple-choice Questions

1. (b)	3. (c)	5. (c)	7. (d)	9. (d)
2. (b)	4. (a)	6. (a)	8. (c)	10. (d)

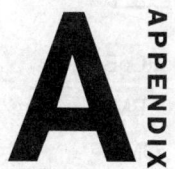

Abbreviations

API	Application Programming Interface
AWS	Amazon Web Services
AEC2	Amazon Elastic Compute Cloud
AMAZON S3	Amazon Simple Storage Service
AMI	Amazon Machine Image
AMAZON EC2	Amazon Elastic Compute Cloud
CC	Cluster Controller
CRM	Customer Relationship Management
CDN	Content Delivery Network
CFS	Completely Fair Scheduler
CLC	Cloud Controller
CM	Cloud Manager
COSO	Committee of Sponsoring Organizations of Treadway Commission
CCaaS	Compute Capacity as a Service
CDC	Cloud Data Center
COTS	Commercial, Off-the-shelf
CPU	Central Processing Unit
CRM	Customer Relationship Management
CaaS	Communications as a Service
DHCP	Dynamic Host Configuration Protocol
DaaS	Desktop as a Service
DBaaS	Database as a Service
EC2	Elastic Compute Cloud
EMI	Eucalyptus Machine Image
EU	European Union
FDS	Fire Dynamics Simulator

FCoE	Fibre Channel over Ethernet
FEM	Finite Element Method
GM	Group Manager
HTB	Hierarchical Token Bucket
HTML	HyperText Markup Language
HTTP	HyperText Transfer Protocol
IAAS	Infrastructure as a Service
IM	Instance Manager
I/O	Input/Output
IM	Information Management
LUN	Logical Unit numbers
MaaS	Monitoring as a Service
NIC	Network Interface Cards
PAAS	Platform as a Service
PDN	Public Data Network
PED	Personal Electronic Device
QoS	Quality of Service
REST	Representational State Transfer
RSA	Rivest, Shamir, and Adleman
RTT	Round-trip Time
RFC	Request For Comment
RFP	Request For Proposal
SMS	Short (or small) Message Service
SAAS	Software as a Service
SC	Storage Controller
SIP	Session Initiation Protocol
SLA	Service Level Agreement
SLO	Service Level Objective
SSD	Solid-State Drive
SSH	Secure Shell
SNMP	Simple Network Management Protocol
SOAP	Simple Object Access Protocol
SSD	Solid-State Drives
SDL	Security Development Lifecycle
SECaaS	Security as a Service

TCP	Transmission Control Protocol
UDP	User Datagram Protocol
VLAN	Virtual Local Area Network
VM	Virtual Machine
VPN	Virtual Private Network
VMM	Virtual Machine Monitor
VOIP	Voice over Internet Protocol
WS3	Walrus Storage Controller
WAP	Wireless Application Protocol. A standard commonly used for the development of applications for wireless Internet devices.
Whitebox test	Test in which the ethical hacking team has full knowledge of the target information system.
Whitehat hacker	An individual who conducts ethical hacking to help secure and protect an organization's information systems.
Wide area network (WAN)	A network that interconnects users over a wide area, usually encompassing different metropolitan areas.
WRG	White Rose Grid
WSDL	Web Services Description Language
WSDM	Web Services Distributed Management
WS	Web Services
XML	Extensible Markup Language

APPENDIX B
Study on Amazon Network

Amazon was one among those corporations which first proposed cloud services to the public. Amazon Web Services (AWS) provides an entire array of infrastructure and other application services which may operate virtually.

Amazon.com is an American multinational electronic commerce corporation with its headquarters in Seattle, Washington, United States. It is a leading online dealer which also manufactures customer electronics, especially the Kindle Fire tablet computer and the Amazon Kindle e-book reader, and is a chief supplier of cloud computing services.

Amazon has discrete trade websites for the following nations—France, United States, United Kingdom, Germany, Canada, Italy, Japan, China, and Spain along with global distribution to other particular nations for a number of its goods. The corporation was titled after the River Amazon, one of the biggest rivers in the world, which was named after the Amazons, the renowned empire of female soldiers in Greek mythology. Amazon.com began as an online bookstore, but later diversified, promoting MP3 downloads, CDs, DVDs, software, electronics, video games, furniture, toys, jewellery, and apparel.

AWS Users Group is a cluster under Amazon, and supports the activities of the world's biggest Cloud Services supplier. This cluster is a space, a medium to get together and share experiences about Cloud Computing, particularly Amazon Web Services. Amazon VPC, RDS, S3, and EC2 are entranced in knowing more regarding how you and your corporation may benefit from AWS. This user group is not only for individuals who are fascinated by the technical features of AWS cloud computing platform.

Information Management (IM) and Customer Relationship Management (CRM) support the business policies of Amazon. The principal technology which persists in Amazon working is Linux based. Amazon possesses the three biggest Linux databases of the world. The principal data storehouse of Amazon is prepared by many Hewlett Packard servers along with four CPUs per node operating Oracle database software. Technology design of Amazon deals with millions of back-end strategies each day, in addition to inquiries from more than half a million third-party retailers. Along with hundreds of thousands of populace transferring their credit card numbers to servers of Amazon each day, safety is of prime importance. Netscape Secure Commerce Server, using the Secure Socket Layer protocol, has been employed by Amazon. This collects all credit card facts in a distinct database. The corporation also documents data on consumer purchases that facilitates them in suggesting or providing personal things as per need.

Reward of cloud computing is the access to switch capital infrastructure costs with low variable expenses which may limit your trade.

Amazon offers the following services:

Elastic Compute Cloud (EC2) Offers extra CPU cycles and virtual machines for your company.

Simple Storage Service (S3) Facilitates you to save matter up to five GB in volume in virtual storage service of Amazon.

Simple Queue Service (SQS) Facilitates your machines to converse with one another using this message-passing API.

SimpleDB A web service for operating inquiries on structured data in actual time. This service operates in secure combination with EC2 and S3, jointly offering the capacity to save, practice, and inquire about data suites in the cloud.

These services may be tough to use, as they have to be made via the command line. Virtual machines of Amazon are editions of Linux allocations. First, applications may be written on your machine and then uploaded to the cloud. The development of cloud computing has been catalyzed by AWS and continues to supply the most available means to fast influence utility computing.

Amazon EC2

Amazon EC2 is a web service which offers resizable compute competence in the cloud. It is intended to make webscale computing simpler for designers.

Easy web service of Amazon EC2 interface facilitates you to attain and organize capabilities with a nominal argument. It supplies you with total power of your computing resources and allows you to perform on a computing atmosphere established by Amazon. It lessens the time needed to attain and boot new server cases to minutes, permitting you to swiftly scale competence, both up and down since your computing necessities vary. Amazon EC2 modifies the economics of computing by permitting you to pay merely for facility which is used by you in reality.

Amazon EC2 Functionality

Amazon EC2 informs a factual virtual computing environment, permitting you to use web service interfaces in order to initiate cases with a variety of operating systems, insert them with your custom application setting, administer access authorizations of your network, and operate your image using few or as many systems as you wish.

We use Amazon EC2 in the following ways:
1. Choose a pre-configured shape Amazon Machine Image (AMI) for instant operation or to generate an AMI enclosing data, applications, libraries, and allied design settings.
2. Design network access and safety on the Amazon EC2 case.
3. Decide which case kind(s) you desire, then begin, finish, and scrutinize as many cases of your AMI as required, using the web service APIs or the administration devices offered.
4. Decide whether you desire to perform in multiple sites, consume static IP, or connect constant block storage to your cases.
5. Simply pay for the resources that were truly utilized by you, like data transfer or instance-hours.

Features of EC2

Elastic Amazon EC2 permits you to reduce or augment competence within minutes, not days or hours. You can deal with a single case, or hundreds and even thousands of server cases concurrently. As this is all manipulated with web service APIs, your application may mechanically scale itself up and down based on requirements.

Completely controlled You have total control over your cases. You have base access for everyone and you may interrelate with them as you can, with every machine. You can prevent your case whilst maintaining the data on your boot panel and then later resume a similar case using APIs web service.

Flexible You have the alternative of multiple case forms, software packages, and operating systems. Amazon EC2 permits you to choose an arrangement of CPU, memory, instance storage, and the boot panel extent which is best possible for your option of application and operating system.

Planned for use with other AWS Amazon EC2 functions in combination with Amazon Simple DB, Amazon S3, Amazon SQS, and Amazon Relational Database Service (Amazon RDS) to offer a complete declaration for storage, inquiry procedures, and computing transversely a broad series of applications.

Reliable Amazon EC2 offers an extremely trustworthy atmosphere where substitution cases may be unavoidably and swiftly commissioned. The service works inside datacenters and network infrastructure established by Amazon. The Amazon EC2 Service Level Agreement obligation gives nearly 100 per cent accessibility for every Amazon EC2 area.

Secure Amazon EC2 offers various means for protecting computer resources. Amazon EC2 comprises web service interfaces to design firewall settings which run network access to and amid clusters of cases. While deploying Amazon EC2 resources inside Amazon Virtual Private Cloud, you can segregate your compute cases by specifying the IP series you desire to use and attach to existing IT infrastructure using industry-standard encrypted. You could as well select to deploy dedicated instances into your VPC. Committed instances are Amazon EC2 instances which work on hardware dedicated to an only client for additional isolation.

Inexpensive Amazon EC2 exceeds the financial advantages of Amazon. You pay an incredibly minimal cost for the compute facility you truly utilize.

On-demand instances On-demand instances allow you to pay for the compute facility (by the hour) without any long-standing responsibility. This makes you free from the expenses and complications of preparing, purchasing, and retaining hardware and converts what are normally huge permanent expenses into a good deal of lesser variable expenses.

Reserved instances Reserved instances provide you the alternative to create a small, one-time imbursement for every case you desire to keep and consecutively obtain considerable concession on the hourly price for that case. Three reserved instance kinds are there (light, medium, and heavy utilization reserved instances) which facilitate you to bear the sum you pay upfront along with your efficient hourly cost.

Spot instances The spot price varies occasionally on the basis of supply and demand, and consumers whose offer meet or exceed it achieve access to the accessible spot instances. Spot instances may considerably lesser your Amazon EC2 expenses, if you have elasticity when your applications operate.

Easy to start Swiftly receive progress along with Amazon EC2 by pop in AWS Marketplace to select preconfigured software on Amazon Machine Images (AMIs).

Amazon S3

Amazon S3 is storage meant for the Internet. It is intended to formulate web-scale computing simpler for designers. It offers an easy web services interface which may be used to save and regain any sum of data, at whatever time, from wherever on the web. It provides every designer access to the similar exceedingly scalable, safe, dependable, speedy, economical infrastructure which is used by Amazon to operate its individual universal network of websites. The service targets to make best use of advantages of scale.

Recently, AWS launched Glacier, a low-priced storage service for the long-standing protection of data. Glacier of Amazon can be used conveniently. Every copy of data may be separated into two common classes—data security and construction.

Amazon announces three new Amazon EC2 features:

1. Now, consumers may deploy 64-bit Amazon Machine Images (AMIs). This facility permits you to scale athwart micro, typical, high memory, and high CPU. This supports cases with only 64-bit AMI.
2. The 13th Amazon EC2 case is perfect for various applications which need a rational sum of memory and CPU, but do not need all the resources.
3. Right now, it provides facility to consumers so they may log into Linux, right from inside the Amazon EC2 administration console, with the requirement to arrange further software customers.

References

1. http://aws.amazon.com/about-aws/whats-new/2012/03/07/three-new-Amazon-EC2-features, last accessed on May 17, 2018
2. http://aws.amazon.com/ec2/benefits of EC2, last accessed on May 17, 2015

APPENDIX C

Microsoft's Cloud

Cloud computing has the facility to provision resources on demand. It helps you to convert your datacenter into an IT as a Service platform. This signifies that you can convey applications to end users quicker than ever, with no investing in novel infrastructure, teaching fresh employees, or certifying innovative software. Cloud computing also assists your business run in the latest markets and converses with consumers in novel ways. You may push down the expenses of doing commerce and amplify your capability to adjust to varying market situations.

As cloud computing modifies the mode your corporation utilizes IT, you may alter the function of IT in your corporation and the manner in which your team conveys business accomplishment.

Be it in your datacenter, along with a service supplier, or from datacenters of Microsoft, the company supplies an alternative, and elasticity and power to accept cloud computing to meet the company's needs, via a personal cloud, a public cloud, or an amalgamation of the two.
Microsoft provides the following cloud computing offerings:

Private Cloud

The personal cloud of Microsoft provides you with flexibility and manages to exploit the influence of the cloud on your conditions. A Microsoft personal cloud offers back-to-back service administration regarding your workloads and applications, as a result of which you can concentrate more on business assessments.

Public Cloud

Microsoft's personal cloud was the initial step towards constructing a cloud, Windows Azure, that facilitates you to join the public cloud. Windows Azure is a cloud platform which authorizes you to build up and perform applications along with unrestrained scalability and user-friendliness. Along with this flexible platform, you can simply scale up or down to meet the needs of your company. Windows Azure permits your designers to build and operate applications swiftly, whilst controlling existing talents to expand applications with Java, or PHP, or .NET.

The future of the cloud seems to be a hybrid amalgamation of private and public cloud, instead of being just one or the other. There will be periods when you wish to operate a workload in a personal cloud and then transfer it up to a public cloud, and afterward transfer it back once more to your personal cloud. Cloud offerings are intended to ensure that the personal cloud and public cloud work jointly.

Along with the Microsoft cloud, you stay in complete power, be it is in the datacenter of Microsoft, a partner datacenter, or your datacenter. With Microsoft cloud, we acquire the following characteristics:
- A general set of administration devices
- The capability to view entire application in your personal, public, and conventional cloud situations from an only console.
- A general set of identity devices.

- As users log in, they acquire access to all the personal, public, and conventional cloud services you have agreed on giving them access to.
- Potential to build up applications that support both the public and personal cloud.

You can control the steady and recognizable knowledge of goods of Microsoft in the cloud, using current IT skill sets and technology you already possess, whilst taking the benefit of the latest assessment offered by the cloud situation. The investments made by you today will work for you in the future with the progress of cloud computing.

Whether the private information of a customer is saved on individual computers or within an online setting, or whether a mission-critical data of a company is saved internally or is on a hosted server and transmitted athwart the Internet, Microsoft comprehends that all of these situations ought to offer a reliable computing skill. As a corporation, Microsoft is at an exclusive position to offer both direction and technology which may propose a safer online experience. It also assists consumers avoid economic loss. Microsoft guarantees that the procedures, populace, and technologies the corporation employs offer more safe and secrecy-improving experiences, services, and goods.

Microsoft provides a trustworthy cloud through focus on three areas:
1. Consuming a risk-based information safety program which prioritizes and assesses safety and operational bullying to the company.
2. Renewing and retaining a thorough suite of safety measures which lessen risk.
3. Operating a framework of acquiescence, which guarantees controls, are intended properly and are working efficiently.

Microsoft saves consumers data and company functions via an inclusive Information Security Program and a grown-up approach for consent and strategy administration, repeated in-house and peripheral assessment of abilities and practices and heavy safety measures athwart the entire service layers. These means and procedures are how Microsoft meets the terms with business principles and maintains regulatory agreement with all the directions, laws, rules, and statutes whilst conveying services online to a universal consumer base.

The Microsoft cloud computing is the rational and physical infrastructure in addition to the hosted platform services and applications. The physical infrastructure comprises the data center amenities themselves, with the hardware and elements which support the networks and services. The rational infrastructure at Microsoft comprises unstructured data storage, routed networks, and operating system cases, whether working on physical or virtual resources.

Online applications operating in the Microsoft cloud comprise easy and versatile goods intended for an array of customers. The online services, secrecy, and safety needs may be set as offerings for the following:
1. Customer and small business services: Microsoft facilitates customer and small businesses using illustrations which comprise Windows Live Messenger.
2. Enterprise services: The Microsoft Business Productivity Online Standard Suite and Microsoft Dynamics CRM Online are the Enterprise Services of Microsoft.
3. Third-party hosted services: This comprises web-based applications which are built and performed by third parties using platform services offered via the Microsoft cloud computing situation.

The principal driver to generate an effectual safety program is to be aware of a safety programme. Microsoft knows that such traditions should be supported and authorized by corporation heads. The Microsoft management team has long been dedicated to building the appropriate encouragement and investments to drive safe activities.

Computing is a principal commercial value at Microsoft, directing everything that the company performs. At the basis of this scheme are the following four pillars:
- Privacy
- Security
- Reliability
- Business practices

Microsoft comprehends that achievement in the swiftly varying trade of online services is dependent upon the secrecy and safety of the data of consumers and the resiliency and the accessibility of the services Microsoft provides. Microsoft carefully intends and examines infrastructure and applications to globally known values so as to disclose these consent with laws and with in-house secrecy and safety strategies. Thus, Microsoft consumers gain from more alert investigating and scrutinizing, automatic patch distribution, price-reduction economies of scale, and continuing safety enhancement.

Microsoft is devoted to defend the safety of private information. The online service distribution groups use a diversity of safety technologies and measures to guard private data from illegal use, disclosure, or access. Microsoft software development groups apply the principles, classified in the Security Development Lifecycle (SDL), all through the progress and operational practices of the company.

Privacy by design Microsoft uses this theory across multiple means throughout the progress, preservation, and discharge of applications to guarantee that the data accumulated from consumers is for a specific reason and that the consumer is given suitable notice to facilitate informed supervisory. When data to be accumulated is categorized as extremely perceptive, further safety procedures like encrypting whilst in transfer, not working, or both, may be taken.

Privacy by default Microsoft offerings enquire with consumers for consent before accumulating or transmitting perceptive data. Once certified, such data is confined by measures like access control lists (ACLs) in amalgamation with identity verification means.

Privacy in deployment Microsoft reveals secrecy means to organizational consumers as suitable to permit them to set up suitable secrecy and safety strategies for their users.

Communications Microsoft keenly connects the public via publication of secrecy strategies, white papers, and other documentations concerning secrecy.

References

1. http://cdn.globalfoundationservices.com/documents/SecuringtheMSCloudMay09.pdf
2. http://www.microsoft.com/enterprise/fr-be/it-trends/cloud-computing/articles/A-Pragmatic-Approach-to-Security-in-the-Cloud.aspx, last accessed in May 2015

Appendix D: Study on Salesforce.com

Salesforce.com Inc. is an international enterprise software corporation having its headquarters in San Francisco, California, United States and best famous for its customer relationship management (CRM) product.

The corporation focuses on Software as a Service (SaaS). The Salesforce.com Foundation was established on a particular thought, resources, and technology to manufacture combined knowledge and facilitate deeds to enhance societies all across the globe.

Salesforce.com is a reliable head in CRM and cloud computing, and is a pioneer in the business world. The salesforce.com foundation formulates salesforce.com goods which are accessible to non-profit corporations via product concession.

The expression 'cloud computing' seems to have been derived from the drawings of clouds used to symbolize the Internet. The idea was derived from telecommunications corporations which moved from point-to-point data circuits to virtual private network (VPN) services. By optimizing resource consumption via load balancing, they might be able to complete their work more economically and proficiently.

Salesforce.com was one of the first delivery services in cloud computing, which was launched by the idea of conveying business applications through an easy website. Later, Amazon's Elastic Compute cloud (EC2), a commercial web service, facilitated people and small corporations to lease computers on which to operate their individual computer applications.

Eucalyptus, the first open source AWS API familiar platform for installing personal clouds, was trailed by OpenNebula, the foremost open source software for installing personal and combination clouds.

Capgemini was one among the first system integration experts to start a bond with SaaS and cloud. It has extensive skills and services, mainly for incorporating cloud applications by means of inheritance systems. Social media and zone specialists have worked with hundreds of customers to build new means for them to perform business, get to consumers, and share data athwart the value series using the benefits of the newest technology innovation.

Capgemini and salesforce.com could turn a business into a spirited social venture with redefined operational procedures, consumer experiences, and business modules. Through amalgamating the Salesforce SaaS platform, you can generate new consumer connections as you wish, now and in the future.

The key features of services include the following:
1. Synchronized consumer views: The entire consumer's information is present in a single place.
2. Always-on consumer service: Business services combine with social networks for an even larger incorporated environment for employees and consumers
3. Flexibility to install novel business projects and convey innovative services to the market.
4. With no disturbance, you may accomplish back-to-back social renovation.

5. Provide salespeople the devices to sell more
6. Observe consumer promotion in new ways.
7. Discovery meetings to assist you to plan the potentials for your association.

Some of the world's largest organizations have been experiencing the benefits delivered by cloud computing technology.

- *Proven Web-services amalgamation*: Cloud computing technology is much faster and simpler to amalgamate with further venture applications.
- *World-class service delivery*: Cloud computing infrastructures provide much better notable uptime numbers, total disaster recovery, and scalability.
- *No hardware or software to launch*: The total infrastructure of cloud computing is very simple and attractive because, in reality, it needs considerably lesser capital expenses in order to start up.
- *Lower-risk and quicker deployment*: You may work along with a cloud computing infrastructure with low risk and high security.
- *Support for deep customizations*: Several IT experts believe that cloud computing technology is unfeasible or complex to modify comprehensively, and thus is not a good option for versatile companies. The cloud computing infrastructure not only facilitates attractive and easy application configuration and customization, but also safeguards the customizations. Cloud computing technology is perfect for application progress in order to support developing requirements of your corporation.
- *Empowered business users*: IT does not use time to bring together slight modifications and operating statements. As cloud computing technology permits all this, point-and-click, easy customization, and state generation for trade users is possible.
- *Automatic upgrades which don't impact IT resources*: If we upgrade to the newest-and-supreme edition of the application, we will be enforced to expend time and resources to reconstruct. Cloud computing technology never compels you to choose amid protecting and upgrading your hard work, as those incorporations and customizations are mechanically conserved through an upgrade.
- *Pre-built, pre-integrated apps for cloud computing technology*: The Force.com AppExchange attributes hundreds of applications developed for cloud computing infrastructure, pre-incorporated with your Salesforce CRM application or your other application progress work on Force.com.

How Can We Create a Community in Salesforce?

Salesforce community is a website where customers and support agents can correspond publicly or privately. It supports an online discussion where people help each other.
Community creation is effortless in this regard. The steps are as follows:

1. From Setup, click Customize > Communities > Settings
2. Choose Enable Communities
3. Type a unique domain name for your community, and click Check Availability, since your company name is recognizable.
4. Click Save
5. Click OK on the confirmation message to enable your community
6. From Setup, click Customize > Communities > Manage Communities; then click New Community
7. Name your community
8. Accept the unique community URL, or type your own. This URL is added to the domain you created previously for your community
9. Click Create

References

1. http://www.cloudtweaks.com/2011/02/a-history-of-cloud-computing, last accessed in May 2018
2. http://www.salesforce.com/cloudcomputing, last accessed in May 2018
3. http://www.salesforce.com/us/developer/docs/workbook_service_cloud/workbook_service_cloud.pdf/create community, last accessed in May 2018
4. Evolution of Cloud Computing and Enabling Technologies, International Journal of Cloud Computing and Services Science (IJ-CLOSER) Vol.1, No.4, October 2012; pp. 182~198 ISSN: 2089-3337
5. http://usa.chinadaily.com.cn/epaper/2013-01/21/content_16148524.htm, last accessed in May 2018

APPENDIX E

Study of Hypervisors

The word 'hypervisor' was first used to refer to software which supplemented IBM 360/65. It permitted the model IBM to reveal its memory, partially as a copy IBM 7080 and partially behaving as an IBM 360. The software marked 'hypervisor' did the swapping among the two forms on a split-time basis. Two kinds of hypervisor are categorized as follows:

- Kind 1 (or local, bare metal) hypervisors work straightforwardly on the hardware of the host in order to manage the hardware and to control guest operating systems. A guest operating system therefore works on a further level over the hypervisor. The current counterpart of this is VMware, Citrix XenServer, Oracle VM Server, Microsoft Hyper-V, KVM hypervisor, etc.
- Kind 2 (or hosted) hypervisors work inside a traditional operating system atmosphere. Having the hypervisor layer as a separate second software level, guest operating systems work at the third level higher than the hardware. Examples of Kind 2 hypervisors are VirtualBox, BHyVe, and VMware Workstation.

Cloud computing was intended to tackle these two matters. Hardware virtualization is the principal technology which has made cloud computing probable. This model of the technology is known as hypervisor. Cloud computing consumes superior high-functioning server systems along with great sums of multiple processors, storage, and memory.

Figure E.1 shows how application and operating systems are linked with each other through virtualization. Hypervisor generates multiple virtual servers inside a physical server. Every virtual server might have its individual operating system (OS) deployed in it. Various virtual servers may be operated independently and concurrently of one another. Hypervisors permit the merging of the memory resources and processor. Deploying a hypervisor on the host server facilitates it in controlling various operating systems concurrently by using virtualization technology. The number of physical servers might be lessened significantly by using server virtualization.

A hypervisor is an operating system that signifies that it understands how to perform in a systematic mode. The hypervisor lies at the lowest levels of the hardware. Since in cloud computing you want to support numerous distinct operating environments, the hypervisor turns out to be a perfect transport means.

In other words, Kind 1 hypervisor operates in a straightforward way on the hardware, whereas Kind 2 hypervisor operates on an additional operating system, like Linux, Windows, or FreeBSD. Microsoft Hyper-V symbolizes a Kind 1. In both instances, the Hyper-V hypervisor loads earlier to the administration operating system and every virtual environment developed performs reliably on the hypervisor, and not by means of the administration operating system. Figure E.2 shows the types of hypervisors.

The hypervisor allows you to demonstrate similar applications on systems without having to physically make applications on every system. As a result of the hypervisor's design, it may be compatible with

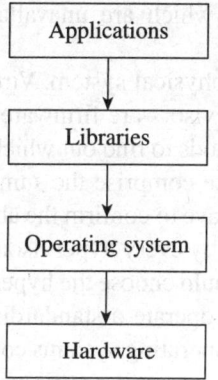

Fig. E.1 Operating system and application linking

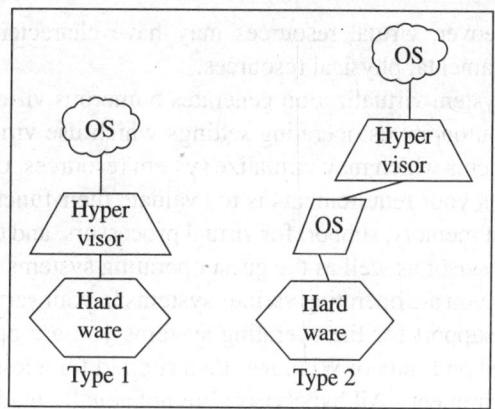

Fig. E.2 Types of hypervisors

any distinct operating system as though it was simply another application. Thus, the hypervisor is a very realistic means of attaining items virtualized proficiently and swiftly.

It is intended to be like a processor OS instead of a Windows operating system. The hypervisor have to decide on basis of some criteria to divide resources like CPU and input-output devices among guest and other operating system. Along with virtualization knowledge, you may use the hypervisor to divide the physical resources of a computer. Resources may be divided 50–50 or 80–20 among two guest OSs. The guest operating system never assumes it is working in a virtual panel; it assumes that it has a computer to itself.

Different Types of Hypervisors in Cloud Computing

Diverse hypervisors support distinct features of the cloud. Different kinds of hypervisors are available:
1. *Native hypervisors*, which rest reliably on the hardware platform, are most probably used to get enhanced functioning for personal users.
2. *Embedded hypervisors* are incorporated into a mainframe on a discrete chip. By using this kind of hypervisor, a service supplier achieves working enhancements.
3. *Hosted hypervisors* work as a different software layer over both the OS and the hardware. This kind of hypervisor is helpful, both in public and personal clouds, to achieve working enhancements.

Virtualization provides logical view to different users of a single physical resource, considering IT resources as rational resources instead of different physical resources. By using virtualization in your setting, you can merge resources such as storage, networks, and processors into a virtual setting that offers the following advantages:
1. Consolidation to lessen hardware charge
2. Workloads optimization
3. IT accessibility and elasticity

Virtualization is the formation of supple alternatives for genuine resources, alternates which have a similar operation and exterior interfaces, but vary in aspects such as performance, price, and amount. These alternates are known as virtual resources and their users are characteristically ignorant of the replacement.

Normally, virtualization is applied to physical hardware resources by merging multiple physical resources into shared groups from which users obtain virtual resources. Along with virtualization, you may create a single physical resource which appears similar to the manifold virtual resources.

Moreover, virtual resources may have characteristics or operations which are unavailable in their fundamental physical resources.

System virtualization generates numerous virtual systems inside a physical system. Virtual systems are autonomous operating settings which use virtual resources. Hypervisors are firmware or software elements which may virtualize system resources. One of the finest methods to find out which hypervisor meets your requirements is to evaluate their functioning metrics. These comprise the sum of host and guest memory, support for virtual processors, and CPU overhead. You have to confirm the abilities of the hypervisor as well as the guest operating systems which are supported by every hypervisor.

If you are operating various systems in your service network, you should choose the hypervisor which has support for the operating systems you are operating now. If you operate a standardized network based on Linux or Windows, then support for a lesser number of guest operating systems could suit your requirements. All hypervisors are not equally made, but each one provides similar attributes.

Factors Before Choosing Suitable Hypervisors

Virtual systems ought to better or atleast meet the working of their physical equivalent, in any case, in relation to the applications inside every server. It is desired that every hypervisor optimizes resources to make best use of the working for every virtual machine.

Live immigration is extremely vital for users, as it supports diagonally distinct platforms and the ability to concurrently use two or more VMs. You would need to think what the personal hypervisors provided in this field are.

There are two primary approaches to virtualization:
- Platform virtualization (e.g., server)
- Resources virtualization (e.g., storage network)

Server virtualization separates the only physical machine into various virtual servers. The major server virtualization classes are complete virtualization, OS-level virtualization, and para-virtualization. Complete virtualization permits hypervisors to operate a basic guest operating system and it is ignorant to think that it can be virtualized. The para-virtualization method comprises the operating system with the intention that it is conscious of being virtualized. Operating system-level virtualization method offers a well-organized design with a single operating system case.

Storage virtualization groups numerous physical storage resources into an only storage resource and it is centrally controlled. Network virtualization merges the accessible resources in a network by dividing the accessible bandwidth into channels.

Note: As you have already studied the various type of virtualization (i.e., Server, Network, and Application in the chapter 6, chapter 7, and chapter 8, respectively), you can implement these concepts by using open source Hypervisor i.e. VirtualBox. Please visit the website https://www.virtualbox.org/manual/UserManual.html/ and download the user manual by following the guidelines for installations of Virtual box. Please keep in mind before installation of VitualBox hypervisor software read carefully how to install VirtualBox and follow the steps mentioned in the manual. Please visit the website https://www.virtualbox.org/wiki/Downloads for download the VirtualBox software.

References

1. Hypervisor performance: www.cc.iitd.ernet.in/misc/cloud/hypervisor_performance.pdf, last accessed in May 2018
2. Hypervisor overview: http://home.ubalt.edu/abento/315/hypervisor/index.html, last accessed in 2015
3. VirtualBox: https://www.virtualbox.org, last accessed in May 2018

APPENDIX F

Study on Eucalyptus

Eucalyptus is a software platform for on-premise (personal) Infrastructure as a Service (IaaS) clouds, with no requirement for retooling the existing IT infrastructure of the company or for initiating any particular hardware. The platform sustains great assurance with the Amazon Web Services (AWS) API, facilitating support for both hybrid and IaaS clouds on-premise. Such compatibility permits every Eucalyptus cloud to be converted into a hybrid IaaS installation, competent of transferring workloads among on-premise data centers and AWS. Eucalyptus is well-matched with prosperity of applications and devices.

Eucalyptus was initially developed as an open source cloud and currently supports venture-group personal cloud with hybrid cloud computing. Presented infrastructure has been used by Eucalyptus in order to generate a scalable, safe web services layer which condenses compute, safety groups, storage and network to provide IaaS. It acquires benefit of current infrastructure virtualization software to generate flexible groups which may be dynamically scaled up or down on the basis of application workloads. Eucalyptus web services are exclusively intended for hybrid clouds by using the business standard AWS API. The advantages are power, extremely proficient scalability, and amplified faith for ItaaS.

Eucalyptus is well-matched with Amazon APIs so as users can control Eucalyptus instructions to administer Eucalyptus or Amazon cases. Cloud users may as well shift among the Amazon public cloud and a Eucalyptus personal cloud in order to make a hybrid cloud. Eucalyptus controls operating system virtualization in order to attain isolation among applications.

Benefits of Eucalyptus

- Reduced Public Cloud expenditure
- Organizational Agility
- Operational Efficiency
- Improved Performance
- Cloud Reliability
- Security and Control
- Infrastructure Flexibility
- Dynamic Scalability
- Hybrid Capability

Currently, Eucalyptus 3.3 is obtainable and the buildup of novel AWS-familiar aspects makes it perfect for examining and growing applications made for AWS. A Eucalyptus personal cloud speeds up time to market by supplying a reliable and consistent setting which covers both public and personal clouds. Eucalyptus supports numerous methodologies for self-service IaaS. The web-based Eucalyptus User Console offers IaaS users secure access to provisioning and demanding cloud images and resources. Likewise, Eucalyptus may offer incorporated self-service portals and cloud service administration for supporting users. The Eucalyptus platform too offers a dynamic compilation of web services for designers to create convention self-service interfaces. Fig. F.1 shows Structure of Eucalyptus.

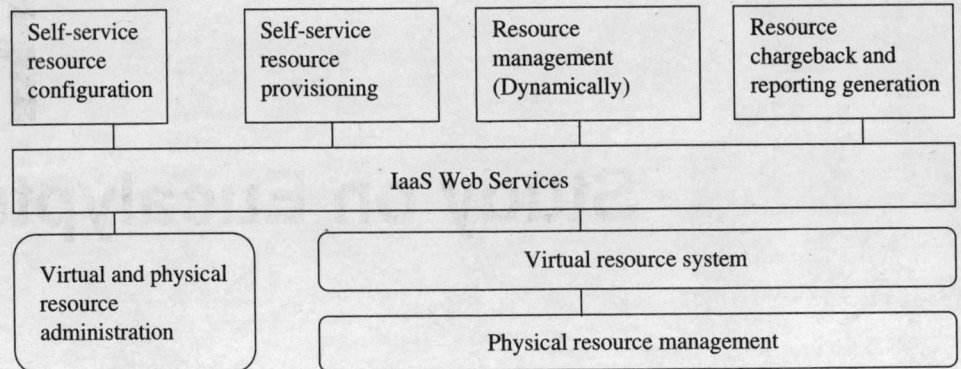

Fig. F.1 Structure of Eucalyptus

The following is an explanation of terminology and concepts used by Eucalyptus:
- *Instances*: When an image is set to use, it is called an instance that can be vigorously implemented at runtime and the cloud organizer determines where the image will work, networking and storage is assigned to meet resource requirements.
- *IP addressing*: Eucalyptus has a personal IP but may too have a public IP. Eucalyptus too supports flexible IPs.
- *Safety*: Eucalyptus too supports safety of layer two.
- *Networking*: There are four forms of networking. In Managed form, Eucalyptus deals a native network of cases, comprising safety pools and flexible IPs. Eucalyptus acquires complete benefit of flexible IPs and safety pools.
- *Access Control*: Eucalyptus user is allotted individuality, and individualities may be pooled collectively for access control.

Cloud computing systems basically offer access to huge sums of computational resources and data via a diversity of interfaces. In general, numerous existing systems possess the idea that resources may be attained and free on-demand and which the user interfaces must be maintained quite easy. Besides, resources offered by cloud computing systems conceal a big pact of data from the user via virtualization.

It is an open source software structure for cloud computing which executes what is usually taken to as IaaS systems, which let users the facility to manage and operate whole virtual machine cases installed athwart a diversity of physical resources.

There are several measures wherein data storage and computational control amenities are offered to users, varying from a user accessing a only laptop to the distribution of thousands of compute connections disseminated all over the globe. Normally users discover resources according to a variety of distinctiveness, comprising the network connectivity, memory and storage capacity, hardware design, and rarely geographic position. Web browsers and tools help us to access Eucalyptus and basic architecture of Eucalyptus consists of cloud controller having different clusters with many nodes.

Since number of cloud computing systems continues to develop, noteworthy study is needed to decide guidelines we may follow toward the aim of creating future cloud computing platforms beneficial. Presently, the majority of accessible cloud-computing offerings are either proprietary or depend on software. Researchers concerned in practicing cloud-computing infrastructure inquiries have a small number of devices by which to work.

Open-source cloud-computing structure is one which uses storage and computational infrastructure universally accessible to intellectual research pools in order to offer a platform. Along with Eucalyptus, it is meant to tackle open inquiries in cloud computing whilst offering a universal open-source structure. Eucalyptus is compiled of numerous elements which interrelate with each another via definite interfaces.

The design of the Eucalyptus system is modular, easy and supple with a hierarchical informative general resource settings discovered in various intellectual situations. Fundamentally, the system permits users to begin control, access, and finish virtual machines using an emulation of query interfaces and Amazon EC2's SOAP. Namely, Eucalyptus users interrelate with the system by using the literal similar interfaces and devices which they use to interrelate with Amazon EC2.

Eucalyptus utilizes a hierarchical intend to reveal fundamental resource topologies. Three high-level elements are there, each with its individual Web-service interface, which includes a Eucalyptus deployment:

- Group Manager collects information concerning and plans implementation of VM on particular instance supervisors, in addition to controls virtual case network.
- Cloud Manager is the access-point into the cloud for managers and users. It questions joint executives for information regarding resources, creates stylish arrangement, and executes them by creating needs to group supervisors.
- An Instance Manager (IM) performs and operates the system software. Every case is allocated a public interface associated to the physical Ethernet, and a personal interface associated to a virtual distributed Ethernet (VDE) in reply to questions and deal requirements from its Group Manager. An IM forms questions to find out the physical resources with the core number, the accessible disk space, and the memory size, and to discover regarding the condition of VM. The data hence composed, is transmitted up to the Group Manager in replies to depict instances needs and resource.

Reference

1. Eucalyptus:http://www.dxc.technology/cloud/offerings/140037/140196-managed_cloud_services, last accessed in May 2018

Study on Cloud Simulators

Cloud computing is a tool to automate businesses that might help business players to alter a few of their IT infrastructure expenditures into a further flexible on-order resource provisioning module. Cloud computing is the foremost technology for transfer of scalable, consistent, sustainable, safe, and error-lenient computational services. Cloud systems are convenient, appropriate for appraisal of novel cloud strategies, and have applications prior to genuine progress of cloud goods.

CloudSim

CloudSim is a simulator used for cloud computing. The aim of CloudSim is to offer an extensible and comprehensive simulation which allows simulated testing and modeling of potential application services and cloud computing infrastructures, permitting its users to concentrate on particular systems.

CloudSim is built in the distributed systems and cloud computing laboratory, at the Computer Science and Software Engineering Department of the University of Melbourne.

Main Features
- Support for simulated and modeling of huge-scale cloud computing data centers
- Support for simulation and modeling of virtualized server hosts, along with customizable strategies for provisioning host resources to virtual machines
- Support for simulation and modeling of energy-conscious computational resources
- Support for simulation and modeling of message-transient applications and data center network topologies
- Support for user-definite strategies for allotment of hosts to virtual machines and strategies for allotment of host resources to virtual machines.

iCanCloud

iCanCloud is a simulation platform meant to copy and imitate cloud computing systems. The chief aim of iCanCloud is to provide a suite of applications implemented in a particular hardware and then offer to users helpful data. iCanCloud may be used by a broad variety of users, from fundamental committed users to designers of great disseminated applications.

The most outstanding attributes of the iCanCloud imitation platform comprise the following:
1. Both accessible and non-accessible cloud computing designs may be copied and imitated.
2. A supple cloud hypervisor unit offers a simple technique for incorporating and experimenting both fresh and existing cloud strategies.
3. Customizable VMs may be used to swiftly imitate multi-core or uni-core systems.
4. iCanCloud offers a broad variety of configurations for storage systems that comprise regional storage systems, isolated storage systems, and equivalent storage systems, such as RAID systems and parallel file systems.

5. iCanCloud offers a comprehensible GUI to relieve the cohort and customization of huge disseminated models. This GUI is particularly helpful for running a depository of pre-configured cloud systems, running a depository of pre-configured VMs, creating graphical reports, installing tests from the GUI, and running a depository of pre-configured tests.
6. Novel elements may be added to the depository of iCanCloud to amplify the functionality of the imitation platform.

Simulation methods have turned out to be a powerful device for determining the finest preliminary situation in 'pay-as-you-go' circumstances. For developing fresh plans targeted at distinct topics related to cloud computing, lots of money and work is needed to establish a sufficiently sized test bed comprising distinct datacenters from public cloud suppliers and distinct companies.

Even though automatic devices subsist to perform such work, it would be extremely hard to create a functioning appraisal in a guarded and repeatable mode, because of the inconsistency of the cloud. Thus, it is simpler to use imitation as a device for studying versatile circumstances. In the area of cloud computing, simulators turn out to be particularly helpful for calculating the trade-offs between cost and working in pay-as-you-go situations.

Installing iCanCloud Simulation Platform

1. Download iCanCloud from www.iCanCloudSim.org.
2. Extract iCanCloud. Now, a folder called omnetpp-4.X is generated. This folder contains the OMNeT++ framework, the INET framework, and iCanCloud.
3. Install OMNeT++. There is a very detailed installation guide in ~/omnetpp- 4.X/doc/installGuide.pdf. Installing OMNeT requires (Flex, bison, tcltk ..).
4. Install INET.
    (a) Launch omnetpp IDE. Select folder ~/omnetpp-4.X as workspace. tar -zxvf iCanCloud-YYYY_MM_DD.tgz
    (b) Import INET to the workspace (File -> Import).
    (c) Compile INET
5. Install iCanCloud
    (a) Launch omnetpp (if not running)
    (b) Import iCanCloud to the workspace.
        (i) File -> Import… -> Existing projects into Workspace
        (ii) Select iCanCloud folder
        (iii) Click Finish
    (c) Compile iCanCloud

References

1. Cloudsim: http://www.cloudbus.org/cloudsim, last accessed in May 2018
2. iCanCloud quickguid installation: https://www.arcos.inf.uc3m.es/old/icancloud/downloads/iCanCloud_installationGuide.pdf, last accessed in May 2018

Study of Aneka

For developing disseminated applications on the cloud, there is a framework and a platform called Aneka which controls the extra CPU cycles of a heterogeneous network of data centers or servers and desktop PCs on a need basis. A rich group of application programming interfaces (APIs) has been offered to developers by Aneka for evidently using such resources and articulating the business logic of applications with the chosen programming abstractions. In order to check and manage the installed infrastructure, system administrators may influence a compilation of tools. This may be a public cloud accessible to anybody via the Internet, or a private cloud comprised by a set of nodes with controlled access.

A computing cloud based on Aneka is a cluster of virtualized and physical resources associated via a network that are either a private intranet or the internet. All of these resources host an instance of the Aneka Container signifying the runtime setting where the disseminated applications are implemented. The necessary management features a single node and leverages all other operations on the services it is hosting and are presented by the container.

Aneka application consists of infrastructure such as database, platform supporting layer, fabric services layer, foundation services supporting layer, application services supporting layer, and middle layer which is an interface between application development layer and other layers as shown in Fig. H.1.

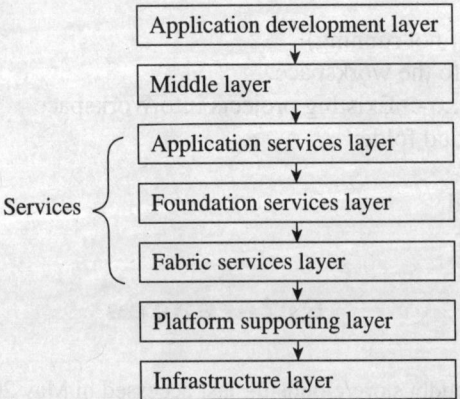

Fig. H.1 Aneka application method

The services are categorized into fabric, foundation, and application services. Fabric services interrelate with the node via the platform abstraction layer (PAL) and execute hardware profiling and dynamic resource provisioning. Foundation services recognize the core system of the Aneka middleware, supplying a set of essential features to facilitate Aneka containers to execute specific and specialized sets of jobs. Execution services unswervingly deal with the scheduling and execution of applications in the cloud.

One of the important characteristics of Aneka is its capability of presenting various ways for articulating circulated applications by presenting various programming models; execution services are generally involved with supplying the middleware with an accomplishment for these models. Further services like safety and persistence are transversal to the whole stack of services which are hosted by the container. At the application level, an array of various devices and components are given to (a) port accessible applications to the cloud, (b) simplify the development of applications (SDK), and (c) run and supervise the Aneka cloud.

An Aneka-based cloud is comprised of an array of interrelated resources which are animatedly customized as per requirements of the user by using resource virtualization or by attaching the extra CPU cycles of desktop machines. If the operation recognizes a private cloud, all the resources are in house, for instance, within the venture. The operation is expanded by adding publicly accessible resources on requirement or by cooperating with other Aneka public clouds offering computing resources associated over the internet.

Aneka is a market-oriented cloud and an expansion platform with speedy application development and workload distribution abilities. It is an incorporated middleware package that permits you to flawlessly build and handle a unified network besides accelerating development, operation, and management of disseminated applications using Microsoft .NET frameworks on these networks. Aneka is market-oriented as it permits you to build, plan, provision, and observe results using accounting, pricing, QoS/SLA services in private and/or public (leased) network settings.

Aneka is a workload allotment and running platform which hastens applications in Microsoft .NET framework settings. A few of the major benefits of Aneka over other GRID or cluster-based workload distribution solutions comprise the following:
1. Speedy disposition tools and framework
2. Support of multiple programming and application settings
3. Capability to control multiple virtual and/or physical machines for hastening application results
4. Built on-top of Microsoft .NET framework, with support for Linux environments via Mono
5. Provisioning on the bases of QoS/SLA
6. Instantaneous support of multiple run-time situations

Aneka has four key constituents—Aneka Master, Aneka Worker, Aneka Management Console, and Aneka programming models as shown in Fig. H.2. The Aneka Master and Aneka Worker are both Aneka containers which characterize the basic arrangement of Aneka based clouds. Aneka containers host various kinds of services depending on their role. Apart from mandatory services various others are also supported such as scheduling, reporting, etc., and worker support for running execution service. The master container is liable for managing the whole Aneka cloud, organizing the performance of applications, while the worker container is responsible for executing the work units, observing the execution, and gathering and forwarding the results of various applications.

The management studio and programming model (client libraries) provide support in handling the Aneka cloud and developing applications for utilizing resources on the cloud. The management studio is an administrative support which can be used to configure Aneka clouds, start or stop various containers, create user accounts, and set permissions for accessing available cloud resources. Aneka PaaS supports three different kinds of cloud programming—Task Programming, Thread Programming, and MapReduce Programming.

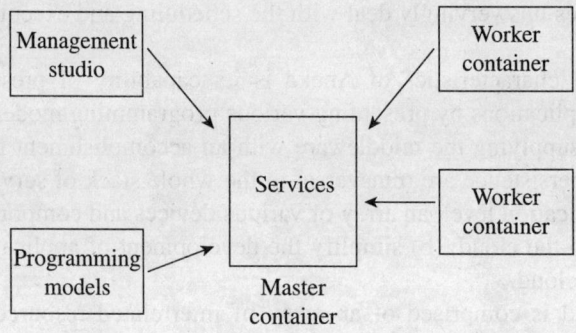

Fig. H.2 Aneka basic architecture

One of the major characteristics of Aneka is its aid for provisioning resources on various public cloud providers, for example, GoGrid, Amazon EC2, and Windows Azure. In this section, we will introduce Aneka platform and its assimilation with one of the public cloud infrastructures, Windows Azure, that permits the usage of Windows Azure Compute Service as a resource provider of Aneka PaaS. The assimilation of the two platforms will permit users to influence the power of Windows Azure Platform for Aneka cloud computing, utilizing a large number of compute cases to manage their applications equivalently. Moreover, consumers of the Windows Azure platform may gain from the assimilation with Aneka PaaS by implementation of the advanced characteristics of Aneka in terms of numerous programming models, application execution services, scheduling and management services, dynamic provisioning services, and accounting and pricing services.

Computing cloud based on the Aneka is a cluster of virtualized and physical resources associated via a network that might be a private intranet or the Internet. All of these resources host a case of the Aneka container, signifying the runtime setting wherein the disseminated applications are accomplished. The container offers the essential management features of the single node and controls all the other operations on the services which it is hosting.

Characteristics of Aneka Cloud Application Development Platform

To Windows Azure application users, the assimilation of Windows Azure Platform and Aneka PaaS permits them to comprise the following advanced features from Aneka PaaS:

Multiple programming models Aneka PaaS offers consumers with three distinct types of cloud programming models that include *Map Reduce programming*, *task programming*, and *thread programming* in order to cover various application circumstances, severely decreasing the time desired to develop cloud-aware applications.

Scheduling and management services Scheduling service of the Aneka PaaS may accelerate the cluster of jobs which make the Aneka application to compute nodes in a totally transparent way. The consumers need not look into the setting up and running of the application execution.

Execution services Execution services of the Aneka PaaS may execute the execution of disseminated application and gather the outcome on the Aneka worker container runtime situation.

Accounting and pricing services Accounting and pricing services of Aneka PaaS facilitate billing the final consumer for using the cloud by maintaining a record of the applications operating and supplying supple pricing approaches which are of profit to both the service providers and the final consumers of the application.

Dynamic provisioning services At present, the pricing model for Windows Azure as is such that consumers have to pay at an hourly rate on the basis of the size of the compute case. Hence, it is logical to add cases to a disposition at runtime as per the load and necessity of the application. Likewise, cases can be animatedly reduced or the whole disposition can be removed for avoiding charges if not being used actively. One of the main characteristics is its support for dynamic provisioning which may be used to influence resources animatedly for scaling up and down Aneka clouds, managing the lifespan of virtual nodes.

The safety layer gives support to the safety infrastructure of Aneka. This layer divides substantiation, which means recognizing who the consumers are—from permission—which means what consumers are permitted to do. The execution of these two functions relies on suppliers that extract the two operations in the framework, and consumer credentials, that have the information needed by the suppliers to verify and permit consumers. Prior to any operation for the user is executed on the Aneka Cloud, its credentials are confirmed against the verification and sanction suppliers, who can refuse or permit the operation. Specific executions of these two suppliers may be flawlessly included into the infrastructure merely by controlling the configuration of the container. In this way, it is probable to operate Aneka on diverse security infrastructure as per the specific needs of the cloud. Specific dispositions may need the use of current safety infrastructures. In this instance, the particular execution of safety suppliers will depend on the current security model and user credentials will have the necessary information for interpreting the consumer in the underlying safety system. This has been the tactic for supporting the Windows authentication in Aneka. In the instance of Windows-based dispositions, Aneka can trust the Windows integrated safety and offer access to the system for specific Windows users. Alternatively, it is likely to set up a cloud with no safety at all, merely by using the unidentified safety providers, which do not execute any safety check for consumer applications. Third parties may establish their own safety suppliers by executing the interfaces named in the Aneka security APIs.

Aneka offers a platform on which it is possible to develop applications for the cloud. All that is necessary from a development point of view is addressed through Software Development Kit; however, this is only a part of the feature collection needed by a cloud computing platform. The support for examining, running, sustaining, and setting up computing clouds is vital. These operations are depicted by the management API and the platform abstraction layer on which all the management devices and interfaces have been planned, of specific interest are the web management interfaces and the Management Studio.

A significant device for system managers is the Management Studio, which is a comprehensive setting which permits them to handle every feature of the Aneka clouds from an accessible graphical user interface. As clouds are comprised of hundreds and even thousands of machines, both virtual and physical, it is unfeasible to reach and set up every single machine by hand. Having a device which permits global and remote management is then an essential necessity. Concisely, the set of operations which can be executed through the Management Studio are as follows:

1. Speedy set-up of computing clouds
2. Remote setting up and arrangement of nodes
3. System load supervising and regulating
4. Remote managing of containers

Further, the remote control characteristics considerably abridge the management of the cloud. It is significant to perceive the support for screening the cumulative dynamic data of Aneka clouds. This assists supervisors to alter the complete performance of the cloud. It is also possible to explore every single node and accumulate data. The memory and CPU load information is gathered from every container and by checking the container arrangement, it is possible to recognize blockages in the cloud. Since in the whole framework, the Management Studio has been planned to be expansible, it is possible to include new services and new features by executing management plugins which are loaded into the milieu and approach the cloud.

The Management Studio is not a single device for running Aneka clouds. The structure offers a set of web interfaces which give a programmatic management of Aneka. Presently, just a constrained set of features—resource reservation and conciliation, task compliance, and observing—is accessible via web services, whereas the others are still under growth and testing.

References

1. David Chappell, Introducing the Windows AzurePlatform.David Chappell & Associates, October 2010.
2. Aneka- Azure Platform: http://www.cloudbus.org/papers/Aneka-AzurePlatform.pdf, last accessed in May 2018

MODEL QUESTION PAPERS

SET A

UNIT – I

Q.1 (a) What do you know about Computing Cluster? [3]
    (b) Distinguish between traditional Computer and Virtual Machine. [4]
    (c) Explain the architecture of Cloud Computing. [4]
    (d) Define MapReduce in detail. [4]
    (e) What is the structure of Cloud Controller? [4]
    (f) Describe the cloud storage system. [3]

UNIT – II

Q.2 (a) Discuss the Virtualization process at Instruction Set Architecture (ISA) level. [8]
    (b) Write a detailed note on Hypervisor. [8]
Q.3 (a) Explain Amdahl's Law in detail. [8]
    (b) Describe the classification of Distributed and Parallel Computing Systems. [8]
Q.4 (a) Differentiate between Public Cloud and Private Cloud. [8]
    (b) Give a brief explanation on various cloud services and their major providers. [8]
Q.5 (a) What are the attractive features of Hadoop? What is a Hadoop Cluster? [8]
    (b) What do you know about the HDFS and MapReduce architecture in Hadoop? [8]
Q.6 (a) What are the various policies of Cloud Resource Management (CRM)? [8]
    (b) Discuss coordination and performance management in cloud computing. [8]
Q.7 Write a detailed note on Amazon simple storage service (S3). [16]

UNIT – III

Q.1 (a) What is Cloud? [3]
    (b) What is a Virtual Machine? [4]
    (c) What are the benefits of using Cloud Computing? [4]
    (d) Provide any four advantages of MapReduce. [4]
    (e) What is Borrowed virtual time? Explain. [4]
    (f) What kind of data is stored in the cloud? [3]

UNIT – IV

Q.2 (a) Distinguish the various mechanisms for the implementation of resource management policies in Cloud. [8]
    (b) What are the control theory applications to CRM? List and explain. [8]

Q.3 (a) Write about Virtualization for Linux and Windows NT Platform. [8]
    (b) Discuss the method of Live Migration of VM from one host to another. [8]

Q.4 Give a detailed description of the various Cloud Service Models. [16]

Q.5 (a) What is a Google file system (GFS)? Explain. [8]
    (b) Describe Hadoop cluster in detail. [8]

Q.6 (a) Explain Service Oriented Layered Architecture in detail. [8]
    (b) What is a Computational Grid? Explain. [8]

Q.7 (a) Explain parallel file systems in detail. [8]
    (b) Provide the limitations of cloud storage. [8]

UNIT – V

Q.1 (a) Define GRID. [3]
    (b) What is Para-virtualization? [4]
    (c) Give some examples of Cloud Computing. [3]
    (d) Describe four uses of MapReduce in research. [4]
    (e) How would you explain resource bundling in cloud computing? [4]
    (f) How would you access My Cloud? [4]

UNIT – VI

Q.2 (a) Explain the various benefits of Cloud over traditional Distributed system. [8]
    (b) Give a detailed description of P2P network and its main categories. [8]

Q.3 (a) Discuss the process of Virtualization in Operating Systems (OS) Level. [8]
    (b) Explain Virtual Clusters in detail. [8]

Q.4 (a) What are the Security and Trust barriers in Cloud Computing? [8]
    (b) What is meant by Platform as a Service (PaaS)? Explain. [8]

Q.5 Provide a detailed description on Data Flow implementation of MapReduce. [16]

Q.6 (a) Provide different control theory applications to CRM. [8]
    (b) Discuss about a utility-based model for Cloud-based web services. [8]

Q.7 (a) What are distributed file systems? Explain. [8]
    (b) What are the business profits of cloud storage? [8]

UNIT – VII

Q.1 (a) What is a P2P Network? [4]
    (b) Explain the various challenges of Memory Virtualization. [4]
    (c) How would you describe the different types of Cloud Computing? [3]
    (d) What is meant by Hadoop? [4]
    (e) Describe Ascending Clock Auction in detail. [3]
    (f) What do you know about distributed file systems? [4]

UNIT – VIII

Q.2 Explain the following in detail:
    (a) Computational Data Grid [8]
    (b) Different types of challenges in Cloud Computing. [8]

Q.3 (a) Elucidate the course of Virtualization at Hardware Abstraction. [8]
    (b) Differentiate between Full Virtualization and Para-virtualization. [8]

Q.4 (a) Explain the Cloud echo system for creating a Private Cloud. [8]
    (b) Write in detail about Infrastructure as a Service (IaaS). [8]

Q.5 (a) Give a detailed description about MapReduce Architecture. [8]
    (b) Discuss Google File System (GFS) Architecture in detail. [8]

Q.6 (a) What is a Utility-based model for cloud-based web services? Give details. [8]
    (b) Explain the scheduling algorithms for computing clouds. [8]

Q.7 (a) Explain how a cloud storage works. [8]
    (b) List out all the personal benefits of cloud storage. [8]

SET B

UNIT – I [10 × 2 = 20]

Q.1 Define data security.
Q.2 What meant by cloud computing?
Q.3 What is risk management?
Q.4 Mention the design challenges in cloud architecture.
Q.5 Explain the mapping applications briefly.
Q.6 Explain the use of Google file system.
Q.7 Provide the features of virtualization.
Q.8 Define resource provisioning.
Q.9 Give a brief description of desktop virtualization.
Q.10 What is Elastic IP Addressing?

UNIT – II

Q.11 (a) (i) Discuss the system models for distributed and cloud computing. [7]
      (ii) Describe the characteristics of PaaS and SaaS. [6]
                    OR
   (b) (i) Differentiate between Public, Private, and Hybrid clouds. [7]
      (ii) Describe the NIST cloud computing reference architecture. [6]

Q.12 (a) (i) Discuss the virtualization structures. [6]
　　　　(ii) How to virtualize CPU? Explain. [7]
　　　　　　　　　　　　　OR
　　(b) (i) Explain the different types of virtualization. [7]
　　　　(ii) What do you know about server virtualization? What is parallel processing? [6]

Q.13 (a) (i) Explain how resources can be managed in inter cloud. [7]
　　　　(ii) Give a detailed description on global exchange of cloud resources. [6]
　　　　　　　　　　　　　OR
　　(b) Describe the architectural design of compute and storage clouds in detail. [13]

Q.14 (a) (i) Describe the Iterative MapReduce programming model using Twister. [7]
　　　　(ii) Differentiate between Parallel and Distributed Programming paradigms. [6]
　　　　　　　　　　　　　OR
　　(b) Write short notes note on:
　　　　(i) Google App Engine [7]
　　　　(ii) Open Nebula [6]

Q.15 (a) (i) What is the security architecture design framework? Explain. [7]
　　　　(ii) Give a detailed description on Virtual Machine security. [6]
　　　　　　　　　　　　　OR
　　(b) (i) Explain the cloud security challenges in detail. [6]
　　　　(ii) What do you know about security monitoring and incident response? Discuss. [7]

UNIT – III

Q.16 (a) Discuss the layered cloud architecture development with its design challenges. [15]
　　　　　　　　　　　　　OR
　　(b) Write a detailed description on Amazon AWS with cloud software environments. [15]

....

SET C

UNIT – I

Q.1 Discuss the cloud reference model in detail, along with its layers and types of clouds. [16]
　　　　　　　　　　　　　OR
Q.1 (a) Provide the architectural design of compute and storage clouds. [10]
　　(b) Explain fractures of cloud programming in brief. [6]

UNIT – II

Q.2 What is meant by cloud computing? Discuss the challenges, risks, and approaches of migration into cloud. [16]
　　　　　　　　　　　　　OR
Q.2 (a) List the ethical issues of cloud computing in detail. [8]
　　(b) Give brief descriptions on ubiquitous cloud and internet of things. [8]

UNIT – III

Q.3 Describe cloud security services along with design principles and security challenges in detail. [16]

OR

Q.3 Discuss data security in cloud in contrast to the following:
(a) Trust Management [5]
(b) SLA (Service Level Agreements) [6]
(b) Risk Mitigation [5]

UNIT – IV

Q.4 What is meant by virtualization technology? Discuss implementation level of virtualization along with the advantages of virtualization. [16]

OR

Q.4 Explain the following in brief:
(a) Virtual cluster and resource management [8]
(b) Virtualization of data-center [8]

UNIT – V

Q.5 Give brief descriptions on following (any two): [8 × 2 = 16]
(a) Cloud application platform-Integration of private and public cloud
(b) CRM and ERP
(c) Cloud scientific application
(d) Third-party cloud services

....

SET D

Q.1 Give short notes on the following: [10]
- Cloud Service Brokerage
- Mobile Cloud Computing
- Amazon Simple DB
- Modes of Eucalyptus

Q.2 (a) List the features of Google file system. [10]
(b) Describe Cloud Data Security in detail. [10]

Q.3 (a) Describe Openstack Architecture in detail. [10]
(b) Give a detailed description of Xen Architecture. [10]

Q.4 (a) State the impact of shared resources and multi-tenancy on cloud applications. [10]
(b) Mention the essential requirements for cloud applications architecture? [10]

Q.5 (a) Mention the techniques used for the risk assessment and management of cloud. [10]
(b) What is the AAA model for cloud? [10]

Q.6 (a) How would you explain cloud deployment models? [5]
(b) State the advantages of virtualization. [5]
(c) What is SaaS Maturity Model? [5]
(d) Describe different types of hypervisor with examples. [5]

Index

A

Administrating clouds   176
   CloudWatch   178
   Kaavo   177
   Morph   178
   RightScale   177
   Scalr   178
   Zeus   178
AJAX   245
   Demerits   246
   Merits   246
Alternative deployment models   92
   Jericho Cloud Cube Model   92
   Linthicum Model   92
Apache Virtual Computing Lab   238
App-specific clouds   259
   Virtualized desktop   259
Application virtualization   167
   Advantages of   168
   Flexera Software Supporting Application Virtualization   169
   Limitations of   168
   Microsoft Application Virtualization (App-V)   168
   Tools used for   168
   VMWare ThinApp   169
Architectural influences on cloud   32
   Autonomic computing   33
   High-performance computing   32
   High-scalability architecture   35
   Horizontal scaling   34
   Service consolidation   33
   Utility and enterprise grid computing   32
   Web services   35
Azure cloud services   272

B

Banking on cloud economics   193
Bigtable   273
   Columns   275
   Construction of   275
   Development of   276
   Structure of   274
   Tablets   274
   Timestamps   274
Business and information technology perspective   16
   Accounting and online banking   17
   Commerce on clouds   17
   Distributed hosting on clouds   17
   Electronic faxing   17
   Voice on clouds   17
Business continuity   107
Business intelligence   232
   Calculation of three financial RoI metrics   234

C

Challenges to cloud security   215
   Confidential information requiring safer storage   216
   Insecure applications   216
   Internal clouds intrinsically insecure   216
   Lack of risk awareness and security visibility   216
   More vigorous authorization and authentication   216
Characteristics of cloud computing   62
   Broad network access   63
   Calculated service   64
   Dynamic computing infrastructure   65
   Elasticity and scalability   66
   IT service-centric approach   65
   Multi-persistence   64
   On demand self services   63
   Quick elasticity   64
   Resource pooling   64
   Self-managed platform   66
   Self-service based usage model   65

Index

Standardized interfaces 66
Chubby 275
Clouds 17
   How to access 187
   News on 17
   Vulnerability assessment tools 213
   Workload patterns for 268
Cloud access control issues 223
   Browser security 223
   Cloud malware injection attack 224
   Data protection 224
   Flooding attacks 224
   Incomplete data deletion 224
   Lock-in 224
   XML signature element wrapping 223
Cloud analytics 114
Cloud and disaster recovery 108
Cloud and dynamic infrastructure 66
Cloud application development 36
   Challenges faced 36
   Design patterns 37
Cloud architectural consideration 213
   Micro architecture 213
Cloud architecture and applications 35
   Issues in scalability of 35
Cloud backup 107
Cloud computing 1, 4, 9, 18, 23, 31, 62, 72, 196, 219, 254
   Advanced technologies in 254
   Benefits of 18
   Characteristics of 62
   Essentials of 1
   Factors that affect 31
   History of 9
   Legal matters in 219
   Limitations of 18
   Models of 72
   Need of 4
   Security issues of 196
   Vendors of 23
Cloud computing architecture 48, 51
   On the basis of cloud balancing 58
   On the basis of disk provisioning 54
   On the basis of failure detection and recovery 59
   On the basis of hypervisor installed 55
   On the basis of load balancing 53
   On the basis of migration 56
   On the basis of service relocation 57
   On the basis of storage management 55
   On the basis of virtual switches load balancing 59
Cloud computing environment open-stack 264
Cloud computing sub service models 83
   Compliance as a service 83
   Everything as a service 83
   IaaS: compute capacity as a service (CCaaS) 84
   IaaS: database as a service (DBaaS) 84
   Identity as a service 84
   PaaS: desktop as a service (DTaaS) 84
   Paas: storage as a service (STaaS) 84
   SaaS: communications as a service (CaaS) 84
   SaaS: monitoring as a service (MaaS) 84
   SaaS: security as a service (SECaaS) 84
Cloud computing trends 254
   Cloud computing information security 255
   Dedicated cloud applications for mobile 255
   High commercial importance 254
   Hybrid cloud computing 255
Cloud data center requirements 31, 98
   Cloud data center 31
Cloud deployment models 85
   Community 89
   Hybrid 90
   Private 87
   Public 86
Cloud descriptor language 265
   Perl 266
   Python 266
   Scripting languages 266
Cloud information security objectives 199
   Client-side computing environment requirement 201
   Cloud computing environment and accessibility 200
   Cloud security services 201
   Confidentiality 200
   Integrity 201
   Organizational security and privacy requirements 200
Cloud infrastructure 21
Cloud infrastructure management and migration 176
Cloud management products 179
   Cloud infrastructure management and service creation tools 180
   Applications and platform software 180
   Physical infrastructure 179
   Virtual infrastructure 179

Cloud Mashup 241
    Platform Mashups 241
Cloud performance monitoring tools 235
Cloud providers and traditional it service
        providers 185
    Data limits and availability 186
    Performance 186
    Security 186
Cloud security design principles 201
    Complete mediation 203
    Defence in depth 202
    Defence in multiple places 203
    Deploy intrusion detection systems 203
    Deploy KMI/PKI 203
    Economy of mechanism 203
    Fail-safe 203
    Layered defences 203
    Least privilege 202
    Leveraging existing components 203
    Security robustness 203
    Separation of duties 202
Cloud security services 204
    Accountability 205
    Auditing 204
    Authentication 204
    Authorization 204
Cloud service models 72
    Cluster as a service 82
    Infrastructure as a service 80
    Platform as a service 76
    Software as a service 73
Cloud service suppliers and threats 247
CloudStack 93
Cloud storage 93
Cloud testing environment 208
    Cloud-based application testing over
        clouds 209
    Cloud/SaaS-oriented testing 208
    Online-based application testing
        on clouds 209
Cloud tools 256
Cloud usage for Big Data analytics and
        Internet of Things 276
    Big Data 277
Cloud with DiverseLook 256
Cluster as a service 82
    Design description 83
    Design issue needs 83
Cometcloud 282

Computer security incident response team 216
Common threats and vulnerabilities 221
Computing on demand 115
Computing platforms 230
Core components of traditional
        data centers 22
Core elements 98
    Application 99
    Compute 100
    Database management systems 99
    Network 103
    Storage 100

D

Database integrity issues 218
Desktop virtualization 160
    Advantages of 161
    Components for 166
    Infrastructure of 165
    Limitations of 162

E

Elastic computing 24
EMC 246
Enomaly Elastic Computing Platform 239
Enterprise cloud computing 25
Exploring cloud management products 231
Exploring network virtualization 143
    Benefits of 145
    Tools used in 145

F

Features of network components 146
    Virtual LAN 148
    Virtual switches 146
Force.com and Salesforce.com 238
Fragmentation attacks 223

G

Google App Engine 242
    Selecting an app engine environment 243
Green computing 267
Grid architecture 49
    Advantages of 50
    Challenges of 51
Grid and cloud computing 60
    Similarities and differences 60
Grid framework overview 48
Groupware clouds 260

H

Hadoop 240
Hardware virtual machine (HVM) 169
Hypervisor taxonomy 129

I

Identity management and access control 214
Impediments to cloud adoption 68
Inappropriate system uses 222
Independent software vendor 234
    Apica 234
    Chef 234
    CloudOpt 234
    CloudPassage 235
    CodeFutures 235
Influence of cloud computing on
        business companies 42
    Business alignment 43
    Governance 43
Information life cycle management 112
Information privacy and laws 221
Infrastructure as a service 80
    Machine virtualization 81
    Primary facets of 81
    Various service providers of 82
Input validation and content injection 218
Intercloud 236, 271
Internet of Things 277
    Applications of 278
    Architecture of 279
    Challenges of 279
    Different aspects of 281

K

Key design aspects of cloud architecture,
        cloud services, and cloud applications 59
    Issues at design level 60
    Issues related to the implementation 60

L

Limitations of cloud computing 18
    Availability of services 19
    Data location 20
    Data lock-in 19
    Data segregation 19
    Deletion of Data 21
    Offline clouds 21
    Privilege neglect 20
    Recovery and backup 21
    Scaling resources 20
    Unpredictable performance 21
Logical partitioning 134
Logon abuse 221

M

Machine imaging 171
Mapreduce 239
Media clouds 257
Microsoft Azure 244
    Media services 245
Microsoft Hyper-V 243
Migrating to clouds 191
    Advantages 192
    Challenges 192
    Disadvantages 192
Mobile cloud computing 262
    Advantages of 263
    Applications 264
    Disadvantages of 264
    Examples 264

N

Need of cloud computing 4
    Autonomic computing 14
    Client-server technology 9
    Disaster relief 7
    Distributed computing 11
    Ease of implementation 7
    Easy to customize 8
    Fully automated storage tiering—FAST 9
    Parallel computing 15
    Peer-to-peer technology 10
    Platform virtualization 14
    Reduced costs 5
    Remote access 6
    Response time 8
    Scalability 6
    Service oriented architecture—SOA 14
    Skilled vendors 8
    Utility computing 15
    Virtual provisioning 8
NetApp 247
Network attached storage 138
    Comparison between SAN and NAS 139
Network intrusion 222
Nimbus 242

O

Object-based storage technologies 105
Online analytical processing 232
Opennebula 241
Operational influences on cloud 40
    Automation 42
    Consolidation 40
    Information technology service management 42
    Outsourcing 41

P

Physical machine to virtual machine (P2V) conversion 131
    Conversion process 132
    Converter components 132
Physical security of systems 217
Platforms 187
Platform as a service 76
    Download 78
    Features of PaaS for application developers 79
    Google App Engine 78
    PaaS selected as per requirement 79
    Uniqueness in 77
    Using GoogleApp (first application) to make application 78
    Various service providers of 80
Porting application 171
Processes in cloud service management 182
    Availability administration 184
    Capacity administration 183
    Compliance administration 185
    Financial management 185
    Incident administration 183
    Performance administration 183
    Problem administration 184
    Service benefit and configuration administration 183
    Service catalog administration 184

Q

Quality of service issues in clouds 235

R

Regulatory issues 218
Remote desktop services 164
    Advantages of 165
    Disadvantages of 165

Replication technologies 109
Resource management and tools 129
Risk issues 217

S

Secure cloud software requirements 209
Secure cloud software testing 205
    Forms of 207
    Importance of 207
    Internet-based software testing vs cloud testing 208
    Need for 206
    Types of 206
Secure development practices 210
    Code practices 211
    Handling data 211
    Language options 212
    Physical security of systems 212
Secure execution environment and communications 214
Security clouds 258
Selection of cloud application 265
Server/compute virtualization 120, 121, 122, 125, 127
    Advantages of 127
    Before virtualization 121
    Components 122
    Need of 125
    Techniques of 127
    Virtual components in a virtual machine 121
Service level agreement 248
    Requirements of 248
Session hijacking attacks 222
Sky computing 236
SOA and cloud computing 231
Social networking 25
Software as a service 73
    Importance of 75
    Uniqueness in 76
    Various providers of 76
Storage area network 136
Storage network technologies and virtualization 104
    Components of fibre channel SAN 104

T

T-Systems 283
Techniques of server/compute virtualization 127

Full virtualization   127
Hardware assisted virtualization   127
Para virtualization   127
Technological influences on cloud   38
   Commoditization   39
   Open-source software   39
   Universal connectivity   39
   Virtualization   40
Third-party technology   249, 270
   Examples of third parties   271
Threats to infrastructure, data, and access control   198
   Cross site scripting   199
   Denial of service   198
   Man in the middle attack   198
   Network sniffing   198
   Port scanning   199
   SQL injection attack   199
Tplatform   237
Traditional data center management   110
Traffic management and its techniques   149
   Proposed load balancing in cloud computing   153
   Technique 1: balancing client workload—hardware   150
   Technique 2: balancing client workload—software   150
   Technique 3: storm control   151
   Technique 4: NIC teaming   152
   Technique 5: limit and share   152
   Technique 6: traffic shaping   152
Types of virtualization   134
   Data center   134
   Sensor   136
   Server   135
   Storage   135

U

Unified management software   180
Unified storage   106

V

Vendors of cloud computing   23
   Amazon Web Services—IaaS   23
   Google—SaaS, PaaS   23
   Microsoft Azure Service Platform—PaaS   23
   Rackspace—Cloud Hosting   24
   Salesforce.com—SaaS, PaaS   24
Virtual clusters   126
Virtual machine and hardware components   128
Virtual machine migration services   155
   Energy efficient   155
   Fault tolerant   155
   Load balancing   155
Virtual machine provisioning   172
Virtualization   163
   Drivers used in   163
   Features of   163
   Techniques used for   163
Virtualization reference model   119
Virtualization technology   119, 143, 160
   Advantages   120
   At desktop and application   160
   At network   143
   At server   119
VM security   214, 215
   Recommendations   214
   Techniques   215

W

Web Applications   187
Web Application Programming Interface   188
   Google Gadgets   189
Web Browsers   189
   Chrome   191
   Chrome Cloud   191
   Internet Explorer   190
   Mozilla Firefox   190
   Safari   190

X

Xen Cloud Platforms   237

About the Author

Shailendra Singh is presently Professor, Computer Science and Engineering, National Institute of Technical Teachers' Training and Research (Under Ministry of Human Resource Development, Govt. of India), Bhopal. Earlier, he was associated with Rajiv Gandhi Proudyogiki Vishwavidyalaya (RGPV), Bhopal, India.

With more than 20 years of experience in teaching as well as training for human resource and development, Dr Singh is on the panel of examiners of different Indian universities for the evaluation of doctoral and masters' level research work.

Dr Singh received his M.Tech. and Ph.D. degrees in Computer Science and Engineering in 2004 and 2010, respectively, from RGPV, Bhopal. He is senior member of IEEE, USA.

Prof. Singh has been bestowed with several honours and awards such as Eminent Educationist award, Bharat Ratna Dr APJ Abdul Kalam Excellence Award, Bharat Jyoti Award, and Best Research Paper Award in International Conference held in San Francisco USA.

Related Titles

Digital Image Processing, Second Edition [9780199459353]
S. Sridhar, Associate Professor, Department of Information Science and Technology, College of Engineering Guindy Campus, Anna University, Chennai.
This second edition of Digital Image Processing is designed as a textbook for undergraduate engineering students of Computer Science, Information Technology, Electronics and Communication, and Electrical Engineering.

Features

- A chapter on wavelet transforms and multiresolution analysis
- Topics such as image security, visual effects, Radon transform, digital image forensics, and computer vision
- Colour plates illustrating the effect of different image processing operations and image processing applications such as visual effects
- Additional illustrations, solved examples, and MATLAB exercises

Soft Computing with MATLAB Programming [9780199455423]
N.P. Padhy, faculty, Department of Electrical Engineering, Indian Institute of Technology Roorkee
S. P. Simon, Assistant Professor, Department of Electrical and Electronics Engineering, National Institute of Technology, Tiruchirappalli.
Soft Computing with MATLAB Programming is a textbook designed for undergraduate students of computer science, information technology, electrical and electronics, and electronics and communication engineering as well as those pursuing an MCA degree.

Features

- Discusses swarm intelligence systems with their fundamental concepts of exploration and exploitation
- Elaborates on Artificial Bee Colony algorithm and Cuckoo Search algorithm with suitable applications
- Provides more than 25 MATLAB programs with step-by-step comments and 75 solved problems
- Discusses swarm intelligent systems

Software Testing, Second Edition [9780199465873]
Naresh Chauhan, Professor, Department of Computer Engineering, YMCA University of Science & Technology, Faridabad
This second edition of Software Testing serves as a textbook for students of computer science, information technology, and computer applications.

Features

- A chapter on Agile Testing focusing on the agile testing methodology which has gained importance in recent years
- Strengthened coverage of dynamic testing techniques, with the inclusion of robust worst-case testing method, orthogonal array testing strategy, predicate coverage, and path sensitization
- Testing techniques such as reliability testing and system testing based on use-cases
- An appendix (available online) which provides an overview of the working environment and components of CAST tools such as JMeter, JUnit, and Selenium

Cyber Forensics [9780199489442]
Dejey, Assistant Professor, Department of Computer Science and Engineering, Anna University Regional Campus, Tirunelveli
S. Murugan, Inspector General of Police and Joint Director, Vigilance and Anti-corruption, Chennai
Cyber Forensics is a textbook designed for the undergraduate engineering students of Computer Science and Information Technology programmes for the related course.

Features

- Provides a perfect balance of discussion on cybercrime, forensics, and cyber laws (both Indian and International)
- Discusses principles, processes, and case studies for a better grasp of concepts
- Introduces a fundamental chapter on computer networks and security
- Provides a model case example report as an appendix for a better understanding of how forensic examination findings are reported and documented

Other Related Titles

9780195692327 *Natural Language Processing & Information Retrieval* by U.S. Tiwary & Tanveer Siddiqui	9780195671544 *Artificial Intelligence & Intelligent Systems* by N.P. Padhy
	9780198093480 *Distributed Computing* by Sunita Mahajan & Seema Shah